Interdisciplinary Public Finance, Business and Economics Studies Volume III

Adil AKINCI (ed.)

Interdisciplinary Public Finance, Business and Economics Studies Volume III

PETER LANG

Bibliographic Information published by the Deutsche Nationalbibliothek

The Deutsche Nationalbibliothek lists this publication in the Deutsche Nationalbibliografie; detailed bibliographic data is available online at http://dnb.d-nb.de.

Library of Congress Cataloging-in-Publication Data

A CIP catalog record for this book has been applied for at the Library of Congress.

ISBN 978-3-631-81896-1 (Print)
E-ISBN 978-3-631-83427-5 (E-PDF)
E-ISBN 978-3-631-83428-2 (EPUB)
E-ISBN 978-3-631-83429-9 (MOBI)
DOI 10.3726/b17540

Peter Lang – Berlin · Bern · Bruxelles · New York · Oxford · Warszawa · Wien

This publication has been peer reviewed.

www.peterlang.com

Foreword

The book "Interdisciplinary Public Finance, Business and Economics Studies-Volume III", by bringing together the works of academics and researchers working in the area of economics and administrative sciences, carries an aim to reveal the actual and historical developments experienced in economics and administrative sciences in Turkey and in the world, and produce solution proposals and make a general evaluation.

I express my gratitude to the authors of the book chapters that contributed to the book "Interdisciplinary Public Finance, Business and Economics Studies-Volume III" without losing their research spirit in spite of the Covid-19 epidemic, which is on the global agenda.

The book "Interdisciplinary Public Finance, Business and Economics Studies-Volume III" consists of 32 valuable book chapters consisting of theoretical and empirical studies. The topics studied in the book chapters are presented below.

In her study, Kıran Baygın made a convergence analysis of health expenditures per capita in OECD countries. In his study, Tüzüntürk examined the subject of organizational network analysis. In her study Ayas made the econometric analysis of the relationship between public spending and economic growth in Turkey. In his study, Ciğerci examined actos in the electoral system and their behavioral tendencies. In his study, Güney made a causality analysis in order to be able to determine the relationship between bank loans and money supply. In his study, Hacıhasanoğlu, by examining the Kuznet curve literature, has evaluated its effects on green finance. In his study, Canbay analyzed the relationship between research-development expenditures and economic growth in G-7 countries. In her study, Özen examined the relationship between urbanization and poverty. In his study, Gemici examined the cryptocurrency market. In her study, Kılınçer analyzed the relationship between BIST-100 index and monetary policy practices. In his study, Korkmaz examined the economic dimensions of cultural diversity. In their study Obiero and Şengür analyzed the relationship between inflation and economic growth in Kenya. In his study Bozkurt examined the Wealth Tax collected in Turkey during World War 2. In their study Göksu and Özçelik made an econometric analysis on the determinants of poverty. In his study, Sarıtaş analyzed the impact of globalization on economic growth in scope of Turkey. In his study, Oksak analyzed the relationship between Islam and poverty. In her study, Yılmaz analyzed the effects of total factor productivity, patent applications and exportation of ICT (information-communication technologies) on per capita income within OECD countries. In her study, Taşkın examined the İstanbul Mukataas in the Ottoman State between the years 1550–1605. In their work, Erdoğan and Karakoç examined the parlimentary government system. In their studies, Ögel and Aşıkoğlu examined the effects of the 2001 financial crisis on the manufacturing industry with the help of financial ratios analysis. In their study, Bengül and Çelikkol examined the effects of perceived financial risks on customers' purchasing decisions, satisfaction and loyalty in online shopping process. In their study, Kaya and Utku examined the application of integrated reporting in the Turkish banking sector. In her study, Öztürk evaluated consumer preferences for chain coffee shops. In his study, Düğer examined contemporary leadership styles within the framework of social change theory. In her study, Mısırdalı Yangil examined the concept of holacracy. In his study, Cıranoğlu examined the management of after-sales services in the durable goods market. In her study, Bayar examined the relationship between the organizational performance and loyalty levels and the leadership and power sources. In her study, Varışlı evaluated leadership styles and organizational culture in modern management systems. In her study, Yağmur examined the subject of business judgment rule in terms of turkish commercial code. In their study, Durgut and Bulut examined the subject of contract of carriage for passenger, luggage and cargo by ınternational airline. In their study, Kurnaz and Kestane examined the effect of artificial intelligence on internal audit. In his study, Gümüş analyzed economic and social effects of minimum wage determination

All publishing rights of the published book chapters belong to the publisher, and the content responsibility of the published articles belongs to the author. The opinions in the book chapters are the personal opinions of the authors; it is not an official opinion of any institution or organization.

Assoc. Prof. Adil AKINCI
Kutahya/Turkey, 2020

Contents

List of Contributors

Rıza Aşıkoğlu
Ph.D., Prof., Afyon Kocatepe University, Faculty of Economics and Administrative Sciences, Department of International Trade and Finance, riza@aku.edu.tr, ORCID: 0000-0003-4282-4561

Işıl Ayas
Ph.D., Assist. Prof., Sakarya University, Faculty of Political Sciences, Department of Public Finance, iyeter@sakarya.edu.tr, ORCID: 0000-0002-5441-006X

Münevver Bayar
Ph.D., Manager, Social Security Institution, munevverbayar@hotmail.com, ORCID: 0000-0002-8077-2160

Selahattin Bozkurt
Ph.D., Assist. Prof. Dr., Kütahya Dumlupınar University, History of the Republic of Turkey, selahattin.bozkurt@dpu.edu.tr, ORCID: 0000-0001-7676-7206

Şerif Canbay
Ph.D., Assist. Prof., Duzce University, Faculty of Political Sciences, Department of Economic, canbay.serif@gmail.com, ORCID: 0000-0001-6141-7510

İsmail Ciğerci
Ph.D., Assist. Prof., Afyon Kocatepe University, Faculty of Economics and Administrative Sciences, Department of Public Finance, icigerci@aku.edu.tr, ORCID: : 0000-0002-8858-5685

Mehmet Cıranoğlu
Ph.D., Research Assistant, Bursa Uludag University, Inegol Faculty of Business, Department of Business Administration, ciranoglu@uludag.edu.tr, ORCID: 0000-0002-7798-7099

Ramazan Durgut
Ph.D. iur., Assist. Prof., Istanbul University, Business School, Commercial Law Department, rdurgut@istanbul.edu.tr, ORCID: 0000-0002-9037-2005

Selami Erdoğan
Ph.D., Assist.Prof., Kutahya Dumlupınar University, Faculty of Administrative and Economics Sciences, Department of Public Administration, Kutahya-Turkey, selami.erdogan@dpu.edu.tr, ORCID: 0000-0002-2245-4105

İbrahim Ethem Güney
Ph.D., Doha Representative, Central Bank of the Republic of Turkey, ethem.guney@tcmb.gov.tr, ORCID: 0000-0001-6890-205X

Eray Gemici
Ph.D., Assist. Prof., Gaziantep University, Islahiye Faculty of Economics and Administrative Sciences, Department of Business Administration, gemici@gantep.edu.tr, ORCID: 0000-0001-5449-0568

Serkan Göksu
Ph.D., Lecturer. Afyon Kocatepe University, Vocational School of Dazkırı. sgoksu@aku.edu.tr, ORCID: 0000-0003-3261-6769

Ebru Gül Yılmaz
Ph.D., Assist. Prof., İstanbul Gelişim University, egyilmaz@gelisim.edu.tr, ORCID: 0000-0002-3610-4982

İskender Gümüş
Ph.D., Assist. Prof., Kirklareli University, Faculty of Economics and Administrative Sciences, Department of Labor Economics and Industrial Relations, iskender.gumus@klu.edu.tr, ORCID: 0000-0002-1428-0512

Erkam Hasim Bulut
Research Assistant, Istanbul University, Business School, Commercial Law Department,erkam.bulut@istanbul.edu.tr, ORCID: 0000-0001-8579-509X

Fikret Karakoç
Ph.D. Student, Kutahya Dumlupinar University fikret.karakoc@ogr.dpu.edu.tr, ORCID: 0000-0001-7974-3103

Yusuf Kaya
Ph.D., Assist.Prof., Pamukkale University, Department of Banking and Insurance, ykaya@pau.edu.tr, ORCID: 0000-0002-2076-9808

Ali Kestane
Ph.D., Kilis 7 Aralık Üniversitesi,, Faculty of Economics and Administrative Sciences, Department of Management, alikestane@kilis.edu.tr, ORCID: 0000-0002-7049-0354

Beyhan Kılınçer
Ph.D., Lecturer, Adiyaman University, Vocational School of Social Sciences, Department of Accounting and Tax, bkilincer@adiyaman.edu.tr, ORCID: 0000-0002-5638-8177

Burcu Kıran Baygın
Ph.D., Prof., Istanbul University, Faculty of Economics, Department of Econometrics, 34452, Beyazit, Istanbul, Turkey. Tel: (212) 440-00-00 /11211. E-mail: kburcu@istanbul.edu.tr, ORCID: 0000-0002-4258-0870

İlhan Korkmaz
Ph.D., Assist. Prof., Kütahya Dumlupinar University, Faculty of Economics and Administrative Sciences, Department of Economics, ilhan.korkmaz@dpu.edu.tr, ORCID: 0000-0002-7503-6505

Niyazi Kurnaz
Ph.D. Prof., Kütahya Dumlupınar University,, Faculty of Economics and Administrative Sciences, Department of Management, niyazi.kurnaz@dpu.edu.tr, ORCID: 0000-0001-7019-0119

Wilkista Lore Obiero
Eskisehir Osmangazi University, Institute of Social Sciences, Department of Economics, lwilkista@gmail.com, ORCID: 0000-0002-0498-3142

Mediha Mine Çelikkol
Ph.D., Assist. Prof., Kütahya Dumlupinar University, Kütahya Vocational School of Social Sciences, Department of Banking and Insurance, mine.celikkol@dpu.edu.tr, ORCID: 0000-0001-7876-9483

Fulya Mısırdalı Yangil
Ph.D., Assoc. Prof., Dumlupınar University, Altıntaş Vocational School, Management&Organization, fulya.myangil@dpu.edu.tr, ORCID: 0000-0002-5746-3458

Serdar Ögel
Ph.D., Assist. Prof., Afyon Kocatepe Üniversity, Faculty of Economics and Administrative Sciences, Department of Business Administration, serdarogel@aku.edu.tr, ORCID: 0000-0002-7151-1671

Yüksel Okşak
Ph.D., Assist. Prof., Bursa Uludağ University, İnegöl Faculty of Business, yukseloksak@uludag.edu.tr, ORCID: 0000-0001-8794-4597

Özer Özçelik
Ph.D., Assist. Prof., Kütahya Dumlupınar Üniversitesi, Faculty of Economics and Administrative Sciences, Department of Economics, ozer.ozcelik@dpu.edu.tr, ORCID: : 0000-0001-9164-5020

Eda Özen
Ph.D., Assist. Prof., Bilecik Seyh Edebali University, Faculty of Economics and Administrative Sciences, Department of Economics, eda.ozen@bilecik.edu.tr, ORCID: 0000-0002-0818-1040

Derya Öztürk
Ph.D., Assoc.Prof., Ordu University, Unye Faculty of Economics and Administrative Sciences, Department of Business, deryaozturk@odu.edu.tr, ORCID: 0000-0001-5287-6600

Tufan Sarıtaş
Ph.D., Assist. Prof., Karamanoğlu Mehmetbey University, Faculty of Economics and Administrative Sciences, Department of Economics, tufansaritas@kmu.edu.tr, ORCID: 0000-0003-1728-2377

Yavuz Selim Düger
Ph.D., Assist. Prof., Kütahya Dumlupinar University, Faculty of Economics and Administrative Sciences, Department of International Trade and Finance, yselim.duger@dpu.edu.tr, ORCID: 0000-0003-3523-9671

Yavuz Selim Hacıhasanoğlu
Ph.D., Economist, Central Bank of the Republic of Turkey, yavuz.selim@tcmb.gov.tr. The views in this chapter are only those of the author and should not be interpreted as reflecting those of the Central Bank of the Republic of Turkey.

Mehmet Şengür
Ph.D., Assist. Prof., Eskisehir Osmangazi University, Faculty of Economics and Administrative Sciences, Department of Economics, msengur@ogu.edu.tr, ORCID: 0000-0002-2173-9977

Safiye Süreyya Bengül
Ph.D., Assist. Prof., Kütahya Dumlupinar University, Kütahya Vocational School of Social Sciences, Department of Marketing, ssureyya.bengul@dpu.edu.tr, ORCID: 0000-0003-0773-0690

Figen Taşkın
Ph.D, Assist. Prof., Ordu University, Unye Faculty of Economics and Administrative Sciences, Department of Political Science and Public Administration, figentaskin@odu.edu.tr, ORCID: 0000-0001-9752-3139

Selim Tüzüntürk
Ph.D., Assoc. Prof., Bursa Uludağ University, Department of Econometrics, selimtuzunturk@uludag.edu.tr, ORCID: 0000-0002-8987-2280

Mehmet Utku
Ph.D., Assist.Prof., Pamukkale University, Department of Business Administration, mutku@pau.edu.tr, ORCID: 0000-0002-7076-6891

Nuran Varışlı
Ph.D., Expert, Republic of Turkey Social Security Institution, gulmennuran@hotmail.com, ORCID: 0000-0002-0657-756X

Setenay Yağmur
Ph.D., setenayyagmur@gmail.com, ORCID:0000-0001-5765-5962

Burcu Kıran Baygın

Convergence of Per Capita Health Expenditures: Evidence from Selected OECD Countries

1 Introduction

The concept of human capital is first introduced by Schultz (1961) and means increasing the number of people with skills, education and experience. It is very critical for a country's economic and political development. Therefore, human capital development refers to the investment in human and also creative and productive development of investment. Human capital investments increase both human and physical capital investments by creating an overflow-spreading effect, thus affecting economic growth positively (Barro, 1991). Factors which play a critical role in the increase of human capital stock are considered as components of human capital, and these components are divided into five categories: (i) health services which affect individuals' life expectancy, life force, and energy (ii) educations organized by companies (iii) formal education at primary, secondary and higher education level (iv) working programs which are not organized by companies for adults, especially including agricultural progress programs (v) individual or family migrations to adapt to changing job opportunities. In fact, education and health are the most important of these categorized components. Because healthy, educated and skilled labor force constitute comprehensive and productive capital (Schultz, 1961).

The basic condition for individuals to get education and engage in economic activities is to be healthy. The government plays an active role in this field due to the realization of the growth target of health expenditures. On the other hand, health is semi-public goods. The most important health indicators used in country comparisons are birth rate, mortality rate, infant mortality rate, total fertility rate, life expectancy at birth, share of health expenditures in gross domestic product (GDP) and per capita health expenditures. In recent years, convergence in the healthcare system has become an important research topic with the rapid increase in health expenditures and the increasingly similar health policies.

The term of convergence can be identified as "the result of a process in which the structures of different industrial societies come increasingly to resemble each other" (Jary and Jary, 1991). Economic convergence is based on neo-classical growth theory and has a simple notion. According to neo-classical growth models, if the countries only differ from each other in the initial level of per capita income and capital, they will reach the same steady – state level, since the productivity of capital in the poor countries is higher than that of the rich countries. This means that the poor countries will experience a higher growth rate than rich countries. Consequently, the former will eventually catch-up, the disparity gap will shrink and eventually close over time. On the other side, if the growth rates of the rich countries are higher than the rates of poor countries, the disparity gap will increase over time. In this case, it is said that these countries are diverging from each other (Fallahi, 2011). Over time, the idea of convergence is used to assess the transformations of other areas of economic life. An example of this is the use of convergence in the analysis of health expenditure.

Borrowing convergence concept from neo-classical growth theory, some studies have recently considered health expenditure convergence between countries and reached mixed results (Hitiris, 1997; McCoskey and Selden, 1998; Nixon, 1999; Hitiris and Nixon, 2001; Jewell et al., 2003; Carrion-i-Silvestre, 2005; Narayan, 2007; Aslan, 2008; Kerem et al., 2008; Wang, 2008; Alcalde-Unzu et al. 2009; Fallahi, 2011; Schmitt and Starke, 2011; Panopoulou and Pantelidis, 2012).

This paper examines the convergence of per capita health expenditures for selected 21 Organisation for Economic Co-operation and Development (OECD) countries over the period from 1975 through 2018 by using Papell and Prodan (2006) unit root test with one and two endogenous structural breaks. According to the OECD Health Statistics report published in 2019, health expenditure as a share of GDP was 8.8 %, on average across the OECD countries, in 2017. The share of GDP is expected to stay at 8.8 % in 2018. Health expenditure in 2017 was highest in the United States (17.1 %). The second and third highest spenders were Switzerland (12.3 %) and France (11.3 %), respectively. On the other hand, the lowest spenders in terms of share of GDP were Turkey (4.2 %), Luxembourg (5.4 %) and Mexico (5.4 %). Based on the per capita terms, health expenditure in 2017 is USD 3 854 on average. The averaged health expenditure per capita for the United States was USD 10 206, more than double the OECD average. There are strong reasons for the high levels of per capita health expenditures in the United States. One of them is that the USA has a much higher capacity in high-technology facilities compared to other countries. Second one is that the USA tends to adopt new medical technologies more rapidly than other countries (Anderson et al., 2000, 154). The next highest level of per capita health expenditures, above the OECD average, occurred in Switzerland (USD 7 147) and Norway (USD 6 064) (OECD, 2019).

The remainder of the paper is organized as follows: Section 2 lays out the basics of the Papell and Prodan(2006) unit root test with one and two endogenous structural breaks, while Section 3 describes the data and reports the results. Finally, Section 4 concludes the paper.

2 Papell and Prodan (2006) Unit Root Test with One and Two Endogenous Structural Breaks

Papell and Prodan (2006) suggested unit root tests with one and two structural breaks that both account for structural change and maintain a long-run mean or trend by considering an Additive Outlier (AO) type model to model changes that occur instantaneously. The Additive Outlier model is estimated in two step. As a first step, the deterministic part of the analyzed series (y_t) is removed by using following regression equation for a value of the break point *TB*, with $0.10T < TB < 0.90T$ (where *T* is the sample size):

$$y_t = \mu + \gamma DU_t + \tilde{z}_t$$

Here, the dummy variable DU_t is constructed as follows:

$$DU_t = \begin{cases} 1 & \text{if} \quad t > TB \\ 0 & \text{otherwise} \end{cases}$$

The reason of using $0.10T < TB < 0.90T$ trimming is to avoid finding spurious breaks at the beginning and end of the sample. As a second step, the unit root test is applied by calculating the *t* statistic for *TB* in the following regression:

$$\Delta\tilde{z}_t = \sum_{i=0}^{k} \omega_i D(TB)_{t-i} + \alpha\tilde{z}_{t-1} + \sum_{i=1}^{k} c_i \Delta\tilde{z}_{t-i} + \varepsilon_t$$

where

$$D(TB)_t = \begin{cases} 1 & \text{if} \quad t = TB + 1 \\ 0 & \text{otherwise} \end{cases} .$$

To ensure that *t* statistic on α is invariant to the value of truncation lag parameter *k*, it is needed to include *k* + 1 dummy variables. The recursive procedure of choosing *k* starts with $k_{\max} = 8$ and it is repeated until the last lag is significant by using critical value of 1.645. The break date TB is choosen by minimizing the t-statistic on α. Statistics are calculated for all break dates based on the trimming.

As a different specification, Papell and Prodan (2006) include a time trend to the previous Additive Outlier model and perform unit root tests by permitting shifts in the intercept at an unknown time. They again use two step procedure. As a first step, to remove the deterministic part of the considered y_t series, the following regression is estimated:

$$y_t = \mu + \beta t + \gamma DU_t + \tilde{z}_t$$

Here, 10 % trimming is used to avoid spurious breaks. As a second step, the previous equation

$$\Delta\tilde{z}_t = \sum_{i=0}^{k} \omega_i D(TB)_{t-i} + \alpha\tilde{z}_{t-1} + \sum_{i=1}^{k} c_i \Delta\tilde{z}_{t-i} + \varepsilon_t$$

is re-estimated. The unit root test is applied by using the t statistic for $\alpha = 0$.

By including two endogenous structural breaks, Papell and Prodan (2006) extend the Additive Outlier model. The deterministic part of the y_t series is removed by including two break points TB_1 and TB_2 with $0.10T < TB_i < 0.90T$ (where T is the sample size and i = 1, 2) as follows:

$$y_t = \mu + \gamma_1 DU_{1t} + \gamma_2 DU_{2t} + \tilde{z}_t$$

where

$$DU_{1t} = \begin{cases} 1 & \text{if} \quad t > TB_1 \\ 0 & \text{otherwise} \end{cases}$$

$$DU_{2t} = \begin{cases} 1 & \text{if} \quad t > TB_2 \\ 0 & \text{otherwise} \end{cases} .$$

As a second step of the process with two structural breaks, following regression equation is estimated:

$$\Delta\tilde{z}_t = \sum_{i=0}^{k} \omega_{1i} D(TB_1)_{t-i} + \sum_{i=0}^{k} \omega_{2i} D(TB_2)_{t-i} + \alpha\tilde{z}_{t-1} + \sum_{i=1}^{k} c_i \Delta\tilde{z}_{t-i} + \varepsilon_t$$

Here,

$$D(TB_i)_t = \begin{cases} 1 & \text{if} \quad t > TB_i + 1 \\ 0 & \text{otherwise} \end{cases} .$$

Finally, Papell and Prodan (2006) remove the deterministic part of the y_t series by using regression equation with two structural breaks in below:

$$y_t = \mu + \beta t + \gamma_1 DU_{1t} + \gamma_2 DU_{2t} + \tilde{z}_t$$

Then, they estimate the same regression equation which is estimated in the second step of the other test specifications. The unit root hypothesis is tested as in the previous cases.

3 Data and Empirical Results

This paper investigates per capita health expenditures convergence for selected 21 OECD countries (Australia, Austria, Belgium, Canada, Denmark, Finland, Germany, Iceland, Ireland, Japan, Korea, Netherlands, New Zealand, Norway, Portugal, Spain, Sweden, Switzerland, Turkey, United Kingdom, United States) over the period from 1975 through 2018 by using Papell and Prodan (2006) unit root test with one and two endogenous structural breaks. These countries are selected based on the data availability between 1975 and 2018. The source of the data is OECD Health statistics database.

For testing convergence, we use Carlino and Mills' (1993, 1996) methodology to convert data into the relative per capita health expenditures. Following their methodology, a yearly sample average for considered OECD countries is calculated and then the natural logarithm of relative per capita health expenditures for each countries is computed as follows:

$$H^*_{PC_t} = \ln(H^i_{PC_t} / averageH^{OECD}_{PC_t})$$

where $H^i_{PC_t}$ is the per capita health expenditures for country i at time t, $averageH^{OECD}_{PC_t}$ is the average value of per capita health expenditures for selected OECD countries in the sample period. The obtained relative per capita health

Table 1: *The results of ADF and PP unit root tests*

Countries	ADF	PP
Australia	−2.558 (0)	−2.546 (1)
Austria	−1.206 (0)	−1.521 (3)
Belgium	−3.288[c] (0)	−3.280[c] (3)
Canada	−1.983 (1)	−1.741 (3)
Denmark	−1.617 (0)	−1.368 (3)
Finland	−2.451 (1)	−2.032 (2)
Germany	−1.491 (0)	−1.827 (3)
Iceland	−3.658[b] (1)	−2.384 (3)
Ireland	−1.554 (1)	−1.760 (3)
Japan	−2.470 (1)	−1.781 (3)
Korea	−2.842 (0)	−3.105 (1)
Netherlands	−1.906 (0)	−1.936 (2)
New Zealand	−3.494[b] (0)	−9.017[a] (2)
Norway	−2.329 (0)	−2.383 (3)
Portugal	−0 856 (0)	−0.979 (8)
Spain	−1.777 (1)	−1.440 (2)
Sweden	−0.697 (0)	−0.690 (2)
Switzerland	−1.265 (0)	−1.610 (4)
Turkey	−2.583 (0)	−2.585 (3)
UK	−3.006 (0)	−2.975 (3)
US	−1.695 (1)	−1.966 (2)

Notes: a,b and c denote significance at the 1 %, 5 % and 10 % significance levels, respectively. The numbers in parentheses are the lag orders in the ADF. The lag parameters are selected on the basis of Schwarz (SC) criterion. The truncation lags for the Newey-West correction of the PP test are in parentheses.

expenditures series for each countries is labeled as $H^*_{PC_t}$. As a first step, traditional Augmented Dickey Fuller (ADF) and Philips and Perron (PP) unit root tests, which do not take into account structural breaks are applied to $H^*_{PC_t}$ series with a constant and trend and the results are reported in Table 1.

According to the results in the table, it can be seen that relative per capita health expenditures series for Belgium and New Zealand are stationary based on both ADF and PP unit root tests. On the other hand, there is evidence of stationarity for the relative per capita health expenditures series of Iceland based on ADF unit root test. These results indicate that per capita health expenditures convergence is supported for Belgium, Iceland and New Zealand when the

Table 2: *The results of Papell and Prodan (2006) unit root test with one structural break*

Countries	α	*TB1*	γ_1	*k*	t_α
Australia	−0.306	1984	−0.097	1	−3.484
Austria	−0.410	1988	0.250	0	−4.927[c]
Belgium	−0.760	1988	0.075	1	−5.295[b]
Canada	−0.274	1991	−0.097	2	−3.598
Denmark	−0.452	1987	−0.120	0	−3.859
Finland	−0.282	1982	0.146	1	−3.298
Germany	−0.413	1998	−0.100	3	−3.220
Iceland	−0.365	2006	−0.239	1	−4.918[c]
Ireland	−0.179	1997	0.325	1	−3.145
Japan	−0.243	1994	−0.149	2	−3.950
Korea	−0.578	1982	0.264	3	−3.875
Netherlands	−0.307	1996	0.101	0	−4.319
New Zealand	−0.534	1983	−0.222	3	−4.859[c]
Norway	−0.733	1995	0.116	0	−5.842[a]
Portugal	−0.346	2008	−0.366	1	−3.202
Spain	−0.230	1985	0.136	1	−3.722
Sweden	−0.362	2006	0.253	3	−3.803
Switzerland	−0.265	1984	0.123	3	−3.390
Turkey	−0.446	1991	0.106	3	−4.429
UK	−0.699	1985	−0.105	1	−4.671
US	−0.122	1986	0.143	1	−2.185

Notes: a,b and c denote significance at the 1 %, 5 % and 10 % significance levels, respectively.

structural breaks are not taken into account. Since Perron (1989) claims that ignoring a structural break can lead to false acceptance of the unit root null hypothesis, we update our analysis by taking into account existence of possible structural breaks. For this purpose, Papell and Prodan (2006) unit root test is applied with one and two endogenous structural breaks. The results with one structural break are tabulated in Table 2.

The results show that unit root null hypothesis is rejected for relative per capita health expenditure series of Austria, Belgium, Iceland, New Zealand and Norway, giving evidence on the per capita health expenditure convergence for these countries. The structural breaks occur between 1982and 1988 for Australia, Austria, Belgium, Denmark, Finland, Korea, New Zealand, Spain, Switzerland, UK and US; between 1991 and 1998 for Canada, Germany, Ireland,

Table 3: *The results of Papell and Prodan (2006) unit root test with two structural breaks*

Countries	α	TB_1	γ_1	TB_2	γ_2	k	t_α
Australia	−0.360	1984	−0.078	2001	0.042	1	−3.927
Austria	−1.088	1985	0.086	1992	0.245	3	−5.955[c]
Belgium	−0.906	1985	0.051	1990	0.048	1	−6.490[a]
Canada	−0.449	1993	−0.107	2005	0.048	3	−5.147
Denmark	−0.799	1987	−0.079	2004	0.077	0	−5.669
Finland	−0.451	1982	0.156	1989	−0.041	1	−5.007
Germany	−0.738	1999	−0.099	2012	0.052	3	−4.577
Iceland	−0.456	1989	−0.133	2006	−0.307	1	−5.740[c]
Ireland	−0.370	1996	0.268	2003	0.296	2	−4.255
Japan	−0.312	1990	−0.009	2010	0.148	3	−4.878
Korea	−1.031	1982	0.201	1997	−0.211	3	−6.991[a]
Netherlands	−0.457	1984	−0.094	1996	0.073	0	−4.334
New Zealand	−0.703	1983	−0.179	2007	0.087	3	−6.002[b]
Norway	−0.859	1988	−0.006	1995	0.117	0	−7.574[a]
Portugal	−0.618	2003	−0.172	2010	−0.352	1	−4.391
Spain	−0.324	1985	0.071	2008	−0.126	1	−4.680
Sweden	−0.553	1990	−0.176	2009	0.234	0	−5.452
Switzerland	−0.408	1984	0.096	1998	−0.080	3	−4.490
Turkey	−0.652	1984	−0.199	1996	0.349	0	−5.111
UK	−0.866	2000	0.100	2010	0.054	1	−6.820[c]
US	−0.210	1987	0.124	2012	−0.037	3	−3.643

Notes: a,b and c denote significance at the 1 %, 5 % and 10 % significance levels, respectively.

Japan, Netherlands, Norway and Turkey; between 2006 and 2008 for Iceland, Portugal and Sweden. To compare the findings based on per capita health expenditure convergence, we also apply Papell and Prodan (2006) unit root test with two structural breaks and give the results in Table 3.

Based on the results in the table, we are able to reject the unit root null hypothesis for Austria, Belgium, Iceland, Korea, New Zealand, Norway and UK in the case of two structural breaks. In other words, per capita health expenditure convergence is valid for these countries with structural breaks in mixed dates. In general, these structural breaks for each country refer to some typical events such as recessions, booms, natural disasters, political instability, epidemic contagious disease among others.

4 Conclusions

This paper investigates per capita health expenditure convergence of selected 21 OECD countries over the period from 1975 through 2018. To convert data into the relative per capita health expenditures for each countries, we use Carlino and Mills' (1993, 1996) methodology. In the first step of the analysis, we apply traditional ADF and PP unit root tests which do not take into account structural breaks and find that there is evidence of per capita health expenditure convergence for Belgium, Iceland and New Zealand. By considering that ignoring structural breaks can lead to false acceptance of the unit root null hypothesis, we take into account existence of possible structural breaks as a second step. To reach this aim, Papell and Prodan (2006) unit root test is used with one and two endogenous structural breaks. The test results with one structural break give that per capita health expenditure series of Austria, Belgium, Iceland, New Zealand and Norway are converging to the average value of selected 21 OECD countries. When we update Papell and Prodan (2006) unit root test with two structural breaks, the evidence of per capita health expenditure convergence is found for Austria, Belgium, Iceland, Korea, New Zealand, Norway and UK.

References

Alcalde-Unzu, J., Ezcurra, R. & Pascual, P. (2009). Cross-Country Disparities in Health-Care Expenditure: A Factor Decomposition. Health Economics, 18(4), 479–485.

Anderson, G.F., Hurst, J., Hussey, P.S. & Jee-Hughes, M. (2000). Health Spending and Outcomes: Trends in OECD Countries 1960–1998. Health Affairs, 19,150–157.

Aslan, A. (2008). Convergence of Per Capita Health Care Expenditures in OECD Countries. MPRA Paper, 10592, 1–10.

Barro, R. (1991). Economic Growth in a Cross Section of Countries. Quarterly Journal of Economics, 106(2), 407–443.

Carlino, G.A. & Mills, L.O. (1993). Are US Regional Converging? A Time Series Analysis. Journal of Monetary Economics, 32, 335–346.

Carlino, G.A. & Mills, L.O. (1996). Testing Neoclassical Convergence in Regional Incomes and Earnings. Regional Science and Urban Economics, 26, 565–590.

Carrion-i-Silvestre, J.L. (2005). Health Care Expenditure and GDP: Are They Broken Stationary?. Journal of Health Economics, 24(5), 839–854.

Fallahi, F. (2011). Convergence of Total Health Expenditure as a Share of GDP: Evidence from Selected OECD Countries. MPRA Paper, 51324, 1–22.

Hitiris, T. (1997). Health Care Expenditure and Integration in the Countries of the European Union. Applied Economics, 29(1), 1–6.

Hitiris, T. & Nixon, J. (2001). Convergence in Health Care Expenditure in the EU Countries. Applied Economics Letters, 8, 223–228.

Jary, D. & Jary, J. (1991). Dictionary of Sociology, Glasgow: Harper Collins.

Jewell, T., Lee, J., Tieslau, M. & Strazicich, M.C. (2003). Stationarity of Heath Expenditures and GDP: Evidence from Panel Unit Root Tests with Heterogeneous Structural Breaks. Journal of Health Economics, 22, 313–323.

Kerem, K., Püss, T., Viies, M. & Maldre, R. (2008). Health and Convergence of Health Care Expenditure in EU. International Business & Economics Research Journal, 7, 29–43.

McCoskey, S. & Selden, T.M. (1998). Health Care Expeditures and GDP: Panel Data Unit Root Test Results. Journal of Health Economics, 17, 369–376.

Narayan, P.K. (2007). Do Health Expenditures 'Catch-up'? Evidence from OECD Countries. Health Economics, 16, 993–1008.

Nixon, J. (1999). Convergence Analysis of Health Care Expenditure in the EU Countries Using Two Approaches. Department of Economics and Related Studies, University of York, Heslington, Discussion Papers in Economics, No 1999/03.

OECD. (2019). OECD Health Statistics. (online); http://www.oecd.org/els/health-systems/health-data.htm.

Panopoulou, E. & Pantelidis, T. (2012). Convergence in Per Capita Health Expenditures and Health Outcomes in the OECD Countries. Applied Economics, 44(30), 3909–3920.

Papell, D.H. & Prodan, R. (2006). Additional Evidence of Long-Run Purchasing Power Parity with Restricted Structural Change. Journal of Money, Credit, and Banking, 38(5), 1329–1349.

Perron, P. (1989). The Great Crash, the Oil Price Shock and the Unit Root Hypothesis. Econometrica, 57, 1361–1401.

Schmitt, C. & Starke, P. (2011). Explaining Convergence of OECD Welfare States: A Conditional Approach. Journal of European Social Policy, 21(2), 120–135.

Schultz, T. (1961). Investment in Human Capital. The American Economic Review, 51(1), 1–17.

Wang, Z. (2008). The Convergence of Health Care Expenditures in the US States. Health Economics, 18, 55–70.

Selim Tüzüntürk

A Quantitative Research Method for Business Management: Organizational Network Analysis

1 Networks

Today, the reality of the claim that "networks are everywhere" is more obvious than ever. Coronavirus (COVID-19) disease which causes a respiratory illness has spread all over the world in 2020. It was first detected in the central Chinese city of Wuhan in December 2019. Up to now, 4.641 individuals died depending on this fatal disease in China. John Hopkins University Coronavirus Resource Center declared that the number of the total confirmed cases in the worldwide are 10.487.022 people, 5.366.092 people were recovered and 511.546 people were dead so far (http://coronavirus.jhu.edu/map.html, retrieved online July 1, 2020).. Following other websites statistics such as https://worldometers.info/coronavirus/ and others, these numbers are seen unfortunately increasing day by day. In the end, the global impact of this spread of this disease is sadly deaths of human beings.

Following the figure above, red colors are the countries that confirmed hundred or more cases. As the red color becomes darker, the number of the cases increases for the related country. On the other hand, beige colors show the countries with fewer than hundred cases. In just three months, disease spread fast to all over the world.

The above explained sad truth is a type of biological network[1]. Particularly, Coronavirus (COVID-19) disease is a disease transmitting network such as HIV/AIDS (Human Immunodeficiency Viruses/Acquired Immunodeficiency Syndrome), influenza (flu), malaria and cholera. And, these are known as PANDEMICS[2]. Ecological networks (food webs, river basins and rain forest), metabolic networks, community networks (insect societies, animal herds, bird flocks and schools of fish) and gene expression networks are the other types of

1 Network scientists categorized real world networks into three (Committee on Network Science for Future Army Applications, National Research Council, 2006: 12): (i) biological networks, (ii) physical networks and (iii) social networks. See Tüzüntürk (2012a, 2012b, 2019) for details.

2 A pandemic is the global outbreak of a disease.

Fig. 1: *Coronavirus Spread Map* (https://foreignpolicy.com, *retrieved online April 10, 2020)*

biological networks. The global impact of these networks are respectively, the survival of selected species, sustenance of life for given generation of living entities, survival of selected species and transmission and evolution of life between generations.

Physical networks are distribution grids (electric power, water supply and business supply chains), telecommunications infrastructure (cellular, cable TV and internet), transportation networks (airports, highways, railways and shipping) and electronic financial transaction networks (banking, credit cards and ATMs). The global impact of these networks are respectively, efficient distribution of goods or commodities, instantaneous worldwide information distribution, network-centric warfare and network enabled operations, rapid movement of goods from supplier to market and electronic cashless transactions.

Social networks are affiliation or acquaintance networks (terrorist, community, business, religious and clubs), broadcast networks (radio and TV networks), information exchange networks (mail, local and long distance telephone service), group forming networks (eBay, corporate intranets), supply chains and business networks and social services networks (social security, family services, Medicare and Medicaid). The global impact of these networks are respectively, efficient collaboration and activity coordination, dissemination of identical information to large groups, cheap communications, convenient formation of groups of like-minded people who have never met, coordination of multiple players to achieve common goals and efficient delivery of government services.

Within this framework, organizational networks are included in the third type of real world networks, social networks. As is mentioned above, biological networks may have fatal effects. Besides, physical networks and social networks may have peculiar effects that may have consequences on every day of our lives. For instance, distribution grid is a type of physical network. The electric cut-outs experiences show that inefficient distribution of electric energy may stop the production and thereby may have some economic consequences that can affect the whole economy of related country. On the side, the interactions of individuals in organizational networks have substantial organizational consequences that can affect organizational objectives. Within this scope, the description and explanation of the *organizational networks* and their analyzing method that is called *Organizational Network Analysis Method* is the subject matter of this chapter.

2 Organizational Networks

Organizational networks can be examined in two main levels. These are (Tüzüntürk, 2012 (d): 37): (i) interorganizational and (ii) intraorganizational levels. The focus of the studies in the interorganizational level is the network between a focal organization (ego) and the linked organizations[3] with ego and with each other. This network is called egocentric network (Gulati et al., 2002: 282).

These organizations can be connected to each other through some social and economic relationships such as supplier relationships, resource flows, trade association memberships, interlocking directorates, relationships among individual employees and strategic alliances (Gulati et al., 2002: 282).

The focus of the studies in the intraorganizational level is the network between employees in an organization. The intraorganizational level of the analysis can be conducted in three levels (Raider and Krackhardt, 2002: 62): (1) Dyadic level, (2) Individual network level or ego network level and (3) Group level.

The focus of the studies in dyadic level is the network of two people which is called dyadic network.

A dyad is a group of two people which is considered as the smallest social group in the society. The focus of the studies in dyadic level is the characteristics of the relationship between two people. Whether or not that this relationship

---

3 These organizations are close friends of ego and they are called alters. They have direct connections with ego.

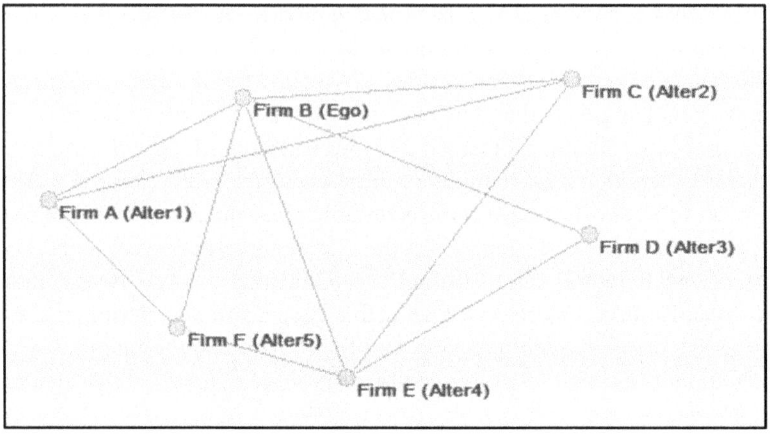

Fig. 2: *Hypothetical Egocentric Network* This network and rest of the hypothetical networks were drawn with PAJEK. This package is free for practitioners and it can be downloaded from the following link: http://mrvar.fdv.uni-lj.si/pajek/. See De Nooy et al. (2007) and Tüzüntürk (2018) for detailed computer applications.

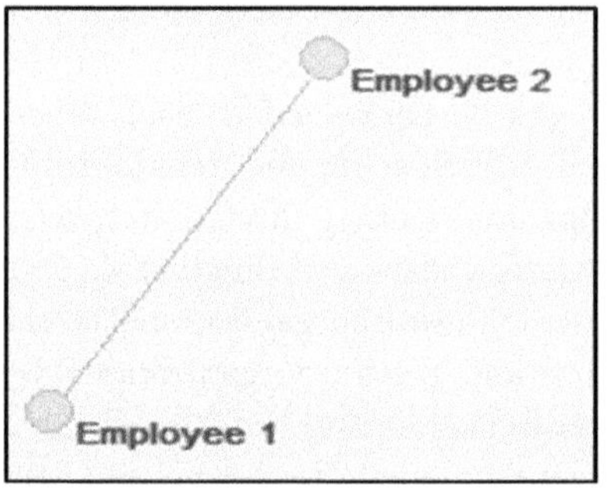

Fig. 3: *Hypothetical Dyadic Network*

connection is a friendship, colleague, affinity, boss or subordinate connection. Especially, these studies focus on the following question:

"*Where do these relations (or connections) come from?*"

It is explained in the literature that the starting point of these connections is related to the notion of "homophily" which refers to the tendency of people to have ties with people to whom they are similar (sex, age, race, occupation)

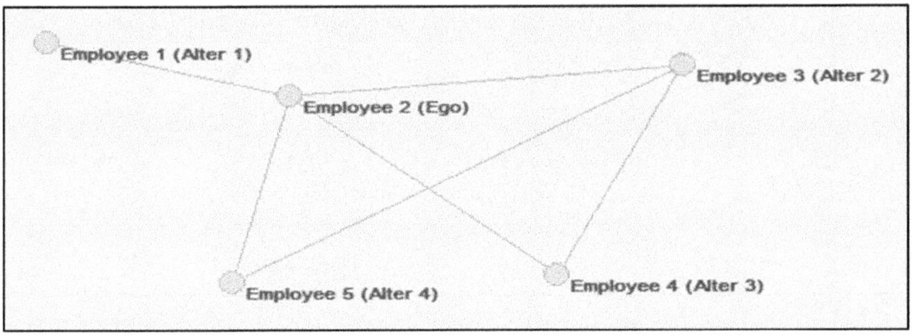

Fig. 4: *Hypothetical Individual Network/Ego Network*

with each other. The idea of similarity leads to connectivity, so it is been thought that homophilous people connect with each other. Besides, the effects of dyadic networks on the career development and job satisfaction, performances of the subordinates depending on the relations between subordinates and bosses and the role of dyadic networks on the performance assessments.

The focus of the studies in individual network level or ego network level is the network of a selected individual. This network is also called egocentric network or ego network that is similar to interorganizational level examination.

In such networks, whether or not the properties of the individual's network affect his/her behaviors or opinions is examined. "Social capital[4]" issue is discussed in two separate ways: (i) Granovetter's (1973) The Strength of Weak Ties Theory and (ii) Burt's (1995) Structural Holes Theory.

In the Strength of Weak Ties Theory, strong ties are frequently contacted individuals such as family members or close friends. Weak ties are rarely contacted individuals such as acquaintances or the people that we are familiar with.

In the figure above, individuals numbered one, two and three are tightly attached close friends who have direct connections with each other. The connections between them are strong ties. Also, it is the same for individuals numbered four, five and six. Individuals three and four are two familiar people. The connection between these two is weak tie. However, this weak tie provides

4 Social capital consists of the stock of active connections among people; the trust, mutual understanding, and shared values and behaviors that bind the members of human networks and communities and cooperative action possible (Anklam, 2007: 15). See Burt (1995, 1997, 2000, 2004, 2005), Lin (1999, 2003), Lin et al. (2008), and Anklam (2007) for detailed discussion of Social Capital issue.

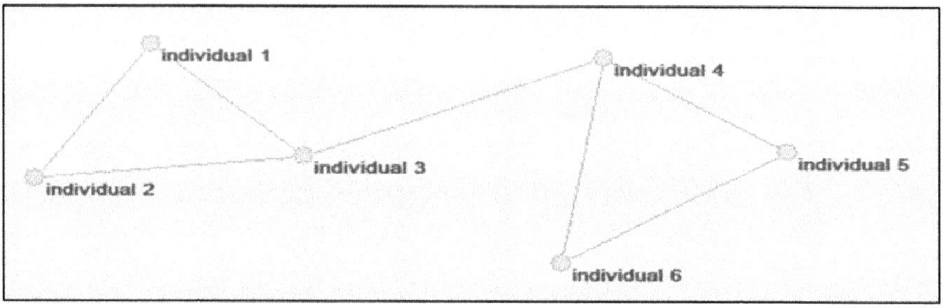

Fig. 5: *Hypothetical Network with Weak and Strong Ties*

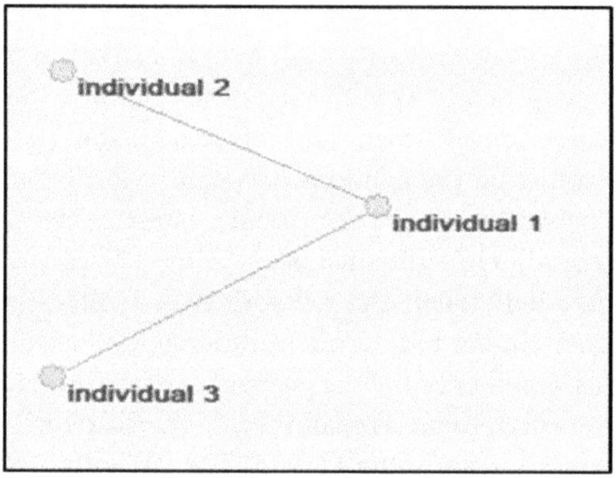

Fig. 6: *Hypothetical Network with Structural Hole*

a connection with different and disparate groups of people which may lead to an important source of information such as finding a job in a fast way. The individual advantage that is gained from the weak tie connection underlines the strength of weak ties.

In the Structural Holes Theory, individuals hold positional advantages or disadvantages in their networks of relationships. A structural hole is explained as a gap between two individuals. For instance, in the figure below there is a lack of tie between individuals two and three which represents a gap between them.

Because of this gap, individual one has the competitive advantage as compared to individuals two and three in the network depending on the flow of the information. The position of individual one makes it available for her/him to access valuable information from both individuals. The control of the information

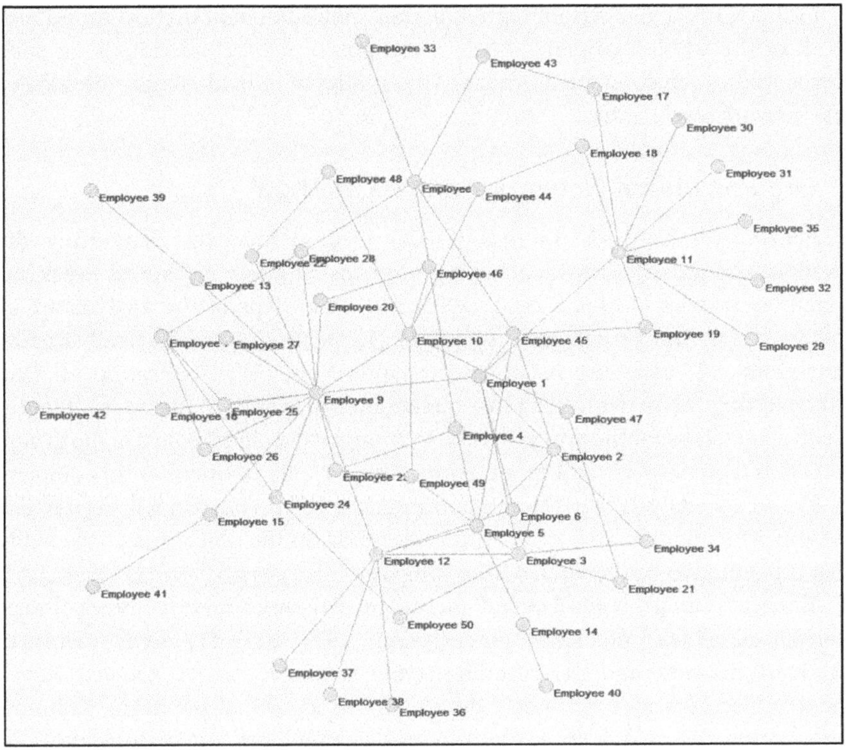

Fig. 7: *Hypothetical Group Network*

that is received from different sources gives her/him power. This advantage gives opportunity to step forward with new ideas among all the individuals participated in the network.

In addition to the issues above, contagion studies which is related to the transmission of knowledge and information through network ties are also conducted with individual networks. It is proposed that the opinions and considerations of individuals' affect the functioning of organizations. Especially, these studies focus on the following question:

"How do the networks affect the transmission of opinions and experiences?"

The focus of the studies in group level is the network of a group of individuals such as a work team or a department in a company or all company staff.

In the figure above, visual representation shows the hypothetical group network of the whole company which is composed of fifty individuals. In such levels, studies can conducted similar to the studies of individual network level or ego network level studies.

3 Organizational Network Analysis Method[5]

Organizational Network Analysis (ONA) is a method for diagnosing the relationships among individuals and groups inside firms and across organizational boundaries (Anklam et al., 2005: 540). The steps of the analysis are as follows (Cross and Parker, 2004: 143–162): (1) identifying a strategically important group, (2) assessing meaningful relationships, (3) visualization of data, (4) analyzing the network data in a quantitative manner, (5) create meaningful feedback sessions for the group, (6) assess progress and effectiveness of the group.

Dyads, ego network and group (work team or a department or all company staff) can be analyzed for intraorganizational level as is explained in previous section. The identification of the group depends on the objectives of the study that is planned to be conducted for a company.

Managers can get a good overall picture by diagramming three types of relationship networks (Krackhardt and Hanson, 1993: 105): (1) Advice network, (2) trust network and (3) communication network. *Advice network* shows the key players whom the others dependent on in case of providing technical information that may help her/him in solving problems and performing tasks (Krackhardt and Hanson, 1993: 105; Koput, 2010: 4). Advice network can be drawn by asking employees such a question: "Whom do you go to for advice at least one a week?". Mapping advice networks can uncover the source of political conflicts and failure to achieve strategic objectives (Krackhardt and Hanson, 1993: 106). *Trust network* shows the important employees who share delicate political information and back one another in a crisis (Krackhardt and Hanson, 1993: 105). Trust network can be drawn by asking employees such a question: "Whom would you trust to keep in confidence your concerns about work-related problems?". *Communication networks* show the employees who

---

5 This method is based on the visual and numerical methods of Social Network Analysis (SNA) Methods. Organizational Network Analysis is often called in different names such as "Organizational Social Network Research", "Social Network Research in Management", "Network Research in Organizations" and "Social Network Analysis for Organizations" (Tüzüntürk, 2012 c; Tüzüntürk, 2012 d).

talk about work-related matters on a regular basis (Krackhardt and Hanson, 1993: 105). Communication network can be drawn by asking employees such a question: "Whom do you talk to everyday at work?". The communication network can help identify gaps in information flow, the inefficient use of resources, and the failure to generate new ideas (Krackhardt and Hanson, 1993: 106).

Visualization and quantitative methods are the methods of SNA that are used together to discover the nature of the networked relationships inside the organizations. Things to look for in SNA are (Cross et al., 2002: 6): (i) *bottlenecks* who are central people and provide the only connection between different parts of the network, (ii) *number of links* that are included or not which should exist in establishing the coordination between departments, (iii) *average distance* which indicates the transmission of the information is fast or slow, (iv) *isolation* which shows the employees who are not connected to network, (v) *high expert people* who cannot be well utilized and (vi) *organizational subgroups or cliques* which can develop their own subcultures and negative attitudes toward other groups.

Feedback sessions with group members are beneficial for management and employees. Network maps are shown to group members and asked them to explain the patterns that they see. By this way, problems are noticed and solutions are tried to develop together with employees. Most central people of the networks can be experts and also can be overloaded employees (bottlenecks). Redistribution of tasks and responsibilities can help overloaded people to take a breath and focus of their own expert area. Peripheral people can be unutilized employees or represent turnover risks for the organization. These people should be moved to the centers of networks in order to win these people. In addition to these, isolated parts of the organizational networks can be integrated to the network and some weak connections of the network can be repaired.

Finally, ONA is conducted again minimally after six months period in order to assess the progress and effectiveness of the analyzed group.

4 Conclusions

Organizations have objectives such as making profits, doing a service to society, giving satisfaction to their customers, maintaining their life, growing and developing their business, being the leader of sector and gaining a reputation (Eryılmaz, 2019: 41). On the other hand, social interactions affect organizational productivity. The configuration or structure of these relationships in an organization significantly impacts organizational performance, as well as individual performance (Lieberman, 2019: 24).

Patterns of individual relationships are analyzed by using ONA. This method provides valuable information to organization managements and employees. From the management stand point, ONA help to find out the solutions to organizational problems. The achievement of collaboration and connectivity among the organization members enables organizations to function well and improve their productivity. From the employee stand point, ONA help them to make use of network opportunities such as finding a new job positions, getting a promotion or taking a position in a new business project. Employees can use network benefits in their career improvement.

References

Anklam, P. (2007). Net Work a Practical Guide to Creating and Sustaining Networks at Work and in the World, Burlington, USA: Butterworth-Heinemann Publisher.

Anklam, P., Cross, R. & Gulas, V. (2005). Expanding the Field of Vision. The Learning Organization, 12(6), 539–551.

Burt, R. S. (1995). Structural Holes: The Social Structure of Competition, USA: Harvard University Press.

Burt, R. S. (1997). A Note on Social Capital and Network Content. Social Networks, 19, 355–373.

Burt, R. S. (2000). The Network Structure of Social Capital. Research Organizational Behavior, 22, 1–93.

Burt, R. S. (2004). Structural Holes and Good Ideas. The American Journal of Sociology, 110(2), 349–399.

Burt, R. S. (2005). Brokerage and Closure: An Introduction to Social Capital, New York, USA: Oxford University Press.

Committee on Network Science for Future Army Applications, National Research Council (2006). Network Science, Washington, USA: The National Academic Press.

Cross, R. & Parker, A. (2004). The Hidden Power of Social Networks: Understanding How Work Really Gets Done in Organizations, Boston, USA: Harvard Business School Press.

Cross, R., Parker, A. & Borgatti, S. P. (2002). A Bird's-Eye View: Using Social Network Analysis to Improve Knowledge Creation and Sharing. IBM Institute for Knowledge-Based Organizations, 1–19.

De Nooy W., Mrvar, A., & Batagelj, V. (2007). Exploratory Social Network Analysis with PAJEK, New York, USA: Cambridge University Press.

Eryılmaz, M. (2019). İşletme Bilimine Genel Bakış. In Mehmet Eryılmaz, Sait Kaygusuz and İsmail Efil (Eds.), İşletme, Kuram ve Pratik, Bursa: Ekin Kitabevi, 3–80.

Granovetter, M. (1973). The Strength of Weak Ties. The American Journal of Sociology, 78(6), 1360–1380.

Granovetter, M. (1983). The Strength of Weak Ties: A Network Theory Revised. The Sociological Theory, 1, 201–233.

Gulati, R., Dialdin, D. A. & Wang, L. (2002). Organizational Networks. In Joel A. C. Baum (Ed.), Companion to Organizations, UK: Blackwell Publishers Ltd., 281–304.

http://coronavirus.jhu.edu/map.html

https://foreignpolicy.com

http://mrvar.fdv.uni-lj.si/pajek/

https://worldometers.info/coronavirus/

Koput, K. W. (2010). Social Capital: An Introduction to Managing Networks. Cheltenham, UK: Edward Elgar Publishing Limited.

Krackhardt, D. & Hanson, J. R. (1993). Informal Networks: The Company Behind the Chart, Harvard Business Review, 71(4), 104–111.

Lieberman, M. (2019). Talent Management: Organizational Network Analysis. Workforce Solutions Review, 24–27.

Lin, N. (1999). Building a Network Theory of Social Capital. Connections, 22(1), 28–51.

Lin, N. (2003). Social Capital: A Theory of Social Structure and Action, New York, USA: Cambridge University Press.

Lin, N., Cook, K. & Burt, R. S. (Eds.) (2008). Social Capital: Theory and Research, New Brunswick, New Jersey, USA: Transaction Publishers.

Raider, H., & Krackhardt D. J. (2002). Intraorganizational Networks. In Joel A. C. Baum (Ed.), Companion to Organizations, UK: Blackwell Publishers Ltd., 58–75.

Tüzüntürk, S. (2012a). Ağ Bilimi, Birinci Baskı, Bursa: Dora Kitabevi.

Tüzüntürk, S. (2012b). What Is Network Science?. 1st International Interdisciplinary Social Inquiry Conference, Uludağ University, 17–21 June, Bursa.

Tüzüntürk, S. (2012c). Organizational Network Analysis: An Illustrative Example in a Textile Firm. 1st International Interdisciplinary Social Inquiry Conference, Uludağ University, 17–21 June, Bursa.

Tüzüntürk, S. (2012d). Organizasyonel Ağ Analizi, Birinci Baskı, Bursa: Dora Kitabevi.

Tüzüntürk, S. (2018). Sosyal Bilimlerde PAJEK Uygulamalı Yapısal Analiz, Bursa: Aktüel 16.

Tüzüntürk, S. (2019). Ağ Bilimi, Genişletilmiş 2. Baskı, Bursa: Dora Kitabevi.

Işıl Ayas

The Relationship between Public Expenditure and Economic Growth in Turkey: Hidden Cointegration Test Allowing Multiple Breaks

1 Introduction

Expenditure made with the purpose of meeting public demands is called public expenditure. Extent of public expenditure historically depends on various ideologies. Economic growth is another variable closely interacted with public expenditure. In general terms, economic growth is defined as the annual increase of goods and services in a country. Countries often target a public expenditure rate that will maximize economic growth. Therefore, the relationship between public expenditure and economic growth has been a matter of discussion from past to present. In this context, two opposing views, Keynesian and Wagner, have come to the fore. According to Keynesian view, public expenditure is a function of economic growth. Thus, economic growth depends on the increase in public expenditure. On the contrary, according to Wagner's Law, economic growth is the function of public expenditure. Public expenditure increases as economic growth is achieved. The goal of this study is to analyze the relationship between public expenditure and economic growth in Turkey in the context of these two views. What distinguishes it from other studies is that structural breaks are taken into account while testing the relationship between positive shocks in public expenditure and economic growth variables.

2 Theoretical Framework

There are various approaches that explain the causes of increase in public expenditure. Of these approaches, Wagner's Law and Keynesian approach are the ones that have come to the fore. Wagner Law is the approach that suggests that share of public expenditure in total economic activities continually increases with economic growth. German Economist Adolp Wagner found out that public expenditure of industrialized countries he observed was in a constant rise. He suggested that production boomed with industrialization, which accordingly increased national income. Additionally, he claimed that the community rose their expectations from the state as a result of their wish to develop and the state increased public expenditure in order to meet this expectation (Önder, 1974:18). According to Wagner, public expenditure was defined as an internal variable and economic growth as an external variable (Singh and Sahni, 1984, 630). It was suggested that the state might fall into financial deficiency in the short term in order to meet the increasing needs but it would be able to overcome this situation in the long term by extending these activities. According to Wagner, public expenditure grows faster than national income. In other words, income elasticity of public expenditure is bigger than 1 (Bulutoğlu, 2003:221).

Keynesian approach was put forward by John Maynard Keynes after 1930 depression. Contrary to Wagner, Keynes claimed that increasing public expenditure would lead to increased economic growth. Public expenditure is regarded as an external variable and he suggests that increasing public expenditure will result in increased national income (Telek and Telek, 2016: 630). What enables this are its multiplier and accelerator mechanisms. Multiplier is a multiple used to calculate to what extent an increase in autonomous expenses influences national income. The multiplier, which was first used by Khan in the context of employment, was used by Keynes for national income calculations (Keynes, 2008:105).

According to Keynes, public expenditure and tax policies are used as economic intervention tools against conjectural fluctuations in economy. Keynes dealt with the demand aspect of economy and suggested that it was necessary to increase public expenditure in order to increase effective demand. Still, intervention of the state in economy in order to remove imbalance in social life is legitimized (Pehlivan, 2008:76).

Public expenditure might influence growth in various ways. The first one is related to whether public expenditure is productive or not. Non-productive public expenditure has a negative influence on economic growth of developed countries in the middle and long term. As for developing countries, it has a positive influence in the short term and negative influence in the middle term (Şit and Karadağ, 2017:34). Another factor that has an influence on economic growth is the type of public expenditure. For example, it is possible to find studies in literature on the influence of educational, health and research-development expenditure on economic growth (Erdal, 2019; Çalışkan et al., 2018:75; İğdeli, 2019: 2517).

3 Literature

There are a lots of studies in literature dealing with the relationship between public expenditure and economic growth. Some of them measure this relationship on the basis of expenditure components while others used total public expenditure as a variable. Literature review involves only studies that deals with Turkey as our study was carried out in the context of Turkey. From a general perspective, Wagner's Law and Keynesian theory were tested. Some studies suggest that Wagner's Law is valid in Turkey (Yıldırım, 1994; Yamak and Zengin, 1996; Terzi, 1998; Sarı, 2003; Işık and Alagöz, 2005; Cergibozan et al., 2017; Mohammadi et al., 2008; Selen and Eryiğit, 2009; Altunç, 2011; Ulusoy and Zengin, 1998; Gacaner, 2005; Arısoy, 2005; Akçoraoğlu 1999; Demirbaş, 1999; Çavuşoğlu, 2005; Aytaç and Güran, 2010; Şanlısoy and Sunal, 2016; Dübüş, 2017; Uzuner et al., 2017). On the contrary, it is claimed in some studies that Keynesian view is valid (Uzay, 2002; Altay and Altın, 2008; Gül and Yavuz; 2011; Ergen and Yavuz, 2017; Yüksel and Songur, 2011; Pata and Tütüncü, 2017; UluTürk, 2001; Artan and Berber, 2004; Uysal and Mucuk, 2009).

Two-way casualty was found between public expenditure and economic growth in some studies that measured the casualty between the two variables (Şimşek, 2004; Taşseven, 2011; Güder et al., 2016; Tülümce and Zeren, 2017; Yavuz ve Doruk, 2018). In the study by Tülümce and Yayla (2017), public expenditure differs according to classification type. It is suggested that Keynesian approach is appropriate in economic classification of public expenditure while Wagner's Law is valid for functional classification. No relationship was found by some studies between the two variables (Bağdigen and Çetintaş, 2004; Başar et al., 2009; Ulucak and Ulucak, 2014). Though few, some studies have concluded that their relationship is negative (Yavuz and Ergen, 2017; Kolçak et al., 2017).

Considering the studies that test the two variables separately in short and long term, Kanca (2011) found that Keynesian approach is valid in the short term and Wagner's Law in the long term in Turkey. Additionally, Kabaklarlı and Er (2014) suggest that increase economic growth causes a decline in public expenditure in the short term but Wagner's Law is valid in the long term. Although short term results of the two studies are different, they carry the same view in the long term.

According to the literature review in general terms, it is observed that the number of studies suggesting that Wagner Law is valid in Turkey is higher than studies suggesting that Keynesian view is valid.

4 Data, Methodology

Data related to Turkey's 1987–2018 public expenditure and economic growth were obtained from World Development Indicators, data set of the World Bank. Inflation-adjusted real forms of variables were used. Logarithmic versions of the variables were used in the analysis. First, stability of variables was tested. Then, Granger and Yoon (2002) and Hatemi-J Irandoust hidden cointegration test were used in order to identify if there was a relationship between public expenditure and economic growth. In addition to that, Maki Cointegration that allows multiple breaks was used in order to identify the structural breaks in this cointegration relationship.

Hidden cointegration tests is based on Engle and Granger (1987) cointegration test. Before carrying out the test, variables were divided into positive/negative components in order to identify the positive or negative shocks. Then cointegration relationship was identified between these components.

When two random walk time series of X_t and Y_t assumed,

$$Xt = Xt - 1 + \varepsilon t = X0 + \sum_{i=1}^{t} \varepsilon i \tag{1}$$

$$Yt = Yt - 1 + \eta t = Y0 + \sum_{i=1}^{t} \eta i \tag{2}$$

In the equation, X_0 and Y_0 indicate preliminary values while, ε_t and η_t indicate zero mean white noise error terms. $X_{t\,\text{and}}$ Y_t are the variables whose cointegration relationship was tested and negative and positive shocks must be defined in order to analyze the hidden cointegration relationship between these two variables.

$$\varepsilon_i^+ = max\,(\varepsilon_i, 0)\ \varepsilon_i^- = min\,(\varepsilon_i, 0) \tag{3}$$

$$\eta_i^+ = max\,(\eta_i, 0)\ \eta_i^- = min\,(\eta_i, 0) \tag{4}$$

Therefore, it is possible to define error terms as (3) $\varepsilon_i = \varepsilon_i^+ + \varepsilon_i^-, \eta_i = \eta_i^+ + \eta_i^-$.

When error terms are placed in the equation,

$$X_t = X_{t-1} + \varepsilon_i = X_0 + \sum_{i}^{t} \varepsilon_i^+ + \sum_{i}^{t} \varepsilon_i^- \tag{5}$$

$$Y_t = Y_{t-1} + \eta_i = Y_0 + \sum_{i}^{t} \eta_i^+ + \sum_{i}^{t} n_i^- \tag{6}$$

models are obtained. Granger and Yoon (2002) assumed that when $X_t^+ = \sum_{i=1}^{t} \varepsilon_i^+$, $X_t^- = \sum_{i=1}^{t} \varepsilon_t^-$, $Y_t^+ = \sum_{i=1}^{t} \eta_t^+$ $Y_t^- = \sum_{i=1}^{t} \eta_t^-$, X_0 and Y_0 were stationary $X_t = X_0 + X_t^+ + X_t^-$ and $Y_t = Y_0 + Y_t^+ + Y_t^-$. Then it might be shown as $\Delta X_t^+ = \varepsilon_i^+$, $\Delta X_t^- = \varepsilon_i^-$, $\Delta Y_t^+ = \eta_i^+$, $\Delta Y_t^- = \eta_i^-$. Granger-Yoon hidden cointegration test results are achieved when these shocks are subjected to Eangle-Granger cointegration test. Again, Hatemi-J and Irandoust (2012) cointegration test results are achieved when these shocks are subjected to Johansen cointegration test.

Cointegration test, introduced by Maki (2012) to the literature by using four different models, allows three or more structural breaks. Below are presented the models.

Model 0: No trend model that allows break in constant term
Model 1: No trend model that allows break in constant term and slope
Model 2: Trend model that allows break in constant term and slope
Model 3: Trend model that allows break in constant term, slope and trend

5 Findings

Stability of data set was tested by unit root tests. Maki Cointegration test was carried out after Hidden Cointegration tests in order to identify the structural breaks in cointegration relationship. Finally, To Do Yamamato casualty test was carried out in order to identify the way of cointegration relationship.

5.1 Unit Root Tests

Stability of variables was tested by Generalized Dickey-Fuller (ADF) and Philips-Peron (PP) unit root tests.

Level values of variables have unit roots. The first difference of the two variables is stationary at I(1).

5.2 Hidden Cointegration Test

Granger Yoon hidden cointegration test was carried out among positive components. Results are presented on Table 2.

There is a hidden cointegration relationship between positive components of public expenditure and economic growth only in constant model. However,

Table 1: *Augmented Dickey-Fuller (ADF) and Philips-Peron (PP) Unit Root Tests*

Variables		ADF		PP	
		Intercept	Trend-Intercept	Intercept	Trend-Intercept
Level	PGDP+	2.141	0.091	2.608	2.586
	PPE+	0.411	−3.125	0.860	−.3.125
First difference	PGDP+	3.826***	−4.521***	6.769***	8.223***
	PPE+	−4.624***	−4.515***	−6.671***	−6.632**

Note: *** indicates %1 significance level,
** %5 significance level,
*%10 significance level.

Table 2: *Granger-Yoon and Hatemi-j and Irandoust Hidden Cointegration Test Results*

Test Statistics				
Dependent Variable	Independent Variable	T statistics Constant	T statistics Constant Trend	Critical Values
PGDP+	PPE+	−3.368*	−0.813	−3.66, −2.96, −2.56
PPE+	PGDP+	−3.400**	−0.817	(%1) (%5) (%10)

Not 1: *** indicates %1 significance level,
** %5 significance level,
*%10 significance level.

Table 3: *Hatemi-J Iradoust Hidden Cointegration Test Results*

Variables	Hypotheses	Trace Statistic	Eigen Value	Prob
$PGDP^{+}$	There is no cointegration	35.1980	25.872	0.0026
PPE^{+}	There is cointegration.	8.1762	12.5179	0.2376

Note: Suitable delay length was obtained by Hannan-Quinn data criteria. Appropriate model was selected according to Pantula principle.

hidden cointegration relationship in constant-trend model is insignificant. Therefore, Hatemi-J and Irandoust (2012) hidden cointegration test, considered to be stronger, was carried out. Hatemi-J Iradoust hidden cointegration test results are presented on Table 3.

There is a long-term hidden cointegration relationship between positive shocks of public expenditure and positive shocks of economic growth according

Table 4: *Maki Cointegration Test Findings*

Model 2	Test Statistics	%1	%5	%10	Break Dates
$PGDP^+$, PPE^+	−7,01	−6,915	−6,357	−6,057	1990 1998 1993 2000 2008

Note: Crirical values were obtained from Maki (2012) Tabe 1.

Table 5: *Toda-Yamamato Casualty Test Results*

Casualty Way	Chi-sq	Prob
$PGDP^+ \rightarrow PPE^+$	25.311	0.0000
$PPE^+ \rightarrow PGDP^+$	1.411	0.4937

to Hatemi-J and Irandoust Hidden Cointegration method. The reason for the differences of Hatemi-J and Irandoust results from Granger-Yoon is the superiority of Johansen cointegration method over Engle-Granger method. Therefore, it might be said that these results are more reliable (Şener et al., 2013: 244).

5.3. Maki Structural Break Cointegration Test

Maki cointegration test results are presented on Table 4. Critical values given on Table 4 are obtained by Monte Carlo Simulation.

According to Table 4, there is a long-term cointegration relationship between public expenditure and economic growth.

5.4. Toda-Yamamato Casualty Test

Toda-Yamamoto casualty test was carried out in order to identify the way of cointegration relationship between the two variables.

According to the test results, there is a casualty relationship from positive shocks of economic growth to positive shocks of public expenditure.

5 Conclusion

The relationship between public expenditure and economic growth has been discussed from past to present. It is possible to say that Wagner's Law and Keynesian theory are the two views that have come to the fore in this context. Although there are various studies that deal with the relationship between public expenditure and economic growth in Turkey, the number of studies revealing that Wagner's Law is valid is higher than the number of studies supporting Keynesian theory. Hidden cointegration test revealed hidden cointegration between positive shocks of public expenditure and positive shocks of economic growth. In Maki multiple break cointegration test carried out with positive shock variables, break dates that influenced the relationship between the two variables were obtained. In 1989, the decision numbered 32 paved the way for financial liberalism in Turkey. The break in 1990 might be regarded as a reflection of this decision. It is possible to suggest that Asia crisis in 1998, the crisis in November, 2000 and mortgage crisis that emerged in the U.S.A. and affected the whole globe in 2008 were the significant developments that influenced Turkish economy. According to the results of Toda-Yamamto Casualty test between variables, a casualty relationship was detected from positive shocks of economic growth to positive shocks of public expenditure. Therefore, we might suggest that Wagner's Law is valid in Turkey between 1987 and 2018.

References

Akçoraoğlu, A. (1999). Kamu harcamaları, kamu gelirleri ve keynesci politikalar: Bir nedensellik analizi. Gazi Üniversitesi İktisadi Ve İdari Bilimler Fakültesi Dergisi, 1(2), 51–65.

Altay, O. N. ve Altın, O. (2008). Türkiye'de kamu harcamalarının ekonomik büyüme ve yatırımlar üzerine etkileri (1980–2005). Ege Akademik Bakış, 8(1), 267–285.

Altunç, F. Ö. (2011). Kamu harcamaları ve ekonomik büyüme ilişkisi: Türkiye'ye ilişkin ampirik kanıtlar. Celal Bayar Üniversitesi İİBF Yönetim ve Ekonomi Dergisi, 18(2), 145–157.

Arısoy, İ. (2005). Wagner ve keynes hipotezleri çerçevesinde Türkiye'de kamu harcamaları ve ekonomik büyüme ilişkisi. Ç.Ü. Sosyal Bilimler Enstitüsü Dergisi, 14(2), 63–80.

Artan, S. ve Berber, M. (2004). Kamu kesimi büyüklüğü ve ekonomik büyüme ilişkisi: Çoklu koentegrasyon analizi. C.Ü. İktisadi ve İdari Bilimler Dergisi, 5(2), 13–29.

Aytaç, D. ve Güran, M. (2010). Türkiye'de kamu sektörü büyüklüğü ve ekonomik büyüme ilişkisinin ampirik analizi. Sosyo Ekonomi, 6(13), 129–152.

Bağdigen, M. ve Çetintaş, H. (2004). Causality between public expenditure and economic growth: The Turkish case. Journal of Economic and Social Research, 6, 53–72.

Başar, S., Aksu,H., Temurlenk, S., ve Polat, Ö. (2009). Türkiye'de kamu harcamaları ve büyüme ilişkisi: sınır testi yaklaşımı. Atatürk Üniversitesi Sosyal Bilimler Enstitüsü Dergisi, 13(1), 301–314.

Bulutoğlu, K. (2003), Kamu Ekonomisine Giriş, Yapı Kredi Yayıncılık, 2003.

Cergibozan,R., Çevik, E. ve Demir, C. (2017) Wagner kanunu'nun Türkiye ekonomisi için sınanması: Çeşitli zaman serisi bulguları, Finans Politik & Ekonomik Yorumlar, Cilt: 54 Sayı: 625.

Çalışkan Ş., Karabacak, M. ve Meçik, O. (2018). Türkiye'de uzun dönemde eğitim ve sağlık harcamaları ile ekonomik büyüme ilişkisi, Dokuz Eylül Üniversitesi İktisadi İdari bilimler Fakültesi Dergisi, Cilt 33, Sayı 1.

Çavuşoğlu, A. T. (2005). Testing the validity of Wagner's law in Turkey: The bounds testing approach. AÜ Siyasal Bilgiler Fakültesi Dergisi, 60(1), 73–87.

Demirbaş, S. (1999). Cointegration analysis – causality testing and Wagner's law: The case of Turkey 1950–1990. University of Leicester Discussion Papers, 99/2, 1–26.

Dübüş, U. (2017). Wagner ve Keynes hipotezlerinin test edilmesi: Türkiye örneği. Yayınlanmamış Yüksek Lisans Tezi, Namık Kemal Üniversitesi, Sosyal Bilimler Enstitüsü

Engle, R. F. ve Granger, C. W. J. (1987). Cointegration and error correction: representation, estimation, and testing. Econometrica, Vol: 55, ss.251–276.

Erdal, H. N. (2019). Eğitimin ekonomik büyümeye etkisi: Türkiye örneği, Yayınlanmamış Yüksek Lisans Tezi, Hacettepe Üniversitesi, Sosyal Bilimler Enstitüsü

Ergen, E. ve Yavuz, E. (2017). Büyüme ile harcama arasındaki ilişkinin Ardl eşbütünleşme ve granger nedensellik testleri ile analizi: Türkiye Üzerine Kanıtlar, Uluslararası Yönetim İktisat ve İşletme Dergisi, ICMEB17 Özel Sayısı, 84–92.

Gacaner, A. (2005). Türkiye açısından Wagner kanunu'nun geçerliliğinin analizi. Dokuz Eylül Üniversitesi İktisadi ve İdari Bilimler Fakültesi Dergisi, 20(1), 103–122.

Granger, C. W. ve Yoon, G. (2002). Hidden Cointegration. University of California, Department of Economics Working Paper. San Diego.

Güder, F., Yücekaya, P. ve Şenyurt A. (2016). Kamu harcamalari ile ekonomik büyüme ilişkisi: Türkiye için keynesyen görüş mü? Wagner kanunu mu geçerli? (2006–2015 Dönemi). ÇOMÜ Uluslararası Sosyal Bilimler Dergisi, 1(1), 47–60

Gül, E. ve Yavuz H. (2011). Türkiye'de kamu harcamaları ile ekonomik büyüme arasındaki nedensellik ilişkisi: 1963–2008 dönemi. Maliye Dergisi, 160, 72–85.

Hatemi-J, A. ve Irandoust, M. (2012). Asymmetric ınteraction between government spending and terms of trade volatility new evidence from hidden cointegration technique. Journal of Economic Studies, 39(3), 368–378.

Işık, N. ve Alagöz, M. (2005). Kamu harcamaları ve büyüme arasındaki ilişki. Erciyes Üniversitesi İktisadi ve İdari Bilimler Fakültesi Dergisi, 24(1), 63–75.

İğdeli, A. (2019). Ar-Ge ve Eğitim harcamalarının ekonomik büyüme üzerindeki etkisi: Türkiye örneği, MANAS Sosyal Araştırmalar Dergisi, Cilt 8, Sayı 3.

Kabaklarlı, E. ve Er, P. H. (2014). Türkiye'de kamu harcamalarının ekonomik büyümeye etkisinin sınır testi yaklaşımı ile analizi. Maliye Dergisi, 166, 268–285.

Kanca, O. C. (2011). Kamu Harcamalarının Ekonomik Büyüme Üzerine Etkisi 1980–2008 (Ampirik Bir Çalışma), Atatürk Üniversitesi, İktisadi ve İdari Bilimler Dergisi, 25(1), 75–92.

Keynes, J. M. (2008). Genel teori faiz istihdam ve paranın genel teorisi, Çev. Uğur Selçuk Akalın, 1. Baskı, Kalkedon Yayınları, İstanbul.

Kolçak, M., Kalabak, A. Y. ve Boran H. (2017). Kamu harcamaları büyüme üzerinde bir politika aracı olarak kullanılmalı mı? Vecm analizi ve yapısal kırılma testleri ile ampirik bir analiz: 1984–2014 Türkiye örneği. Ankara Üniversitesi SBF Dergisi, Cilt 72, No. 2, 467 – 486.

Maki, D. (2012). Tests for cointegration allowing for an unknown number of breaks. Economic Modelling, 29(5), 2011–2015.

Mohammadi, H., Cak, M. ve Cak, D. (2008). Wagner's hypothesis new evidence from Turkey using the bounds testing approach. Journal of Economic Studies, 35(1), 94–106.

Önder, İ. (1974). Türkiye'de kamu harcamalarının seyri: 1927–1967, Fakülteler Matbaası, İstanbul.

Pata, U. K. ve Tütüncü, A. (2017). Yapısal kırılmalarla birlikte Türkiye'de kamu harcamaları ve ekonomik büyüme ilişkisinin analizi. Maliye Dergisi, Ocak-Haziran 2017; 172. 30–51.

Pehlivan, O. (2008). Kamu Maliyesi, Derya Kitabevi, Trabzon.

Sarı, R. (2003). Kamu harcamalarının dünyada ve Türkiye'deki gelişimi ve Türkiye'de ulusal gelir ile ilişkisi. İktisat İşletme ve Finans, 18(209), 25–38.

Selen, U. ve Eryiğit, K. (2009). Yapısal kırılmaların varlığında, wagner kanunu Türkiye için geçerli mi? Maliye Dergisi, 156, 177–198.

Singh, B. ve Sahni B. (1984). Causality between public expenditure and national income. The Review of Economics and Statistic, 66(4), 630–644.

Şanlısoy, S. ve Sunal, O. (2016). Kamu harcamaları-Ekonomik büyüme ilişkisi: Türkiye örneği. Gümüşhane Üniversitesi Sosyal Bilimler Enstitüsü Elektronik Dergisi, Cilt: 7, Sayı: 17.

Şener, S. Yılancı, V. ve Tıraşoğlu, M. (2013). Petrol fiyatlari ile borsa İstanbul'un kapanış fiyatlari arasındaki saklı ilişkinin analizi. Selçuk Üniversitesi İktisadi ve İdari Bilimler Fakültesi Sosyal ve Ekonomik Araştırmalar Dergisi, 231–248.

Şimşek, M. (2004). Kamu Harcamalarını Özel Yatırımlara Etkileri, 1970–2001. Cumhuriyet Üniversitesi İktisadi ve İdari Bilimler Dergisi, 4(2), 1–20.

Şit, M. ve Karadağ, H. (2017). Türkiye ekonomisinde kamu harcamaları ekonomik büyüme ilişkisi: Toda Yamamoto nedensellik testi, Uluslararası Ticaret ve Ekonomi Araştırmaları Dergisi, Cilt: 2, Sayı:1.

Taşseven, Ö. (2011). The Wagner's law: Time series evidence for Turkey, 1960–2006. Doğuş Üniversitesi Dergisi, 12(2), 304–316.

Telek, C. ve Telek, A. (2016). Kamu harcamaları ve ekonomik büyüme ilişkisinin wagner ve keynes hipotezi çerçevesinde incelenmesi, Uluslararsı Yönetim İktisat ve İşletme Dergisi, ICAFR 16 Özel sayısı, 628–642.

Terzi, H. (1998). Kamu harcamaları ve ekonomik kalkınma ilişkisi üzerine ekonometrik bir inceleme. İktisat, İşletme ve Finans Dergisi, 13(142), 67–78.

Tülümce, S. Y. ve Yayla, N. (2017). Türkiye'de kamu harcamalarının bileşenleri ve ekonomik büyüme ilişkisi: Wagner ya da Keynes? Social Sciences (NWSAENS), 3C0164, 12(4), 163–184.

Tülümce, S. Y. ve Zeren, F. (2017). Türkiye'de kamu harcamaları ve ekonomik büyüme arasındaki ilişkinin asimetrik nedensellik testi ile analizi. Uluslararası Yönetim İktisat ve İşletme Dergisi, Cilt 13, Sayı 2.

Ulucak, R. ve Ulucak, Z. Ş. (2014). Kamu harcamaları ve ekonomik büyüme arasındaki nedensellik: Türkiye örneği. Uluslararası Yönetim İktisat ve İşletme Dergisi, 10(23), 81–97.

Ulusoy, A. ve Zengin, A. (1998). Türkiye'de Kamu Ekonomisi ve Mali Kriz. XII. Türkiye Maliye Sempozyumu Bildiri Kitabı, İ. Ü. Maliye Bölümü Yayınları, 83.

Ulutürk, S. (2001). Kamu harcamalarının ekonomik büyüme üzerine etkisi. Akdeniz Üniversitesi İİBF Dergisi, 1, 131 - 139.

Uysal, D. ve Mucuk, M. (2009). Türkiye ekonomisinde kamu harcamaları ve ekonomik büyüme ilişkisi. Finans Politik ve Ekonomik Yorumlar, 46(527), 39–48.

Uzay, N. (2002). Kamu büyüklüğü ve ekonomik büyüme üzerindeki etkileri: Türkiye örneği (1970–1999). Erciyes Üniversitesi İktisadi ve İdari Bilimler Fakültesi Dergisi, 19, 151–172.

Uzuner, G., Bekun, F. V. ve Akadiri, S. S. (2017). Public expenditures and economic growth: was Wagner right? Evidence from Turkey. Academic Journal of Economic Studies, 3(2):36–40

Yamak, R. ve Zengin, A. (1996). Kalman Filtre Yöntemi ve Wagner Yasası. DİE Araştırma Sempozyumu, 133(12), 32–43.

Yavuz, H. Y. ve Doruk, Ö. T. (2018). Türkiye ekonomisi için Keynesyen yaklaşım ve Wagner yasası'nın test edilmesi: 1950–2017 yılları arasında bir inceleme,

Artıbilim: Adana Bilim ve Teknoloji Üniversitesi Sosyal Bilimler Dergisi, 1(2), 79–93.

Yavuz, E. ve Ergen, E. (2017). Impact of Public Expenditures and Economic Classification on Growth: Turkey Analysis, Maliye Araştırmaları Dergisi, Mart, Cilt: 3,Sayı:1.

Yıldırım, Z. R. (1994). Türkiye'de gayrisafi milli hâsıla ile kamu harcamaları arasında nedensellik ilişkisi. Dokuz Eylül Üniversitesi İktisadi ve İdari Bilimler Fakültesi Dergisi, 9(1), 25–40.

Yüksel, C. ve Songur, M. (2011). Kamu Harcamalarının Bileşenleri ile Ekonomik Büyüme Arasındaki ilişki: Ampirik Bir Analiz (1980–2010). Maliye Dergisi, 161, 365–380.

İsmail CİĞERCİ

Actors in the Election System and Their Behavioral Tendencies[1]

1 Introduction

Democracy can be defined as a form of government where citizens have equal rights in shaping state policies. As democracies can be practiced by direct participation of citizens in the government, it can also be practiced through representatives elected by citizens, which is called representative democracy. Representative democracy is in force in most of today's democratic countries. In representative democracies, representatives (MPs or parliamentarians in the current sense) elected by the people gather in the parliament or assembly and make decisions on behalf of the people.

One of the most important elements that connect politics and economy in the form of democratic management is making choices and the other is decision making. Both politicians and economists use a number of tools to achieve specific goals. Both have to choose among these purposes and tools. However, the shortage of resources is one of the problems that arise in the preference of both objectives and tools. Another problem is that individuals have different preferences between different purposes and tools. The preference of these goals and tools also brings social costs. Namely; while these goals and tools bring cost to some parts of the society, they also provide certain income to some parts of the society. At this point, the concept of election economy shows itself. Ruling party/parties or political parties that want to win the election, act to maximize their votes and have to take individual preferences into account in order to achieve this.

In this study, the actors involved in the political process and their behaviors in the political process will be discussed. As it is known, there are four actors in the political process. These are voters, politicians, pressure and interest groups and bureaucrats.

---

1 This study was derived from the doctoral thesis named "The Effect Of Election Economics Applications in Turkey Between 1980 and 2010 on Budget Deficits" written by İsmail CİĞERCİ under the supervision of Prof. Dr. Tülin CANBAY in Celal Bayar University, Institute of Social Sciences.

2 Behaviors of Voters

Knowing the factors that determine voting decisions of voters is crucial for governments. The reason for this is that a government that wants to remain in power has to be informed about the political economic factors, which are accepted as the most important determinants of voter decisions (Telatar, 2004).

2.1 Parties and the Effect of Elections on Voter Behaviors

The behavior of voter is a way of his/her political behavior which is embodied by the effects of some factors like economic growth, employment and they show these behaviors both before and after the elections. Voter's behaviors can also be shaped depending on their choice to vote or not to vote and to make a choice among various alternatives and to change or continue his/her choice after the election (Avşar, 2002).

Voter behaviors have an important place in the political system. Since voter behavior is a phenomenon that can be observed in almost all societies, it is a tool used in comparative political studies.

2.2 Rational or Adapted Expectations of Voters

Whether voters are rational in voting for a politician plays an important role in voters' behavior. Voters want to maximize their personal benefits with their rational behavior. According to the rational voter hypothesis, voters' decision whether to vote or not depends on the benefit and cost to be obtained as a result of the selection and the possibility of voter's vote affecting election result (Dennis, 1976). Accordingly, if the benefit to be obtained from voter voting is greater than the cost of voting, the voter will vote. If the voter benefits from voting are less than the cost of voting, s/he will not vote.

The voter, who takes care of his own interests, appears in two ways as "egoist" and "altruist". In the egoist voter type; voters are those who harm others or others' interests while protecting their own interests. Altruist voters, on the other hand, are the type of voters who do not harm others or the interests of others while protecting their own interests (Onur, 2004).

The fact that rational voting has full knowledge is the most controversial assumption because rational voters need to know some concepts and economic variables in order to determine the success of the ruling politician. These concepts and variables are concepts such as unemployment, inflation, growth, wage and salary increases, tax cuts, budget deficits. The controversial aspect of the assumption is that rational voters cannot have sufficient information about all these variables.

2.3 Indifference and Ignorance of Voters

The ignorance of rational voters means that voters do not have enough information in their demands for public goods and services. The ignorance of voters stems from the fact that individuals in society are not at the same educational and cultural level. Another reason is that voters do not or cannot use mass media adequately or mass media are not sufficiently delivered to voters (Aktan, 2001). The programs of political parties, the propaganda of political parties, the direction of pressure and interest groups can be counted among other reasons that prevent voters from accessing information.

In the literature, instead of the notions of indifference and ignorance of voters, the concept of "Rational Negligence" is also used. By rational negligence, it is thought that voting is unlikely to change the election results alone and it is unnecessary to undertake the information costs to be acquired about the policies that politicians have implemented (Heidhues and Lagerlöff, 2003). Accordingly, as the voter is of the opinion that his/her vote does not have importance during social decision-making process, s/he does not make much effort to obtain the information needed.

The voter, who analyzes the benefits and costs of his/her vote, refuses to reach the information if the costs are high. This is especially true for lower income groups. While some voters groups make their decisions, they decide as a result of the direction of the media and its close circle. Voters who do not want to bear the cost can be directed by other voter groups. In this case, the decisions taken during the social decision-making process will be taken by voters who do not have full knowledge. Downs describes this situation as "Voters' Indifference and Ignorance" (Downs, 1957).

2.4 Voter Myopia

According to a recent widespreading view of the political economy, politicians who want to maximize their votes, create a kind of political conjuncture. According to this view, voting has two features. These are myopia and amnesia. Voters' myopia means that they are not interested in what will happen in the future. It also means voters not being concerned with what will happen in order to be able to use an economic development in the short term to maximize votes.

According to Denzau et al., voter myopia is called voters to vote for policies that will see results quickly in the short term. In other words, voters are called to vote for the policies that will benefit them in the short term, even if their welfare levels will decrease in the long term (Denzau, Arthur and Mackay, 1976). Therefore, voters will act according to their gaining before the elections, and politicians will enter into daily and short-term accounts in their future thoughts (Nordhaus, 1975).

Another aspect of voters' myopia is that voters do not consider policy costs. Namely, in cases where economic variables show a tendency towards voters' desire (such as decrease in unemployment, economic growth), voters will think that their benefit is higher than the costs they incur or other bear the cost. However, the costs of policies that provide improvement in real economic variables are higher than the benefits obtained. For example, if we try to close the deficit in the balance of payments through external borrowing, this will create an unfavorable situation in the long run. Although this preference may seem to be useful in the short term, it will be a costly policy in the long run. The reason why voters are mistaken is because of their 'myopic' feature (Savaş, 2008).

2.5 Voter Amnesia

Voter amnesia is that the voters forget the past and evaluate the economic developments occurring in the short term or on that date (Savaş, 2008). According to ONUR, voters' forgetfulness also causes voters to make mistakes systematically. This enables policy makers to easily implement the policy they want. Therefore, the main reason for voter amnesia is that s/he does not have information about the level of government competency. The voters who do not have enough information about the economic events in the past can delete what they have experienced from their memories easily. The fact that the government in power has the supremacy of knowledge causes voters to be unable to observe economic developments and to become amnesia (Onur, 2004).

2.6 Floating Votes

Another factor affecting voter preferences is floating voting. Considering the success of the rulers/governments at keeping economy free from crisis, "floating voting" appears as a term that means voters can change their votes. It should be assumed that the expectations of the voters are adapted. In other words, based on past economic performances of governments, voters change their votes in the election period as they wish, which is called floating vote (Varım, 1995). Voters are divided into two classes according to whether they change or not their votes during the election period. While the first one, **the flexible voter**, has the feature of fluctuating voting in the elections, the other voter group **the rigid voter** is called the voter who votes for the same party in each election period, especially for ideological reasons (Onur, 2004).

3 The Behaviors of the Government and the Ruling Politician

In democratic regimes, political parties act with the motivation to win elections. Political parties have two purposes. The first is to achieve power and to extend the duration of the power it has (to be re-elected), and the second is to produce the policies desired by the voters whose votes the parties have obtained. For this reason, political parties do not come to power with the aim of implementing certain policies, they use certain policies to come to power.

3.1 The Behaviors of Politicians

One of the tools used in the implementation of the election economy is undoubtedly the behavior of politicians. The aim of politicians is to seize power by maximizing their votes and to have the material and moral powers they will gain.

The behavioral styles of politicians are very important in democratic systems. Politicians try to increase their votes with the decisions they make and the policies they implement. Politicians have the strongest voice in this process. Politicians, who have a voice both in the political and economic processes, have an important place in the formation of political conjuncture fluctuations.

3.1.1 Political Myopia

The aim of politicians is to be re-elected by maximizing their votes. According to politicians or ruling parties, the best policy is the ones that lead to winning the elections. Therefore, instead of choosing projects that will bring great benefits to the economy in the long term, political governments choose projects that will directly benefit voters in the short term, which is called political myopia (Aktan, 2006). In case of political myopia, politicians will follow short-term policies that reflect immediate results, rather than pursuing electoral policies and deep-rooted policies before the elections. As a result of this practice, while public expenditures increase, the way of financing these increases is realized through emission and borrowing (Onur, 2004). In other words, public expenditures are tried to be financed with non-tax revenues. Politicians want to eliminate their political concerns by using non-existing public resources (emissions and borrowing). This is a future election investment for political governments. While this policy may have positive effects on production and employment in the short term, it brings about problems such as inflation and increased tax burden in the long term.

3.1.2 Political Cheating

In the political cheating, politicians mislead voters and try to maximize their votes. Politicians who want to win the elections in election periods go into political cheating by going into extreme secrecy, making false promises, making false statements to voters, applying propaganda or providing excessive information (Aktan, 2001). According to KOVANCILAR, the voters' being free-riders lie behind the basis political cheating. Voters take into account the marginal benefit of public activities rather than the total benefit of public activities and are reluctant to participate in the cost of these public activities while seeking to increase public activities that increase their benefit (Kovancılar, 1997). Therefore, voters' such behavior (free-rider) may result in political manipulation of the economy by politicians and the use of populist practices, especially during election periods.

3.2 The Behaviors of Political Parties

Another actor in the electoral economy is political parties. Political parties are one of the cornerstones of the decision-making mechanism in representative democracies. Political parties can be defined as "political communities that have a permanent and stable organization, seeking to take control and presentation of public activities provided that they receive public support"(Özbudun, 1974).

As it is known, there are more than one political parties in representative democracies and this is because voters' preferences are different. According to BUCHANAN, political parties want to maximize their benefits. Their behavior to maximize their benefits becomes "political income" for political parties. In other words, the benefit of politicians is called political income. Political parties will maximize their political income (benefits) when they seize power (Buchanan, 1975).

DOWNS tried to analyze the political parties' policy determinations by comparing them to the profit maximization behavior of the companies in the market. DOWNS states that as the firms in the market strive to maximize their profits, political parties also make efforts to maximize their vote (to come to power) (Downs, 1957).

3.2.1 The Behaviors of Ruling Party/Parties

Depending on the rule of majority vote in electoral systems, the political party that gets the most votes from the elections takes the lead in the public decision-making mechanism. This political party is called the ruling party. The ruling party can consist of only one political party, or it may be a union consisting of more than one political party, called a coalition. The ruling party or the ruling coalition implements the policies they set up until the next election within the public decision-making mechanism (Çelebi, 2003). Thus, the ruling party or coalition parties have the authority to carry out public activities. In addition to carrying out public activities, the ruling party or coalition will also want to use this mandate to win the next election and will therefore try to meet the demands of the majority of voters (Varım, 1995).

According to ÇELEBİ, the ruling party, by acting in these ways, engages in various interactions. The first interaction occurs within the ruling party itself. That is to say, every representative elected as a member of the ruling party will want to shift public activities to their constituency. In the coalition government, bargaining and voting trade will become important among the coalition parties. The second interaction happens between the pressure groups and the ruling party. The power of pressure groups has an impact on the ruling party's public activities. The third and last interaction takes place between the individuals in the minority and the ruling party. Minority individuals try to benefit from public activities and get rid of their costs (Çelebi, 2003).

3.2.2 Behaviors of Opposition Party/Parties

The party or parties that cannot obtain enough votes to become ruling party/parties and that cannot perform public activities are called opposition party/parties. The aim of the opposition party (s) is to win the next elections, take power and carry out public activities. For this reason, they try to evaluate the reactions coming from various parts of the society and produce policies (Varım, 1995).

According to BULUTOĞLU, these policies, which will be produced by the opposition party/parties, can follow two ways to the ruling party's attitude. As the first way, they adopt the same policies and strategies on all matters with the ruling party and demand votes from voters, claiming that they can make these policies and strategies better than those in power. The second way is that the ruling party fulfills all the choices of the majority, while the opposition party adopts to provide a majority by combining the policy preferences of the minorities (Bulutoğlu, 2004).

4 Behaviors of Pressure and Interest Groups

Other actors in the political economic system are pressure and interest groups. It should be noted that these two concepts are often mixed and used in the same sense. However, these two concepts are defined in different ways in political science.

Interest groups are actors in modern societies and they are a group of people who make certain requests from other groups, have common behaviors and have an actual "interest" relationship between them (Abadan, 1959). Pressure groups, on the other hand, are a special type of interest groups, which are organized groups that unite within the framework of common interests and try to influence political authorities to realize these interests. Pressure groups, on the other hand, are a special type of interest groups, which are organized groups that unite within the framework of common interests and try to influence political authorities to realize these interests (Kapani, 1996). According to KIŞLALI, pressure groups are defined as the communities that affect political power externally and try to ensure that decisions are taken and implemented in line with their own interests or opinions. In short, pressure groups are formed when naturally existing interest groups are organized (Kışlalı, 2000).

In other words, pressure groups are called interest groups that affect government and administration in various ways (Gürbüz, 1980). Trade unions, employer confederations, professional chambers, trade-industry-agriculture and other professional associations, conglomerates, foundations, associations and media can be given as examples to pressure groups.

The pressure groups, which have an effective propaganda power on the public, use the public to reach their goals and targets more quickly and take power and responsible ministers as interlocutors (Aktan, 1994). For this reason, pressure groups want to settle in the decision-making centers of the political structure in order to influence the decision mechanisms. Thus, while acting in the common interest of both themselves and the society, they also affect the economic process (Serin, 1998).

According to SAKAL, pressure groups try to lead the ruling power and its members to believe in their activities. However, if the ruling government and its members are indifferent to these activities, the pressure groups can threaten them by declaring that they will not support the deputies and the candidates for the deputy when the election periods are approaching. With this threat, the interests of the pressure group of some deputies are defended. In practice, the pressure group behaviors that we encounter most often appear in the form of general strikes, lockouts and student movements. Pressure groups can influence political power and bureaucracy in ways such as lobbying, law brokering, election campaign aids, threats, sabotage, bribery and persuasion (Sakal, 1998).

On the other hand, according to ŞENER, the effectiveness of the pressure groups may change according to the power of political parties, the prevalence of democratic social organizations and the level of political culture in the country. If the elections reflect society preferences skewed, we can talk about the effectiveness of pressure groups, especially the effectiveness of pressure groups representing employers. Although the numerical excess of the trade unions and organizational disorder decrease their impact on the political decisions, they can be very effective in making political decisions because of the economic power of employer representatives (Şener, 1996).

4.1 Rent-seeking

The activities that the pressure and interest groups attempt to achieve an artificial transfer created artificially by the state and the expenditures they have made for this purpose are called rent-seeking (Aktan, 1993). In the practice, rent-seeking can be in the form monopolistic, tariff, license, quota, social welfare, incentive and tip-seeking.

As far as pressure and interest groups can influence political decisions, they can prevent individual preferences from turning into social preferences. Pressure and interest groups can influence political power and bureaucracy in various ways by means of pressure. These pressure methods are persuasion, lobbying, aid to the election campaign, bribery, threat, sabotage, collective action and media.

4.2 Transfer Society

Today, the structure of society has become a transfer society in modern democracies. The expression transfer society means increasing amounts of funds are transferred from the state treasury to various interest groups. At the heart of this transformed system lies the efforts to re-elect power. The government wants to guarantee re-election with this fund. This is a way of selling the vote for money (Özbilen, 2012).

4.3 Lobby Activities

One of the methods used by pressure and interest groups in the process of influencing decision makers is lobbying. The most important feature of lobbying is that it is effective on decision-making mechanisms and decisions. In fact, lobbying refers to the activities carried out to make or break a law or decision on legislative and executive powers (Özbaş, 2011).

People dealing with lobbying activities are called lobbyists. Lobbyists can be included in various income groups as well as independent employees. Lobbying activity can be done in two ways, directly and indirectly. In direct lobbying, members of the government or bureaucrats should be contacted directly.

Examples of indirect lobbying activities used by lobbies are face-to-face meetings, presenting information, committee sessions, sending letters, conducting public relations work, cooperation and coalitions between lobbies, providing financial support, supporting pre and post election campaigns. The most effective method is the direct meeting with decision-makers (Bulutoğlu, 2004).

5 Behaviors of the Bureaucracy and Bureaucrats

Bureaucracy can be defined as organizations that have a hierarchical structure and are composed of appoint individuals who implement the policies of political power, fulfill the daily services of the state (Eryılmaz, 1993).

According to ERDOĞAN, bureaucracies have become politicized over time and become unable to perform their essential duties. Namely; The main task of civil servants, namely bureaucrats, who come through appointments in modern states, is to express information about the public activities that they produce and carry out publicly to the political power and the public. But over time, they have been named unqualified officials among the people they have not been able to fulfill their basic duty, as mentioned above (Erdoğan, 2004).

In contemporary societies, bureaucracy acts as a bridge between the public and the state (voters and the government) because the public goods and services offered by the government can only be produced and offered to the public through bureaucracy. As it is seen, important duties fall to the bureaucracy to ensure effectiveness in the political decision-making mechanism. On the other hand, just as the aim of the politician is to maximize his/her vote, the aims of the bureaucrats are to increase their interests, budgets and enlarge their office. Bureaucrats who maximize their budgets can also increase their number of staff and strength, reputation, salary, social security, and other benefits of their staff (Niskanen, 1971).

Besides all these, by achieving this budget maximization, bureaucrats gain benefits such as higher spending in their fields, easy promotion opportunities and comfortable working environment (Savaş, 2008). According to BUCHANAN, bureaucrats can support political parties and politicians who commit or allow to expand their bureau's budget, even if they are against their political views, because they want to maximize their budgets (Buchanan, 1977).

ALESINA and TABBELINI have touched on an important point in the relations between the politician and the bureaucrat in today's sense. Bureaucrats may not always implement the decisions made by politicians. To illustrate, in most countries the President of the Central Bank is a bureaucrat appointed by the government. The President carries out monetary policy independently of those who appoint himself. Bureaucrats may not act in this direction, although sometimes the government wants the president to act on their own accord. The ruling party may ask the Central Bank to cut interest rates, but Central Bank Bureaucrats may not decide accordingly. Therefore, regulatory policies are an application desired by both politicians and bureaucrats. However, the high number of applications to be organized brings the bureaucracy to an important point in the decision making and implementation of these regulations in the legal environment (Alesina and Tabbelini, 2006).

6 Conclusion

There are four actors in the political process: voters, politicians, pressure and interest groups and bureaucrats, each of whom tries to maximize his/her own benefit. In short, politicians (ruling and opposition party/parties) try to maximize their votes in order to be re-elected, voters try to benefit from more public goods, and pressure and interest groups try to maximize their rent and bureaucrats try to maximize their budgets.

If we consider the relationship between political power, bureaucrats, and voters, while the ruling party demands voters to regain power in election times, voters vote for policies that will increase their personal benefits. Therefore, the ruling party tries to maximize its own votes and try to increase the benefit of the voters by adopting the policies demanded by the voters. The ruling party appoints bureaucrats to implement these policies in government programs.

As stated before, in order to take place in higher positions, bureaucrats act to maximize the votes of the ruling party, but this turn into maximizing their own authority. Therefore, budget maximization , which is the intersection of the goals of voters, politicians and bureaucrats , serves to realize the goals of all of these three actors. In other words, rather than maximizing the budget, the act is to increase the public expenditures, because voter will want to get more benefits from public goods and services and the politicians who want to achieve this will develop policy accordingly and put the policy into action through bureaucrats. As a result of such policy, public spending must be increased. By increasing expenditure, budget maximization will be provided, which will result in budget deficit maximization . In this case, it will become an important problem in the financial structure of the country.

References

Abadan N. (1959), Devlet İdaresinde Menfaat Gruplarının Rolü, Ankara Üniversitesi Siyasal Bilimler Fakültesi Dergisi, Cilt: 14, Sayı:5, p: 233.

Aktan C. C. (1993), Politikada Rant Kollama, Amme İdaresi Dergisi, Cilt:26, Sayı:4, pp: 119–125.

Aktan C. C. (1994), Rant Savaşları, TOBB Ekonomik Forum, p: 14.

Aktan C. C. (2001), Siyasal Ahlak ve Siyasal Yozlaşma, Yolsuzlukla Mücadele Stratejileri, Hak-İş Yayınları, Ankara, p: 65.

Aktan C. C. (2006), Devletin Başarısızlığının Anatomisi, Çizgi Kitabevi, Konya.

Alesina A., Tabbelini G. (2006), Bureaucrats or Politicians? Part I: A Singler Policiy Task, Harvard University, NBER and CBER, January, pp: 1–2.

Avşar N. (2002), Seçmen Davranışının Sosyo-Ekonomik Boyutları ve Mesleğin Seçmen Davranışı Üzerindeki Etkileri, Yayımlanmamış Yüksek Lisans Tezi, Süleyman Demirel Üniversitesi, Isparta, p: 80.

Buchanan J. M. (1975), The Limits of Liberty, Between Anarchy and Leviathan, The University of Chicago Press, p: 157.

Buchanan J. M. (1977), Why Does Government Grow?, In T. Borchardin (Ed.), Budgets And Bureaucrats: The Sources of Government Growth, North Carolina, Duke University Press, p: 53.

Bulutoğlu K. (2004), Kamu Ekonomisine Giriş: Demokraside Devletin Ekonomik Bir Kuramı, Batı Türkeli Yayıncılık, 8.Baskı, İstanbul, pp: 112–113.

Çelebi K. A. (2003), Liberal Ekonomik Düşüncede Kamu Kesiminin Büyüklüğü Sorunu, Emek Matbaası, Manisa, Birinci Baskı, p: 122.

Denzau T., Arthur R. and Mackay J. (1976), Benefit Shares and Majority Voting, The American Review, Vol.66, p: 69–72.

Downs A. (1957), An Economic Theory of Democracy, Harper And Row, New York, p: 69.

Erdoğan S. (2004), Siyaset-Ekonomi İlişkileri, Değişim Yayınları, İstanbul, p: 27.

Eryılmaz B. (1993), Bürokrasi, Anadolu Matbaacılık, İzmir.

Gürbüz Y. (1980), Siyasal Sistemler, MAY Yayınları, İstanbul, p: 62.

Heidhues P., Lagerlöff J. (2003), Hiding Information in Electoral Competetion, Games and Economic Behavior, Vol:42, pp: 48–49.

Kapani M. (1996), Politika Bilimine Giriş, Bilgi Yayınevi, Ankara, p:193.

Kışlalı A. T. (2000), Siyaset Bilimi, Sekizinci Basım, İmge Kitabevi, Ankara, p:295.

Kovancılar B. (1997), Çağdaş Liberal Düşüncede Demokratik Karar Alma Mekanizması ve Bütçe Harcamalarında Popülist Eğilimler, Celal Bayar Üniversitesi İ.İ.B.F. Yönetim ve Ekonomi Dergisi, Sayı:3, pp: 211–212.

Mueller D. C. (1976), Public Coice: A Survey, The Journal Of Economic Literature, Vol:14, No:2, p: 403.

Niskanen W. A. (1971), Bureaucracy and Representative Government, Aldine-Atherton, Chicago.

Nordhaus W. (1975), The Political Business Cycle, Review of Economic Stduies, Vol.42, pp: 169–185.

Onur S. (2004), Seçim Ekonomisi, Asil Yayın Dağıtım Ltd.Şti., 1.Basım, Ankara, p: 40

Özbaş O. (2011), STK'ların Karar Alıcıları Etkileme Aracı Olarak Lobicilik Faaliyetleri, İdarecinin Sesi Dergisi, pp: 35–37.

Özbilen Ş. (2012), Siyasal Yozlaşmadan Ekonomik Yozlaşmaya: Demokrasi Açısından Analitik Bir Yaklaşım, http://www.econturk.org/Turkiyeekonomisi/yozlasma.pdf, Erişim Tarihi:15/06/2012.

Özbudun E. (1974), Siyasal Partiler, Sosyal Bilimler Derneği Yayınları, Birinci Basım, Ankara, p: 32.

Sakal M. (1998), Siyasal Karar Alma Sürecinde Yer Alan Ajanlar ve Roller, Dokuz Eylül Üniversitesi İktisadi ve İdari Bilimler Fakültesi Dergisi, Cilt:13, Sayı: 1, pp: 214–217.

Savaş V. (2008), Politik İktisat, Beta Yayım Evi, 6.Baskı, İstanbul, pp: 153–154

Serin V., (1998), İktisat Politikası, Alfa Basım Yayım Dağıtım Ltd.Şti., İstanbul.

Şener O. (1996), Kamu Ekonomisi, Beta Basım Yayım Dağıtım A.Ş., İstanbul, p: 173.

Telatar, F. (2004), Politik İktisat Politikası, İmaj Yayınevi, Ankara, p: 391.

Varım S. (1995), Türkiye'de Popülizm ve Seçim Ekonomisi, Egovizyon Dergisi, Sayı:10, p: 9.

İbrahim Ethem Güney

Time-Varying Causality between Bank Loans and Money Supply in Turkey

1 Introduction

There exists a prolonged discussion about the money creation process in the economics literature. Monetarists and neo-Keynesians argue that money supply is exogenous and the monetary authorities have complete control over money supply by managing monetary base via their policy tools. However, the post-Keynesian view, which has become increasingly popular among central bankers and academics in recent decades, posits that money supply in an economy is endogenously determined. More specifically, in addition to central banks' policy actions, the demand for bank loans, credit activities of commercial banks, and investment/consumption decisions of firms and households also play a crucial role in the money creation process.

The theoretical literature developed three different views about endogenous money theory. According to the accommodationist view based on Kaldor (1982), Kaldor and Trevichik (1981), and Moore (1989a, 1989b) studies, commercial banks utilize the central bank's policy rate to determine loan rates and then they try to meet all loan demands of borrowers. Monetary authorities are assumed to have control only on interest rates but not on reserves and they have to fully accommodate the liquidity needs of commercial banks to preserve the healthy functioning of the financial system. Hence, the demand for bank loans is assumed to be the main driver of the money supply. On the other hand, the structuralist view depending on Chick (1977, 1983), Minsky (1982), and Rousseas (1986) papers claims that central banks can restrict bank loans by partly accommodating the reserve needs of the banking system. Commercial banks could meet the remaining funding needs by external finance or via asset/liability management (Pollin, 1991; Palley, 1994, 1998). In this approach, central banks partly play a role in the money creation process and the monetary base, which is controlled by central banks, has an impact on bank credits. The third view is the liquidity preference approach, which objects to the assumption of identical supply and demand functions of loan money implied by the first two views. Howells (1995) emphasized differing liquidity preferences of different economic players and stated that one may not observe an identical increase in deposits resulting from loan increases. Some parts of deposits may be converted into other instruments, which will result in insufficient deposits supply to meet loan demand. This will imply a rise in deposit rates to close the mismatch between deposit supply and loan demand.

In addition to the abovementioned theoretical money supply literature, starting with the seminal papers of Moore (1988, 1989b), numerous studies tried to empirically examine the money creation process in different countries with different methods. The results strongly support the endogenous money supply theory. Pollin (1991) worked with the U.S. data for the period 1953–1988 and confirmed the structuralist view. Howells and Hussein (1998) utilized causality tests to show endogenous money in G7 economies. In a concurrent paper, Panagopoulos and Spiliotis (1998) found evidence for the accommodationist view in Greece. Nell (2000) used the South African data for the period 1987–1998 and showed that all three endogenous theoretical views are present in South Africa. Vera (2001) revealed the endogeneity of money supply in Spain for the period 1987–1998. Shanmugam et al. (2003) supported the liquidity preference view of endogenous money theory for Malaysia. Similarly, Lavoie (2005) showed that bank credits drive money supply in Canada. Haghighat (2012) established the endogenous money hypothesis for Iran. Tas and Togay (2012) worked with the data of GCC countries and disclosed the endogenous money theory for all GCC countries except Bahrain and Kuwait. Nayan et al. (2013), utilized a large data set of 177 countries for the period 1970–2011. They employed a dynamic panel data analysis which revealed the endogenous money hypothesis as post-Keynesians proposed. Badarudin et al. (2013) andØrataş et al. (2015) investigated the nature of the money supply for G7 countries and found evidence for the endogenous money hypothesis. In a recent study, Işık et al. (2018) showed the role of credits in the money creation process for 13 European Union countries for the period 2001–2015.

There are also many papers in the empirical literature that investigated the money creation process in Turkey. Çavuşoğlu (2003) studied the relationship between money supply, inflation and budget deficits for the period 1985–2005 and revealed the endogenous money structure. Çifter and Ozun (2007) confirmed the accommodationist view in Turkey for the period 1997–2006. Işık and Kahyaoğlu (2011) examined the endogenous money hypothesis for the 1987–2007 period and showed the impact of bank loans on the monetary base and money supply in Turkey. Similarly, Köksal (2016) proved the endogenous money structure for the period of 2006–2014. Çepni and Güney (2017) empirically tested the endogenous money supply hypothesis for the period 2006–2015. Their results are strongly supportive of the hypothesis that money supply is loan-driven and demand-determined in Turkey. Dedeoğlu and Öğüt (2018) employed an asymmetric causality test and showed that causality runs from bank loans to money supply for the positive components so loan cuts may not result in a fall in the money supply. Finally, in a recent study, Koç Yurtkur (2019) investigated the causal relationship between loans, money supply and monetary base for the period of 2006–2018. The results confirmed the bi-directional causal relationship between credit and money multiplier which supports the liquidity preference view.

The majority of the existing literature employed different types of causality and cointegration tests to check the endogenous money supply hypothesis for different countries. However, to the best of my knowledge, there does not exist a study that utilizes the time-varying Granger causality method in this literature. Motivating from the fact that the nature of money supply and bank loans could change significantly in the observation period, in this chapter I utilize the time-varying Granger Causality test developed by Rossi and Wang (2019) to examine the nature of money supply in Turkey for the period 2007–2019. This test is robust to the presence of instabilities, allows for controlling other variables and can capture the periods in which Granger-causality either arises or fades away in the data. This provides me the chance to observe the endogeneity structure dynamically. The empirical analysis shows that there exists bi-directional causality between bank loans and money supply in Turkey, which supports the endogenous money hypothesis. Besides, causality from money supply to bank loans becomes very weak especially after the beginning of 2014. This implies that the Central Bank fully accommodates the liquidity needs of the banking system and has imperfect control in the money creation process in recent years.

2 Data

In the empirical analysis, I use monthly data of total bank loans (BL), deposits (DEP), and the money supply[1] (M2) over the period January 2007–December 2019. I download the data from the electronic data delivery system of the Central Bank of the Republic of Turkey (CBRT) and Bloomberg. All data are seasonally adjusted and transformed into a natural logarithmic form.

1 I also employ empirical analysis with M1 and M3 monetary aggregates. The results are similar. For simplicity, I proceed only with M2, which is mostly used in the literature.

3 Methodology

Granger (1969) causality tests, which are extracted from reduced-form Vector Autoregressive (VAR) models, are frequently used to examine interdependencies between different time series in the empirical literature. However, this methodology is subject to serious practical challenges. First, instabilities in time series data may appear (Stock and Watson, 2006). Second, predictive content could be unstable over time (Rossi, 2013). In particular, a successful predictor in one period may not perform well in other subsequent periods. Third, a good in-sample predictor may not have an out-of-sample forecasting ability (Rossi, 2013). Considering such problems, Granger causality tests depending on stationarity assumptions may provide incorrect inferences (Rossi, 2005).

Therefore, in this chapter, I utilize the time-varying Granger causality test developed by Rossi and Wang (2019), which is robust to the abovementioned instabilities. Following the theoretical framework in Rossi and Wang (2019), firstly a reduced-form VAR with time-varying parameters is utilized as follows:

$$B_t\left(L\right)y_t = u_t \tag{1}$$

$$B_t\left(L\right) = I - B_{1,t}L - B_{2,t}L^2 - \ldots - B_{k,t}L^k \tag{2}$$

$$u_t \overset{iid}{\sim} \left(0, \Sigma\right) \tag{3}$$

where $B_{i,t}$, $i = 1, .., k$represent (nxn) time-varying coefficient matrix and $y_t = \left[y_{1,t}, y_{2,t}, \ldots, y_{n,t}\right]'$ is $(nx1)$ vector of endogenous variables, whereas u_t stands for error terms[2]. One should note that error terms can comply with idiosyncratic shocks which are assumed to be heteroscedastic and serially correlated.

Secondly, following Jordà (2005) I utilize a direct multistep VAR-linear projections (VAR-LP) forecasting model with time-varying parameters. Iteration of equation (2) and projection of y_{t+h} onto the linear space created by $(y_{t-1}, y_{t-2}, \ldots, y_{t-k})'$ derives the following equation:

$$y_{t+h} = \alpha_{1,t}y_{t-1} + \alpha_{2,t}y_{t-2} + \ldots + \alpha_{k,t}y_{t-k} + \varepsilon_{t+h} \tag{4}$$

2 The lag length is chosen as 1 according to the Schwarz Information Criterion (SIC).

where $\alpha_{i,t}, i = 1, \ldots k$ is a function of time-varying coefficients, $\left[y_{t+h}, y_{t-1}, \ldots, y_{t-k}\right]'$ represent the variables in the model, and ε_{t+h} is moving average of errors u from t to $t + h$, h=3,6,9 months.
Finally, taking λ_t as an appropriate subset of the vector including $(\alpha_{1,t}, \alpha_{2,t}, \ldots, \alpha_{k,t})$, then in both specifications, robust Granger causality test figure out the validity of the null hypothesis in equation (5):

$$H_0 : \lambda_t = 0, \qquad for\ all\ t = 1, \ \ldots, T \tag{5}$$

The null hypothesis is checked by using four test statistics as given in Rossi (2005); namely, the optimal exponential Wald test statistic (ExpW), optimal mean Wald test statistic (MeanW), Nyblom test statistic (Nyblom), and Quandt likelihood test statistic (SupLR). ExpW and MeanW were proposed in Andrews and Ploberger (1994). Nyblom test was introduced by Nyblom (1989) and the SupLR test statistic is based on the Sup-LR test proposed by Andrews (1993). I examine the time-varying causality between bank loans and money supply by using the following vector of endogenous variables:

$$y_t = [BL_t, DEP_t, MS_t]' \tag{6}$$

where BL_t is the total bank loans, DEP_t represents deposits and MS_t is the M2 money supply indicator composed of currency in circulation, sight deposits, and time deposits. DEP_t is included as a control variable since bank deposits may have an impact on both bank loans and money supply, which may affect empirical results.

4 Empirical Findings

I start the empirical analysis with a stylized fact. Figure 1 illustrates the relationship between the year-on-year (YoY) percent change in total bank loans and the money supply (M2) in Turkey. These two series have followed similar patterns in my observation period.

Motivating from this observation, I employ reduced-form VAR-based robust Granger causality tests to examine which variable drives the other. Empirical results are summarized in Table 1. The key observation from Table 1 is that there exists a definitively statistically significant bi-directional Granger causality between total bank loans and money supply in Turkey. This result is in favor of the liquidity preference view of the endogenous money supply theory. According

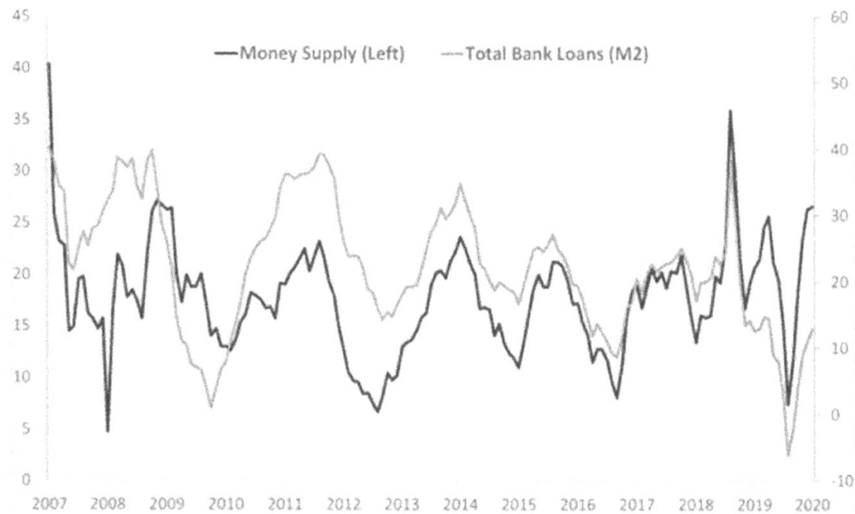

Figure 1: *Total Banks Loans – Money Supply Relationship (YoY % Change)*

Table 1: *Time-Varying Parameter Granger Causality Test Results (VAR Model)*

Direction of Causality	Test Type	Test Statistic	p-value
$BL_t \to MS_t$	ExpW	132.42	0.00
	MeanW	169.62	0.00
	Nyblom	108.44	0.00
	SupLR	274.14	0.00
$MS_t \to BL_t$	ExpW	123.63	0.00
	MeanW	74.70	0.00
	Nyblom	190.01	0.00
	SupLR	256.79	0.00

to different tests' results, observed bi-directional causality is intrinsically time-varying. This result is intuitive since several domestic or foreign shocks have been experienced in Turkey during the sample period, which might affect the degree and nature of the relationship between bank loans and money supply through time.

To have a more detailed analysis, I draw the track of Wald statistic over the sample period, as presented in Figures 2 and 3. We observe three episodes from

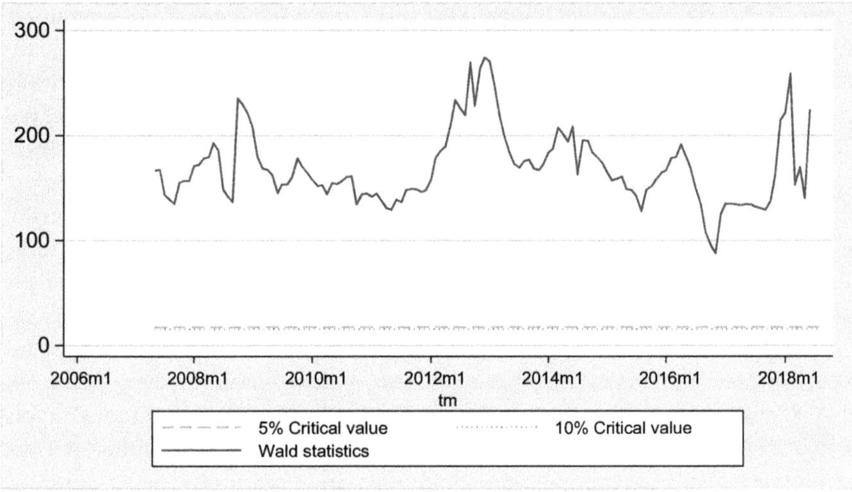

Figure 2: *Time-Varying Wald Statistics (VAR Model, Testing BL Granger Causes MS)*

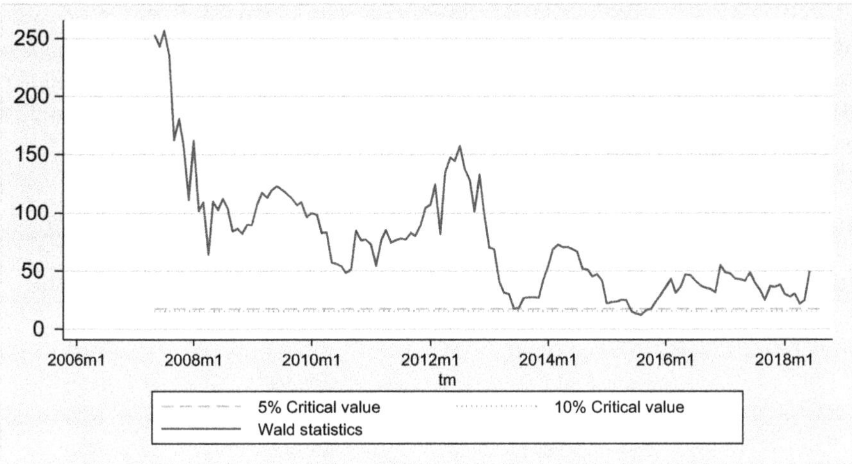

Figure 3: *Time-Varying Wald Statistics (VAR Model, Testing MS Granger Causes BL)*

Figure 2 during which the Granger causality from bank loans to money supply strengthens. Firstly, during the global financial crisis, an increase in bank loans could be quickly reflected into deposits which might affect money supply via the monetary base channel. The second increase in causality is observed during FED's quantitative easing period during which portfolio flows to emerging countries including Turkey increased dramatically with rising risk appetite. However, causality then weakened with the effect of FED's taper tantrum starting at the end of 2013 and macro-prudential regulations implemented by Turkish regulators in that period. Finally, during 2017 bank loans grew sharply with the effect of new credit guarantee fund limits. That increase quickly reflected in monetary aggregates, which implied strong causality from bank loans to the money supply. On the other hand, the main observation from Figure 3 is that starting from the beginning of 2014, Granger causality from money supply to bank loans gets weaker and vanishes at some episodes. During that period, changing global risk appetite and supply/demand conditions in the domestic credit market could be the main drivers of weakening causality from monetary aggregates to bank loans.

The final step is to check the out-of-sample predictive performance of bank loans and money supply variables. For this purpose, I repeat the abovementioned analysis with a multistep VAR-LP forecasting model over 3, 6 and 9 -months ahead horizons, assuming heteroscedastic and serially correlated shocks. The results are summarized in Table 2. All test statistics confirm the predictive ability of bank loans for money supply and vice versa. Hence, both variables can predict each other both in- and out-of-sample.

Table 2: *Time-Varying Parameter Granger Causality Tests (VAR-LP Forecasting Model)*

Direction of Causality	Test Type	Test Statistic	p-value
3-Months Ahead			
$BL_t \rightarrow MS_t$	ExpW	70.92	0.00
	MeanW	48.55	0.00
	Nyblom	126.85	0.00
	SupLR	151.19	0.00
6-Months Ahead			
$BL_t \rightarrow MS_t$	ExpW	136.79	0.00
	MeanW	119.78	0.00
	Nyblom	103.98	0.00
	SupLR	283.28	0.00

Table 2: Continued

Direction of Causality	Test Type	Test Statistic	p-value
9-Months Ahead			
$BL_t \rightarrow MS_t$	ExpW	199.55	0.00
	MeanW	170.33	0.00
	Nyblom	957.45	0.00
	SupLR	408.71	0.00
3-Months Ahead			
$MS_t \rightarrow BL_t$	ExpW	145.07	0.00
	MeanW	115.33	0.00
	Nyblom	862.49	0.00
	SupLR	299.92	0.00
6-Months Ahead			
$MS_t \rightarrow BL_t$	ExpW	628.75	0.00
	MeanW	247.91	0.00
	Nyblom	288.43	0.00
	SupLR	1267.24	0.00
9-Months Ahead			
$MS_t \rightarrow BL_t$	ExpW	211.78	0.00
	MeanW	127.12	0.00
	Nyblom	452.44	0.00
	SupLR	433.24	0.00

5 Conclusion

In this chapter, I try to examine the time-varying relationship between bank loans and money supply in Turkey for the period 2007–2019. For this purpose, I utilize the time-varying Granger causality framework proposed by Rossi and Wang (2019), which allows me to observe how the causality between these variables changes through the sample period. The empirical evidence shows that there exists a significant causality relation from bank loans to the money supply in Turkey, which emphasizes the role of commercial bank credits in the money creation process. Observed causality gets stronger in some episodes with the effect of rising global risk appetite and/or easing in domestic financial conditions. I also detect a Granger causality from money supply to bank loans which becomes weaker after 2014. All in all, empirical results validate the liquidity preference view and partly the accommodationist view of the endogenous money supply hypothesis for Turkey.

References

Andrews, D. W. (1993). Tests for Parameter Instability and Structural Change with Unknown Change Point. Econometrica: Journal of the Econometric Society, 61(4), 821–856.

Andrews, D. W., and Ploberger, W. (1994). Optimal Tests When a Nuisance Parameter Is Present Only under the Alternative. Econometrica: Journal of the Econometric Society, 62(6), 1383–1414.

Badarudin, Z. E., Ariff, M., and Khalid, A. M. (2013). Post-Keynesian Money Endogeneity Evidence in G-7 Economies. Journal of International Money and Finance, 33, 146–162.

Chick, V. (1977). The Theory of Monetary Policy. Oxford: Parkgate Books.

Chick, V. (1983). Macroeconomics After Keynes: A Reconsideration of the General Theory. Oxford: Philip Allan.

Cifter, A., and Ozun, A. (2007). The Monetary Transmission Mechanism in the New Economy: Evidence from Turkey (1997–2006). South East European Journal of Economics and Business, 2, 15–24.

Çavuşoğlu, A. T. (2003). The Endogenous Money Growth: An Outcome of High Budget Deficits in Turkey. HÜ İktisadi ve İdari Bilimler Fakültesi Dergisi, 21(1), 111–127.

Çepni, O., and Guney, I. E. (2017). Endogeneity of Money Supply: Evidence from Turkey. Finance & Banking Studies, 6(1), 1–10.

Dedeoğlu, D., and Ogut, K. (2018). Examination of Money Supply Endogeneity in Turkey: Evidence from Asymmetric Causality Test. Cogent Economics & Finance, 6: 1518956.

Erataş, F., Başçı Nur, H., and Çınar, S. (2015). Para Arzının Post Keynesyen Yorumu: Gelişmiş Ülkeler Örneği. Akademik Sosyal Araştırmalar Dergisi, 3(15), 398–409.

Granger, C. W. (1969). Investigating Causal Relations by Econometric Models and Cross-Spectral Methods. Econometrica: Journal of the Econometric Society, 37(3), 424–438.

Haghighat, J. (2012). The Endogenous Money in Iran: What It is and Why It Matters. International Journal of Trade, Economics and Finance, 3(2), 82.

Howells, P. G. A. (1995). Endogenous Money. International Papers in Political Economy, 2(2), 1–41.

Howells, P. G. A., and Hussein, K. (1998). The Endogeneity of Money: Evidence from the G7. Scottish Journal of Political Economy, 45(3), 329–340.

Işık, S., and Kahyaoğlu, H. (2011). The Endogenous Money Hypothesis: Some Evidence from Turkey (1987–2007). Journal of Money, Investment and Banking, 19, 61–71.

Işık, S., Alkin, H., ve Uluğ, M. (2018). Avrupa Birliği Üyesi 13 Ülkede Post-Keynesyen Para Arzının İçselliği Hipotezinin Test Edilmesi. Kafkas Üniversitesi İktisadi ve İdari Bilimler Fakültesi Dergisi, 9(17), 1–20.

Jordà, O. (2005). Estimation and Inference of Impulse Responses by Local Projections. American Economic Review, 95(1), 161–182.

Kaldor, N. (1982). The Scourge of Monetarism. London: Oxford University.

Kaldor, N., ve Trevithick, J. (1981). A Keynesian Perspective on Money. Lloyds Bank Review, 139(1), 1–19.

Koç Yurtkur, A. (2019). Para Arzının İçselliği Hipotezi: Türkiye için Ampirik Bir Analiz (2006–2018). International Journal of Economic and Administrative Studies, 24, 131–150.

Köksal, B. (2016). Türkiye Ekonomisinde Para Arzının İçselliği: 2006–2014 Dönemi Üzerine Bir Uygulama. Ataturk University Journal of Economics & Administrative Sciences, 30(2), 455–471.

Lavoie, M. (2005). Monetary Base Endogeneity and the New Procedures of the Asset-Based Canadian and American Monetary Systems. Journal of Post Keynesian Economics, 27(4), 689–709.

Minsky, H. P. (1982). Can 'It' Happen Again? Essays on Instability and Finance. New York: M. E. Sharpe.

Moore, B. J. (1988). Horizontalists and Verticalists: The Macroeconomics of Credit Money. Cambridge: Cambridge University Press.

Moore, B. J. (1989a). A Simple Model of Bank Intermediation. Journal of Post Keynesian Economics, 12(1), 10–28.

Moore, B. J. (1989b). The Endogeneity of Credit Money. Review of Political Economy, 1(1), 65–93.

Nayan, S., Kadir, N., Abdullah, M. S., and Ahmad, M. (2013). Post Keynesian Endogeneity of Money Supply: Panel Evidence. Procedia Economics and Finance, 7, 48–54.

Nell, K. S. (2000). The Endogenous/Exogenous Nature of South Africa's Money Supply under Direct and Indirect Monetary Control Measures. Journal of Post Keynesian Economics, 23(2), 313–329.

Nyblom, J. (1989). Testing for the Constancy of Parameters over Time. Journal of the American Statistical Association, 84(405), 223–230.

Palley, T. (1994). Competing Views of the Money Supply Process. Metroeconomica, 45(1), 397–403.

Palley, T. I. (1998). Accommodationism, Structuralism and Superstructuralism. Journal of Post Keynesian Economics, 21(1), 171–173.

Panagopoulos, Y., and Spiliotis, A. (1998). The Determinants of Commercial Banks' Lending Behavior: Some Evidence for Greece. Journal of Post Keynesian Economics, 20(4), 649–672.

Pollin, R. (1991). Two Theories of Money Supply Endogeneity. Journal of Post Keynesian Economics, 13(3), 366–96.

Rossi, B. (2005). Optimal Tests for Nested Model Selection with Underlying Parameter Instability. Econometric Theory, 21(5), 962–990.

Rossi, B. (2013). Advances in Forecasting under Model Instability. In: G. Elliott and A. Timmermann (eds.), Handbook of Economic Forecasting, Volume 2B. Elsevier Publications, pp. 1203–1324.

Rossi, B., and Wang Y. (2019). Vector Autoregressive-Based Granger Causality Test in the Presence of Instabilities. The Stata Journal: Promoting Communications on Statistics and Stata, 19(4), 883–899.

Rousseas, S. (1986). Post Keynesian Monetary Economics. New York: M. E. Sharpe.

Shanmugam B., Nair M., and Wee Li O. (2003). The Endogenous Money Hypothesis: Empirical Evidence from Malaysia. Journal of Post Keynesian Economics, 25(4), 599–611.

Stock, J. H., and Watson, M. W. (2006). Forecasting with Many Predictors. Handbook of Economic Forecasting, 1, 515–554.

Tas, B. K. O., and Togay, S. (2012). A Direct Test of the Endogeneity of Money: Implications for Gulf Cooperation Council (GCC) Countries. Economic Modelling, 29, 577–585.

Vera, A. P. (2001). The Endogenous Money Hypothesis: Some Evidence from Spain (1987–1998). Journal of Post Keynesian Economics, 23(3), 509–526.

Yavuz Selim Hacıhasanoğlu

Review of the Environmental Kuznets Curve Literature and the Implications for Green Finance

1 Environmental Kuznets Curve Hypothesis

One of the key trade-offs in today's world is between economic growth and environmental protection. In the early stages of growth-pollution nexus, a linear relationship is considered because more growth requires more usage of energy which brings environmental pollution. For example, Limits to Growth (Meadows et al. 1972) idea considers the consumption of natural resources as a limit to sustainable development. Opposite to this argument, at the beginning of the 1990s, some researchers asserted that there is a non-linear relationship between economic growth and environmental degradation.

Traditional Kuznets' curve (KC) based on the seminal paper by Kuznets (1955) hypothesizes that inequality follows an inverted U-shaped path through the rise in income per capita. Adopted from this, the environmental Kuznets curve (EKC) shows the relationship between income and pollution which asserts an in-verted U-shaped relationship between them, meaning that in the initial steps of economic growth environmental pollution increases up to a certain point, and then it starts decreasing implying that economic growth causes an environmental recovery (Grossman and Krueger, 1991). That is to say, up to a certain point economic growth is the cause of environmental deterioration, and after reaching that point economic growth is the source of the environmental quality.

2 Explanations for the Shape of the EKC

Grossman and Krueger (1995) use scale, composition, and technique effects to explain the form of the EKC. In the early stages of growth, an economy produces more using more resources with brown energy and this displays environmental pollution which shows the scale effect. In the second stage, the production composition of the economy converts from energy-intensive industrial production to environmentally friendly technology and service-intensive production (composition effect). Finally, in the technique effect, a wealthy economy transforms old pollutive technologies to clean technologies and use green energy. In addition to production explanations, with increasing environmental awareness for high-income consumers, the composition and technique effects are supported by consumers in wealthy economies (Selden and Song 1995; McConnell 1997). Consumers in these countries consider more about environmental quality, and they have a higher demand for environmentally friendly products (Dinda 2004; Bagliani et al. 2008). In other words, there are structural differences in consumer preferences while their income is low and high based on different stages of economic development (Hervieux and Darne 2015; Dietz et al. 2012). The relative intensity of these effects through economic growth determines the shape of the EKC.

Starting with Grossman and Krueger (1991), the EKC hypothesis is one of the most investigated hypotheses. Using reduced-form models with time series or panel data, the relationship was tested for many countries (Ang 2007 for France; Narayan and Narayan 2010 for 43 developing countries; He and Richard 2010 for Canada; Acaravci and Ozturk 2010 for Europe; Pao and Tsai 2011 for BRIC countries; Wang 2012 for 98 countries; Sephton and Mann 2013 for Spain; Tiwari et al. 2013 for India; Osabuohien et al. 2014 for African economies; Apergis and Ozturk 2015 for Asian economies; Ajmi et al. 2015 for G7 countries other than Germany; Wang et al. 2016 for China; Azam et al. 2016 for the US, China, India, and Japan; Saidi and Mbarek 2016 for 19 emerging countries; Bilgili et al. 2016 for OECD countries; Rafindadi 2016 for Japan; Apergis et al. 2017 for 48 US states).

3 Environmental Pollution Indicators in the Literature

Most of the studies in the empirical EKC literature use CO2 emission as a proxy for environmental pollution. However, CO2 emission is not enough to represent environmental degradation. As emphasized by Stern (2014) with technological innovations and environmental regulations, the composition of effluent has shifted which implies the necessity of considering different environmental variables in the analysis. Alternatively, ecological footprint – first developed by Rees (1992) and improved by Wackernagel and Rees (1998) to measure the environmental influence of countries or individuals – calculates the consumption of resources and absorption of waste in terms of equal parts of the biosphere, that is, biologically productive land and sea area or in other words biocapacity. If biocapacity is greater than the ecological footprint then there is an ecological surplus for that country. A relatively small number of studies utilize ecological footprint as a measure of environmental degradation. Bagliani et al. (2008),

Wang et al. (2013), Al-Mulali, Tang, and Ozturk (2015), Acar and Aşıcı (2016), and Charfeddine and Mrabet (2017) are some of the examples testing the EKC hypothesis for groups of countries using ecological footprint. Another measure used in the literature is carbon footprint is defined as "A measure of the total amount of CO2 and CH4 emissions of a defined population, system or activity, considering all relevant sources, sinks, and storage within the spatial and temporal boundary of the population, system or activity of interest." in Wright et al. (2011). This measure is used in some recent papers such as Pablo-Romero and Sanchez-Braza (2017) and Charfeddine (2017).

4 Methodologies in the EKC Literature

Starting with Grossman and Krueger (1991), a huge empirical literature accumulated to test the EKC hypothesis for developing and developed countries. The literature mainly focuses on the relationship between per capita income and environmental pollution indicators. To test the nonlinearity or quadratic nature of the relation, most of the papers include both income and square of income as explanatory variables using a single country or group of countries with different econometric estimation techniques. Single country studies utilize time-series methodologies while panel data is used for groups of countries based on the degree of development of countries. Finally, some studies include control variables in their analysis. Basically, EKC papers differentiate from each other in four dimensions: type of environmental pollutant variables used, the econometric methodology implemented, set of countries and time periods in the analysis, and type of control variables in the model.

4.1 Cross-Sectional Studies

Early studies are based on cross-sectional data while panel data and time series methodologies have started to be used in recent years. Papers from Rothman (1998) for a group of countries, York et al. (2003) for 142 countries, Gondran and Brodhag (2006) for 131 countries, Bagliani et al. (2008) for 141 nations, and Wang et al. (2013) for 150 countries do not find evidence to support the EKC hypothesis. On the other hand, Panayotou (1993) support the EKC hypothesis for 68 countries.

4.2 Panel Data Studies

Apart from the cross-sectional studies, conclusions from the papers using panel data models are more in line with the EKC hypothesis. For instance, Kaufmann et al. (1998) for 22 countries in the 1974–1989 period, Song et al. (2008) for Chinese provinces from 1985 to 2005, Bilgili et al. (2016) for 17 OECD countries in the period 1977–2010, Richmond and Kaufmann (2006) for 36 developed and emerging countries with a different turning point for different income levels find supporting evidence for the EKC. Similarly, Ulucak and Bilgili (2018) confirm the EKC hypothesis for high-, middle-, and low-income countries. On the other hand, Al-Mulali et al. (2015) by classifying 93 countries according to their income levels in the period 1980–2008 favor the EKC hypothesis for high- and middle-income countries but not for the low-income countries. Ozturk et al. (2016) find similar results for 144 countries over the period 1988–2008 for the tourism sector. On the other hand, using fixed and random effects panel data models for 58 countries from 1961 to 2003, Dietz et al. (2012) show that there is a U-shaped relationship between environmental measure and income which is the opposite of what EKC implies. Similarly, using data for the 15 Middle East and North African (MENA) economies, Charfeddine and Mrabet (2017) indicates that the GDP per capita and environmental footprint have an inverted U-shaped relationship for oil-exporting economies and U-shaped relationship for non-oil-exporting economies in the period 1975–2007. Caviglia-Harris, Chambers and Kahn (2009) and Al-Mulali et al. (2016) are two examples of papers providing evidence against the EKC hypothesis for 146 countries and 58 countries respectively. Finally, differentiating from these panel studies, Akbostancı, Asik, and Tunc (2009) find an N-shaped relationship between income and pollution.

4.3 Time-Series Studies

Because of the country-specific dynamics which are not considered in cross-sectional and panel data models, some researchers (Stern et al. 1996; Friedl and Getzner 2003) argue that these models have misleading results. Taking this into consideration, many researchers have started using time-series methodologies for individual countries and finding unsupportive (Hervieux and Darne 2015; Hervieux and Darne 2016), supportive for some countries and not supportive for others (Wang 2017), supportive for some environmental variables (Mrabet and Alsamara 2017), and U-shaped (Charfeddine 2017) evidence. In this time series methodological part of the literature, some studies try to investigate a causal relationship between environmental degradation and income using different types of Granger causality tests. Applying a vector error correction model (VECM) Granger causality test, Bello et al. (2018) find evidence of the EKC hypothesis in Malaysia. Similarly, Iwata et al. (2010) support an inverted U-shaped relationship between income and environmental variables for France via running the Granger causality test with the ARDL model. Some studies find one-way causality from income to environmental variables (Hamit-Haggar 2012; Govindaraju and Tang 2013; Yuan et al. 2008; Saboori and Jamalludin 2013; Jebli et al. 2016; Arouri et al. 2013; Kivyiro and Arminen 2014; Rafindadi 2016), while others show a bi-directional causality (Pao and Tsai 2011; Ang 2007; Tiwari et al. 2013; Magazzino 2016; Destek and Sarkodie 2019). Some recent studies initiated time-varying Granger causality frameworks for their EKC analysis. Some of the examples of these papers are Ajmi et al. (2015), Shahbaz et al. (2016), Tzeremes (2018), and Yilanci and Ozgur (2019). Of these studies, Shahbaz et al. (2016) find evidence for EKC in Turkey and Indonesia. Yilanci and Ozgur (2019) make their analysis for G7 countries and confirm the validity of EKC in Japan and the USA but not in the UK, Germany, France, Italy, and Canada. On the other hand, Ajmi et al. (2015) and Tzeremes (2018) find an N-shaped relationship for G7 countries except for Germany and the 50 USA states respectively.

4.4 Studies Using Control Variables

The latest papers in the EKC literature have incorporated additional control variables to check the robustness of their results. As explained in Ozturk et al. (2016), potential control variables in the literature are energy consumption (Pao and Tsai 2010; Lean and Smyth 2010; Shahbaz et al. 2014; Baek 2015), renewable energy production (Bento and Moutinho 2016), nuclear energy (Iwata et al. 2010), political freedom (Torras and Boyce 1998), employment ratio (Sari and Soytas 2009; Ghosh 2010), international trade (Suri and Chapman 1998; Tiwari et al. 2013; Arouri et al. 2013; Ozturk and Al-Mulali 2015; Bento and Moutinho 2016), investment (Ghosh 2010) and urbanization (Hossain 2011; Al-Mulali et al. 2015).

3 Conclusion

The main conclusion from this review is that evidence of the EKC hypothesis is mixed depending on the estimation method, countries and time period in the analysis, and the type of environmental variables utilized in the models. There are positive, negative, linear, U-shaped, and N-shaped results between the environmental indicators and economic growth in the literature. These results show that the EKC hypothesis is valid only for few countries and for a few types of footprints, meaning that economic growth is not the source of the environmental quality. This also implies that countries need additional environmental regulations such as enhancing energy efficiency and decreasing greenhouse effects to reduce environmental degradation. For this reason, green finance has an important role in financial systems that may improve environmental quality.

References

Acar S, Aşıcı AA (2016) Does income growth relocate ecological footprint? Ecol Indic 61:707–714.

Acaravci A, Ozturk I (2010) On the relationship between energy consumption, CO2 emissions and economic growth in Europe. Energy 35(12):5412–5420. https://doi.org/10.1016/j.energy.2010.07.009

Ajmi AN, Hammoudeh S, Nguyen DK, Sato JR (2015) On the relationships between CO2 emissions, energy consumption and income: the importance of time variation. Energy Econ 49:629–638. https://doi.org/10.1016/j.eneco.2015.02.007

Akbostancı E, Asik S, Tunc GI (2009) The relationship between income and environment in Turkey: is there an environmental Kuznets curve. Energy Policy 37(3):861–867. https://doi.org/10.1016/j.enpol.2008.09.088

Al-Mulali U, Solarin SA, Ting LS, Ozturk I (2016) Does moving towards renewable energy cause water and land inefficiency? An empirical investigation. Energy Policy 93:303–314. https://doi.org/10.1016/j.enpol.2016.03.023

Al-Mulali U, Tang CF, Ozturk I (2015) Does financial development reduce environmental degradation? Evidence from a panel study of 129 countries. Environmental Science and Pollution Research, forthcoming. http://link.springer.com/article/10.1007/s11356-015-4726-x

Al-Mulali U, Weng-Wai C, Sheau-Ting L, Mohammed AH (2015) Investigating the environ-mental Kuznets curve (EKC) hypothesis by utilizing the ecological footprint as an indicator of environmental degradation. Ecol Indic 48:315–323. https://doi.org/10.1016/j.ecolind.2014.08.029

Ang JB (2007) CO2 emissions, energy consumption, and output in France. Energy Policy 35(10):4772–4778. https://doi.org/10.1016/j.enpol.2007.03.032

Apergis N, Ozturk I (2015) Testing environmental Kuznets curve hypothesis in Asian coun-tries. Ecol Indic 52:16–22. https://doi.org/10.1016/j.ecolind.2014.11.026

Apergis N, Christou C, Gupta R (2017) Are there environmental Kuznets curves for US state-level CO2 emissions? Renewable and Sustainable Energy Reviews, Elsevier 69(C): 551–558.

Arouri M, Shahbaz M, Onchang R, Islam F, Teulon F (2013) Environmental Kuznets curve in Thailand: cointegration and causality analysis. J Energy Dev 39(1/2):149–170.

Azam M, Khan AQ, Abdullah HB, Qureshi ME (2016) The impact of CO2 emissions on economic growth: evidence from selected higher CO2 emissions economies. Environ Sci Pollut Res 23:6376–6389.

Baek J (2015) A panel cointegration analysis of CO2 emissions, nuclear energy and income in major nuclear generating countries. Appl Energy 145:133–138. https://doi.org/10.1016/j.apenergy.2015.01.074

Bagliani M, Bravo G, Dalmazzone S (2008) A consumption-based approach to environmental Kuznets curves using the ecological footprint indicator. Ecol Econ 65:650–661. https://doi.org/10.1016/j.ecolecon.2008.01.010

Bello MO, Solarin SA, Yen YY (2018) The impact of electricity consumption on CO2 emis-sion, carbon footprint, water footprint and ecological footprint: the role of hydropower in an emerging economy. J Environ Manag 219:218–230. https://doi.org/10.1016/j.jenvman.2018.04.101

Bento JPC, Moutinho V (2016) CO2 emissions, non-renewable and renewable electricity pro-duction, economic growth, and international trade in Italy. Renew Sustain Energy Rev 55:142–155. https://doi.org/10.1016/j.rser.2015.10.151

Berenguer-Rico V, Gonzalo J (2013) Co-summability: From linear to non-linear cointe-gration. Universidad Carlos III de Madrid working paper (no. 13–12).

Bilgili F, Koçak E, Bulut Ü (2016) The dynamic impact of renewable energy consumption on CO2 emissions: a revisited environmental Kuznets curve approach. Renew Sustain Energy Rev 54:838–845. https://doi.org/10.1016/j.rser.2015.10.080

Caviglia-Harris JL, Chambers D, Kahn JR (2009) Taking the 'U' out of Kuznets. A comprehen-sive analysis of the EKC and environmental degradation. Ecol Econ 68(4):1149–1159.

Charfeddine L (2017) The impact of energy consumption and economic development on eco-logical footprint and CO2 emissions: evidence from a markov switching equilibrium cor-rection model. Energy Econ 65:355e374. https://doi.org/10.1016/j.eneco.2017.05.009

Charfeddine L, Mrabet Z (2017) The impact of economic development and social-political fac-tors on ecological footprint: a panel data analysis for 15 MENA countries. Renew Sust En-erg Rev 76:138–154. https://doi.org/10.1016/j.rser.2017.03.031

Destek MA, Sarkodie SA (2019) Investigation of environmental Kuznets curve for ecological footprint: the role of energy and financial development. Sci Total Environ 650:2483–2489. https://doi.org/10.1016/j.scitotenv.2018.10.017

Dietz T, Rosa EA, York R (2012) Environmentally efficient well-being: is there a Kuznets curve? Appl Geogr 32:21–28. https://doi.org/10.1016/j.apgeog.2010.10.011

Dinda S (2004) Environmental Kuznets curve hypothesis: a survey. Ecol Econ 49(4):431–455. https://doi.org/10.1016/j.ecolecon.2004.02.011

Friedl B, Getzner M (2003) Determinants of CO2 emissions in a small open economy. Ecol Econ 45(1):133–148. https://doi.org/10.1016/S0921-8009(03)00008-9

Ghosh S (2010) Examining carbon emissions-economic growth nexus for India: a multivariate cointegration approach. Energ Pol 38:2613–3130.

Gondran N, Brodhag C (2006) Local environmental quality versus (global) ecological carrying capacity: what might alternative aggregated indicators bring to the debates about environ-mental Kuznets curves and sustainable development? Int J Sustain Dev 9(3):297–310. https://doi.org/10.1504/IJSD.2006.012850

Govindaraju VC, Tang CF (2013) The dynamic links between CO2 emissions, eco-nomic growth and coal consumption in China and India. Appl Energy 104:310–318.

Grossman GM, Krueger AB (1991) Environmental impacts of a North American free trade agreement. National Bureau of Economic Research. Working papers no. 3914.

Grossman, GM., Krueger, AB (1995). Economic growth and the environment. Q J Econ 110(2): 353–377.

Hamit-Haggar M (2012) Greenhouse gas emissions, energy consumption and economic growth: a panel cointegration analysis from Canadian industrial sector perspective. Energy Econ 34:358–364. https://doi.org/10.1016/j.eneco.2011.06.005

He J, Richard P (2010) Environmental Kuznets curves for CO2 in Canada. Ecol Econ 69:1083–1093.

Hervieux M-S, Darné O (2015) Environmental Kuznets curve and ecological footprint: a time series analysis. Econ Bull 35(1):814–826.

Hervieux MS, Darne O (2016) Production and consumption-based approaches for the envi-ronmental Kuznets curve using ecological footprint. J Environ Econ Policy 5(3):318–334. https://doi.org/10.1080/21606544.2015.1090346

Hossain S (2011) Panel estimation for CO2 emissions, energy consumption, economic growth, trade openness and urbanization of newly industrialized countries. Energ Pol 39:6991–6999.

Iwata H, Okada K, Samreth S (2010) Empirical study on the environmental Kuznets curve for CO2 in France: the role of nuclear energy. Energy Policy 38(8):4057–4063. https://doi.org/10.1016/j.enpol.2010.03.031

Jebli MB, Youssef SB, Ozturk I (2016) Testing environmental Kuznets curve hypothesis: the role of renewable and non-renewable energy consumption and trade in OECD countries. Ecol Indic 60:824–831. https://doi.org/10.1016/j.ecolind.2015.08.031

Kaufmann RK, Davidsdottir B, Garnham S, Pauly P (1998) The determinants of atmospheric SO2 concentrations: reconsidering the environmental Kuznets curve. Ecol Econ 25(2):209–220. https://doi.org/10.1016/S0921-8009(97)00181-X

Kivyiro P, Arminen H (2014) Carbon dioxide emissions, energy consumption, economic growth, and foreign direct investment: causality analysis for sub-Saharan Africa. Energy 74:595–606. https://doi.org/10.1016/j.energy.2014.07.025

Kuznets S (1955) Economic growth and income inequality. Am Econ Rev 45(1):1–28.

Lean HH, Smyth R (2010) CO2 emissions, electricity consumption and output in ASEAN. Appl Energy 87:1858–1864.

Magazzino C (2016) The relationship between CO2 emissions, energy consumption and eco-nomic growth in Italy. Int J Sustain Energy 35(9):844–857. https://doi.org/10.1080/14786451.2014.953160

McConnell KE (1997) Income and the demand for environmental quality. Environ Dev Econ 2(4):383–399.

Meadows DH, Meadows DL, Randers J, Behrens WW (1972) The limits to growth. New York: Universe Books.

Mrabet Z, Alsamara M (2017) Testing the Kuznets curve hypothesis for Qatar: a comparison between carbon dioxide and ecological footprint. Renew Sust Energ Rev 70:1366–1375. https://doi.org/10.1016/j.rser.2016.12.039

Narayan PK, Narayan S (2010) Carbon dioxide emissions and economic growth: Panel data evidence from developing countries. Energy Policy 38(1):661–666.

Osabuohien ES, Efobi UR, Gitau CMW (2014) Beyond the environmental Kuznets curve in Africa: evidence from panel cointegration. J Environ Pollut 16:517–538. https://doi.org/10.1080/1523908x.2013.867802

Ozturk I, Al-Mulali U (2015) Investigating the validity of the environmental Kuznets curve hypothesis in Cambodia. Ecol Indic 57: 324–330.

Ozturk I, Al-Mulali U, Saboori B (2016) Investigating the environmental Kuznets curve hy-pothesis: the role of tourism and ecological footprint. Environ Sci Pollut Res 23(2):1916–1928. https://doi.org/10.1007/s11356-015-5447-x

Pablo-Romero M, del P, S_anchez-Braza A (2017) The changing of the relationships be-tween carbon footprints and final demand: panel data evidence for 40 major countries. En-ergy Econ 61:8e20. https://doi.org/10.1016/j.eneco.2016.10.018

Panayotou T (1993) Empirical tests and policy analysis of environmental degradation at different stages of economic development. International Labour Organization.

Pao HT, Tsai CM (2010) CO2 emissions, energy consumption and economic growth in BRIC countries. Energ Pol 38:7850–7860.

Pao HT, Tsai CM (2011). Multivariate Granger causality between CO2 emissions, ener-gy consumption, FDI (foreign direct investment) and GDP (gross domestic product): evidence from a panel of BRIC (Brazil, Russian Federation, India, and China) countries. Energy 36(1):685–693. https://doi.org/10.1016/j.energ y.2010.09.041

Rafindadi AA (2016) Revisiting the concept of environmental Kuznets curve in period of en-ergy disaster and deteriorating income: empirical evidence from Japan. Energy Policy 94:274–284. https://doi.org/10.1016/j.enpol.2016.03.040

Rees WE (1992) Ecological footprints and appropriated carrying capacity: what urban eco-nomics leaves out. Environ Urban 4(2):121–130. https://doi.org/10.1177/095624789200400212

Richmond AK, Kaufmann RK (2006) Is there a turning point in the relationship between in-come and energy use and/or carbon emissions? Ecol Econ 56(2):176–189. https://doi.org/10.1016/j.ecolecon.2005.01.011

Rothman DS (1998) Environmental Kuznets curves—real progress or passing the buck? A case for consumption-based approaches. Ecol Econ 25:177–194.

Saboori B, Jamalludin S (2013) CO2 emissions, energy consumption and economic growth in Association of Southeast Asian Nations (ASEAN) countries: a cointegration ap-proach. Energy 55:813–822.

Saidi K, Mbarek MB (2016) The impact of income, trade, urbanization, and financial devel-opment on CO emissions in 19 emerging economies. Environ Sci Pollut Res Int. https://doi.org/10.1007/s11356-016-6303-3

Sari R, Soytas U (2009) Are global warming and economic growth combatable? Evidence from five OPEC countries. Appl Energy 86:1887–1893.

Selden TM, Song D (1995) Neoclassical growth, the J curve for abatement, and the inverted U curve for pollution. J Environ Econ Manag 29(2):162–168. https://doi.org/10.1006/jeem.1995.1038

Sephton P, Mann J (2013) Further evidence of an environmental Kuznets curve in Spain. Energy Econ 36:177e181. https://doi.org/10.1016/j.eneco.2013.01.001

Shahbaz M, Khraief N, Uddin GS, Ozturk I (2014) Environmental Kuznets curve in an open economy: a bounds testing and causality analysis for Tunisia. Renew Sust Energ Rev 34:325–336.

Shahbaz M, Mahalik MK, Shah SH, Sato JR (2016) Time-varying analysis of CO2 emissions, energy consumption, and economic growth nexus: statistical experience in next 11 coun-tries. Energy Policy 98: 33–48. https://doi.org/10.1016/j.enpol.2016.08.011

Song T, Zheng T, Lianjun T (2008) An empirical test of the environmental Kuznets curve in China: a panel cointegration approach. China Econ Rev 19(3):381–392. https://doi.org/10.1016/j.chieco.2007.10.001

Stern DI, Common MS, Barbier EB (1996) Economic growth and environmental degradation: the environmental Kuznets curve and sustainable development. World Dev 24(7):1151–1160. https://doi.org/10.1016/0305-750X(96)00032-0

Stern DI (2014) The environmental Kuznets curve: A primer (No. 450-2016-34062).

Suri V, Chapman D (1998) Economic growth, trade and the environment: implications for the environmental Kuznets curve. Ecol Econ 25:195–208.

Tiwari AK, Shahbaz M, Hye QMA (2013) The environmental Kuznets curve and the role of coal consumption in India: cointegration and causality analysis in an open economy. Re-new Sustain Energy Rev 18:519–527. https://doi.org/10.1016/j.rser.2012.10.031

Torras M, Boyce JK (1998) Income, inequality, and pollution: a reassessment of the environ-mental Kuznets curve. Ecol Econ 25:147–160.

Tzeremes P (2018) Time-varying causality between energy consumption, CO2 emissions, and economic growth: evidence from US states. Environ Sci Pollut Res 25(6):6044–6060. https://doi.org/10.1007/s11356-017-0979-x

Ulucak R, Bilgili F (2018) A reinvestigation of EKC model by ecological footprint measure-ment for high, middle and low income countries. J Clean Prod 188:144–157. https://doi.org/10.1016/j.jclepro.2018.03.191

Wackernagel M., Rees W (1998) Our ecological footprint: reducing human impact on the earth (Vol. 9). New Society Publishers.

Wang K-M (2012) Modelling the nonlinear relationship between CO2 emissions from oil and economic growth. Econ Model 29:1537e1547. https://doi.org/10.1016/j.econmod.2012.05.001

Wang MN (2017) Investigating the environmental Kuznets curve of consumption for develop-ing and developed countries: a study of Albania and Sweden. Bachelor's diss., Aalto University.

Wang Y, Kang L, Wu X, Xiao Y (2013) Estimating the environmental Kuznets curve for eco-logical footprint at the global level: a spatial econometric approach. Ecol Indic 34:15–21. https://doi.org/10.1016/j.ecolind.2013.03.021

Wang S, Li Q, Fang C, Zhou C (2016) The relationship between economic growth, energy consumption, and CO2 emissions: empirical evidence from China. Sci Total Environ 542 (Part A):360–371. https://doi.org/10.1016/j.scitotenv.2015.10.027

Wright LA, Kemp S, Williams I (2011) 'Carbon footprinting': towards a universally accepted definition. Carbon Manag 2(1):61–72. https://doi.org/10.4155/cmt.10.39

Yilanci V, Ozgur O (2019) Testing the environmental Kuznets curve for G7 countries: evidence from a bootstrap panel causality test in rolling windows. Environ Sci Pollut Res 26:24795–24805. https://doi.org/10.1007/s11356-019-05745-3

York R, Rosa EA, Dietz T (2003) Footprints on the earth: the environmental consequences of modernity. Am Sociol Rev 68(2):279–300.

Yuan JH, Kang JG, Zhao CH, Hu ZG (2008) Energy consumption and economic growth: Evidence from China at both aggregated and disaggregated levels. Energy Econ 30(6):3077–3094.

Şerif CANBAY

Examining the Relationship between Research and Development Expenditures (R&D) and Economic Growth by Kónya Causality Analysis Test in G7 Countries

1 Introduction

One of the chief goals of policymakers is to reach a consistent growth trend. Many instruments have been inserted in growth models to that end until today. One of those instruments is technological progress. Technological developments can mostly be created as a result of Research and Development (R&D).

Representatives of Classical and Neo-classical economics have added technological progress in growth models as an external variable; however, they have not endogenized technology to their models. Some countries, as from the last century, have provided significant technological progress achievements as the result of R&D activities. Related achievements cause a consistent economic growth trend and endogenous growth models to emerge. These models are the first ones that evaluate technology and R&D activities as an endogenous variable in economic growth models.

This study aimed to research the relationships between R&D expenditures and economic growth. G7 countries were scrutinized in line with this purpose. In the study, the variables between R&D expenditure and GDP will be analyzed with Kónya (2006) panel causality test with the help of the data of 1990–2019 period.

2 Literature Review

There are many researchers who review the effects of R&D expenditures on economic growth. Studies that belong to Griliches (1985), Lichtenberg (1992), Park (1995), Luh and Chang (1997), Freire-Serén (1999), Yanyun and Mingqian (2004), Falk (2007), Wu and Zhou (2007), Sadraoui and Zina (2009), Peng (2010), Kim (2011), Zhou, He, and Shen (2012), Sokolov-Mladenović, Cvetanović, and Mladenović (2016), Freimane and Bāliņa (2016), Dam and Yıldız (2016), Feng and Ke (2016), Bond and Guceri (2017), Minniti and Venturini (2017),

Uçak et al. (2018) show the positive and statistically significant effect of R&D expenditures on economic growth.

Guloglu and Tekin (2012), Wu and Zhou (2007), Dereli and Salğar (2019) conducted studies and found a two-way causality relation between R&D expenditures and economic growth. There was found a causality relation from R&D expenditures to economic growth in studies that belong to Altın and Kaya (2009), Akıncı and Sevinç (2013), Bozkurt (2015), Taş et al. (2017) with Duman and Aydın (2018). A one-way causality relation from economic growth to R&D expenditures was observed in studies that belong to Genç and Atasoy (2010).

Goel and Ram (1994) conducted a study only for developed countries and found a statistically significant relationship between R&D expenditures and economic growth in the long term while Sylwester (2001), Samimi and Alerasoul (2009), Tuna, Kayacan and Bektaş (2015), Shen, Lin and Wu (2019) could not observe a statistically significant relationship between R&D expenditures and economic growth. Moreover, for Silaghi et al. (2014), R&D expenditures of the private sector positively affect economic growth; on the other hand, there is no statistically significant relationship between R&D expenditures of the public sector and economic growth. Wang et al. (2013) did a research and found that R&D expenditures have no significant effect on economic growth in low and middle-income countries; the same expenditures have a remarkable impact on the economic growth of high-income countries. Again, Inekwe (2014) who worked by classification for income groups of countries, observed that R&D expenditures positively affect economic growth in middle-income countries; however, this impact is insignificant for middle-low income countries.

Many studies that review the relationships between R&D expenditures and economic growth show different results. The root causes of these differences are the differences in the development level of the relevant country or country groups, period, and analysis type. Although it is seen that there are different results among variables, there are significant interactions between related variables and economic growth.

3 Data

R&D expenditures[1] and gross domestic product (GDP)[2] variables of G7 that were obtained from the OECD database were utilized in analyzes in line with the

1 https://stats.oecd.org/OECDStat_Metadata/ShowMetadata.ashx?Dataset=GERD_FORD&ShowOnWeb=true&Lang=en

2 https://stats.oecd.org/index.aspx?queryid=60702

purpose of this study. Two variables as R&D expenditures (lrd) and GDP (lgdp) were inserted in analyzes by taking logarithm to be million US dollars (constant prices and PPPs). The investigation period of study was selected as 1990–2016 because of the restriction of data of R&D expenditures.

4 Econometric Methodology

This study tested the relationships between variables with the help of a panel causality test that was developed by Kónya (2006). The key reason for selecting this test is that the test reveals causality relations for each of the countries one by one; moreover, there is no need to perform a unit root and/or cointegration test first. However, the prior conditions for this test are the presence of cross-sectional dependence in models and the requirement for models to be in a heterogeneous structure. This is because, before the Kónya (2006) causality test, we first tested the presence of cross-sectional dependence in the models. Secondly, we tested the homogeneity/heterogeneity of the slope coefficient in the models.

4.1 Cross-Sectional Dependence Tests

We tested the relationships between variables with the help of Models 1 and 2. Before the cross-sectional dependence, first, these two models are estimated by the least-squares method; the presence of a cross-section is tested in the residual terms of $u_{i,t}$ and $e_{i,t}$ belonging to these models.

$$lgdp_{i,t} = \beta_0 + \beta_i lrd_{i,t} + u_{i,t} \tag{1}$$

$$lrd_{i,t} = \alpha_0 + \alpha_i lgdp_{i,t} + e_{i,t} \tag{2}$$

In the models, β_0 and α_0 are constant terms; β_i and α_i are slope coefficients. β_i shows the effect of 1 % change in *lrd* on *lgdp*; α_i shows the effect of 1 % change in *lgdp* on *lrd*. The *i* index is the country dimension of the models; t is the time dimension of the models. The total number of countries (N) means that the total number of all *i* in the models is 7 countries; T indicates that the whole time dimension is 27.

For example, in Model 1, the residual terms ($u_{i,t}$) of the model should be inserted in the model in the case of testing cross-sectional dependence. Afterwards, cross-sectional dependence is tested by producing Model 3.

$$u_{i,t} = \alpha_i + \beta_i' x_{i,t} + _{i,t}$$

$x_{i,t}$ in the model shows independent variables at the k × 1 dimension. There is $x_{i,t} = (u_{i,t-1}, \ldots u_{i,t-p})$ in cross-sectional dependence tests for the model. α_i is the constant term coefficient; β_i' is the slope coefficient. It is assumed that the residual term for each of the countries is $(\varepsilon_{i,t} = \varepsilon_{1,t}, \ldots, \varepsilon_{N,t})_{i,t} \sim IID\left(0, \sigma_{i,\varepsilon}^2\right)$. Test statistics that are obtained in this way inform us about whether there is a cross-section with the help of the below hypotheses. Cross-sectional dependence in the models means that a shock in one country will create a shock in other countries.

4.2 Homogeneity Test

The model has a homogeneous structure if the slope coefficients of each of the countries in the panel data are equal to a single slope coefficient. The model has a heterogeneous structure if the coefficients of each of the countries are different. Determining this situation is both econometrically and economically significant. This study used a homogeneity test developed by Pesaran and Yamagata (2008) and based on the random coefficients model. Unlike Swamy's (1970) study, the homogeneity test developed by Pesaran and Yamagata (2008) gives reliable results at larger N and T dimensions. We can say for this study that the T = 19 dimension is a long period in terms of panel data models.

H_0: $\alpha_i = \alpha$, i = 1,. . .,N for all i. (Model is homogenous.)
H_1: $\alpha_i \neq \alpha_j$, some of i ≠ j (The coefficient of at least one country is different. Model is heterogeneous.).

Pesaran and Yamagata (2008) suggest $\tilde{\Delta}$ and $\tilde{\Delta}_{adj}$ are asymptotically powerful to test these hypotheses. H_0 is denied if the probability values of these test statistics are lower than statistical significance values such as 10 %, 5 %, and 1 %. This means that the slope coefficients of the models vary by country.

4.3 Kónya (2006) Panel Causality Test

The panel causality test developed by Kónya (2006) reviews relationships between variables based on the SUR developed by Zellner (1962).

The SUR system that includes *lgdp* and *lrd* variables whose causality relationships are analyzed is as follows:

$$\left.\begin{aligned}
lgdp_{1,t} &= \varphi_{1,1} + \sum_{l=1}^{ml_lgdp_1} \alpha_{1,1,l} lgdp_{1,t-1} + \sum_{l=1}^{ml_lrd_1} \beta_{1,1,l} lrd_{1,t-1} + \xi_{1,1,t} \\
lgdp_{2,t} &= \varphi_{1,2} + \sum_{l=1}^{ml_lpgdp_1} \alpha_{1,2,l} lgdp_{2,t-1} + \sum_{l=1}^{ml_lrd_1} \beta_{1,2,l} lrd_{2,t-1} + \xi_{1,2,t} \\
&\cdot \\
&\cdot \\
&\cdot \\
lgdp_{2,t} &= \varphi_{1,2} + \sum_{l=1}^{ml_lpgdp_1} \alpha_{1,2,l} lgdp_{2,t-1} + \sum_{l=1}^{ml_lrd_1} \beta_{1,2,l} lrd_{2,t-1} + \xi_{1,2,t}
\end{aligned}\right\} \quad (4)$$

and

$$\left.\begin{aligned}
lrd_{1,t} &= \varphi_{2,1} + \sum_{l=1}^{ml_lrd_2} \beta_{2,1,l} lrd_{1,t-1} + \sum_{l=1}^{ml_lgdp_2} \alpha_{2,1,l} lgdp_{1,t-1} + \xi_{2,1,t} \\
lrd_{2,t} &= \varphi_{2,2} + \sum_{l=1}^{ml_lrd_2} \beta_{2,2,l} lrd_{2,t-1} + \sum_{l=1}^{ml_lpgdp_2} \alpha_{2,2,l} lgdp_{2,t-1} + \xi_{2,2,t} \\
&\cdot \\
&\cdot \\
&\cdot \\
lrd_{N,t} &= \varphi_{2,N} + \sum_{l=1}^{ml_lrd_2} \beta_{2,N,l} lrd_{N,t-1} + \sum_{l=1}^{ml_lgdp_2} \alpha_{2,N,l} lgdp_{N,t-1} + \xi_{2,N,t}
\end{aligned}\right\} \quad (5)$$

Wald test statistics are computed for each country's VAR equalities in a causality test. Just as in Kónya (2006), these test statistics are compared using critical bootstrap values.

5 Empirical Findings

This part of the study shows the refindings that were obtained using the methods above. The test results for cross-sectional dependence can be seen in Table 1.

There is cross-sectional dependence in both Model 1 and Model 2. It is inevitable for a shock that occurs in one country in the world to affect other countries. Moreover, this result proves the first condition required for the Kónya (2006) panel causality test. Table 2 shows the homogeneity test results.

The coefficients for both models vary from country to country; that is, they are heterogeneous in structure. This result provides the second condition required for the Kónya (2006) panel causality test. Table 3 shows The Kónya causality test results.

Table 1 : *Cross-Section Dependence Test Results*

Models	Model 1		Model 2	
Test	**Test Statistics**	**P-value**	**Test Statistics**	**P-value**
BP_{LM}	34.230*	0.0001	41.782*	0.0001
CD_{LM}	11.524*	0.0001	14.608*	0.0001
LM_{BC}	11.467*	0.0001	14.550*	0.0001
LM_{adj}	−0.506***	0.6125	−1.879***	0.0602

Note: *, *** indicates the rejection of the null hypothesis at the 1 % and 10 % significance level, respectively.

Table 2: *Cross-Section Dependence Test Results*

Modeller	Model 1		Model 2	
Test	**Test Statistics**	**P-value**	**Test Statistics**	**P-value**
$\tilde{\Delta}$	22.568*	0.0001	26.528*	0.0001
$\tilde{\Delta}_{adj}$	23.884*	0.0001	28.075*	0.0001

Note: * indicates the rejection of the null hypothesis at the 1 % significance level.

The causality test results in Table 3 show a one-way causality relation from lgdp to lrd is seen in Italy and Japan. The sign of causality relationships is negative for Italy and positive for Japan. The one-way causality relation from *lrd* to *lgdp* for UK and US. We also see that the sign of these causality relations is positive. Besides, there seems to be a bi-directional causality between lgdp and lrd for France. Also, there is a relation between negative from *lgdp* to *lrd* and positive from *lrd* to *lgdp*.

6 Conclusion

This study investigated the relationship between R&D expenditures and GDP of the G7 countries' (Canada, France, Germany, Italy, Japan, the UK, and the US) for the period 1990–2016. According to Kónya (2006) panel causality results, a one-way causality relationship is seen from GDP to R&D expenditures in Italy and Japan. The sign of causality relationships is negative for Italy and positive for Japan. The one-way causality relation from R&D expenditures to *GDP* in the UK and US. We also see that the sign of these causality relations is positive. Besides, there is bi-directional causality between GDP and R&D expenditures in France.

Table 3: *Kónya (2006) Panel Causality Test Results*

H_0: lgdp is not the Granger causality for lrd (Model 1)					
Countries	**Coefficients**	**Test Statistics**	**Critical Values** ****		
	lgdp	Wald	10 %	5 %	1 %
Canada	0.033	2.348	6.148	9.068	18.060
France	**−0.083**	**7.855*** **	**6.584**	**9.674**	**18.957**
Germany	0.050	0.518	11.857	17.085	32.025
Italy	**−0.075**	**8.667** **	**5.785**	**8.446**	**15.379**
Japan	**0.231**	**7.340*** **	**5.870**	**8.937**	**17.302**
UK	−0.114	4.022	6.409	9.578	18.588
US	−0.101	3.891	6.353	9.474	19.603
H_0: lrd is not the Granger causality for lgdp (Model 2)					
Countries	**Coefficients**	**Test Statistics**	**Critical Values** ****		
	lrd	Wald	10 %	5 %	1 %
Canada	−0.129	1.208	6.179	8.943	17.890
France	**0.268**	**10.650** **	**5.252**	**7.680**	**14.675**
Germany	0.459	3.037	6.567	9.493	18.446
Italy	0.017	0.164	5.323	7.855	15.023
Japan	0.336	0.532	5.816	8.738	16.234
UK	**0.772**	**21.393***	**5.406**	**7.937**	**14.238**
US	**0.715**	**38.509***	**6.354**	**9.248**	**17.813**

Note1: *,**,*** *, **, and *** indicate rejection of the null hypothesis at the 1, 5, and 10 % levels of significance, respectively.

Note2: **** the bootstrap is based on 1000 replications.

Also, there is a relation between negative from *GDP* to R&D expenditures and positive from R&D expenditures to *GDP. Finally,* there is a no bi-directional causality between GDP and R&D expenditures in *Canada and Germany.*

For analysis results, an increase in the GDP of Italy decreases the R&D expenditures. Regarding data of The World Bank database, the GDP of Italy increased approximately by 0.74 % in the 1990–2016 period, that is the time interval of our analysis. This growth rate is so low for a developed country as well as the Italian economy tightened in the 2008 global crisis, 2009, 2012, 2013 and 2014. However, there is seen a steady increase (even if just a drop) in share for R&D expenditures in the GDP of Italy as of 1995. This result shows that the 2008 global crisis may be a reflection of ignoring R&D expenditures and tighten the Italian economy. The share for R&D from GDP, in Italy, was at 1.39 % in 2016;

this is the lowest ratio in G7 countries. For analysis results, Italy reserves a so little share for R&D expenditures from GDP; this may be the reason for the lack of causality from R&D expenditures to GDP.

Regarding Japan, analyzes show that an increase in GDP, namely a one-way causality, increases R&D expenditures. Japan reached an approximately 1.12 % growth rate in the 1990–2016 period. Japan, especially since 1994, has followed an increasing trend on share for R&D expenditures from GDP. Related share was the highest ratio among the shares of G7 countries and almost 3.26 % in 2016. This table confirms the analysis results as well. Accordingly, we can say that Japan prefers to reserve more share for R&D in line with GDP increasing rate day by day.

There was found a one-way and positive marked causality relation from R&D expenditures to GDP in the United Kingdom and the United States. The growth rate of the UK and the US respectively were 2.06 % and 2.46 % for the analysis period. Moreover, the share that was reserved for R&D expenditures from inside of GDP in the UK was 1.70 % in 2016 while this ratio was as high as 2.82 % for the US in the same year. It can be said that both countries use R&D expenditures in productive areas; this situation, thus, accelerates economic growth.

A two-way causality relation was observed between variables for France. Any increase in GDP negatively affects R&D expenditures; any increase in R&D expenditures positively affects GDP. The average growth rate in France for the 1990–2016 period was 1.59 %. Regarding R&D expenditures, the related share reached a plateau from 1990 and remained at 2.2 % in GDP by 2016. France could not increase R&D expenditures under the present conditions; however, France accepts keeping the share of R&D expenditures in GDP at 2 % levels as a policy. It is seen that this 2 % threshold value that is specified for R&D expenditures is enough to positively affect the GDP of France.

There was not found a causality relation between variables for Canada and Germany. R&D ratio that was 2 % for Canada in 2001 regressed to 1.54 % till 2016. Although Canada reached an economic growth rate as almost 2.6 % from 2001 to 2016 and is in a tendency to increase R&D expenditures around the world, a decrease in R&D expenditures can still be seen. This table may result from the focal point that is another field rather than R&D expenditures in Canada. Regarding Germany, the share for R&D expenditures in GDP was 2.1 % in 1994 while this ratio increased to 3.13 % in 2016. Germany seems like a country that considers and increases R&D expenditures. Again, the economic growth rate of Germany approximately was 1.44 % in the 1994–2016 period. For Germany, it is a surprising result that there is no causality relation on GDP, although R&D expenditures are such a high. Discussing this issue by evaluating different variables may reveal much more reliable results.

References

Akıncı, M. & Sevinç, H. (2013). The Relationship between R&D Expenditures and Economic Growth: The Case of Turkey 1990–2011, The Journal of International Social Research, 6(27), 7–17.

Altın, O. & Kaya, A. (2009). Analysis of the Casual Relationship between R&D Expenditures and Economic Growth for Turkey, Ege Academic Review, 9(1), 251–259.

Bond, S. R. & Guceri, I. (2017). R&D and Productivity: Evidence from Large UK Establishments with Substantial R&D Activities, Emerging Markets Finance and Trade, 26, 108–20.

Bozkurt, C. (2015). R&D Expenditures and Economic Growth Relationship in Turkey, International Journal of Economics and Financial Issues, 5(1), 188–198.

Dam, M. M. &Yıldız, B. (2016). Impact of R&D and Innovation on Economic Growth at BRICS-TM Countries: An Econometric Analysis, Akdeniz Üniversitesi İktisadi ve İdari Bilimler Fakültesi Dergisi, 16(33), 220–236.

Dereli, D. D. & Salğar, U. (2019). Relationship between R&D Expenditures and Economic Growth: An Evaluation on Turkey, Journal of Life Economics, 6(3), 345–360.

Duman, K. & Aydın, K. (2018). The Relationship between R&D Expenditure and Gdp in Turkey, Gazi İktisat ve İşletme Dergisi, 4(1), 49–66.

Falk, M. (2007). R&D Spending in the High-Tech Sector and Economic Growth, Research in Economics, 61(3), 140–47. https://doi.org/10.1016/j.rie.2007.05.002.

Feng, P. & Ke, S. (2016). Self-selection and Performance of R&D Input of Heterogeneous Firms: Evidence from China's Manufacturing Industries, China Economic Review, 41, 181–95. doi:10.1016/j.chieco.2016.10.003.

Freimane, R. & Bāliņa, S. (2016). Research and Development Expenditures and Economic Growth in the EU: A Panel Data Analysis. Economics and Business, 29(1), 5–11.

Freire-Serȩn, M. J. (1999). Aggregate R&D Expenditure and Endogenous Economic Growth, UFAE and IAE Working Papers, WP 436–99.

Genç, M. C. & Atasoy, Y. (2010). The Relationship between R&D Expenditure and Economic Growth: Panel Data Analysis, The Journal of Knowledge Economy & Knowledge Management, 5(2), 27–34.

Goel, R. K. & Ram, R. (1994). Research and Development Expenditures and Economic Growth: A Cross-Country Study, Economic Development and Cultural Change, 42(2), 403–11.

Griliches, Z. (1985). Productivity, R&D, and Basic Research at the Firm Level in the 1970's, American Economic Review, 76(1), 141–54.

Guloglu, B. & Tekin, R. B. (2012). A Panel Causality Analysis of the Relationship among Research and Development, Innovation, and Economic Growth in High-Income OECD Countries, Eurasian Economic Review, 2(1), 32–47.

Inekwe, J. (2014). The Contribution of R&D Expenditure to Economic Growth in Developing Economies, Social Indicators Research, 124(3), 727–745.

Kim, J. W. (2011). The Economic Growth Effect of R&D Activity in Korea, Korea and the World Economy, 12(1), 25–44.

Kónya, L. (2006). Exports and Growth: Granger Causality Analysis on OECD Countries with a Panel Data Approach, Economic Modelling, 23(6), 978–992.

Lichtenberg, F. R. (1992). R&D Investment and International Productivity Differences, Working Paper No. 4161, National Bureau of Economic Research, Cambridge.

Luh, Y. H. & Chang, S. K. (1997). Building the Dynamic Linkages between R&D and Productivity Growth, Journal of Asian Economics, 8(4), 525–545.

Minniti, A. & Venturini, F. (2017). The Long-run Growth Effects of R&D Policy, Research Policy, 46, 316–26. doi:10.1016/j.respol.2016.11.006.

Park, W. G. (1995). International R&D Spillovers and OECD Economic Growth. Economic Inquiry, 33(4), 571–591.

Peng, L. (2010). Study on Relationship between R&D Expenditure and Economic Growth of China, In Proceedings of the 7th International Conference on Innovation & Management, 1725–1728.

Pesaran, M. H. & Yamagata, T. (2008). Testing Slope Homogeneity in Large Panels, Journal of Econometrics, 142(1), 50–93. https://doi.org/10.1016/j.jeconom.2007.05.010.

Sadraoui, T. & Zina, N. B. (2009). A Dynamic Panel Data Analysis for R&D Cooperation and Economic Growth, International Journal of Foresight and Innovation Policy, 5(4), 218–233.

Samimi, A. J. & Alerasoul, S. M. (2009). R&D and Economic Growth: New Evidence from Some Developing Countries, Australian Journal of Basic and Applied Sciences, 3(4), 3464–3469.

Shen, X., Lin, B. & Wu, W. (2019). R&D Efforts, Total Factor Productivity, and the Energy Intensity in China, Emerging Markets Finance and Trade, 55(11), 2566–2588, DOI: 10.1080/1540496X.2019.1579709.

Silaghi, M., Alexa, D., Jude, C. & Litan, C. (2014). Do Business and Public Sector and Development Expenditures Contribute to Economic Growth in Central and Eastern European Countries? A Dynamic Panel Estimation, Economic Modeling, 36, 108–119.

Sokolov-Mladenović, S., Cvetanović, S. & Mladenović, I. (2016). R&D Expenditure and Economic Growth: EU28 Evidence for the Period 2002–2012, Economic Research, 29(1), 1005–1020. https://doi.org/10.1080/1331677X.2016.1211948.

Swamy, P. A. (1970). Efficient Inference in a Random Coefficient Regression Model, Econometrica, 38(2), 311–323. https://doi.org/10.2307/1913012.

Sylwester, K. (2001). R&D and Economic Growth, Knowledge, Technology, & Policy, 13(4), 71–84.

Taş, Ş., Taşar, I. & Açcı, Y. (2017). Relationship between R&D Expenditures and Economic Growth: Example of Turkey, Ömer Halisdemir Üniversitesi İktisadi ve İdari Bilimler Fakültesi Dergisi, 10(2), 197–206.

Tuna, K., Kayacan, E. & Bektaş, H. (2015). The Relationship between Research & Development Expenditures and Economic Growth: The Case of Turkey, Procedia – Social and Behavioral Sciences, 195, 501–507.

Uçak, S., Kuvat, Ö. & Aytekin, A. (2018). The Relationship between R&D Expenditures and Growth in Turkey: ARDL Approach, Manisa Celal Bayar Üniversitesi Sosyal Bilimler Dergisi, 16(2), 129–160.

Wang, D. H.-M., Yu, T. H.-K. & Liu, H.-Q. (2013). Heterogeneous Effect of High-Tech Industrial R&D Spending on Economic Growth, Journal of Business Research, 66(10), 1990–1993.

Wu, Y. & Zhou, L. (2007). Cointegration and Causality between R&D Expenditure and Economic Growth in China: 1953–2004, In International Conference on Public Administration. Available at: http://citeseerx.ist.psu.edu/viewdoc/download?doi= 10.1.1.612.4329&rep=rep1&type=pdf (28.03.2020).

Yanyun, Z. & Mingqian, Z. (2004). R&D and Economic Growth: Panel Data Analysis in ASEAN+3 Countries, A Joint Conference of AKES, RCIE, and KDI: Korea and the World Economy, III, July 3–4, Sungkyunkwan University, Seoul, Available at: Korea https://faculty.washington.edu/karyiu/confer/seoul04/papers/zhao.pdf (28.03.2020).

Zellner, A. (1962). An Efficient Method of Estimating Seemingly Unrelated Regressions and Tests for Aggregation Bias, Journal of the American Statistical Association, 57(298), 348–68. https://doi.org/10.1080/01621459.1962.10480664.

Zhou, Y., He, X. & Shen, Y. (2012). An Evaluation of the Efficiency of Chinese Industry Enterprises' Innovation Performance, Economic Research Journal, 5, 107–119.

Eda ÖZEN

Does Urbanization Play Role on Poverty?: Empirical Evidence

1 Introduction

The term poverty, which is used by Seebohm for the first time, means the failure to meet the minimum physical needs required for the continuation of the biological being with total income (Seccombe, 2002). The concept of poverty is a situation where a person does not have sufficient resources and income to meet basic human needs such as food, shelter, health, clothing, water, and security required to sustain his/her life. These needs may vary according to regions and cultures (Kentleşme Şurası, 2009, 35).

Along with the increase in population, the situation of not meeting the basic requirements occurs and people migrate to the regions where the industry is located in order to meet these needs. However, this change has created an essential condition for the population to meet its necessary needs. The condition of the migrated cities causes the growth of existing cities and more cities. With industrialization, the concept of the city creates idle workforce in different professions and migration of people to the industrialized regions as well as differences between income levels. These differences cause the questioning of the relationship between urbanization and the concept of poverty.

For example, when the population changes in our country are analyzed by years, the urbanization created by the increasing population can be observed (DİE Nüfus sayımı, Işık, 2005).

The issue of poverty has an important place in the economy. There are many studies in the literature on its causes and solutions. Generally, macroeconomic factors and their effects on poverty are the most frequently studied topics. In this study, how poverty is affected by urbanization is analyzed with the help of unbalanced panel data. Six different poverty indicators, Random Effect Model and Fixed Effect Model are used in the panel analysis. Four different multiple regression models are used in the study. Analysis carried out in the study indicate that that there is a negative relationship between urbanization and poverty indices.

2 Literatur Review

Ravallion (2002: 435) conducted an empirical analysis on urbanization and poverty for developing countries. In the analysis, cross section data for 39 countries and time series data for India were used. The predicted empirical model displays that the urban poverty rate increase slowly compared to the rural poverty rate. When half of the developing world population lives in urban areas, it is estimated that 60 % of the poor will still live in rural areas.

In his study, Rakodi (2014: 46) draws attention to the details of livelihoods in urban areas. Urbanization trends are explained and details about poverty and inequality in urban areas are highlighted. In addition, he argues that urban centers can't be considered alone. He states that economic growth and poverty in towns and cities have been closely linked to both national economic performance and national development policies. Therefore, before examining the urban situation, he draws attention to the relations between economic growth, inequality and poverty reduction. Flango and Sherbenou (1976: 331) deals with urbanization and poverty in a different dimension whereby they include the crime factor in their study. They analyzed the data of 840 American cities to assess the situational determinants of crime. In this analysis, principal components analysis was used to reduce 59 demographic and socio-economic characteristics to six independent factors (welfare, stage in life cycle, economic specialization, spending policy, poverty and urbanization). As a result of the study, surprising results were obtained in small and large cities. Agarwal et al. (2007) examined the concept of urbanization and poverty from the health point of view. They draw attention to urban poverty and slum areas. In the study, it was emphasized that strengthening community capacity would help in improving awareness of health services in slum areas.

Muggah (2012: 45), who approaches poverty and urbanization with a different perspective, draws attention to the factor of violence in his study in 2012. This study brings together conflicting examples of complex relationships between urbanization, poverty and violence.

Although cities are disproportionately wealthy, they are also associated with poverty. It is very important to find a solution to the urbanization-poverty dilemma in order to achieve sustainable development. This study employs cross-sectional regressions to understand the relationship between urbanization and poverty indicators. The results of the study indicate that increases in gross domestic product per capita significantly reduce poverty and narrows rural-urban gaps (Liddle, 2017: 35).

Urban poverty in developing countries, which is different from rural poverty, has not been discovered at developing national level. The study by Khan et al. (2016: 439) addresses urban poverty at the national level in Pakistan. It emphasizes the urbanization of poverty in the multi-dimensional spectrum at the regional level in Pakistan and suggests policy inputs to prevent urbanization of poverty.

In the literature, there are studies dealing with the poverty factor from different aspects other than urbanization. For example, there are empirical studies examining the cause of poverty in different aspects such as banking crises and poverty, deforestation and poverty, corruption and poverty (See Yalcinkaya Koyuncu & Yilmaz, 2018; Koyuncu & Yilmaz, 2013; Yalcinkaya Koyuncu & Oksak, 2019; Yalcinkaya Koyuncu & Unver, 2016). Another remarkable study (Koyuncu & Yilmaz, 2010) on poverty examines the impact of imports from China on the importing country's poverty level. The results of the cross-sectional data analysis suggest that imports from China help reduce the poverty levels of the economies importing from China.

Finally, there are a number of studies that bring together the urbanization of poverty in Turkey, some of which are outlined below. In his study in 2006, Sipahi evaluated the globalization of poverty and urban poverty on the case of Konya province. In their study in 2005, Erkan and Bağlı examine the relationship of migration and poverty with urbanization on Diyarbakır province case. Es and Güloğlu addressed the increasing problem of urban poverty in their study in 2004. In the study, causes and implications revealed by the urban mismatch are discussed, in the case of Istanbul, Turkey's largest city.

3 Data and Metodology

This part of the study examines how poverty is affected by urbanization with panel data analysis. To analyze how poverty is affected by urbanization, the following multi-time fixed effect models are estimated by using the unbalanced panel dataset:

$$X34_{it} = (\beta_1 + \tau_t) + \beta_2 X45_{it} + \beta_3 X72_{it} + \beta_4 X66_{it} + \beta_5 X55_{it} + u_{it} \quad (1)$$

$$(-1 * X4)_{it} = (\beta_1 + \tau_t) + \beta_2 X45_{it} + \beta_3 X72_{it} + \beta_4 X66_{it} + \beta_5 X55_{it} + u_{it} \quad (2)$$

and also the following multi-time random effect model is estimated:

$$X35_{it} = (\beta_1 + \tau_t) + \beta_2 X45_{it} + \beta_3 X72_{it} + \beta_4 X66_{it} + \beta_5 X55_{it} + u_{it} \quad (3)$$

$$X36_{it} = (\beta_1 + \tau_t) + \beta_2 X45_{it} + \beta_3 X72_{it} + \beta_4 X66_{it} + \beta_5 X55_{it} + u_{it} \quad (4)$$

it sub-index in the above models is the observation value of the i.th country regarding the relevant variable in t year; β_1 is the constant of the model; τ_t is the

Table 1: *Definitions and Sources of Variables*

x4	Human Development Index (HDI)	(WDI) World Bank
x34	(Headcount) poverty indicator, Percentage of people below the poverty line	(WDI) World Bank
x35	(Pov. Gap) poverty indicator, Poverty gap. Measures average distance below poverty line	(WDI) World Bank
x36	(Watts index) poverty indicator, It is the average of proportionate poverty gaps in the population, measured by proportioning the average of the poverty line in proportion to income, by counting the poor in the poverty line	(WDI) World Bank
X45	Urban Population	(WDI) World Bank
x55	GDP Deflator (base year varies by country)	(WDI) World Bank
X66	Domestic general government health expenditure (% of general government expenditure)	(WDI) World Bank
X72	School enrollment rates, gross	(WDI) World Bank

time-specific effect, which affects all countries in the same way but varies from time to time; u_{it} represents the error term of the regression model. Table 1 below presents the dependent and independent variables used in the models above.

4 Estimation Results

	Model 1	**Model 2**	**Model 3**	**Model 4**
Dependent Variable	**x4**	**x34**	**x35**	**x36**
Constant	-0,3999	38,5368	13,6101	19,8946
P-Value	*0,0000*	*0,0000*	*0,0000*	*0,0000*
x45	-0,0032	-0,2665	-0,0985	-0,1551
P-Value	*0,0000*	*0,0000*	*0,0000*	*0,0000*
x72	-0,0027	-0,2428	-0,0999	-0,1447
P-Value	*0,0000*	*0,0000*	*0,0000*	*0,0000*
x66	-0,0033	-0,2500	-0,0168	0,0206
P-Value	*0,0000*	*0,0313*	*0,7502*	*0,8037*
x55	0,0000	0,0047	0,0026	0,0041
P-Value	*0,2640*	*0,0001*	*0,0000*	*0,0000*
Number of shades	1719	733	733	733
Hausman Test Statistics	16,6821	9,6582	8,3555	6,7019
Hausman Test P-Value	0,0022	0,0466	0,0794	0,1525
Selected Model	**FEM**	**FEM**	**REM**	**REM**

Estimation results of multiple regression model are given above. According to Hausman Test statistics, it is seen that the Fixed Effect Model (FEM) is selected in Model 1 and Model 2 while the Random Effect Model (REM) is selected in Model 3 and Model 4 among the four models employed in the analysis. The variables x45, x72, and x66 are statistically significant in Model 1 while the x55 variable isn't significant. All variables are statistically significant in Model 2. In Model 3, the variables x45, x72, and x55 are statistically significant while the x66 variable isn't significant.

5 Conclusion

Poverty and urbanization are two demographic factors that are mostly discussed in the literature. Our literature review revealed that urbanization and poverty are analyzed with different variables. It is generally seen in all studies that the urban and rural distinction affects the poverty factor in different ways.

In this study, as a result of panel analyzes conducted by using four different poverty indicators, it was observed that poverty decreased in the societies dominated by the urban population. This finding appears to be statistically significant in multiple regression models of four different poverty indicators. As a result of this study, it is possible to say that there is a negative relationship between urban population and poverty.

References

Agarwal, S., Satyavada, A., Kaushik, S., & Kumar, R. (2007). Urbanization, urban poverty and health of the urban poor: status, challenges and the way forward. Demography India, 36(1).

DİE, Genel Nüfus Sayımları 1935,1940, 1945, 1950, 1955, 1960, 1965, 1970, 1975, 1980, 1985, 1990, 2000.

Erkan, R., & Bağlı, M. (2005). Göç ve yoksulluk alanlarında kentle bütünleşme eğilimi: Diyarbakır örneği. Hacettepe Üniversitesi Edebiyat Fakültesi Dergisi, 22(1).

Es, M., & Güloğlu, T. (2004). Bilgi toplumuna geçişte kentlileşme ve kentsel yoksulluk: İstanbul örneği. Bilgi Sosyal Bilimler Dergisi, (8), 79–93.

Flango, V. E., & Sherbenou, E. L. (1976). Poverty, urbanization, and crime. Criminology, 14(3), 331–346.

Işık, Ş. (2005). TÜRKİYE'De Kentleşme Ve KentleşmeModelleri, Ege Coğrafya Dergisi, 14, 57–71.

Kentleşme Şurası (2009). Kentsel Yoksulluk, Göç ve Sosyal Politikalar. Ankara: T.C. Bayındırlık ve İskân Bakanlığı.

Khan, A. U., Saboor, A., Ali, I., Malik, W. S., & Mahmood, K. (2016). Urbanization of multidimensional poverty: empirical evidences from Pakistan. Quality & Quantity, 50(1), 439–469.

Koyuncu, C. & Yilmaz, R. (2010). China's Export Surge and World Poverty, Transformation in Business and Economics, Volume: 9, 2(20), 86–94.

Koyuncu, C. & Yilmaz, R. (2013). Impact of private forest ownership on deforestation and poverty. Quality&Quantity, 47(3), 1657–1664.

Liddle, B. (2017). Urbanization and inequality/poverty. Urban Science, 1(4), 35.

Muggah, R. (2012). Researching the urban dilemma: Urbanization, poverty and violence.

Rakodi, C. (2014). Economic development, urbanization and poverty, In Urban Livelihoods, 46–58.

Ravallion, M. (2002). On the urbanization of poverty. Journal of Development Economics, 68(2), 435–442.

Seccombe, K. (2002). Beating the odds, versus, changing the odds: Poverty, resilience and family policy. Journal of Marriage and Family, 64(2).

Sipahi, E. B. (2006). Yoksulluğun Küreselleşmesi Ve Kentsel Yoksulluk: Ekonomik Ve Sosyal Boyutlarıyla Konya Örneğinde Yoksulluk. Sosyal Ekonomik Araştırmalar Dergisi, 6(11), 172–189.

Yalçinkaya Koyuncu, J. & Okşak, Y. (2019). The Impact of Banking Crises on Poverty: Panel Evidence. In Studies on Balkan and Near Eastern Social Sciences-Volume 3 Edited by Rasim Yilmaz and Günther Löschnigg, 255–262.

Yalcinkaya Koyuncu, J. & Unver, M. (2016). The Impact of Poverty on Corruption. Journal of Economics Library, 3(4), 632–642.

Yalcinkaya Koyuncu, J. & Yılmaz,R. (2018). The Contribution of ICT to Poverty Reduction: A Panel Data Evidence. Social Sciences Research Journal, 7(4), (December 2018), 63–75.

Eray Gemici

Testing for Multiple Bubbles in Cryptocurrency Market

1 Introduction

Bitcoin emerged with an article published by the person or persons named Satoshi Nakamoto nickname and is the first known digital currency. Digital currencies are defined as electronic currencies that allow one person to another to pay online without any financial intermediary (Kılıç and Çütcü 2018:235–36). Digital currencies, also called cryptocurrencies, are financial assets that have gained popularity in recent years. Baek and Elbeck (2015) state that Bitcoin is an alternative to money and a hedging method for high-inflation economies, which can replace financial institutions (Baek and Elbeck 2015:30). Although Bitcoin is called money, volatility in its price makes it difficult to defend this claim. It is claimed by researchers that Bitcoin is a speculative investment tool rather than an exchange tool (Baur, Hong, and Lee 2018; Yermack 2013). Volatilities in the price of digital currencies attract both investors and researchers. For this reason, the existence of bubbles in the digital money market is frequently examined. As financial historians argue, the asset market bubble or widespread credit growth occur prior to the financial crises (Phillips, Shi, and Yu 2015:1043). Bubbles are defined as part of the market price that exceeds or falls below the fundamental value of an asset (Cheung, Roca, and Su 2015:2350). Therefore, in order to detect the presence of bubbles, it is first necessary to determine the fundamental value of the asset. Asset price bubbles are not easy to estimate in real time, even historical empirically, and have been the source of controversy among academics and professionals for decades (Caspi 2017:1). Economists and financial market participants often have different views on the pricing of assets. Economists generally believe that given the rational behavior and rational expectations, the value of an asset reflects information only in the market, that is, the price of the asset can only depend on information about the current and future returns of the asset. Market participants believe that information in the market is only one factor in determining asset prices. If herd psychology is accepted by foreign participants, external events can also be an important determinant of the price (Blanchard and Watson 1982:1). The role of rationality in the formation of prices, behavioral finance, or the tendency towards the behavioral economy, or alternative psychological, sociological and epidemiological factors play an important role (Shiller 2014:1486). Therefore, it can be said that traditional finance theories cannot be enough alone in determining the asset price.

There are many studies in the literature that test the presence of bubbles for various markets, such as the stock markets (Diba and Grossman 1988; Evans 1991; Homm and Breitung 2012), housing prices (Abraham and Hendershott 1994; Goodman and Thibodeau 2008), foreign exchange markets (Woo 1987; Wu 1995), crude oil prices (Miller and Ratti 2009), real estate markets (Herring and Wachter 2003; Kim and Suh 1993), agricultural commodity prices (Gutierrez 2013) and in recent years there are studies examining bubbles in the crypto money markets. Cheah and Fry (2015) examined the bubble in Bitcoin prices for the prices of July 18, 2010 and July 17, 2014, determined that speculative bubbles exist in the Bitcoin markets and the fundamental price of Bitcoin is zero. Cheung et al. (2015) have identified a series of short-lived bubbles in the periods specified for the period of 17 July 2010–18 February 2014. The most important of these bubbles was identified in the last part of the 2011–2013 period, three large bubbles that lasted between 66 and 106 days. The last bubble detected coincides with the collapse of the Mt Gox exchange. Gunji (2016) tested the existence of bubbles in terms of Chinese Yuan, US Dollar, Euro, and Japanese Yen in Bitcoin prices, used the data period between 2011 and 2013. Findings show that Bitcoin prices are rational bubbles. Ceylan et al. (2018) studied the bubbles for the period between 1 January 2015 and 31 March 2018 for Bitcoin and Ethereum prices. The findings have revealed that there are many bubbles in Bitcoin and Ethereum currencies. Corbet et al. (2018) analyzed Bitcoin and Ethereum cryptocurrencies for the period of 9 January 2009- 9 November 2017 and found bubble periods. Delikanli and Vogiazas (2018) examined the existence of bubbles in Bitcoin prices between June 2010 and February 2018, detected speculative bubbles in Bitcoin prices. Geuder et al. (2019) tested the bubble behavior in the Bitcoin prices for the period of 19 March 2016–19 September 2018 and found that bubble behavior clearly exists and re-occurs. Li et al. (2019) investigated the existence of bubbles in USA and China Bitcoin markets for the period of June 16, 2011 – September 18, 2017. The findings indicated that there were six bubbles in the Chinese market and five in the USA market. The authors stated that Bitcoin can be used as a hedge tool against market risk. Chaim and Laurini (2019) examined the bubbles in the Bitcoin market from January 2013 to September 2018. They detected the presence of a bubble in Bitcoin prices from the beginning of 2013 to mid-2014. But interestingly, they couldn't find the bubble in late 2017. Cretarola and Figà-Talamanca (2019) studied the existence of the bubble effect for the periods of 1 January 2012–20 January 2018, proved the bubble effect in the first years of Bitcoin, 2012–2013 and in the last period of 2017. Fendi et al (2019) analyzed the bubbles in Bitcoin prices and returns for the 2010–2018 periods. Unlike many other studies, they found no evidence of the presence of speculative bubbles. Moosa (2020) used price and volume data to examine whether Bitcoin entered a bubble that peaked between 2010 and 2017 and found that Bitcoin trading volume can be explained by price dynamics; Bitcoin trading is based on positive price changes in the past; and Bitcoin price has shown an explosive process. These findings support the existence of a price bubble.

This study aims to examine the existence of bubbles in crypto money markets by using PSY method. The rest of the article is organized as follows: Section 2 describes methodology employed. Section 3 discusses the empirical findings. Finally, some concluding remarks are given in Section 4.

2 Methodology

There are many statistical tests developed to detect bubbles in the literature. Diba and Grossman (1988) tested the presence of explosive rational bubbles at stock prices using unit root and cointegration based tests. Evans (1991) stated that Diba and Grossman (1988) tests did not have enough power to detect periodically collapsed bubbles. Later, Phillips, Wu, and Yu (2011, hereafter PWY) and Phillips, Shi, and Yu (2015, hereafter PSY) further expanded the methods of Diba and Grossman (1988) and applied the ADF test as a recursive and rolling basis for defining bubbles and data-stamp bubbles. Since the sup augmented Dickey-Fuller test (SADF) test developed by PWY (2011) failed to detect more than one bubble formation, generalized ADF (GSADF) test was presented by PSY (2015). PSY (2015) stated that according to the findings obtained from Monte Carlo test simulations, the PSY strategy performed better in detecting multiple bubbles compared to the PWY strategy.

This study employs, the generalized SADF (GSADF) and backward supreme ADF (BSADF) test proposed by PSY (2015) to detect the multiple bubbles with a rolling window ADF approach.

The recursive ADF regression as follows;

$$\Delta y_t = \hat{\alpha}_{r_1,r_2} + \hat{\beta}_{r_1,r_2} y_{t-1} + \sum_{i=1}^{k} \hat{\psi}^i_{r_1,r_2} \Delta y_{t-i} + \hat{\varepsilon}_t \tag{1}$$

where k is the (transient) lag order. r_1 and r_2 represent the start and end points of the total sample window in the regression.

Phillips et al. (2015) defined generalized sup ADF(GSADF), as the largest ADF statistic obtained as a result of double recursion in the r_1 and r_2 range. In other words, this test is based on the idea of repeating the ADF regression in equation (1) for sub-samples.

$$GSADF\ (r_0) = \underset{\substack{r_2 \in [r_0, 1] \\ r_1 \in [0, r_2, r_0]}}{sup} \{ADF_{r_1}^{r_2}\}. \tag{2}$$

where r_0, the smallest sample window,

r_1, the starting point of the sample sequence,

r_2, the end point of each sample.

PSY proposed the backward supremum ADF (BSADF) test to determine the start and end dates of bubbles during the sample period.

$$BSADF_{r_2}\ (r_0) = \underset{r_1 \in [0, r_2, r_0]}{sup} \{ADF_{r_1}^{r_2}\} \tag{3}$$

The start and end date – stamp of the bubbles are estimated as follows;

$$\hat{r}_e = \underset{r_2 \in [r_0, 1]}{\inf} \left\{ r_2\ : BSADF_{r_2}\ (r_0) > cv_{r_2}^{\beta_{T_{r_2}}} \right\}, \tag{4}$$

$$\hat{r}_f = \underset{r_2 \in [r_e, 1]}{\inf} \left\{ r_2\ : BSADF_{r_2}\ (r_0) < cv_{r_2}^{\beta_{T_{r_2}}} \right\}, \tag{5}$$

where $cv_{r_2}^{\beta_T}$ shows the 100 % (1-βT) critical value of BSADF statistic for the number of observations r_2 in full sample (T).

3 Data and Empirical Findings

The bubbles of cryptocurrencies are examined using the weekly data from August 09, 2015, to March 29, 2020, for Bitcoin, Ethereum, Litecoin and Ripple. The number of observations for each series is 243, and the data were obtained from www.coinmarketcap.com.

GSADF and backwards supreme ADF (BSADF) test developed by PSY (2015) were used to detect multiple bubbles and the minimum window size was determined using $r_0 = 0.01 + 1.8/\sqrt{T}$ recommended by Phillips and Shi (2020).

Table 1: *GSADF Test Results*

Variable	Test Statistics	CV %1	CV %5	CV %10
Bitcoin	10.247***	9.820	7.237	6.034
Ethereum	10.689**	12.164	8.981	7.693
Litecoin	9.940*	15.741	10.580	8.287
Ripple	24.254**	35.934	23.121	17.615

***, ** and * indicate that the H_0 hypothesis was rejected at the right-tailed 1 %, 5 %, and 10 % significance levels, respectively. The critical values of GSADF test statistics (The critical values were obtained using the "exuber package" developed by Vasilopoulos in R software.) have been obtained by Harvey et al. (2016) with 2000 bootstrap simulation.

Table 2: *Bubble Duration*

	BTC	ETH	LTC	XRP	Sum
2016	3	2	0	0	5
2017	31	16	25	7	79
2018	4	7	3	0	14
2019	6	6	0	0	12
Sum bubble weeks	44	31	28	7	110

Harvey et al. (2016) method, which considers the heteroscedasticity problem in the process of obtaining critical values, was followed.

Shown in Table 1, GSADF test statistics for cryptocurrencies examined in the study are above critical values. Therefore, it has been determined that there has a bubble formation. Bubble dates and figures for each cryptocurrency examined in the study are given below.

Table 2 shows that the frequency of formation of bubbles occurred in 2017. Based on the data on a weekly basis, BTC and ETH are the cryptocurrencies with the highest bubble frequency, 44 and 31 weeks, respectively. The shaded areas in the following graphs regarding the cryptocurrencies examined in the study indicate that the PSY test statistic is greater than the critical values calculated in the 95 % confidence interval. In other words, it shows the periods when the bubbles occurred. The charts also show that all cryptocurrencies have experienced a sharp decline after a sharp rise. The start and end periods of the bubbles for each cryptocurrency are shown in detail in the tables below.

As shown in Table 3, the longest bubble period in Bitcoin is between 30 July 2017 and 11 November 2017 (18 weeks). When the prices on these dates

Table 3: *Bitcoin Bubble Dates*

Start End	Duration
2016–06–12 2016–06–12	1 week
2016–07–03 2016–07–03	1 week
2016–12–25 2017–01–01	2 weeks
2017–04–30 2017–06–18	8 weeks
2017–07–30 2017–11–26	18 weeks
2017–12–10 2018–01–28	8 weeks
2019–05–26 2019–06–30	6 weeks

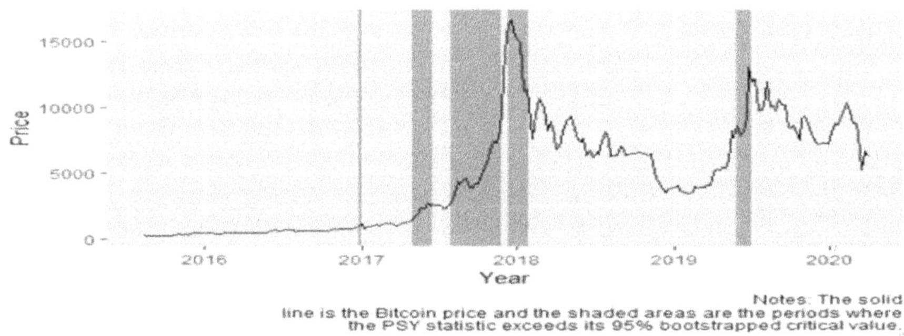

Figure 1: *Bitcoin Price and Bubbles Periods*

are analyzed, it was 1 BTC = $ 2,710 on July 30 and 1BTC = $ 9,888 on November 26. Figure 1 draws attention to the rapid increase in the price of Bitcoin between the dates specified. This increase was approximately 264 %. Similarly, price increases in Ethereum, Litecoin, and Ripple are seen in Figures 2, 3 and 4, respectively.

In Table 4, the longest period of bubble effect for Ethereum is the 7-week period between 2017–12–10 and 2018–01–21. This period was followed by a period of 6 weeks between 2019–05–26 and 2019–06–30. When the prices on these dates are analyzed, it was 1 ETH = $ 702.77 on December 10 and 1 ETH = $ 1058.78 on January 21. This increase was approximately 51 %. In addition, on the date of 26–05–2019, while it was 1 ETH = $ 8659.49, it was realized as 1 ETH $ 11961.27 on 2019–06–30 with an increase of 38.1 %.

When the Litecoin bubble dates in Table 5 were examined,, the existence of a bubble that started on 2017–08–20 and lasted for 9 weeks was determined.

Table 4: *Ethereum Bubble Dates*

Start End	Duration
2016–02–28 2016–03–06	2 weeks
2017–04–30 2017–05–07	2 weeks
2017–05–21 2017–06–25	6 weeks
2017–07–09 2017–08–06	5 weeks
2017–09–24 2017–10–01	2 weeks
2017–12–10 2018–01–21	7 weeks
2018–02–25 2018–02–25	1 weeks
2019–05–26 2019–06–30	6 weeks

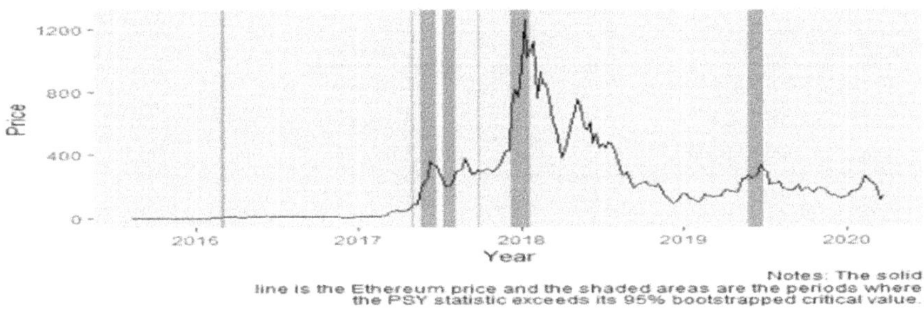

Figure 2: *Ethereum Prices and Bubble Periods*

Table 5: *Litecoin Bubble Dates*

Start End	Duration
2017–04–23 2017–05–07	3 weeks
2017–06–18 2017–07–09	4 weeks
2017–07–23 2017–07–23	1 weeks
2017–08–06 2017–08–06	1 weeks
2017–08–20 2017–10–15	9 weeks
2017–11–19 2018–01–21	10 weeks

This was followed by a second bubble, which started in 2017–11–19 and lasted 10 weeks. While 1 LTC = $ 53.25 at the beginning of the 9-week bubble period, the last week of the bubble period reached 1 LTC = $ 60.73, an increase of about 14 %. The increase rate was more severe in the second bubble period. While it

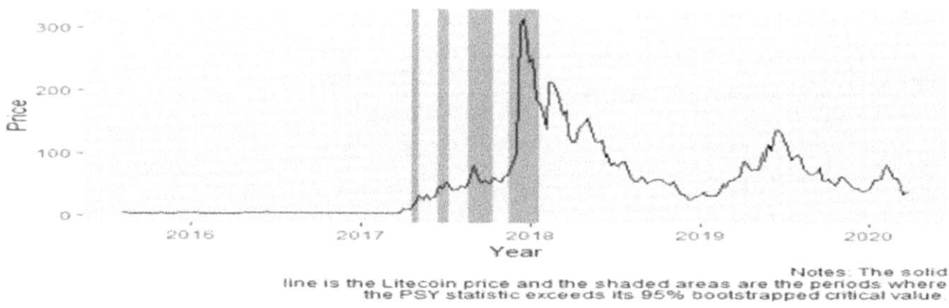

Figure 3: *Litecoin Prices and Bubble Periods*

Table 6: *Ripple Bubble Dates*

Start End	**Duration**
2017–04–02 2017–04–02	1 weeks
2017–04–30 2017–05–14	3 weeks
2017–12–17 2017–12–31	3 weeks

was 1 LTC = 71.89 in 2017–11–19, it increased by approximately 150 % and reached 1 LTC = 179.99 $ in 2018–01–21.

In this study, the cryptocurrency in which the least bubble was detected was Ripple. As shown in Table 6, the maximum bubble duration was determined as 3 weeks. However, the effect of this 3-week bubble on prices is quite evident. While 1 XRP = 0.060 $ in 2017–04–30, it was realized as 1 XRP = 0.394 $ in 2017–05–14 with an increase of 551 %. When the second three-week bubble period is analyzed, it was 1 XRP = $ 0.775 in 2017–12–17, with an increase of approximately 300 %, it was 1 XRP = 3.11 $ in 2017–12–31.

4 Conclusion

Estimating asset prices in real markets as well as financial markets is a constant interest of economists, regulators, investors and researchers. The Efficient Market Hypothesis (Fama, 1970), which has been operating in the finance literature for many years, has become open to discussion with anomalies, behavioral bias and bubbles. For this reason, it is of great importance for market participants who want to estimate asset prices to determine the periods in which they can yield above normal returns.

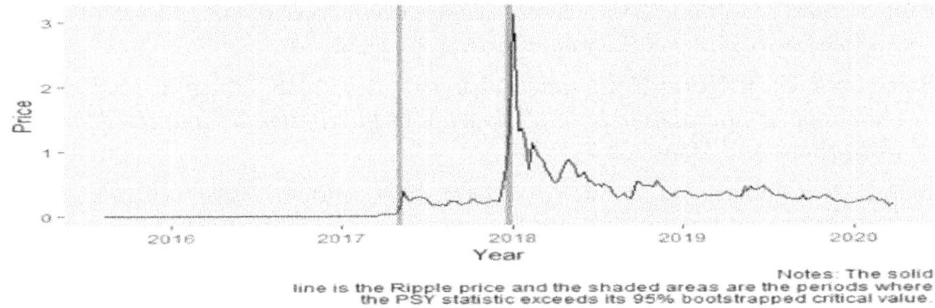

Figure 4: *Ripple Prices and Bubble Periods*

Financial instruments diversity is constantly changing in global markets and technology and financial product diversity is also increasing. Bitcoin, the first digital currency that emerged after the 2008 global crisis, was not known at first, but attracted the attention of investors with high risk appetite a few years later. Volatility in the prices of cryptocurrencies has turned into a speculative investment tool rather than an exchange tool for investors who want to achieve high returns in a short time. Accordingly, an increase has been observed in the researches about crypto money.

This study aims to investigate the presence of bubbles for Bitcoin, Ethereum, Litecoin and Ripple. In doing so, the weekly period from August 9, 2015, to March 29, 2020, is examined with Phillips, Su and Yu (2015) test procedure. Research findings have shown that there are long-term bubbles in Bitcoin (44 weeks) and Etherium (31 weeks). The bubbles were relatively shorter in Litecoin (28 weeks) and Ripple (7 weeks). At this point, risk-taker investors who want to take advantage of the high price movements caused by the bubbles may turn to Bitcoin more and investors who avoid the risk will turn to more Ripple.

These results show that investors who invest in the cryptocurrency market may have higher than normal returns. However, when the graphics in the findings are analyzed, the decreases in prices after the bubble periods are as fast as rises, which poses a risk to investors. Therefore, investors must direct their investments by correctly interpreting whether there are rises or bubbles that should be price rises with risk-return analyzes.

References

Abraham, Jesse M., and Patric H. Hendershott. 1994. *Bubbles in Metropolitan Housing Markets. Working Paper*. 4774. National Bureau of Economic Research.

Baek, C., and M. Elbeck. 2015. "Bitcoins as an Investment or Speculative Vehicle? A First Look." *Applied Economics Letters* 22(1):30–34.

Baur, Dirk G., KiHoon Hong, and Adrian D. Lee. 2018. "Bitcoin: Medium of Exchange or Speculative Assets?" *Journal of International Financial Markets, Institutions and Money* 54:177–89.

Blanchard, Olivier J., and Mark W. Watson. 1982. *Bubbles, Rational Expectations and Financial Markets*. National Bureau of Economic Research, 1–28. https://www.nber.org/papers/w0945

Caspi, Itamar. 2017. "Rtadf: Testing for Bubbles with EViews." *Journal of Statistical Software* 81:1–16.

Ceylan, Fatih, Ramazan Ekinci, Osman Tüzün, and Hakan Kahyaoğlu. 2018. "Kripto Para Piyasasında Balonların Tespiti: Bitcoin ve Ethereum Örneği." *Business & Management Studies: An International Journal* 6(3):263–274.

Chaim, Pedro, and Márcio P. Laurini. 2019. "Is Bitcoin a Bubble?" *Physica A: Statistical Mechanics and Its Applications* 517:222–32.

Cheah, Eng-Tuck, and John Fry. 2015. "Speculative Bubbles in Bitcoin Markets? An Empirical Investigation into the Fundamental Value of Bitcoin." *Economics Letters* 130:32–36.

Cheung, Adrian (Wai-Kong), Eduardo Roca, and Jen-Je Su. 2015. "Crypto-Currency Bubbles: An Application of the Phillips–Shi–Yu (2013) Methodology on Mt. Gox Bitcoin Prices." *Applied Economics* 47(23):2348–58.

Corbet, Shaen, BrianLucey, and Larisa Yarovaya. 2018. "Datestamping the Bitcoin and Ethereum Bubbles." *Finance Research Letters* 26:81–88.

Cretarola, Alessandra, and Gianna Figà-Talamanca. 2019. "Detecting Bubbles in Bitcoin Price Dynamics via Market Exuberance." *Annals of Operations Research*, 1–21. https://doi.org/10.1007/s10479-019-03321-z

Delikanlı, İhsan Uğur, and Sofoklis Vogiazas. 2018. "Testing for the Presence of Speculative Price Bubbles in Bitcoin." *İstanbul Ticaret Üniversitesi Sosyal Bilimler Dergisi* (33):511–23.

Diba, Behzad T., and Herschel I. Grossman. 1988. "Explosive Rational Bubbles in Stock Prices?" *The American Economic Review* 78(3):520–30.

Evans, George W. 1991. "Pitfalls in Testing for Explosive Bubbles in Asset Prices." *The American Economic Review* 81(4):922–30.

Fama, Eugene. 1970. "Efficient Capital Markets: A Review of Theory and Empirical Work." *The Journal of Finance* 25(2):383–417.

Fendi, Usama Adnan, Asem Tahtamouni, Yaser Jalghoum, and Jamal Mohammad Suleiman. 2019. "The Study of Bubbles in Bitcoin Behavior." *Banks and Bank Systems* 14(4):133.

Geuder, Julian, Harald Kinateder, and Niklas F. Wagner. 2019. "Cryptocurrencies as Financial Bubbles: The Case of Bitcoin." *Finance Research Letters* 31:179–184.

Goodman, Allen C., and Thomas G. Thibodeau. 2008. "Where Are the Speculative Bubbles in US Housing Markets?" *Journal of Housing Economics* 17(2):117–37.

Gunji, Hiroshi. 2016. "Are Bitcoin Prices Rational Bubbles." *The Empirical Economics Letters* 15(9):819–824.

Gutierrez, Luciano. 2013. "Speculative Bubbles in Agricultural Commodity Markets." *European Review of Agricultural Economics* 40(2):217–38.

Harvey, David I., Stephen J. Leybourne, Robert Sollis, and A. M. Robert Taylor. 2016. "Tests for Explosive Financial Bubbles in the Presence of Non-Stationary Volatility." *Journal of Empirical Finance* 38:548–74.

Herring, Richard, and Susan Wachter. 2003. "Bubbles in Real Estate Markets." *Asset Price Bubbles: The Implications for Monetary, Regulatory, and International Policies* 217(6):217–230.

Homm, Ulrich, and Jörg Breitung. 2012. "Testing for Speculative Bubbles in Stock Markets: A Comparison of Alternative Methods." *Journal of Financial Econometrics* 10(1):198–231.

Kılıç, Yunus, and İbrahim Çütcü. 2018. "Bitcoin Fiyatları Ile Borsa İstanbul Endeksi Arasındaki Eşbütünleşme ve Nedensellik İlişkisi." *Eskişehir Osmangazi Üniversitesi İktisadi ve İdari Bilimler Dergisi* 13(3):235–250.

Kim, Kyung-Hwan, and Seoung Hwan Suh. 1993. "Speculation and Price Bubbles in the Korean and Japanese Real Estate Markets." *The Journal of Real Estate Finance and Economics* 6(1):73–87.

Li, Zheng-Zheng, Ran Tao, Chi-WeiSu, and Oana-Ramona Lobonț. 2019. "Does Bitcoin Bubble Burst?" *Quality & Quantity* 53(1):91–105.

Miller, J. Isaac, and Ronald A. Ratti. 2009. "Crude Oil and Stock Markets: Stability, Instability, and Bubbles." *Energy Economics* 31(4):559–68.

Moosa, Imad A. 2020. "The Bitcoin: A Sparkling Bubble or Price Discovery?" *Journal of Industrial and Business Economics* 47(1):93–113.

Phillips, Peter. C. B, Yangru, Wu, and Jun, Yu. 2011. "Explosive behavior in the 1990s Nasdaq: When Did Exuberance Escalate Asset Values?." *International Economic Review*, 52(1), 201–226.

Phillips, Peter C. B., ShupingShi, and Jun Yu. 2015. "Testing for Multiple Bubbles: Historical Episodes of Exuberance and Collapse in the S&p 500." *International Economic Review* 56(4):1043–78.

Phillips, Peter CB, and Shuping Shi. 2020. "Real Time Monitoring of Asset Markets: Bubbles and Crises." Pp. 61–80 in *Handbook of Statistics*. Vol. 42. Elsevier.

Shiller, Robert J. 2014. "Speculative Asset Prices." *American Economic Review* 104(6):1486–1517.

Woo, Wing Thye. 1987. "Some Evidence of Speculative Bubbles in the Foreign Exchange Markets." *Journal of Money, Credit and Banking* 19(4):499–514.

Wu, Yangru. 1995. "Are There Rational Bubbles in Foreign Exchange Markets? Evidence from an Alternative Test." *Journal of International Money and Finance* 14(1):27–46.

Yermack, David. 2013. "Is Bitcoin a Real Currency? An Economic Appraisal." *NBER Working Papers*.

Beyhan Kılınçer

The Relationships between Borsa Istanbul Stock Exchange (Bist100) Index and Monetary Policy Implementations: An Empirical Analysis in Turkey

1 Introduction

Central Banks (CB) are the central monetary bodies of countries. Central banks, which are also known as the bank of banks due to the duties and authorities added day by day, are the most important institutions in charge of working in coordination with various policies to control inflation in the long term, in other words, to achieve price stability, also full employment and sustainable growth.

Besides printing money needed by the financial and economical system,, central banks are the most important institutions that directs financial system. They also have duties and powers that vary from country to country, over time. In this context, adjusting the liquidity of the markets in accordance with the monetary policy and ensuring stability in the markets are among the primary functions of CB.

Central Banks aim to keep financial risks under control especially due to international disparities. The many duties and powers place Central Banks on the center of the financial system. Therefore, Central Banks provide extensive services to banks, which are the backbone of the financial system. It makes it easier for banks to provide easy credit to the market in line with reliability and interest rates. Accordingly, financial stability is a supportive goal for Central Banks.

In Turkey, the main duties and authorities of Central Bank, in Law Number of 1211, dated 01.14.1970 with the change of Law Number of 4651 dated 04.25.2001 are listed in detail, in Article 4. According to the first clause of the related article of law, the fundamental aim of CB is to ensure price stability. It has the authority to directly determine its monetary policy and instruments to be practiced in order to ensure price stability. Stability at the overall price level, which is the fundamental objective of CB, is crucial for the long-term stable development of countries, their efficient use of resources and the fair distribution of welfare. Acting as the banker of the state, Central Bank, in accordance with the policies implemented by the government, issuing banknotes in accordance with the requirements of the country's economy, managing money supply and foreign exchange reserves, regulating money and foreign exchange markets to ensure financial stability, carrying out monetary and credit policies, supervising the banking system. It performs tasks such as determining the loan volume and regulating the distribution of loans to units. For example, with the application of credit expansion, which is one of the non-traditional monetary policies, the aim is to reduce the monetary congestion and risk premium and to revive stagnant markets. Moreover, as the head of the banking system in the country, it is also responsible for keeping banks under control and supervision, counselling the authorities of state on financial and economic issues, and lending to the banking system as the last lending authority in the economy.

Due to these duties and responsibilities, the central bank cannot be considered separately from the political and social developments of the country in which it operates and the economic policies carried out. Therefore, while performing these duties and responsibilities, it plays a supporting role in the government's growth and employment policies.

2 Literature Review

One of the vital indicators for import and export within the macroeconomic system is the exchange rate. Because, the losses in the value of the national currency will have positive effects on exports, while it will have the opposite effect on imports. It is clear that this situation will create an advantage over the stock market companies working for export. However, the increase in the exchange rate may be the reason for an increase in the rates of inflation due to the effects of increasing the costs of domestic products for a country dependent on imported products. However, the increase in inflation rates will have negative effects on stock market companies due to the decrease in domestic demand (Gençtürk, 2009). Therefore, in this case, it will be important for companies whether stock market companies are working mainly for domestic or foreign markets. Central banks reduce their loan costs by directly lending to the markets with the widening of the credit conditions, especially during the economic and financial crisis periods, and also to reduce the monetary congestion and risk premium and to revive stagnant markets. Consequently, positive effects of these applications of the central bank are expected on the stock market.

When the literature is reviewed that it has a lot of surveys and important evidence that the in the fields of exchange rate, inflation, stocks, stock market on the correlation between each other and also the results of credit expansion policy. For example, credit expansion has vital effects on the real economy, such as banking crises, housing market crashes, stock market, current account deficit, and economic recessions (For example, Binici and Köksal, 2012; Borio and Lowe, 2002; Gacener Atış and Saygılı, 2014; Kindleberger and Aliber, 2011; L'opez-Salido, Stein and Zakraj, 2017; Mian and Sufi 2009; Minsky, 1982; Schularick and Taylor, 2012; Tornell and Westermann, 2002).

In studies where the relationship between stock market performance and inflation was examined, a positive relationship was found between these two variables (Al-Abbadi & Abdel Khaliq, 2017; Karamustafa & Karakaya, 2004). Whereas, Pindyck (1984) reached to the results of the effects of raise in the aritmetich mean and variance of the inflation rate leads to a declination of firms' expected return on capital.

However, there are different results in studies examining the relationship between stock price and exchange rate. For example, while Adjasi, Harvey & Agyapong (2008) argue that there is a negative relationship between the two variables mentioned. There are also studies in which no relation can be reached between stock price or stock index and exchange rate (Rahman & Uddin 2009; Kendirli & Cankaya 2016). But, Zhao (2010) argued that only the cross volatility effects between these variables.

In the literature, studies that deal with the relationship between stock market, interest rates, consumer price index, economic growth, and capacity utilization rates are available. Of these, there are studies that conclude that there is a short and long-term and negative relationship between the consumer price index (Eyuboglu & Eyuboglu, 2018), and a positive long-term relationship between the stock market and capacity utilization rate (Sahin & Kırıcı, 2019) and also, the stock market affects economic growth positively(Levine & Zervos, 1998; Likewise, Beck & Levine, 2004). In addition to this information, in researches with relation of inflation, exchange rate and interest rate, it has been founded that there is a corelation of each variable with another variable (Doğan, Eroğlu & Değer, 2016; Torun & Karanfil, 2016).

As can be seen, there are many studies in which are handled stock exchange, exchange rate, inflation and credit variables in different combinations. Our study, unlike the others, aims to examine the results of central bank monetary policy practices in this respect by considering these four variables together.

3 Data and Metodology

This study examined whether is a long-term and causality relationship between BIST100 indices, inflation rate, credits by banks, the Dolar/TL exchange rate for the period 2004:01–2020:03, in Turkey. E-views statistics program were used for the statistical time series analyzes. In this study, since the inflation rates are based on 2003, the whole data set was started in January 2004. All data for the period 2004:01–2020:03 are obtained from the electronic data distribution system of the Central Bank of Republic of Turkey. Variables choosed in the study and details about the data set are presented in the table below.

Table 1: *Data Set*

Variables	Descriptions
BIST100	BIST 100 index level values according to closing prices ((January 1986 = 1) -Level)
INF	Inflation rates(CPI), which represent an increase compared to the same month of the previous year (2003 base)
EXCR	Dollar / TL expressing the buying value of the US Dollar
CREDIT	Domestic credits by banks

In this study, the natural logarithm of the all series was taken in order to ensure that the series close to normal distribution. First of all, whether the time series have stationary or stationary levels were tested by Augmented Dickey Fuller (ADF) and Philip-Perron (PP) Stationarity and Unit Root tests. After performing the stationary test, the Johansen Cointegration test was used to examine the long-term relationship between the variables. In addition, the causality relationship between variables was investigated by applying Toda Yamamoto Causality Test. The methodology handled is briefly mentioned below.

3.1 Stationarity and Unit Root Tests

Firstly, we examined Augmented Dickey Fuller (ADF) and Philips-Perron (PP) (1981) unit root tests. The empirical equations used for the regressions in which the Dickey-Fuller (DF) Test is applied regarding the theory and practice are briefly given below.

Table 2: *Empirical Equations for Unit Root Test and Descriptions*

without constant&trend $\Delta Yt = \alpha Yt\text{-}1 + \varepsilon t$. . . . .(1)	In equations (1), (2) and (3) indicates; Δ. . . . . .Difference operator and linear time trend,
with constant $\Delta Yt = b0 + \alpha Yt\text{-}1 + \sum_{i=1}^{k} \alpha \Delta Y_i + \varepsilon t$. . . . . (2)	Y. . . . . The variable of the time series is applied the stationary test, b0. . . . . .Constant term, b1 and α . . ...Coefficients, t. . . . . .Time trend,
with constant&trend $\Delta Yt = b0 + b1t + \alpha Yt\text{-}1 + \sum_{i=1}^{k} \alpha \Delta Y_i + \varepsilon t$ ...(3)	Yt-1. . . . . .The first difference of the variable applied stationary analysis, i=1,2,3. . . k,. . .. it is the optimal lag length that prevents the autocorrelation problem between the variables, ε . . . .The error term.

In the survey, in addition to the ADF test, PP test is carried out to strengthen the findings. In PP test, the following regression is taken into account (Tarı, 2015: 400).

$$Y_t = b_0 + \alpha_1 Y_{t-1} + \varepsilon_t \text{. . . . .(4) and } Y_t = b_0 + \alpha_1 Y_{t-1} + \alpha_2 (t\text{-}T/2) + \varepsilon_t \text{. . . . .(5)}$$

Here, T shows the number of observations, ε_t the distribution of error terms and the expected average of this error term is equal to zero (Beşel, 2017). Hypotheses related to unit root and stationary tests are formed as follows: (Şenturk and Akbas, 2014; Kılınçer, 2019).

H_0: α= 0, Time series is not stationary, so Y has unit root.
H_1: α ≠ 0, Time series is stationary, Y has no unit root.

3.2 Cointegration Test

Cointegration analysis is one of the methods that can be used to determine whether there is a long-term relationship between the series. According to Johansen and Juselius (1990) cointegration approach, despite the short-term deviations, the variables may have a long-term balance. Since we have more than two variables in the study, Johansen and Juselius (1990) cointegration test was used because of the possibility of having more than one cointegrating vector. To explain this method with the help of the vector autoregression (VAR) method below;

$$Xt = \Pi 1\ Xt\text{-}1 + \Pi 2\ Xt\text{-}2 + \text{. . . . . . .} + \Pi k\ Xt\text{-}k + \varepsilon t \quad t= 1, 2, \text{. . . ....} T \text{ (4)}$$

Here, Xt; Vector showing Linf, Lexcr, Lcredit variables, k; number of lags, ε; represents the error term. In addition, the level of stationarity of our variables must be the same. According to ADF and PP stationarity tests, since all series become stationary at I (1) level, equation (4) turns into equation (5) below (Şenturk and Akbas, 2014).

$$\Delta Xt = \Gamma 1\ \Delta Xt\text{-}1 + \Gamma 2\ \Delta Xt\text{-}2 + \ldots\ldots + \Gamma k\text{-}1\ \Delta Xt\text{-}k\text{+}1 + \Pi\ Xt\text{-}k + \varepsilon t \quad \textbf{(5)}$$

Here,

Γi = -(I – Π1 – Π2 -. . . . . .- Πi) (i= 1, 2, ...k-1) and
Π = -(I – Π1 – Π2 -. . ...-Πk) I = Unit matrix, express.

In the Johansen & Juselius (1990) method, Trace statistics and Max Eigenvalue statistics are used to determine the number of cointegration vectors and whether they are significant or not. There are two tests equations in this approach (Tarı, 2015).

$$\text{TraceTest} : \lambda_{\text{trace}} = -T.\sum_{i=1}^{n} \ln\left(1 - \hat{\lambda}_i\right) \quad (6)$$

$$\text{MaxTest} :: \lambda\text{max} = -T.\ln\left(1 - \hat{\lambda}_{r+1}\right) \quad (7)$$

If Trace Statistics and MaxEigenvalue statistics results is greater than the critical table value, the H_0 hypothesis is not accepted. In the other hand, in Trace and Max Tests, H_0 hypothesis is equal to or less than r whereas H_1 hypothesis is the number of cointegrated vectors is r + 1 (r expresses the number of cointegrated vectors) (Enders, 1995: 391). Accordingly, hypotheses are created as follows.

The hypotheses in the Trace Test;	The hypotheses in the Max Test;
$H_0: r \leq r_0$	$H_0: r = r_0$
$H_1: r \geq r_0 + 1$	$H_1: r = r_0 + 1$

The tests's hypotheses are as follows:

H_0= There is no cointegrating equation. and H_1= There is/are cointegrating equation(s).

In these tests, if the calculated value is greater than the critical table values, the H_0 hypothesis is rejected. Then, VAR model is established and cointegration status is checked by estimating the relevant model. The model with the smallest

Akaike and Schwarz information criterion is considered as the most suitable model (Ayvaz, 2006: 6–10).

3.3 Vector Error Correction Model

If any cointegration is found in the research, it must be shown the short term movements of the variables. Short-term analysis of the VAR model is examined with the vector error correction mechanism (VECM). The model is as follows.

$$\Delta Y_t = \alpha_0 + \alpha_{-1}\Delta X_t + \alpha_2 e_{t-1} + v_t \qquad (7)$$

$e_{t=}$ Yt-Ŷt, refers to the error correction term.

e_{t-1} . . . is the error correction model. α_2 refers to the coefficient as the adjustment rate and, if it is statistically significant, there is a deviation. α_2 shows how much short-term imbalance in the Y series can be corrected after one period (Tarı, 2015).

3.4 Toda Yamamoto Causality Test

Regression analysis gives the relationship of independent variables with dependent variable, but this relationship does not show causality. If there is a relationship between variables, knowing the direction of this is important for the decisions to be taken. The Granger test is influenced by the size of the sample, the annual or seasonal data of and the non-stationarity of the series. In addition, when there is any cointegrating equation between the non-stationary series, Granger causality test is performed on VECM models, not VAR. But, seasonal effects, stationarity, co-integration in series are not important in Toda-Yamamoto (1995) causality test. What important in the Toda-Yamamoto causality test is the VAR model's lag length (k) and the greatest stationary degree of the series studied (dmax). After determining these two values, a VAR model in size (k + dmax) can be established and the Toda-Yamamoto test can be performed (Sentürk & Akbas, 2014: 5825). In the Toda-Yamamoto (1995) causality test, the following VAR model is taken into consideration.

$$Y_t = \alpha_{10} + \sum_{i=1}^{k} \alpha_{1i} X_{t-i} + \sum_{i=1}^{k} \beta_{1i} Y_{t-i} + \sum_{j=k+1}^{dmax} \delta_{1i} X_{t-i} + \sum_{j=k+1}^{dmax} \lambda_{1i} Y_{t-i} + e_{1t} \qquad (8)$$

$$X_t = \alpha_{20} + \sum_{i=1}^{k} \alpha_{2i} X_{t-i} + \sum_{i=1}^{k} \beta_{2i} Y_{t-i} + \sum_{j=k+1}^{dmax} \delta_{2i} X_{t-i} + \sum_{j=k+1}^{dmax} \lambda_{2i} Y_{t-i} + e_{1t} \quad (9)$$

First Model	**Second Model**
$H_0 = \alpha_{1i} = 0$ X is not the cause of Y.	$H_0 = \beta_{2i} = 0$ Y is not the cause of X.
$H_1 = \alpha_{1i} \neq 0$ X is the cause of Y.	$H_1 = \beta_{2i} \neq 0$ Y is the cause of X.

Hypotheses are tested by testing with Wald test.

4 Empirical Findings

4.1 ADF-PP Tests Results

ADF-PP unit root tests results are presented in the table below.

Table 3: *ADF-PP Unit Root Tests Results*

At Level			LBIST	LCREDIT	LEXCR	LINF	At First Difference			LBIST	LCREDIT	LEXCR	LINF
With Constant	ADF	t-Statistic	-2.3715	-2.1278	1.1309	-0.6238	With Constant	ADF	t-Statistic	-4.9038	-5.6019	-7.2416	-8.8336
		Prob.	0.1512	0.2341	0.9977	0.8611			***Prob.***	0.0001	0.0000	0.0000	0.0000
	PP	t-Statistic	-2.3662	-3.7138	1.2452	-3.0253		PP	t-Statistic	-13.2838	-10.3495	-9.4638	-10.7379
		Prob.	0.1528	0.0046	0.9984	0.0343			***Prob.***	0.0000	0.0000	0.0000	0.0000
With Constant & Trend	ADF	t-Statistic	-3.5753	-2.5871	-1.513	-1.4332	With Constant & Trend	ADF	t-Statistic	-5.0506	-5.8169	-7.5379	-8.9592
		Prob.	0.0348	0.2868	0.8221	0.8481			***Prob.***	0.0003	0.0000	0.0000	0.0000
	PP	t-Statistic	-3.0942	-3.1042	-1.4248	-3.465		PP	t-Statistic	-13.3299	-10.8157	-9.4426	-10.7027
		Prob.	0.1106	0.1083	0.8509	0.0461			***Prob.***	0.0000	0.0000	0.0000	0.0000
Without Constant & Trend	ADF	t-Statistic	1.4465	4.3482	2.5699	0.5857	Without Constant & Trend	ADF	t-Statistic	-4.686	-1.8096	-6.776	-8.8246
		Prob.	0.9632	1.0000	0.9976	0.842			***Prob.***	0.0000	0.067	0.0000	0.0000
	PP	t-Statistic	1.3987	8.2249	2.9242	-0.3166		PP	t-Statistic	-13.1669	-6.694	-9.5636	-10.7746
		Prob.	0.9595	1.0000	0.9992	0.5704			***Prob.***	0.0000	0.0000	0.0000	0.0000

According to the test results;

In the model with constant; Lcredit variable is stationary at the level of 1 % significance only in the PP test. In addition, logarithmized inflation data is stationary at a level of 5 % significance only in the PP test. Other variables have a unit root according to ADF and PP tests. In other words, they are not stationary.

In the model with constant & trend; Lbist data is stable at 5 % significance level, according to ADF test, and Linflation data set is stable at 5 % significance level only according to PP test. Other variables are not stationary.

In the model without constant & trend; It is concluded that all variables are unit-rooted and not stationary.

Due to the differences in the test results in general, the first differences of each variable were taken and it was determined that they became stationary at I (1) level.

4.2 Johansen-Juselius Cointegration Test Results

Before the Johansen Cointegration Test, for the VAR model was determined to 2 lag lenght with most asterisk according to the all information criteria and the 3th model (linear deterministic intercept (no trend) as cointegration model. r = 0 indicates the null hypothesis that there is no cointegration. Trace and Max–Eigen Statistic Test have similar results, test results were given in Table 4.

Table 4: *Johansen Cointegration Test Results*

Hypothesized	Hypotesis	Trace	0.05		Max-Eigen	0.05	
No. of CE(s)	H_0 H_1	Statistic	Critical Value	Prob.**	Statistic	Critical Value	Prob.**
None *	r=0 r=1	86.77323	47.85613	0.0000	51.9289	27.58434	0.0000
At most 1 *	r≤1 r=2	34.84433	29.79707	0.012	23.88302	21.13162	0.02
At most 2	r≤2 r=3	10.96131	15.49471	0.2139	10.66632	14.2646	0.1717
At most 3	r≤3 r=4	0.29499	3.841466	0.587	0.29499	3.841466	0.587

According to the cointegration test results, the H_0 hypothesis is rejected, suggesting cointegration between series. Trace test and Max test findings point on that, there is a long-term relationship between Linflation, Lexchange rate, Lcredit variables and Lbist.

Therefore, according to Johansen cointegration test results, it can be said that these variables are balanced together in the long term. According to the econometric theory, series having a cointegrated relationship are expected to return to equilibrium in the long term even if they are subject to some deviations. The error correction model is also affected by the short-term equilibrium deviations of the variables in the system, and the equation of this model includes lag errors of the co-integration regressions as well as the primary differences of the variables (Şahbaz, 2009, p.140). Whereat, the an equation to be created with normalized cointegrating coefficients according to the test results are as follows.

Table 5: *Normalized Cointegration Coefficients*

Cointegrating Equation(s):		Log likelihood	1984.434
Normalized cointegrating coefficients (standard error in parentheses)			
LBIST	LCREDIT	LEXCR	LINF
1.000000	−0.730164	0.526696	−0.354071
Std.dev.	(0.04752)	(0.11874)	(0.10145)
t-ist	15,365	4,435	3,49

LBIST=0,73LCREDIT-0,52LEXCR+0,35LINF

Therefore test results express that credit (LCREDIT) and inflation (LINF) have a positive impact on Bist100 (stock market) indices (LBIST) in the long run. Whereas, exchange rate (LEXCR) has a negative impact on Bist100 indices, with statistically significant, on average, ceteris paribus. Attention, the effect of credit variable is higher than inflation, more than doubled. It marks the requirement of the central bank's policies to show the sensitivity required for credit expansion applications.

4.3 Vector Error Correction Model

Vector Error Correction Model Results are presented in the table below. We comment by looking at the coefficient of the error term (ECM). According to VECM results, only inflation data between variables is not significant as statistically. Credit data is significant at a level of 10 %. The coefficient of the error correction model (Ecm) is negative and statistically significant.

Table 6: *Vector Error Correction Model Resuts*

Dependent Variable: DLBIST				
Variable	**Coefficient**	**Std. Error**	**t-Statistic**	**Prob.**
C	0.021707	0.007453	2.912600	0.0040
DLINF	0.000395	0.005016	0.078719	0.9373
DLEXCR	−0.114175	0.048325	−2.362658	0.0192
DLCREDIT	−0.498819	0.278593	−1.790496	0.0750
ECM(-1)	−0.081590	0.033555	−2.431527	0.0160

The coefficient of the error term shows us how much the balance deterioration has improved over the past year. In other words, approximately 8 % of 1 unit deviation improves in the next period, and the deviation from the average decreases. Short-term imbalances decrease by 8 % every month. Accordingly, deviations will come to equilibrium after 100/8 = 12.5 periods (about 1 year). Accordingly, despite some short-term deviations between the series, the equilibrium situation re-occurs in the long run.

4.5 Toda Yamamoto Causality Test Results

The causality directions between variables are exhibited in Table 7. The findings show that, the causality relationships between the Bist100 and the credit variables are bidirectional at 5 % significance level. Moreover, there is a causality relationship between exchange rate and inflation variables at a level of 1 % significance. All together of the Bist100, the exchange rate and the credit variables are the cause of inflation. In addition, the results shows while there is no causality relationship from each variables to exchange rate, but; all together of the Bist100 indices, the inflation and the credit variables are the cause for the exchange rate. Moreover, there is a causality relationship at the level of 10 % significance from the exchange rate variable to the credit variable. However, the all together variables of the Bist100, the inflation and the exchange rate are the cause of the credit variable.

Table 7: *Toda Yamamoto Causality Test Results*

	Independent Variables		Dependent Variable	Prob.	Decision
FROM	INF	TO	BIST	0.4964	There is no causality.
	EXCR			0.8572	There is no causality.
	CREDIT			0.0501	There is causality.
	INF+EXCR+CREDIT			0.1389	There is no causality.
FROM	BIST	TO	INF	0.3208	There is no causality.
	EXCR			0.0006	There is causality.
	CREDIT			0.1650	There is no causality.
	BIST+EXCR+CREDIT			0.0000	There is causality.
FROM	BIST	TO	EXCR	0.2069	There is no causality.
	INF			0.2596	There is no causality.
	CREDIT			0.1244	There is no causality.
	BIST+INF+CREDIT			0.0176	There is causality.
FROM	BIST	TO	CREDIT	0.0373	There is causality.
	INF			0.5777	There is no causality.
	EXCR			0.0715	There is causality.
	BIST+INF+EXCR			0.0002	There is causality.

5 Conclusion

Our fundamental objective is to examine the relationship between Borsa Istanbul stock market (BIST100) indices and, domestic credit given by banks, Dolar/TL exchange rate, inflation rate over the period 2004:01–2020:03 in Turkey.

As a outputs of the our analysis, it was determined that each of the series used in this study is unit rooted and becomes stationary when the first differences are taken. In addition, according to the cointegration test results, a long-term relationship has been reached between Bist100 and other variables. And also, the coefficients of VECM are statistically significant in terms of short and long term relationship as generally. Moreover, according to our findings, the positive relationship between inflation and the stock market is similar to the results of Karamustafa and King (2004) and also the negative relationship between foreign exchange rate and the stock market is similar to the results of Adjasi, Harvey & Agyapong (2008).

Accordingly, it was determined that credit policies of the central bank had mutually positive effects on Borsa İstanbul 100 indices, but credit variable has not directly a causal connection with exchange rate or inflation variables.

This conclusion shows that exchange rate and inflation are not the cause of the Bist100 index alone is similar to the work of Durukan (1999) and Kendirli & Cankaya (2016).

However, this study explains that, it is important that causality relationship between credit and Bist100. Each of credit, exchange rate and inflation variables are separately caused by the coexistence of 3 other variables except themselves. We can express that credit-related policy practices support the markets positively, but exchange rate negatively. The necessity to take care of these results may be suggested to policy makers.

References

Adjasi, C. K. D., Harvey, S. K., & Agyapong, D. A. (2008). Effect of Exchange Rate Volatility on the Ghana Stock Exchange (December 28, 2008). African Journal of Accounting, Economics, Finance and Banking Research, Vol. 3, No. 3, December 2008. Available at SSRN: https://ssrn.com/abstract=1534178.

Al-Abbadi, H., & Abdel Khaliq, S. (2017). The Relationship Between Inflation and Stock Market Performance in Jordan. European Journal of Business and Management, Vol. 9, pp. 142–150.

Ayvaz, Ö. (2006). Döviz Kuru ve Hisse Senetleri Fiyatları Arasındaki Nedensellik İlişkisi. Gazi Üniversitesi İktisadi ve İdari Bilimler Fakültesi Dergisi, Vol. 8, No. 2, pp. 1–14.

Beck, T., & Levine, R. (2004). Stock Markets, Banks and Growth: Panel Evidence. Journal of Banking & Finance, Vol.28, Issue 3, March, pp. 423–442.

Beşel, F. (2017). Energy Consumption and Unemployment Nexus in Turkey. The International Journal of Economic and Social Research, Vol. 13, Year 13, No. 2.

Binici, M., & Köksal, B. (2012). Türkiye'de Aşırı Kredi Genişlemeleri. TCMB Ekonomi Notları, No:2012/15, 10 July 2012.

Borio, C., & Lowe, P. (2002). Asset Prices, Financial and Monetary Stability: Exploring The Nexus.. BIS Working Papers Monetary and Economic Department, July, No.114.

Dickey, D. A., ve Fuller, W. A. (1981). Likelihood Ratio Statistics for Autoregressive Time Series with a Unit Root. Econometrica, Jul, 49, 4; ABI/INFORM Global, pp. 1057–1072.

Doğan, B., Eroğlu, Ö., & Değer, O. (2016). Enflasyon ve Faiz Oranı Arasındaki Nedensellik İlişkisi: Türkiye Örneği. Çankırı Karatekin Üniversitesi İİBF Dergisi, Vol. 6, No. 1, pp. 405–425. Geliş / Received: 26.06.2015 Kabul / Accepted: 16.09.2015 Çevrimiçi Erişim / Available Online: 28.09.2015 DOI: 10.18074/cnuiibf.258.

Durukan, M.B. (1999). İstanbul Menkul Kıymetler Borsasında Makroekonomik Değişkenlerin Hisse Senedi Fiyatlarına Etkisi. İMKB Dergisi, Vol. 3, No. 11, 19–47.

Enders, W. (1995). Applied Econometric Time Series, John Wiley&Sons, Third Edition, University of Alabama, 1995. https://tr.scribd.com/doc/180318659/ (Erişim Tarihi:01.04.2020).

Eyuboglu, S., & Eyuboglu, K. (2018). Enflasyon Oranı ile Borsa İstanbul Sektör Endeks Getirileri Arasındaki İlişkinin İncelenmesi. Anadolu Üniversitesi Sosyal Bilimler Dergisi, Vol. 18, pp. 89–100. DOI:10.18037/ausbd.552686.

Gacener Atış, A., & Saygılı, F. (2014).Türkiye'de Kredi Hacmi ve Cari Açık İlişkisi Üzerine Bir İnceleme. Business and Economics Research Journal, Vol. 5, No. 4, ISSN: 1309–2448, ss. 129–141.

Gençtürk, M. (2009). Finansal Kriz Dönemlerinde Makroekonomik Faktörlerin Hisse Senedi Fiyatlarına Etkisi. Suleyman Demirel University Journal of Faculty of Economics & Administrative Sciences, Vol. 14, No. 1.

Johansen, S., & Juselius, K. (1990). Maximum Likelihood Estimation and Inference on Cointegration-with Application to the Demand for Money. Oxford Bulletin of Economics and Statistics, Vol. 52, pp. 169–210.

Karamustafa, O., & Karakaya, O. (2004). Enflasyonun Borsa Performansı Üzerindeki Etkisi. Kocaeli Üniversitesi Sosyal Bilimler Enstitüsü Dergisi, (7). 2004 / 1: 23–35.

Kendirli, S., & Çankaya, M. (2016). Döviz Kuru ve Enflasyonun Bist Banka Endeksi Üzerindeki Etkisi. MANAS Journal of Social Studies, Vol. 5, No. 3, ISSN: 1624–7215.

Kılınçer, B. (2019). Doğrudan Yabancı Yatırım Girişlerinin Türkiye'nin Finansal Göstergeleri Üzerine Etkileri. Mart, (Yayınlanmamış Doktora Tezi), İnönü Üniversitesi, İİBF, İşletme ABD, Malatya, ss. 315.

Kindleberger, C. P. ve Aliber, R. Z. (2011). Manias, Panics, and Crashes: A History of Financial Crises, Sixth Edition. Palgrave Macmillan, Hampshire.

Levine, R., & Zervos, S. (1998). Stock Markets, Banks, and Economic Growth. The American Economic Review, Vol. 88, No. 3, pp. 537–558. Retrieved April 10, 2020, www.jstor.org/stable/116848.

López-Salido, D., Stein, J., & Zakrajsek, E. (2017). Credit-Market Sentiment and the Business Cycle. Quarterly Journal of Economics, Vol. 132, pp. 1373–1426. doi:10.1093/qje/qjx014.

Mian, A., & Sufi, A. (2009). The Consequences of Mortgage Credit Expansion: Evidence from the U.S. Mortgage Default Crisis. The Quarterly Journal of Economics, Vol. 124, Issue 4, November pp. 1449–1496, https://doi.org/10.1162/qjec.2009.124.4.1449.

Misnky, H. P. (1982). Can 'It' Happen Again? Essays on Instability and Finance. New York, M.E. Sharpe, February, pp. xxiv+301.

Phillips, P. C. B., ve Perron, P. (1988). Testing for a Unit Root in Time Series Regression. Biometrika, Vol. 75, No. 2, pp. 335–346.

Pindyck, R. S. (June 1984). Risk, Inflation, and the Stock Market. The American Economic Review, Vol. 74, No. 3, pp. 335–351.

Rahman, M. L., & Uddin, J. (2009). Dynamic Relationship between Stock Prices and Exchange Rates: Evidence from Three South Asian Countries. International Business Research, April, Vol. 2, No. 2, pp. 167–174.

Sahin, S., & Kirici, A. (2019). Association between Bist Sector Indices and Capacıty Utilizatıon Rates in Turkey. Osmaniye Korkut Ata University Journal of Economics and Administrative Sciences, Vol. 3, Issue: 1, June 2019, pp. 72–86.

Schularick, M., & Taylor, A. M. (2012). Credit Booms Gone Bust: Monetary Policy, Leverage Cycles, and Financial Crises, 1870–2008. American Economic Review, Vol. 102, No. 2, April, pp. 1029–61.

Sentürk, M., & Akbas, Y. E. (2014). İşsizlik-Enflasyon Ve Ekonomik Büyüme Arasındaki Karşılıklı İlişkinin Değerlendirilmesi: Türkiye Örneği. Journal of Yasar University, Vol. 9, No. 34, ss.5820–5832.

Şahbaz, A. (2009). Gelişmekte Olan Ülkelerde Kur Değişimlerinin Toplam Çıktı Üzerine Etkileri: Türkiye Üzerine Bir Uygulama. (Yayımlanmamış doktora tezi). Çukurova Üniversitesi Sosyal Bilimler Enstitüsü, Adana.

Tarı, R. (2015). Ekonometri. Umuttepe Yayınları, 11. Baskı, Kocaeli, s.400.

Toda, H. Y., & Yamamoto,T. (1995). Statistical Inference in Vector Auto Regressions with Possibly Integrated Processes. Journal of Econometrics, Vol. 66, pp. 225–250.

Tornell, A., ve Westermann, F. (2002). Boom-Bust Cycles in Middle-Income Countries: Facts and Explanation. IMF Staff Papers, National Bureau of Economic Research, September, Vol. 49, pp. 111–155. http://www.nber.org/papers/w9219.

Torun, M., & Karanfil, M. (2016). 1980–2013 Dönemi Türkiye Ekonomisinde Enflasyon ve Faiz Oranı Arasındaki İlişki. Journal of Administrative Sciences, Vol. 14, No. 27, pp. 473–490.

Uyar, U., Kangallı Uyar, S., & Gokce, A. (2016). Gosterge Faiz Oranı Dalgalanmaları ve Bist Endeksleri Araındakı Iliskinin Esanlı Kantil Regresyon Ile Analizi. Ege Academic Review, Ege University Faculty of Economics and Administrative Sciences, Vol. 16, No. 4, pp. 587–598.

Zhao, H. (2010). Dynamic Relationship Between Exchange Rate and Stock Price: Evidence from China. Research in International Business and Finance, Vol. 24, No. 2, 103–112.

Zhu, H. (2006). An Empirical Comparison of Credit Spreads between the Bond Market and the Credit Default Swap Market. Journal of Financial Services Research, Vol. 29, Issue 3, pp. 211–235.

İlhan Korkmaz

A Literature Review on Economic Dimensions of Cultural Diversity[1]

1 Introduction

Cultural diversity phenomenon, formed by people from different cultures sharing the same geography, is not a new issue in the world history, but has become more common with the globalization process after 1980s. Globalization made easier individuals to move around the world in an extra-ordinary level. According to United Nations' International Migrant Stock Report (2019), the number of international migrants worldwide has reached nearly 272 million in 2019, an increase of 51 million since 2010. A great majority of all international migrants reside in developed countries. Consequently, countries in the world are becoming more and more culturally diverse. While this situation concerns the developed countries more closely in the first place, with the acceleration of the globalization process, it has started to affect the developing countries.

Economic analysis of cultural diversity requires an interdisciplinary approach. The topic is closely related to a wide range of fields such as social psychology, national and international migration, economic geography, regional and urban economics. In early studies, it has been found that high cultural heterogeneity causes poor economic performance (Easterly & Levine, 1997; Alesina et al., 2003; Alesina & La Ferrara, 2005). In the following period, some researchers have shown that under certain conditions, cultural diversity can provide positive economic outcomes (Florida, 2002; Ottaviano & Peri, 2006; Bellini et al. 2008). The basic view underlying the positive approach to cultural diversity refers to the diversity of ideas is higher in a group of individuals with different cultural backgrounds. This creates a talent complementary effect among individuals and culturally heterogeneous group performs better in a problem solving than the homogeneous group (Hong & Page, 2001; Hong & Page, 2004). Recent studies show that cultural diversity generally affects economic development through per capita income, factor productivity, innovation and entrepreneurship.

1 This paper is based on author's Ph.D thesis named "Spatial Analysis of the Effect of Cultural Diversity on Regional Development in Turkey".

The rest of the paper is organized as follows. Section 2 includes the definitions and measurement of the cultural diversity. Section 3 answers the question why cultural diversity important for economies and describes theoretical background. Section 4 provides a critical review of the literature and final section concludes and makes suggestions for further research.

2 Definition and Measurement of Cultural Diversity

Cultural diversity is a complex concept that may vary depending on the context in which it is studied. However, it can generally be expressed as differences in race, language, national origin or ethnic origin (Elias & Paradies, 2016:19). Due to its multidimensional nature, it has been widely discussed in the literature that what will be the criteria for differentiating people living in a region from a cultural perspective. Obviously, what makes an individual different from others can be a combination of different features such as race, religion, language and birthplace. However, these features are difficult to express quantitatively. Therefore, a practical definition is often used in economic models of cultural diversity (Ozgen et al., 2013:7).

While measuring cultural diversity, it is necessary to determine one or more 'identity markers' as a criterion for the definition of the cultural groups (Bellini et al., 2008:9). The availability of data plays an important role in quantitative research in the choice of cultural identity marker. Therefore, it is seen that the two most common representative variables used to express cultural diversity in the literature are the birth place (country) and ethnicity (Nathan, 2011:8). It is clear that neither ethnicity nor birth place completely capture the full meaning of culture. They can only reflect some aspects of it. Each one of them has several advantages and disadvantages. According to Extra and Yağmur (2004), while country of birth criteria is objective and easy to reach data but it does not always mean ethnicity and does not capture second generations in immigrant country. On the other hand, ethnicity depends on self categorization and self categorization may change in time. It is not also possible to collect ethnicity data for each case.

Various forms of cultural diversity no matter which criterion is preferred is generally measured with *fractionalizaton index*. Using birth place criteria, it can be written as:

$$Fracitonalization_j = 1 - \sum_{r=1}^{R} n_j^2$$

Where n is the proportion of people lives in city j who were born in country r; and R is the number of different countries (Kemeny, 2013:8). The index is also known as "*Ethnolinguistic fractionalization (ELF) Index*", which measures the possibility that two randomly selected individuals from the population belong to different ethnic groups (Bove & Elia, 2017:228). The index takes values between 0 and 1. While nearing to 0 indicates a decrease in diversity, approaching to 1 indicates an increase in diversity. Although it is a widely used measure of diversity the fractionalization index tends to be more affected by the largest group in the population (Cheng & Li, 2012).

3 Why Does Cultural Diversity Matter for Economies?

The impacts of cultural factors on economic performance of countries or regions have been examined in a large number of studies in the economic literature (Granato et al., 1996; Welzel, et al., 2003; Inglehart & Welzel, 2005; Beugelsdijk & Maseland, 2010). However, urban researcher Jacobs (1961) first pointed out that the concept of culture in the context of diversity could have an economic significance. Jacobs (1961, 1969) took a wider approach to diversity and emphasized that diversity in economic activities, urban population, skills, tastes and demands are the engines of the economic development of cities.

Micro level group studies in organizational sciences (Watson et al., 1993; Cox, 1993; McLeod et al., 1996) and economics (Hong & Page, 2001; Hong & Page, 2004) have supported Jacobs' vision. The basic hypothesis of these works is based on the fact that heterogeneous groups will perform better in problem solving than homogeneous groups due to their high (cultural-ethnic) diversity.

According to Cox (1993), diversity based on race, ethnicity, gender and citizenship can directly affect creativity, innovativeness, problem solving and organizational effectiveness of communication. On the one hand, the emergence of these positive effects depends on the good management of diversity. On the other hand, it is inaccurate to expect the benefits of diversity to appear quickly. In a study conducted by Watson et al. (1993) over a 17-week period, initially, homogeneous groups performed better than high-diversity groups. However, with the dissolution of communication barriers over time, it has been observed that high-diversity groups perform better than homogeneous groups.

In their study, McLeod et al. (1996) applied an experimental brainstorming to two groups of students with different structures in terms of ethnic diversity. They found that ethnically diverse groups developed higher quality and more feasible ideas than ethnically homogeneous groups. Hong and Page (2004) observed that the differences in demographic characteristics, cultural identities and experiences of individuals, effect how they perceive and solve problems. They also found that identity-diverse groups outperform homogeneous groups in problem solving. It can be said that a diverse groups can create externalities which is also known as Jacobian knowledge spillovers.

From an economic perspective, the main question is whether a culturally diverse society performs better or worse than homogeneous one. The answer is not clear and equally double faced (Baycan-Levent, 2010). Cultural diversity may create a social environment that opens to change and different pereferences. According to Florida (2002), cultural diversity is crucial for a tolerant society. By eliminating social barriers that hinder participation in society for people with different characteristics cultural diversity provides suitable social conditions for creative thinking, innovation and entrepreneurial ideas to flourish.

A culturally diverse population also tends to demand a wider variety of goods and services (Quigley, 1998; Ottaviano & Peri 2006) and creates a demand side effect that offers new opportunities for entrepreneurs and producers. Another diversity-related channel that influences entrepreneurship is immigrant entrepreneurship. Baycan-Levent and Nijkamp (2009) stated that immigrants are more likely to be entrepreneur than similarly skilled native residents.

Another economic opportunity of cultural diversity is related to diaspora relations and business networks. Individuals who have multicultural connections can provide convenience in terms of access to different markets for companies (Nathan, 2011). However, this dimension of diversity has relatively modest impacts on economic development in comparison to others (Syrett & Sepulveda, 2011).

On the other hand, cultural diversity may cause several problems for societies such as, lower interpersonel trust and social cohesion problems. According to conflict theory, diversity may foster the in-group – out-group distinction and intensifies in-group solidarity or bonding social capital, thus increasing ethnocentrism (Putnam, 2007). However, these drawbacks of diversity largely depend on some circumstances such as income, institutions and political regime (Collier, 2001; Alesina & La Ferrara, 2005).

4 Literature Review on Economic Dimensions of Cultural Diversity

Based on the group level studies examining the effects of cultural diversity mentioned above, Economists began to study the issue at the level of countries, regions and cities[2]. Despite the positive vision of Jacobs (1961, 1969) early studies in the literature have generally reached negative results (Easterly & Levine, 1997; Alesina et al., 2003; Alesina & La Ferrara, 2005). Later on, with the studies of Florida (2002) and Ottaviano and Peri (2006) it is paid attention on the positive economic effects of cultural diversity in the literature.

Easterly and Levine (1997) claimed that ethnic divisions are responsible for economic growth trgedy of Africa. They observed a 2.3 % decrease in economic growth in transition from full homogeneity to full heterogeneity for African countries. They also argued that negative impact of diversity may have resulted from polarization caused by ethnic diversity. In a polarized society, each group could demonstrate a rent seeking behavior, and in such an environment, it would be very difficult to compromise on public goods and public policies.

Collier (2001), on the other hand, examined the findings related to the negative effects of ethnic diversity by examining the types of diversity and political conditions. Collier emphasized that the negative effects of ethnic diversity on growth occur only in non-democratic regimes and where a social group is dominant in the components of diversity.

Alesina et al. (2003) analyzed the effect of ethnic, linguistic and religious diversity on economic growth, institutions and policy quality for 190 countries using fractionalization indices. According to the findings, while ethnic and linguistic diversity negatively affects policy quality, religious diversity affects positively. This situation was interpreted by the authors that religious diversity had a positive effect through increasing tolerance in the society. In addition ethnic diversity is negatively associated with economic growth.

Florida (2002), which approaches cultural diversity differently in terms of both measurement and impact mechanisms, has an important place in the literature. In his Creative Class Theory, Florida has argued that social diversity affects regional development through its impact on the regional distribution of human capital and even the creative class. However, Florida's diversity measurement differs from others by taking into account the share of foreign born in the population, as well as the share of the homosexual population living in a region and those (bohemians) engaged in creative-artistic activities. Florida's work has received great attention in the literature, but has been criticized for its inability to expose causality between variables (Nathan, 2015).

2 Table 1 provides basic information on selected substantial cross-country and regional studies in the literature.

The study of Montalvo and Reynal-Querol (2005) represents an important milestone in the literature in several respects. The authors emphasized the difference between the concepts of ethnic diversity and polarization, which are sometimes used interchangeably in the literature. In cases where ethnic diversity is low, the probability of polarization is high, whereas ethnic diversity increases, polarization decreases. Other findings demonstrate that while ethnic diversity has a negative effect on growth, religious diversity has no effect. Polarization indirectly affects growth, causing a decline on investments, an increase in public spending and an increase in internal conflicts by fueling rent-seeking behavior.

Another significant study in the literature belongs to Ottaviano and Peri (2006). They investigated the effects of cultural diversity on labor market across US states for the period 1970–1990. The main finding of the study is that cultural diversity has a positive effect on the productivity of citizens born in the United States, as it has a positive correlation with both the average wage earned and the average rent paid by individuals born in the USA. One feature that makes the study special in the literature is that it solves the potential problem of endogeneity in the relationship between cultural diversity and economy.

After Ottaviano and Peri's paper, it can be said that a new interest has emerged in the literature that focuses the effects of diversity on wages and rents. Following Ottaviano and Peri (2006), Bellini et al. (2008) examined the economic dimensions of cultural diversity for the NUTS3 level in 12 of the EU15 countries and reached the conclusion that cultural diversity affects production and consumption through positive and negative externalities.

Suedekum et al. (2009) analyzed the effects of this diversity for native employees for a panel of 326 German regions. The study finds positive relationship between diversity of high-skilled foreign workers and local wages and employment for native workers. On the other hand for low-skilled foreign workers negative size effect is found. In the UK context, Longhi (2013) and Nathan (2011) found similar impacts of birth place diversity on wages and employment.

An important outcome that cultural diversity may cause is innovation. Niebuhr (2010) put cultural diversity into knowledge production function and examined the relationship between the birthplace diversity of the workforce population and patent applications at regional level for Germany. The results reveal that the variations in the knowledge and skills of workers from different cultural backgrounds increase the performance of regional R&D sectors. In addition, education levels are also important and quality of diverse workers is the strongest factor on innovation outcomes.

Similarly Ozgen et al. (2011) investigated the effects of migrant diversity on innovation for the periods of 1991–1995 and 2001–2005 on 170 regions in

Table 1: *Cross-country and Regional Studies on Economic Dimensions of Cultural Diversity*

Study	Observation	Period	Diversity Criteria	Dependent Variable	Effect
		Cross-country Studies			
Easterly & Levine (1997)	African countries	1960,1970, 1980	Etnicty	GDP per capita	(–)
Alesina &. (2003)	190 countries	1960–1995	Ethnicty, language, religion and polarizaton	GDP per capita growth, institution and policy quality	(–)
Alesina & La Ferrara (2005)	190 countries and USA cities	1960–2000 (10 years periods)	Ethnicity	GDP per capita growth	(–)
Montalvo & Querol (2005)	138 countries	1960–1989 (5 years periods)	Ethno-linguistic, religion and polarization	Real GDP per capita growth	(+) (–)
Alesina et al. (2013)	195 countries	1990, 2000	Ethnicity, language, religion and birth place	GDP per capita and patent applications	(+)
Gören (2014)	100 developed and 100 developing countries	1960–1999 (5 years periods)	Ethnicity and polarization	Real GDP per capita growth	(–)
Bove & Elia (2017)	135 countries	1960–2010	Birth place and polarization	Real GDP growth	(+)
		Regional Studies			
Florida & Gates (2003)	USA – 50 states	1990	Birth place	High-Tech firm concentration	(+)
Ottaviano & Peri (2006)	USA – states	1970–1990	Birth place	Wages and rents	(+)
Bellini vd. (2008)	12 EU15 countries – regions	1991, 2001	Birth place	GDP per capita wages and rents	(+)
Suedekum vd. (2009)	West Germany 326 regions	1995–2006	Birth place	Wages and employment	(+)
Nathan (2011)	England – cities	2001, 2006	Name classifications	Wages, employments and housing prices	(+) (–)

(*continued on next page*)

Table 1: Continued

Study	Observation	Period	Diversity Criteria	Dependent Variable	Effect
Niebuhr (2010)	Germany – Regions	1995–2000	Birth place	Patent applications	(+)
Ozgen et al. (2011)	EU NUTS2	1991–1995, 2001–2005	Birth place	Patent applications	(+)
Audretsch et al. (2010)	Germany – Regions	1998–2005	Birth place	Tech-oriented startups	(+)
Cheng & Li (2012)	USA – Districts	2001–2003	Birth place, race	Startups	(+)
Rodriguez-Pose &Hardy (2015)	England – Districts	1991, 2001	Birth place, ethnicity	Startups	(+)
Dhose & Gold (2014)	27 EU contries -regions	2002–2011	Birth place	GDP per capita growth and patents per capita	(+)
Limonov & Nesena (2016)	Russia – regions	2002–2010	Ethno-linguistic, Birth place (foreign and domestic)	GDP per capita, wages and rents	(+) (–)
Elias & Paradies (2016)	Australia – regions	2001–2011	Birth place	Wages	(+)

Europe. According to the findings, while the increase in the share of foreigners does not affect innovation, an increase in diversity of it affects positively. This finding is important in terms of emphasizing the effect of not the share of migrants but the diversity of it.

Entreprenurial effects of cultural diversity are also another case. Audretsch et al. (2010) have examined determinants of entrepreneurship in German regions for the period 1998–2005. In the study, it is pointed out that various economic agents with different backgrounds and abilities create knowledge externalities which are essential for entrepreneurship. Results indicate that technology level, human capital and regional (cultural and sectoral) diversity affect entrepreneurship significantly.

Rodríguez-Pose and Hardy (2015) also investigated the link between diversity and entrepreneurship in a cross section of England and Wales districts. Cultural diversity is measured based on ethnicity and birthplace datas. The diversity composition of the skilled workforce is also taken into account. According to the findings, birthplace diversity is more effective on entrepreneurship than ethnic diversity. In addition, the skill level of diversity plays an important at the level of influencing entrepreneurship.

Cultural diversity, innovations and entrepeneurship are factors that tend to create spillover effects. These spillovers can be revealed by spatial analysis. Spatial interactions among regions are taken into account by Niebuhr (2010), Audretsch et al. (2010), Ozgen et al. (2011) and Rodríguez-Pose and Hardy (2015). The results indicate that spatial depence plays an important role on knowledge spill-over across regions.

It can be said that apart from cross-country studies, the studies usually concentrated on the USA, EU countries, UK and Germany cases in the literature. There are few studies on other countries. Limonov and Nesena (2016) found no significant relationship between ethnic diversity and growth, for Russian regions. In addition, they measured two types of birth place diversity based on respectively country of origin and region of origin. They found positive relationship between birth place diversities and growth. On the other hand, unlike the literature, both diversity indices are inversely proportional to wages and rents. The authors state that this may be due to structural factors specific to Russia. This study is original in terms of considering internal migration as a different form of cultural diversity. In Australian case, using a large longitudinal data, Elias and Paradies (2016) examined the impact of cultural diversity on wages. Findings indicate that cultural diversity positively affected wages. Delgado Gómez-Flors and Alguacil (2018) analyzed the effects of immigrant diversity on wages for Spanish regions. The study finds a positive relationship between birth place diversity of workers and wages.

5 Conclusion

This paper represents a review of a growing literature on economic impacts of cultural diversity. As can be seen in the review that cultural diversity especially diversity of skilled migrants in the workforce effects economic growth, regional productivity, innovation and entrpereneurial activities positively in many cases. Studies show that the types of diversity matters for economic performance. In some cases ethnic diversity may have neutral or negative impacts while birth place diversity mostly has positive effects.

When evaluating the results obtained in the literature, it should be taken into consideration that the birth place variables used to measure cultural diversity represent a limited part of the real cultural diversity in the samples. Birth place is generally preferred as a cultural identity marker in most studies because of the available data possibilities. In fact, cultural diversity is a more complex concept and it would be better if there is opportunity to collect data based on self-definition of individuals by surveys. Institutions and researchers should pay more attention to do survey based studies. Lastly, it should be noted that internal migrations in a country may also create a different form of diversity. Therefore, further studies may also investigate internal diversity with together international diversity.

References

Alesina, A., Devleeschauwer, A., Easterly, W., Kurlat, S., & Wacziarg, R. (2003). Fractionalization. Journal of Economic Growth, 8(2), 155–194.

Alesina, A., & Ferrara, E. L. (2005). Ethnic Diversity and Economic Performance. Journal of Economic Literature, 43(3), 762–800.

Alesina, A., Harnoss, J., & Rapoport, H. (2013). Birthplace Diversity and Economic Prosperity IZA Discussion Paper, No. 7568.

Audretsch, D., Dohse, D., & Niebuhr, A. (2010). Cultural Diversity and Entrepreneurship: A Regional Analysis for Germany. The Annals of Regional Science, 45(1), 55–85.

Baycan-Levent, T. (2010). Diversity and Creativity as Seedbeds for Urban and Regional Dynamics. European Planning Studies, 18(4), 565–594.

Baycan-Levent, T., & Nijkamp P., (2009). Characteristics of Migrant Entrepreneurship in Europe, Entrepreneurship and Regional Development, 27(4), 375–397.

Bellini, E., Ottaviano, G. I., Pinelli, D., & Prarolo, G. (2013). Cultural Diversity and Economic Performance: Evidence from European Regions. In Geography, Institutions and Regional Economic Performance (pp. 121–141). Springer, Berlin, Heidelberg.

Beugelsdijk, S., & Maseland, R. (2010). Culture in Economics: History, Methodological Reflections and Contemporary Applications. Cambridge University Press.

Bove, V., & Elia, L. (2017). Migration, Diversity, and Economic Growth. World Development, 89, 227–239.

Cheng, S., & Li, H. (2012). New Firm Formation Facing Cultural and Racial Diversity. Papers in Regional Science, 91(4), 759–774.

Collier, P. (2001). Ethnic Diversity: An Economic Analysis. Economic Policy, 32(16), 128–166.

Cox, T. (1993). Cultural Diversity in Organizations: Theory, Research and Practice. Berrett-Koehler Publishers.

Delgado Gómez-Flors, M., & Alguacil, M. (2018). The Impact of Immigrant Diversity on Wages. The Spanish experience. Sustainability, 10(9), 3312.

Dohse, D., & Gold, R. (2014). Determining the Impact of Cultural Diversity on Regional Economies in Europe (No. 58). WWWforEurope working paper.

Easterly, W., & Levine, R. (1997). Africa's Growth Tragedy: Policies and Ethnic Divisions. The Quarterly Journal of Economics, 112(4), 1203–1250.

Extra, G., & Yağmur, K. (Eds.). (2004). Urban Multilingualism in Europe: Immigrant Minority Languages at Home and School (Vol. 130). Multilingual Matters.

Elias, A., & Paradies, Y. (2016). The Regional Impact of Cultural Diversity on Wages: Evidence from Australia. IZA Journal of Migration, 5(1), 12.

Fichter, J. (2000). Sosyoloji Nedir?, Translator: Nilgün Çelebi, Attila Kitabevi, 4. Baskı, Ankara.

Florida, R. (2002). The Rise of the Creative Class, and How It Is Transforming Work, Leisure, Community and Everyday Life. New York: Basic Books.

Florida, R., & Gates, G. (2003). Technology and Tolerance: The Importance of Diversity to High-Technology Growth. Research in Urban Policy, 9(1), 199–219.

Gören, E. (2014). How Ethnic Diversity Affects Economic Growth. World Development, 59, 275–297.

Granato, J., Inglehart, R., & Leblang, D. (1996). The Effect of Cultural Values on Economic Development: Theory, Hypotheses, and Some Empirical Tests. American Journal of Political Science, 40(3), 607–631.

Hong, L., & Page, S. E. (2001). Problem Solving by Heterogeneous Agents. Journal of Economic Theory, 97(1), 123–163.

Hong, L., & Page, S. E. (2004). Groups of Diverse Problem Solvers Can Outperform Groups of High-Ability Problem Solvers. Proceedings of the National Academy of Sciences, 101(46), 16385–16389.

Inglehart, R. (1997). Modernization and Postmodernization: Cultural, Economic, and Political Change in 43 Societies. Princeton University Press.

Inglehart, R., & Welzel, C. (2005). Modernization, Cultural Change, and Democracy: The Human Development Sequence. Cambridge University Press.

Jacobs, J. (1961). The Death and Life of Great American Cities, Vintage.

Jacobs, J. (1969). The Economy of Cities, Vintage.

Kemeny, T. (2013). Immigrant Diversity and Economic Development in Cities: A Critical Review, SERC Discussion Paper, No:149.

Limonov, L., & Nesena, M. (2016). Regional Cultural Diversity in Russia: Does It Matter for Regional Economic Performance?. Area Development and Policy, 1(1), 63–93.

Longhi, S. (2013). Impact of Cultural Diversity on Wages, Evidence from Panel Data, Regional Science and Urban Economics, 43(5), 797–807.

McLeod, P. L., Lobel, S. A., & Cox Jr, T. H. (1996). Ethnic Diversity and Creativity in Small Groups. Small Group Research, 27(2), 248–264.

Montalvo, J. G., & Reynal-Querol, M. (2005). Ethnic Diversity and Economic Development. Journal of Development economics, 76(2), 293–323.

Nathan, M. (2011). The Economics of Super-Diversity: Findings from British Cities, 2001–2006, SERC Discussion Papers, SERCDP0068. Spatial Economics Research Centre, London School of Economics and Political Sciences, London, UK.

Nathan, M. (2015). After Florida: Towards an Economics of Diversity, European Urban and Regional Studies, 22(1), 3–19.

Niebuhr, A. (2010). Migration and Innovation: Does Cultural Diversity Matter for Regional R&D Activity?, Papers in Regional Science, 89(3), 563–585.

Ottaviano, G. I., & Peri, G. (2006). The Economic Value of Cultural Diversity: Evidence from US Cities. Journal of Economic Geography, 6(1), 9–44.

Ozgen, C., Nijkamp, P., & Poot, J. (2011). Immigration and Innovation in European Regions. IZA DP, No:5176.

Putnam, R. D. (2007). E Pluribus Unum: Diversity and Community in the Twenty-First Century the 2006 Johan Skytte Prize Lecture. Scandinavian Political Studies, 30(2), 137–174.

Quigley, J. M. (1998). Urban Diversity and Economic Growth. Journal of Economic Perspectives, 12(2), 127–138.

Rodríguez-Pose, A., & Hardy, D. (2015). Cultural Diversity and Entrepreneurship in England and Wales, Environment and Planning A, 47(2), 392–411.

Suedekum, J., Wolf, K., & Blien, U. (2014). Cultural Diversity and Local Labour Markets. Regional Studies, 48(1), 173–191.

Syrett, S., & Sepulveda, L. (2011). Realising the Diversity Dividend: Population Diversity and Urban Economic Development. Environment and Planning A, 43(2), 487–504.

United Nations, Department of Economic and Social Affairs. (2019). International Migration Stock. https://www.un.org/en/development/desa/population/migration/publications/migrationreport/docs/MigrationStock2019_TenKeyFindings.pdf

Watson, W. E., Kumar, K., & Michaelsen, L. K. (1993). Cultural Diversity's Impact on İnteraction Process and Performance: Comparing Homogeneous and Diverse Task Groups. Academy of Management Journal, 36(3), 590–602.

Welzel, C., Inglehart, R., & Kligemann, H. D. (2003). The Theory of Human Development: A Cross-Cultural Analysis. European Journal of Political Research, 42(3), 341–379.

Wilkista Lore Obiero & Mehmet Şengür

Inflation and Economic Growth in Kenya

1 Introduction

Many economists believe that escalating prices lead to slower growth and that when prices are excessively high, the economy suffers losses (Judson and Orphanides, 1999). This is however not in line with the Mundell-Tobin Effect which states that when there is a high inflation level in the economy, people will hold less cash and invest more which will lead to lower loans rate and thus economic growth. However, conclusive evidence to prove these beliefs have not been put forward and thus the need for this study which will determine whether a link exists and the nature of the association specifically for the Kenyan economy. Kenya is one of the countries in Sub Saharan Africa experiencing averagely low inflation rates. However, these values keep changing, for instance, average inflation in 2011 was 14.02 % compared to 4.31 % in the year 2010. One of the main economic development goals of the country is to have a high level of economic growth which can only be achieved when the inflation levels are kept low because high inflation distorts the price system and render the market system to function below optimal levels.

Inflation fluctuations in Kenya can be partly attributed to changes in oil prices in the world since all petroleum products used in the country are imported. Other sources could be attributed to the weather conditions since the country's agricultural sector is rain-fed. It is important to know the impact of inflation on growth as this will help in economic policy formulation necessary to achieve the goal of economic growth.

The paper seeks to determine whether a link exists between escalated price levels and growth and to analyze the trends in inflation and GDP growth in Kenya. The estimation strategy used in this analysis is the ARDL Model. As a dynamic model, this strategy allows me the leeway to analyze not just the present effect of inflation fluctuations on growth but the relationship between the lag values of inflation and growth as well. The study uses annual time series data obtained from the Kenya National Bureau of Statistics for the period 1984–2017. The study's various sections are listed below; the first section is the introduction which gives a brief background about inflation dynamics in Kenya. The second section examines into details the concept of inflation focusing on the various types of inflation in the context of Kenya. The third section is dedicated to economic growth with much emphasis on the Kenyan growth dynamics over the years. Section four is dedicated to establishing a theoretical nexus between growth and inflation. By applying various methods of analysis, the empirical link between the variables is established in the fifth part followed by an analysis of the results obtained and a conclusion will be arrived at in the last section of the paper.

2 Economic Growth and Inflation in Kenya

Stability in periods of high inflation as explained by "The Fisher Effect", living costs increase and interest rates rise proportionally. The rise in the policy rates will cause a considerable increase in the cost of borrowing money from different financial institutions and therefore the economy is seen to be underperforming. Putting the inflation levels to controllable amounts and rates is, therefore, the economic goal of many policymakers. For growth to be reported in an economy, the given GDP figures for the period have to be adjusted for inflation. Policymakers, therefore, consider inflation to be detrimental to economic growth and apply either expansionary or contractionary measures depending on the level of inflation present or the rate of growth desired in the economy. To know the level of growth that is desirable for the economy, different growth models put forward by different economists can be applied. One of these includes the Solow Growth Model developed by Robert Solow in 1954 (Mishkin, 2014).

The model states that the factors that influence growth in the economy include investment levels and capital accumulation levels. However, the capital accumulations are subject to yearly depreciation and so for growth to occur, the rate of capital stock accumulation has to exceed the depreciation levels. When the levels of investment are less than the depreciation level the economy will grow but in the long run, a steady-state will be arrived at where the rate of depreciation equals the levels of investment (Sellgren et al., 1999).

Kenya is one of the developing countries in Africa. The countries main economic agenda is to achieve stable economic growth rates by the year 2025. The country has been characterized by high economic performance and medium to low inflation rates in most of the years except during some periods of either extreme droughts or external shocks like international oil prices and border wars. There are many determinants of growth like the level of capital investment and levels of imports and imports but all these have been held constant in order to find out how the economy reacts to changes in inflation (www.bloomberg.com).

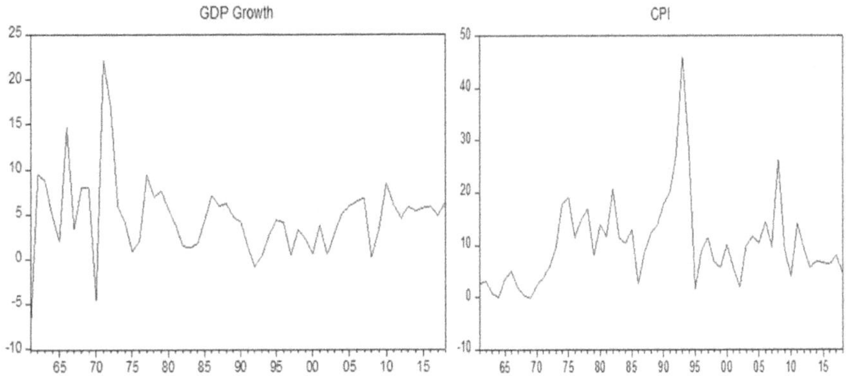

Figure 1: *GDP Growth Trends and Inflation Levels in Kenya for the Period 1961–2018*
Source: *(KNBS, Author's computation)*

From the graph above, it is clear that the growth of the Kenyan Gross domestic product (GDP) has no particular trend but is fluctuating, in 1970 for instance, the Kenyan economy was hardly hit by the world crisis as shown by the sharp reduction in the GDP growth. The 2008/2009 recession is also likely to have had an impact on the growth of the Kenyan economy which can clearly be observed in the Figure 1 above. The economy generally has been characterized by increased output and demand. Most of the income in Kenya is dependent on agriculture and so changes in weather conditions will have an influence on the GDP levels either positively or negatively. Most of the income in Kenya is dependent on agriculture and so changes in weather conditions will have an influence on the GDP levels either positively or negatively. In periods of serious droughts, there is little or no output which leads to the levels of growth reducing and inflation increasing rapidly. During the years 2013–2016 capital accumulation and advancements in technology led to an improvement in the economy as was reflected in the increasing levels of growth and GDP. The capital improvement contributed to an increase in supply which was backed up by an equal increase in demand. These periods of growth were also marked by medium inflation (OEC, 2017).

Inflation levels were particularly high in 2011 coupled with moderate growth levels. This could be an indication that growth and inflation could be positively related up to some levels normally explained by many studies as the benchmark inflation. The lowest level of inflation was experienced in the year 1995 where the levels of inflation fell to only 1.55 % while the highest level of GDP growth was experienced at 28.8 % in 1994. During periods of low inflation, the Kenyan economy, experienced accelerated growth as depicted in the graph.

3 Model, Data and Findings

The study used annual time series data from 1961 to 2018 and where only monthly data existed, it was averaged to obtain the yearly values. Consumer Price Index (CPI) data was used to measure the inflation rates in Kenya while GDP data captured the economic growth rate. Consumption data was used as a control variable since economic growth in Kenya is affected by other factors other than inflation only. The data was sourced from the National Statistics Bank of Kenya (KNBS) and World Bank (WB).

Time series analysis, in finding the nexus between the variables using economic data for the period 1961–2018 since there is only one country under consideration was used. One desirable quality of time series data that is useful in producing quality and reliable data is stationarity. A stationary data is one whose characteristics do not change with changes in time. A strongly stationary series is one whose distribution does not change with changes in time. When non-stationary data is used in the analysis, the conclusions obtained are likely to be wrong and misleading. Therefore, the first step using time series data is to check for stationarity and if stationarity exists then the data can be used for analysis. There are many approaches to use when testing for stationarity including the Dickey-Fuller test (1979), KPSS test and Phillips-Perron (Phillips and Perron, 1988) test. In this study, the ADF approach is used to test the variable's stationarity properties and to avert the possibility of producing spurious results. To establish the relationship between the variables, the functional representation is used;

$$\text{GDP} = \text{f}\,(\text{CPI, CONS}) \tag{i}$$

This is further expressed econometrically as follows;

$$\begin{aligned}\Delta GDP_t = {} & \beta_0 + \beta_1 GDP_{t-1} + \beta_2 CPI^{+}_{t-1} + \beta_3 CPI^{-}_{t-1} + \beta_2 CONS^{+}_{t-1} \\ & + \beta_3 CONS^{-}_{t-1} + \sum_{t=1}^{p} \varphi_i \Delta GDP_{t-i} + \sum_{i=1}^{q} (\varnothing^{+}_{i} \Delta CPI^{+}_{t-i} + \varnothing^{-}_{i} \Delta CPI^{-}_{t-i}) \\ & + \sum_{i=0}^{q} (\varnothing^{+}_{i} \Delta CONS^{+}_{t-i} + \varnothing^{-}_{i} \Delta CONS^{-}_{t-i}) + \varepsilon_t\end{aligned} \tag{ii}$$

Table 1: *Descriptive Statistics*

Variable	Obs.	Expec.	Deviations	Minvalue	Max value
CPI	58	10.22144	8.273576	−0.171501	45.97888
GDP	58	4.768236	4.501644	−7.774635	22.17389
CONS	58	4.864651	6.508936	−6.939824	38.30553

Source: Author's calculations.

Here; GDP is the Gross Domestic Product as a determinant of economic growth, CPI is the Consumer Price Index as a determinant of inflation, CONS is the consumption data.

β_0 is the constant term, t is the time trend, ε_t is the random error term. CPI has been used to measure inflation rate because during inflation there is a difference in the prices paid by consumers over time thus, using a fixed basket of goods measured over time inflation can be measured as follows: Inflation = $\{(P_0 - P_{t-1})/P_{t-1}\} * 100$

Where; P_0 is the current average price level and $P_{t-1}$is the average price level for the previous year. To explain the relationship between inflation and growth, GDP data and CPI data from 1984 to 2017 was used.

From Table 1 above, it can be seen that the expected yearly inflation experienced in Kenya is 10.22 %. The expected yearly growth of GDP in Kenya is 4.77 % and the rate of consumption growth rate in Kenya is averagely 4.86 %. A negative growth rate of 7.77 % was the least value experienced in the country for the period 1984–2017 while a positive growth rate of 22.17 % was the highest. The least value of CPI was observed at −0.17 with the highest of the period was at 45.98. This shows the instability position of inflation in the country.

Due to the time series nature of consumer price index, consumption and GDP data used above, the interconnection of the variables in the period under study 1961–2018 cannot be determined without carrying out the stationarity test. This is particularly important due to the fact that use of non-stationary data gives undesirably spurious results. To test for stationarity of the data, the ADF test by Dickey and Fuller (1979) is applied to help in this analysis. The null hypothesis underlining this test is the presence of unit root in the series.

H_0: Unit root exists. H_1: Unit root does not exist

The structural equation underlining the ADF test is given below:

$$\Delta Y_t = B_0 + \alpha_t + B_1 \Delta Y_{t-1} + B_2 \Delta Y_{t-2} + \ldots\ldots\ldots\ldots\ldots B_p \Delta Y_{t-p} + \varepsilon_t \quad \text{(iii)}$$

Table 2: *Results of ADF Test*

Variables	Lvl		1st Diff	
	Int	Int & Trend	Int	Int&Trend
CONS	−8.438342*	−8.387737*	−5.513847*	−5.444873*
CPI	−3.759966	−3.711754	−7.991089*	−7.987940*
GDP_GRWTH	−5.175133*	−5.371488*	−4.767559*	−4.816319*

The * indicates significance at the 5 % level.

From Table 2, the results of the ADF shows that the variables are integrated of different orders, that is I (0) and (1). A situation where there exists a mixture of variables integrated of different orders some methods of cointergration like Johansen cannot be implemented. However, Autoregressive-Distributed Lag (ARDL) and Nonlinear Autoregressive-Distributed Lag (NARDL) can allow for testing of the presence of cointergrating relationship irrespective of whether all the variables are I(0), I(1) or a mixture of both. To help in creation of this model, a test has to be carried out to determine the optimal number of lags for the model. The results from the test carried out automatically in Eviews reveal the data as ARDL (1,1,1,1, 4).

NARDL captures both non-linear and asymmetric cointergration between variables. Asymmetries both in the long run and in the short run are captured and this can help in explaining the linkages between the variables. Sometimes, linear combinations like ARDL fail to properly detect the cointergrating relationship between the variables. NARDL takes care of this shortcoming and hence allow for detection of omitted cointergrating relationships (Mohd, 2018).

H_0: Long run relationship dose not exist H_1: Long run relationship exist

The results of this test is displayed in Table 3 below;

It can be seen from the table above that the F- statistic of the bounds test is 15.03020 far higher than the upper bound at the 5 % level rendering the rejection

Table 3: *NARDL Bounds Test*

Test statistic	Value	Sig	level	1st Diff
F stat	15.03020	10 %	2.2	3.09
		5 %	2.56	3.49
		1 %	3.29	4.37

Source: Author's calculations

of the Ho of the bounds test. This means long-run relationship exists among the variables and therefore CPI and Consumption still have the potential to explain the growth rate of GDP in Kenya even in the long run.

The NARDL model analysis carried out produced the following results. Following the conclusion from the bounds test approach, the long run report of the ARDL model is reported as shown in Table 4. From the table, it can be seen that a positive shock in CPI has a negative and significant effect on the rate of economic growth in Kenya which implies that any positive shock to inflation will discourage economic growth rate in Kenya. A negative shock to CPI, on the other hand, has a positive and significant effect on the rate of economic growth. These results are in tandem with other previous researches which found that inflation discourages economic growth.

Table 4: *NARDL Long-run Results*

Variable	Coefficient	Std. Error	t-Statistic	Prob.*
GDP_GROWTH(-1)	−0.310402**	0.139300	−2.228304	0.0315
CPI_POS	−0.192799**	0.093355	−2.065229	0.0454
CPI_POS(-1)	0.214354	0.129851	1.650771	0.1066
CPI_NEG	0.20778*	0.103736	2.003036	0.0520
CPI_NEG(-1)	−0.20656**	0.071177	−2.902096	0.0060
CONS_POS	0.433210***	0.059115	7.328281	0.0000
CONS_POS(-1)	0.351373**	0.131557	2.670880	0.0109
CONS_NEG	0.444055***	0.123608	3.592441	0.0009
CONS_NEG(-1)	0.182878	0.109644	1.667923	0.1031
CONS_NEG(-2)	0.33794**	0.108512	3.114402	0.0034
CONS_NEG(-3)	0.001828	0.096246	0.018995	0.9849
CONS_NEG(-4)	−0.140478*	0.074553	−1.884273	0.0668
C	9.054849***	1.688422	5.362907	0.0000
R-squared	0.771512	Mean dependent var		4.889114
Adjusted R-squared	0.702965	S.D. dependent var		4.277120
S.E. of regression	2.331069	Akaike info criterion		4.739684
Sum squared resid	217.3552	Schwarz criterion		5.222963
Log likelihood	−112.6016	Hannan-Quinn criter.		4.925530
F-statistic	11.25531	Durbin-Watson stat		1.806042
Prob(F-statistic)	0.000000			

Source: Author's calculations. ***shows significance at 1 %;** shows significance at 5 %; *shows significance at 10 %

Table 5: *ARDL Short-run Results*

Variable	Coefficient	Std. Error	t-Statistic	Prob.
D(CPI_POS)	−0.19279**	0.070918	−2.718620	0.0096
D(CPI_NEG)	0.20778***	0.057593	3.607870	0.0008
D(CONS_POS)	0.43321***	0.050264	8.618629	0.0000
D(CONS_NEG)	0.44405***	0.070285	6.317942	0.0000
D(CONS_NEG(-1))	−0.19929**	0.082461	−2.416885	0.0203
D(CONS_NEG(-2))	0.13865**	0.060579	2.288733	0.0275
D(CONS_NEG(-3))	0.14047**	0.063929	2.197413	0.0338
CointEq(-1)*	−1.3104***	0.130098	−10.07243	0.0000

Source: Author's calculations

A positive shock in consumption has a positive and significant effect on the rate of economic growth in Kenya which implies that any positive shock to consumption will encourage the rate of economic growth rate in Kenya. A negative shock in consumption also has a positive and significant effect on the rate of economic growth. Both negative and positive shocks to consumption have significant effects on the rate of economic growth implying the great role that consumption plays in the Kenyan economy and this implies that policies targeting increased consumption should be adopted to ensure increased economic growth.

ARDL Short-run Results reported as shown in Table 5. A positive shock in CPI has a negative and significant effect on the rate of economic growth in Kenya. However, a negative shock of CPI has a positive and significant effect on the rate of economic growth in Kenya. This finding indicates that the economy immediately suffers from positive shocks to inflation while it takes time to adjust to the negative shocks to inflation.

A positive shock in consumption, CONS has a positive and significant link to the rate of economic growth in the short run while a negative shock in consumption has a positive and significant link to the short run rate of economic growth in Kenya. This implies that both positive and negative shocks to consumption have significant effects on economic growth in Kenya. The value of the Cointegration equation however indicates that the errors are being over corrected.

The results of diagnostic test is displayed in Table 6. Breusch-Pagan test carried on the data indicate the absence of heteroscadasticity, Breusch-Godfrey test also indicates the absence of autocorrelation, the normality test indicates that the data is normally distributes while the Ramsey test proves that there was no misspecification of the model.

Table 6: *Diagnostic tests*

	F value/ Jacque Berra	Prob
Heteroscedasticity	1.727995	0.1871
Autocorrelation	0.293289	0.7470
Normality	1.735364	0.419924
Ramsey Reset	0.995841	0.3228

Source: Author's own computations

4 Conclusion

The paper's focus was on determining the relationship between inflation and growth in Kenya. Before checking the nature of this relationship, variables were tested for the order of integration and were found to be integrated differently. This led to the conducting of the NARDL model of integration which allows for the testing of hidden cointergration among the variables. From the empirical results, an asymmetric cointergrating relationship is observed to exist between the variables under study. The disintegration of the impacts of explanatory variables in terms of positive and negative shocks is important since it allows for the policy makers to know which policies to undertake in the event of a shock.

From the results obtained positive shocks on inflation was found to be detrimental to growth in Kenya evidenced by reduction in economic growth at least in the study period of 1961–2018.These results are similar to results obtained by Hala and Kheir-El-Din (2011) and Hodge (2006) who found an inverse relationship between inflation and economic growth. According to Keynesian Economic theory, Government, in order to promote economic growth, will increase spending on the economy and thereby consumption will also be higher and finally output increases too.

The government increases its participation by increased spending on education, infrastructure, and health. The main disadvantage of increasing consumption in this way however is that as output increases, inflation levels also tend to increase. This has been shown from the results obtained in the study because the Kenyan government has been increasing its expenditure over the years leading to increased consumption and output in the country. This expansion however also led to increasing inflation levels in the period under study.

Since high inflation was found to be an inverse contributor of growth, the government through its policymakers should come up with ways of maintaining a low inflation percentage in the country and ensure that the economy is making steps towards better development results. Increased consumption was ascertained to be drawing the Kenyan economy closer to achieving its development goals which is in line with the economic policies and thus consumption should be encouraged by the government by lowering interest rates and thus ensure growth in the economy.

The AD-AS model shows that when there is an increase in aggregate demand, an increase in consumption will lead to an increase in output but this will also increase the inflation levels so that in the long run both inflation levels and output levels will be high (Parkin et al., 2005).

These results can be used by the policymakers to help in maintaining the inflation levels below the threshold level and thus ensure economic growth in Kenya. Monetary policies are more responsive than fiscal policies and so these can be applied. This study only sought to identify the nature of the relationship between inflation and growth. It did not find out the level of inflation that is necessary for economic growth to be experienced in Kenya but further research can be conducted to determine this level and thus adjust the policies accordingly.

References

Dickey, D. A., & Fuller, W. A. (1979). Distribution of the Estimators for Autoregressive Time Series with a Unit Root. *Journal of the American Statistical Association*, 74(366), 427.

Hala, A.-A., & Kheir-El-Din, H. (2011). Inflation and Growth in Egypt: Is There a Threshold Effect? *What Drives Prices in Egypt?*, 8120, 83–108.

Hodge, D. (2006). Inflation and Growth in South Africa. *Cambridge Journal of Economics*, 30(2), 163–180.

Judson, R., & Orphanides, A. (1999). Inflation, Volatility and Growth. *International Finance*, *2*(1), 117–138.

Mishkin, F. S. (2014). *Macroeconomics: Policy and Practice*. Pearson, *London*.

Mohd, N. (2018). The Relationship between Energy Consumption and Economic Growth : Evidence from Thailand Based on NARDL and Causality Approaches. *Munich Personal RePEc Archive*, 86384,1–23.

OEC – Kenya (KEN) Exports, Imports, and Trade Partners. (2017). Retrieved September 29, 2019, from https://oec.world/en/profile/country/ken/

Parkin, M., Powell, M., & Matthews, K. (2005). *Economics 6th Edition*. Pearson, *London*.

Phillips, P. C. B., & Perron, P. (1988). Testing for a Unit Root in Time Series Regression. *Biometrika*, *75*(2), 335–346.

Sellgren, A. W., Doepke, M., & Lehnert, A. (1999). *Macroeconomics.* University of Chicago Publish, Illinois.

https://www.Knbs.or.ke/Knbs-data/, Retrieved: 20.11.2019.

https://www.Knbs.or.ke/Knbs-data/, Retrieved: 20.11.2019.

http://datatopics.worldbank.org/world-development-indicators, Retrieved: 20.11.2019.

https://www.bloomberg.com/news/articles/2019-10-31/kenya-s-annual-inflation-rate-accelerates-to-5-in-october, Retrieved: 20.11.2019.

Selahattin Bozkurt

Government Rationale on the Road to Wealth Tax Issued during World War II

1 Introduction

Although not actually entering the Second World War, Turkey felt especially its economic effects too much. The war, which deeply affected all the nations of the world, brought economic problems to the Turkish society as well. While the social welfare level of the society decreased, a new wealthy class emerged as a result of unfair gain in war conditions. Black-marketeering, hoarding and profiteering created a separate group. While the capital was gathered in the hands of this group, the increasing money in circulation made the government anxious.

The single-party government of the period wanted to fix Turkey's deteriorating financial structure and draw the increasing money in circulation from the market. At the same time, it decided that it would be appropriate to impose extraordinary taxes in order to punish the people it thought were making unfair profits. The government thus wanted both to cover the increasing costs due to the war and to control the market. For this purpose, in November 1942, a tax law called "Wealth Tax" was introduced.

Wealth Tax remained in force for sixteen months. It was agreed that the tax would be collected only once, within the framework of the procedures and principles determined by law. To what extent the law would be applied to whom and how long it would be collected were clearly stated. Although the law was clear, it was later seen that a number of problems arouse in practice. Therefore, the tax in question has been heavily criticized for its application method rather than its technique. The rumors of injustice and corruption in its implementation, especially criticisms about minorities, made arguments inevitable.

Rather than the arguments, the objective of this study is to analyze for which reasons the government enacted this tax law. Why was there a need for such a law? The issue will be examined on the basis of the government rationale upon the minutes of the parliament itself. Thus, through emphasis on Turkey's economic situation before and during the war, the introduction of the tax law will be discussed.

2 Turkish Economy Before the Second World War

The Republic of Turkey, although appearing a new state in 1923 in general terms, is in fact continuation of the Ottoman Empire. This is the case in economic terms, as in many other fields. Therefore, a good economic heritage was not left to the new republic from the Ottoman Empire. From the establishment phase on, liberalism was adopted in the economy in line with the decisions of the Izmir Economic Congress in 1923. However, the lack of sufficient capital in the country and the bourgeois class to invest in hindered the expected economic development. Although some efforts were made to support the private enterprise (e.g. the establishment of İşbank, enactment of the Industrial Incentive Law, Cabotage Law), they weren't successful.

Upon the failure of the liberal system, a new era began in the early 1930s in which the state played a more active role in the economy. This can be called the statist or mixed economy model, but the state is more effective here. Therefore, the understanding of "national economics", which was tried to be implemented until the 1930s, was replaced by statism to realize the industrialization movement.[1]

Emre Kongar expresses this situation as follows:

> *"As a principle within the Kemalist ideology, statism was not an economy controlled by the state, but to the extent possible, a national economy independent of foreign control. Statism was a principle that complemented the social and political economic aspect of the transition from the Ottoman social structure to modern state characteristics. It was meant to be a tool to create the West's rapid development period of the 18th and 19th centuries artificially in Turkey".*[2]
>
> Çetin Yetkin says "*The revolutionary CHP prevented the poor classes from protecting their interests with the principle of "populism" and with the principle of "statism", enriched some people by the state at the expense of the people's poverty and sweat, and as the "national chief" institution clearly showed, saw the public as a flock to be herded*".[3]

While Kongar says that this is a national industrialization movement in which foreigners are not active, Yetkin argues that it is a project to create a new rich class by exploiting the poor by the state. However, it is seen in both views that a domestic industrialization and bourgeois class is tried to be created. This

1 Alpaslan Işıklı, Türkiye'de Sendikacılık Hareketleri İçinde Demokrasi Kavramının Gelişimi, Kültür Bakanlığı Yayınları, Ankara, 1994, p.124.

2 Emre Kongar, İmparatorluktan Günümüze Türkiye'nin Toplumsal Yapısı, Remzi Kitapevi, İstanbul, 1981, p. 127.

3 Çetin Yetkin, Türk Halk Hareketleri ve Devrimler, Milliyet Yayınları, May 1980, p.487.

situation is not unique to Turkey. Many states, especially Germany and the USA, went this way before World War II.

In the early years of the Republic, the economic situation emerging as appropriate for Turkey's social structure was agricultural production. While exports were agricultural products in foreign trade, imports were mainly industrial products like machinery and equipment as well as such products as textiles, ready-made clothing and sugar.

With statist policies, Turkey switched to the planned development model. With the law enacted on April 17th 1934, the First Five-Year Industrial Plan was put into effect. In this way, investments were made in the fields of textile, mining, soil industry and chemistry. On the other hand, efforts were made to develop the transportation network by working on the construction of railways, roads and aviation. Although the Second Five-Year Development Plan was prepared before World War II, it could not be implemented due to the war.

In this period, railways, ports and municipal services were taken from foreigners and nationalized. In addition to nationalization in the service sector, there were also businesses taken from foreigners in the industry like Bomonti Brewery and American Match Company. In the mining field, Ergani Copper Enterprise was taken from the Germans and Zonguldak Coal Enterprise was taken from the French. With the establishment of Etibank, mining management was tried to be taken under state control.[4]

3 Turkish Economy during the Second World War

While the economic policies introduced in the 1930s provided some relief, though relatively, in the country, increasing political tensions and armament in the world also started to affect Turkey significantly. Due to the possibility of entering the war at any moment, the government left investments and put military activities in the foreground. While this situation caused a contraction in production, it also created a heavy burden on the budget with the import of arms.

Although Turkey did not enter World War II, it had to implement a "war economy" between 1940 and 1945. The most important reason for this was the declaration of mobilization as if going to war at any moment. Thus, it had to recruit the productive youth of the population. Arming this sector, which was especially important in agricultural production, disrupted agriculture, the most

4 Yahya S. Tezel, Cumhuriyet Döneminin İktisadi Tarihi, Yurt Yayınları, Ankara, 1986, p. 177.

important production area for the country. At the same time, the subsistence problem of those who were under armament put a heavy burden on the budget.

While the share allocated from budget to defense increased, production fell rapidly in all areas. Many areas were restricted and money was transferred to defense. The fact that the adult population was recruited, that the oxen, which were important for the peasant, were seized on behalf of the army and that farmers were forced to sell their product to the state below the market value all revealed the depression of the war conditions.[5]

This reduced production. While total demand increased rapidly, supply remained insufficient. Price increases were out of control. Rapidly uncontrolled increase in prices led to the emerging of war profiteers and their creation of a new black market by making black market and hoarding.[6]

Throughout the War, Turkey experienced significant difficulties in foreign trade. Loans received from foreign banks and firms between 1930 and 1939, the installments of debts from the Ottoman Empire in the same period and debts arising from nationalization transactions became an important burden on the budget. Likewise, increasing arms imports seem to have been an important expense in the budget too.[7]

Dependency on Germany in foreign trade was another problem. Especially the Nazi's economic pressure on the Balkans and their imperialist ambitions in the region if they were to win the war forced Turkey to strengthen its relations with the UK and France. Therefore, "Mutual Aid Agreement" was signed with England and France in October 1939.[8]

Moreover, during the Second World War years, Turkey was faced with difficulties in directing its foreign trade to countries other than Germany because of the high price of the products it exported, the trade of Britain with its own countries, and the geographical distance of the USA and hence Turkey's dependence on Germany continued until the end of the war. After the war, Germany was replaced by other western countries, especially the USA and the UK.[9]

The difficulties caused by the war led the government to new searches. This situation caused the governments to intervene in economic life more. The "National Protection Law" adopted on January 18th, 1940 was the basis of the economic

5 Korkut Boratav, Türkiye İktisat Tarihi, Savaş Yayınları, Ankara, 1982, p. 223.
6 H. Cahit Yalçın, (17.11.1942), "Varlık Vergisi", Yeni Sabah Gazetesi.
7 Tezel, a.g.e., p. 189.
8 Tezel, a.g.e., p. 189–192, Tevfik Çavdar, Türkiye'nin Demokrasi Tarihi, İmge Kitapevi, Ankara, 1999, p. 359–367.
9 Tezel, a.g.e., pp. 184–189.

and fiscal rules to be applied in this period. The Deputies, who spoke during the negotiations of the law in the parliament, expressed a positive opinion. Speaking on behalf of the Temporary Committee, Bingöl Deputy Feridun Fikri Bey said;

> "*. . . in the negotiation of this law, our committee, especially against the great economic crisis that burns the world, regards enforcing the necessary powers to protect both the people and the National Defense within the legal framework as the first aim of the government . . . citizen's law is fully guaranteed . . . illegitimate profits during the war isn't allowed and the country's extraordinary conditions won't be exploited . . . .*"[10]. He argued that the aim of this law was to protect the interests of the people and the state under war conditions in full constitutionality.

Istanbul Deputy Ali Rana Tarhan, on the other hand, supported the law by saying that it is correct to mobilize all the facilities of the nation and the state for the benefit of the state and the nation in such extraordinary situations.[11] Expressing that the law was for the benefit of the state and the nation, Berç Türker, Afyon Deputy, pointed out that certain issues were paid special attention while introducing this law. He said that these issues were in line with the spirit of the Constitution, that the measures mentioned in the law arose in extraordinary conditions, and that the law should disappear with the disappearance of these conditions. He added that the obligations on the citizens were reasonable and prudent, that the 25 million lira loan given to the government should be used when needed, and that all provisions in the law should be used when needed. In the continuation of his speech, Türker stated that with the measures taken by the government against profiteering (to stock up goods to raise the market), the most severe punishment should be given to the profiteers. He asked the government to pay special attention to the part of the law that concerned the villagers, to keep officers fair and just, and to take the necessary precautions not to put villagers under pressure.[12]

Prime Minister Refik Saydam stated that this law was enacted and put into practice immediately due to the economic problems brought by the war. While applying the law, attention would be paid not to affect the normal life of the citizens as much as possible. The normal commercial life of the business citizens would not be interfered. He explained that the private businesses would be discussed with the business owners and decided accordingly.[13]

---

10 TBMMZC, 6. Dönem, C 8, 18.01.1940, p. 139.
11 TBMMZC, 6. Dönem, C 8, 18.01.1940, p. 139.
12 TBMMZC, 6. Dönem, C 8, 18.01.1940, p. 139.
13 TBMMZC, 6. Dönem, C 8, 18.01.1940, pp. 140–141.

With the National Protection Law, it was aimed to get rid of the damage caused by the war to the country, to reduce the difficulties suffered by the citizen in the supply of basic consumer goods and to prevent price increases. In addition, measures aimed at increasing tax revenues needed by the state were aimed. For this purpose, a wide tax increase was made by law, and pricing of basic consumer goods was tried to be taken under state control.[14]

In 1941, when World War II was still in progress, the measures taken to prevent the crisis in the political and economic fields in Turkey weren't working well. Problems such as inflation, excessive price increase and inability to access basic consumer goods all affecting the daily life of the people started to destroy the economic life and social structure. This situation increased black market as well as causing hoarding, speculative movements, new wealthy groups in the society, and big gains. The worse income distribution in the country deteriorated further.

A solution was needed for the punishment of the wealthy who earned unfair profits in war conditions, who became wealthy by doing black market and profiteering, to provide social justice in social life and to increase the tax needed by the state. Thus, the economic burden brought by the war conditions would be distributed to the society in a balanced way and the increasing expenditures of the state, budget deficit and inflation would be taken under control. The market would be regulated and those who earned unfair profits would be punished, while those who stocked goods would launch their product and thus, excessively rising market would be balanced.

4 Wealth Tax and Government Rationale

With deteriorating financial condition during the Second World War, Turkey decided to withdraw the money in the market through an extraordinary tax. Before the tax was issued, public opinion was tried to be prepared with the articles published in the press. At the same time, the public reaction against the profiteers was tried to be prevented with these articles.

In an article dated 14.01.1942, Tan Newspaper published a report titled "A tax will be collected from the institutions whose earnings are increasing"[15]. Zekeriya Sertel said in his article "Where Should the State Search for New Income Sources" in the same newspaper "... *The principle to follow when searching for new sources*

---

14 Bülent Duru, "1941; Kıtlık Yılında Milli Korunma Kanunu Uygulamaları", Açıklamalı Yönetim Zaman Dizini 1940–1949, Ankara, 2008, p. 175.

15 Tan Gazetesi, 14.01.1942.

of income should be . . . avoiding the ways that will strand the low-income people and the civil servant class with already lower level of life and catching the excess wealth caused by the abnormal situation."[16] In his article dated 17.05.1942, Sertel said "*Today, egregious wealth accumulation should be prevented.*"[17] He wanted the state to prevent the emergence of the wealthy of the war. Ahmet Emin Yalman, on the other hand, dealt with similar issues in his article "Taxes on War Gains".[18]

The articles in the newspapers published in 1942 in favor of collecting new taxes are seen to have increased. In addition, through such articles, especially non-Muslim merchants were targeted; for example in the news of Tasvir-i Efkar newspaper dated 01.09.1942, "A Jewish contractor put the treasure in a loss of thousands of liras", and in the news dated 09.09.1942, "Jews were caught with the Hoarder"[19].

While preparing the public with the publications, the letter sent from the Ministry of Finance in September 1942 was remarkable. It was stated that excessive earnings obtained through profiteering (hoarding) couldn't be taxed by existing laws due to war conditions. For this reason, it was stated that minorities made great fortunes. Therefore, the Istanbul Provincial Treasurer Faik Ökte was urgently ordered to investigate who had made excessive profits in the market. He identified those who earned this kind of unfair gains and listed them according to their religious and ethnic origin.[20]

Thus, while completing the studies on the tax to be issued, President İsmet İnönü mentioned in the speech at the opening of the new year of the Turkish Grand National Assembly on November 1st, 1942 about the economic problems of the country and their reasons and stated that the measures to be taken would be explained by Prime Minister Saraçoğlu.

İnönü said that the peasant was protected by raising the price of agricultural products in a reasonable manner. In his speech, saying "*. . . an unconscious trading atmosphere, a scourge of expensiveness overpowering legitimate reasons keeps our homeland in pain today,*" he pointed out that the Government would

---

16 Tan Gazetesi, 15.05.1942, Necati Aksanyar vd., "II. Dünya Savaşında Çıkarılan Varlık Vergisinin Türk Basınında ve Kamu Oyunda Yansımaları (11 Kasım 1942–15 Mart 1944), Dumlupınar Üniversitesi Sosyal Bilimler Dergisi, Ağustos 2008, p. 385, Rıdvan Akar, Aşkale Yolcuları, Varlık Vergisi ve Çalışma Kampları, Belge Yayınları, İstanbul, 1999, p. 55.

17 Zekeriya Sertel, Tan Gazetesi, 17.05.1942.

18 Vatan Gazetesi, 29.05.1942.

19 Faik Ökte, Varlık Vergisi Faciası, Nebioğlu Yayınları, İstanbul, 1951, p. 48.

20 TBMMZC, 6. Dönem, C 28, 11.01.1942, p. 4.

find a solution. "*The most dangerous disease we have seen is the poisonous air in our society that has been blown for two years in order not to succeed the Republican Governments... A few politicians who think all these troubles are great opportunities for policy ambitions and which foreign nation they work for isn't known, the old-time knocker aghas who regard this fuzzy atmosphere an irretrievable opportunity and the insatiable profiteering traders who attempt to make the air we breathe commercial commodity, if they can, are trying to wreck the whole life of a big nation in arrogance. There is of course a way to remedy the obvious harm of these people, who do not exceed three, five hundred, against the homeland.*"[21]

İnönü, with his speech, pointed out that the high cost of living in the country was threatening even the Republic. He also said that the reason for this was the opposition politicians who were cooperating with foreigners. He also heavily blamed large landowners and traders and signaled that they would be punished. This penalty would be the Wealth Tax Law to be issued.

Wealth Tax Draft Law that explained that this one-time tax would be levied on the assets and extraordinary earnings of income and asset holders was submitted to the Grand National Assembly by the Prime Minister Saraçoğlu on 11.09.1942. It is seen that those subject to this tax were divided into four groups:[22]

1 Earning taxpayers and some taxpayers who are exempt from this tax but subject to depression tax,
2 Farmers with profit,
3 Those with buildings and lands above a certain gross earning and value,
4 Those who remained outside of these groups but left their jobs on the date when the law came into effect even though they were engaged in trade and art since 1939.

With the explanation "*Within the scope of this classification, the tax targets earning and income owners, especially those who do not pay (proportionally) taxation with their earnings, despite their high earnings by exploiting the difficulties arising from the tightness of the economic conditions, and aims to see them participate in the sacrifice required by the current dire conditions.*", from whom and for what purpose the tax would be charged was explicitly stated. At the same time, taxpayers should see this as a sacrifice for the interests of the country.

---

21 TBMMZC, 6. Dönem, C 28, 11.01.1942, p. 4.

22 Varlık Vergisi Kanunu Lâhiyası ve Muvakkat Encümen Mazbatası (1/877), Başbakanlık Arşivi, T.C. Başvekâlet Kararlar Dairesi Müdürlüğü, Sayı 6/4067, TCMM2C, 6. Dönem, C. 28, p. 43.

In the draft, "... *those who have mediated commercial affairs and received commission or money regardless of whatever name even for once since 1939 even though they are not traders, brokers, middlemen or agents, are deemed to be suitable for the purpose of the taxation ... It is an appropriate measure to exempt those who receive the allowance, salaries and wages from the public, private or municipal budgets and the institutions subject to the law numbered 3659, and those who are employed per diem upon a position from the Wealth Tax compared to their income rates*".

In the draft, all kinds of income were taxed, while civil servants who received a salary were excluded. In addition, it is understood that the employees in the economic institutions whose capital was fully owned by the state and municipal employees were excluded from the tax. The draft was adopted as 17 articles by unanimous vote of 350 deputies who attended the General Assembly with minor amendments on 11th November 1942.[23] Speaking during the discussion of the draft law in the General Assembly, Prime Minister Saraçoğlu made detailed explanations to the members of the council and explained their rationale:

> "... *every citizen who leaves his bed every morning faces new price increases by talking to his friend or reading his newspaper and asks himself:*
> *-Where are we going?*
> *Another part of the public, seeing that the Government does nothing and stands by, asks:*
> *-Where is the Government?*
> *We are neither Adam Smith's student nor Karl Marx's apprentice. We are the children of a political group whose only social religion is Populism and economic sect is Statism.*"[24]

While the Prime Minister expressed the desperation of the citizens in the face of the uncontrollable price increase in the country, he pointed out that the public held the government responsible for this situation. He stated that the philosophy of his party, which formed the government, was populism and statism. He answers the question "Where's the government?" as follows:

> "... *The explanation I will make now and decisions you are making will show that the government is always at work ... Today, our country is fully surrounded by combat states. If we overlook this truth in our works and decisions, we will make great mistakes in the provisions and precautions we will take ... As the war strings out, it is necessary to see that our hardship and troubles will increase, to be prepared and take precautions accordingly. The deprivations our country is obliged to bear today are almost negligible compared to those of other nations*".[25]

---

23 TBMMZC, 6. Dönem, C. 2, 11.11.1942, p. 25–36.
24 TBMMZC, 6. Dönem, C. 1, 11.11.1942, p. 14.
25 TBMMZC, 6. Dönem, C. 1, 11.11.1942, p. 15.

In his speech, the Prime Minister stated that the government is at work and that the decisions to be taken due to the war should be like going to war at any time. He also added that the country had experienced these problems more comfortably from the beginning of the war compared to other countries. However, he emphasized that more measures should be taken as the prolonged war would increase the troubles. Besides, while saying that the biggest pressure was on the budget in this process, he said the reason for this was "*... in order to protect and save our peace, we were obliged to immediately take and maintain a huge Turkish army into its arms.*"[26]

The first years of the war were comfortable, but later troubles began due to the rapid rise in prices, harder imports and the feeding of a large army taken into arms. Production decreased. He mentioned that the previous Refik Saydam government had taken some precautions for such reasons. However, he stated that due to the inadequacy of these decisions, tougher and tighter decisions would be put into practice: "*...The new decisions made stricter and tougher decisions necessary and after a series of new decisions, the many goods were seized within the country. These decisions did not give the desired result. In a short time, it became impossible to find some goods at official prices and a huge black market settled in the country.*".

The Prime Minister said that the most important issue the government emphasized when making any decision was paying particular attention to whether the decision was fair and feasible. He pointed out that the tax burden would be distributed to every sector in a balanced way. Otherwise, he pointed out that if a balanced tax regulation was not made in this way, it would cause very important social problems in the country.

In his speech, Saraçoğlu brought his words directly to the Wealth Tax and explained the situation as follows "*... in today's insane increase in the prices of goods ... there are large shares of production scarcity, lack of import, wrong measures, especially insatiable ambition and profiteering. But there is another fact as much as the effect of all this; the continuous increase in Turkish currency in circulation....*"[27] and explained the measures to be taken against them. He stated that, while dealing with other problems, the increased money in circulation should be withdrawn from the market by introducing new taxes. This tax should be upon those who gained a lot of money especially exploiting the war years.

---

26 TBMMZC, 6. Dönem, C. 1, 11.11.1942, p. 15.
27 TBMMZC, 6. Dönem, C. 2, 11.11.1942, p. 21.

"As merchants earn the most money during the war years, they will surely bear the biggest burden of this wealth tax... we do not hesitate to ask for a part of the money they earn appreciated by the commission as the tax given by and the work done by the members of this class is obvious.

Our second base for this tax is inns, Turkish baths, and apartments. Their owners are liable for this tax.

The third tax base is big farmers... These are taxpayers and this taxpaying will never exceed five percent of a farmer's assets".[28]

While Prime Minister Saraçoğlu stated from which sectors the tax would be collected, he also explained how to determine and collect the tax. The said tax would be determined by the commissions to be created. However, in order not to cause any abuse, it was desired to be determined and collected quickly. Thus, it was aimed to meet the needs of the country by collecting the money in circulation as soon as possible,, to increase the value of the Turkish currency and to eliminate the reaction in the society.

Deputies who spoke about the draft law also supported this bill by finding it positive. İstanbul Deputy Ali Rana Tarhan said:

> *"Regarding the mentioned Wealth Tax, we find this proposal of the government appropriate in financial, economic and social aspects. We expect other bills (law drafts) that will reach the same goal and benefit continuously.*
> *We also deem it admirable that they do not hesitate to take responsibility for the law application by requesting wide powers for the enforcement of the Law; we rely on their good practice and we wish them success".*[29]

In these words, Tarhan expressed their support to the government's legislative proposal. He also said that they relied on the government to implement the law correctly and would support new laws to be enacted accordingly.

Manisa deputy, Refik İnce, also made a speech supporting the enactment of the law.

> *"... I think that we can deal with the crisis we are in and prevent profiteering with the laws that are offered to us and we can destroy every profiteer with the conscience of a common mentality like treating a microbe that harms the nation... I deem the government thankworthy for bringing a law like this."*[30]

In his speech, İnce thanked the government for making such a law. He also responded to criticism that this tax law might be against the law by saying this

---

28 TBMMZC, 6. Dönem, C. 1, 11.11.1942, p. 22.
29 TBMMZC, 6. Dönem, C. 1, 11.11.1942, p. 22.
30 TBMMZC, 6. Dönem, C. 1, 11.11.1942, p. 23.

law should not be evaluated too much legally because it was issued for extraordinary reasons, and what matters was the interests of the state and the nation.

In his speech, Bursa Deputy Muhittin Baha Pars also thanked the government for the law. *"I would like to thank Saraçoğlu for keeping the promise he gave us and thinking like a nation as a child of the nation. Many of the decisions and proposals made today were wandering in the mind and heart of this nation. By doing this, he thought what the nation wanted and did what the nation loved"*.[31]

Antalya Deputy Rasih Kaplan, while expressing a positive opinion about the bill, definitely recommended to act fairly and honestly in practice.

> "... *The Turkish nation will never sacrifice either its homeland or its independence for the sake of somebody's gain or entertainment. But there is only one thing I want from the government. It is a fair application of the law. If there are those who abuse the implementation of the law, I demand they be punished in the most severe way.*"[32]

Istanbul Deputy General Kazım Karabekir supported the law offer, but requested that its name be changed. Because this tax would be collected from those who gained excessive profits, not from those who had wealth, he proposed that its name be changed to "Excess Profit Tax". However, this offer was not accepted.[33]

Bitlis Deputy Süreyya Özgeevren stated that the bill was correct and that this should be a warning to malicious people.

> "... *This law is a warning to those who are bad and bigoted, who want to exploit the air that people breathe as a better earning way that they will not be able to eat the excessive wealth which is not the work of their own intelligence and capital but they have acquired with the insidious mentality and precautions they have taken against this nation and the homeland.*"[34]

Parliamentarians who spoke during the meetings held in the parliament also emphasized the necessity of the Wealth Tax Law. They supported the law and even said it was a bit late. The common point of the views was that it would be correct to punish those who attempted to earn excessive profits by hoarding goods due to war conditions and black-marketing.

---

31 TBMMZC, 6. Dönem, C. 1–2, 11.11.1942, p. 24–25.
32 TBMMZC, 6. Dönem, C. 2, 11.11.1942, p. 27.
33 TBMMZC, 6. Dönem, C. 2, 11.11.1942, p. 27.
34 TBMMZC, 6. Dönem, C. 2, 11.11.1942, p. 29.

5 Conclusion

The government wanted to collect the increased money in the market by tax, thereby balancing the deteriorated economic situation. It was aimed to meet the increasing expenditures and to transfer the money accumulated in the hands of those who earned illegal and excessive income to the budget. The pressure of the public reaction caused by price increases was tried to be overcome. The Act was essentially enacted to charge more taxes from the rich and less taxes from the poor. Under such war conditions, it was the most correct act. However, problems in practice are still being discussed even today. So much so that the problem is not in law but in practice.

References

Akar R., Aşkale Yolcuları, Varlık Vergisi ve Çalışma Kampları, Belge Yayınları, İstanbul, 1999.

Aksanyar N.- Biçer M., "II. Dünya Savaşında Çıkarılan Varlık Vergisinin Türk Basınında ve Kamu Oyunda Yansımaları (11 Kasım 1942–15 Mart 1944)", Dumlupınar Üniversitesi Sosyal Bilimler Dergisi, Ağustos 2008.

Boratav K., Türkiye İktisat Tarihi, Savaş Yayınları, Ankara, 1982.

Çavdar T., Türkiye'nin Demokrasi Tarihi, İmge Kitapevi, Ankara, 1999.

Duru B., "1941; Kıtlık Yılında Milli Korunma Kanunu Uygulamaları", Açıklamalı Yönetim Zaman Dizini 1940–1949, Ankara, 2008.

Işıklı A., Türkiye'de Sendikacılık Hareketleri İçinde Demokrasi Kavramının Gelişimi, Kültür Bakanlığı Yayınları, Ankara, 1994.

Kongar E., İmparatorluktan Günümüze Türkiye'nin Toplumsal Yapısı, Remzi Kitapevi, İstanbul, 1981.

Ökte F., Varlık Vergisi Faciası, Nebioğlu Yayınları, İstanbul, 1951.

Sertel Z., Tan Gazetesi, 17.05.1942.

Tan Gazetesi, 14.01.1942.

Tan Gazetesi, 15.05.1942.

TBMMZC, 6. Dönem, C. 1.

TBMMZC, 6. Dönem, C. 2.

TBMMZC, 6. Dönem, C 8

TBMMZC, 6. Dönem, C.28

Tezel Y.S., Cumhuriyet Döneminin İktisadi Tarihi, Yurt Yayınları, Ankara, 1986.

Varlık Vergisi Kanunu Lâhiyası ve Muvakkat Encümen Mazbatası (1/877), Başbakanlık Arşivi, T.C. Başvekâlet Kararlar Dairesi Müdürlüğü, Sayı 6/4067.

Vatan Gazetesi, 29.05.1942.

Yalçın H.C., (17.11.1942), "Varlık Vergisi", Yeni Sabah Gazetesi.

Yetkin Ç., Türk Halk Hareketleri ve Devrimler, Milliyet Yayınları, May 1980.

Serkan Göksu & Özer Özçelik

Panel Data Analysis on the Determinants of Poverty: A Case of OECD Countries[1]

1 Introduction

It can be said that the way that developed countries follow in ensuring their development is not very different, and that there are many different reasons for the underdevelopment of underdeveloped countries although some of those reasons are common. These differences bring along the lack of a common prescription for the development strategies of the countries. It is natural that there is no uniformity in terms of the distribution of production factors in the world. This unbalanced distribution in factor distribution can make both the form and the dimensions of the social problems of the countries different from each other.

When looking at the world atlas as a reflection of this situation, it is observed that the welfare levels of some countries are quite high while some countries are in poverty. Some countries between such two extreme poles have a moderate level of life standard and welfare (Aktan, 2002:1). If the science of economics describes its most important goal as an increase in welfare level and claims that this increase in welfare does not just mean an income growth, and if the presence of rights that people should have because they are human have been accepted since 1215, it is clear that every step taken towards eliminating poverty in the world and inequality in income distribution will provide a great service to humanity.

When the concept of poverty is examined in the historical process, it is one of the most important issues on the agendas of both policymakers and policy practitioners. The phenomenon of poverty is one of the common problems for which all countries, whether they are developed or developing, seek solutions although its scope and content are not the same. According to the report published in January 2018 by the international aid organization Oxfam, which is headquartered in England, the wealth of the 26 richest people in the world is more than the wealth of the poorest 3.6 billion people in the world. In fact, even only this data will be enough to reveal that there is a problem in the distribution of resources, not in resource shortage in the world.

1 This study was produced from the doctoral thesis prepared by the first author.

The policies to fight against poverty should be primary development projects supported by all levels of the state. Because the higher the welfare level of the individuals in the society is, the higher the welfare level of the society will be. Failure to effectively fight against poverty is one of the biggest obstacles to becoming a developed society. Because when looking at the developed economies, the sector with high-income grows with significant contributions they make to their economies. The poor, who have limited ability to contribute to public revenues, also make a low contribution to the development of the country. Therefore, it can be concluded that countries develop to the extent that the income gap between the poor and the wealthy in society is reduced. The phenomenon of ensuring sustainability in growth, which is one of the basic macroeconomic policies that every country tries to achieve, is an issue which is highly associated with poverty, and inequality in income distribution should be resolved and the principle of sustainability in growth should be implemented in order to eliminate this problem (Kılıç and Çetinkaya, 2012: 93).

Many attempts are made both at the national and international levels in the fight against poverty and inequality problems. When it is considered in terms of the countries, reduction of poverty and increasing the welfare levels of the poor have been among the main objectives of public authorities in many countries. When it is considered on an international scale, it is observed that global organizations have taken various steps to fight against this problem. Perhaps the most important of these steps are the "Millennium Declaration" announced at the United Nations General Assembly that gathered by the meeting of 147 heads of state or governments between 6 and 8 September 2000, and then, the "Sustainable Development Goals" including the targets envisaged to be achieved between 2015 and 2030 which are the continuation of the millennium development goals. In fact, it should be immediately indicated that the reason why global organizations take an active role in fighting against poverty and hunger is not only increase the welfare of the poor countries, but they also aim to increase the welfare of the developed countries indirectly. Since countries are connected to each other through foreign trade and other economic relations in today's world, the fact that poor countries cannot get enough shares from foreign trade directly or indirectly affects the developed countries (Küçükaksoy and Şen, 2011:3).

In the study, the conceptual framework on the subject was first provided, and then, certain studies on the subject were included. In the analysis part of the study, the human development index (HDI) was used as a dependent variable since it is regularly published to represent the poverty levels of OECD countries and is frequently used as an indicator of poverty in other studies (Ünver and Koyuncu, 2016: 636). The effects of the variables of distribution of income (GINI), growth rate (GROWTH), inflation rate (INFR), unemployment rate (UNEMPL), exchange rate (ER), trade openness (OPEN), foreign direct investments (FDI) and tax burden (TAX), which are considered to be effective on the dependent variable, on the level of human development was attempted to be tested by the panel data analysis method. Within the scope of the analysis, the descriptive statistics tables and correlation matrices of the series to be used in the models to be established were first provided, then their cross-sectional dependence was examined, "unit root tests" were performed and whether these series were stationary or not was tested. Hausman test, F test and Breusch-Pagan LM tests were performed to test which of the pool, random effects and fixed effects models would be more appropriate for the models established. Basic diagnostic tests were performed to test whether the results obtained from the estimators were reliable, and as a result of these tests, since there were heteroscedasticity and autocorrelation problems in most of the models established, the "Driscoll-Kraay (1998)" estimator, which gives resistant estimators in such cases, was used.

2 Certain Studies on the Subject

In the literature, there are different conceptual frameworks regarding the relationship between income inequality and growth (Fisher and Roach Rivas, 2013: 5). The first of these is "neutral growth", which means that all social classes get an equal share of the increasing growth. This approach was developed by Solow and Dollar-Kraay. The second of this conceptual framework is "pro-poor or poor-oriented growth". The relevant studies carried out by Kakwani (2001) and Son and Kakwani (2003) revealed that economic growth is not neutral. They argued that those with production factors tended to take more advantage of the blessings of growth, and therefore, public policies should focus on increasing the income of poor individuals. Finally, according to "inclusive growth" which is an alternative concept developed by the World Bank (2009), "Growth should cover all sectors in the economy, should be spread more widely and should include the vast majority of the country's current workforce". While it is only aimed to increase the welfare of the poor people in the poor-oriented perspective, it aimed to expand the opportunities for the majority of the workforce in the poor or middle class in the inclusive growth approach. In order for growth to be inclusive, it is necessary to provide new employment opportunities and higher productivity rather than just the policies for the poor (Ianchovichina et al., 2009).

McGillivray (1991:1461–1468) analyzed the relationship of human development indicators among themselves and their relationships with economic developments using the 1990 UNDP data by spearman correlation technique.

In the study, it was determined that there was a significant and positive relationship between life expectancy of human development, literacy rates of adults and GNP per capita in all countries analyzed. However, the relationship between the literacy rates of adults and GNP per capita was low.

Bhanojirao (1991:1451–1452) analyzed the relationship between human development levels and income distributions for developing countries in 1990. In the study, it was concluded that a fair income distribution provided together with economic growth significantly and positively affected the human development, that significant developments in human development could be achieved by well planning of education and health expenditures, and that income distribution and social expenditure deficiencies constituted a significant obstacle to human development, while ensuring rapid economic growth.

Ravallion and Chen (2003: 95) emphasized that the income of the population, who are considered poor in the society, should grow faster than the income of the non-poor so that growth would be poorly oriented, and inequality and poverty could be reduced simultaneously only in such a case.

In the study in which Son and Kakwani analyzed the relationships between growth, poverty and income inequality, they indicated that economic growth would be more effective in fighting against poverty in the countries where the poor have more chances in the labor market and are relatively more integrated into the economy and where there is a fairer distribution of income (Son and Kakwani, 2003: 425–426).

François Bourguignon called the relationship between growth, poverty and inequality as "Poverty-Growth-Inequality (PGI) Triangle". Bourguignon (2004:4) explained the "PGI Triangle" as follows: "Poverty can be reduced by increasing income (growth) or with a better income distribution. A percentile decrease in poverty rate can be achieved by a certain growth rate or a certain reduction in inequality. More importantly, an increase in income does not have to conflict with a decrease in inequality. In other words, policymakers can focus on inequality and growth simultaneously in order to reduce poverty, instead of just focusing on growth". Bourguignon (2004: 4) argues that these 3 (three) variables interact with each other and that income distribution is as important as growth in the reduction of poverty.

In the study entitled "growth elasticity of poverty" carried out by Heltberg (2004: 82–90), it was determined that inequality in income distribution was quite effective on poverty. Inequality in income distribution has a significant effect on poverty growth elasticity, and the fact that the level of inequality is initially high is added to economic growth as a negative condition. Therefore, it was concluded that inequality in income distribution should be reduced or solution proposals that would prevent the increase in inequality should be preferred so that economic growth would make positive contributions to poverty reduction.

In their study, Dolar and Kraay used 40-year data set of 80 countries and concluded that the income of the population, which constitutes the poorest 20 % of the society, was increasing as much as the growth rate. In other words, it is understood that the people who were described as the poor in the countries analyzed benefited from the economic growth at the same rate.

The same authors, in their another study including 92 countries between the years 1960 and 2000, found that there was no systematic relationship between income distribution and economic growth. Furthermore, they also concluded that economic growth only apparently improved the income of the lowest income groups, therefore, economic growth alone could not be sufficient for the improvements in the quality of life of the poor (Dollar and Kraay, 2004: 56–57).

In Ravallion's study including 47 countries between the years 1980 and 1990, emphasized that the poor in developing countries took advantages of the increasing welfare if there was an increase in welfare, and they were exposed to the negative consequences of economic contraction if there was economic contraction. It was concluded that the initial conditions were the determining factor in the relationship between growth and poverty rate. In the study, it was emphasized that the most favorable situation in poverty reduction was the reduction of inequality together with economic growth (Ravallion, 2004: 77).

In the study on 16 sub-Saharan African countries carried out by Fosu in 2008, it was indicated that a fairer income distribution positively affected the economic growth, and that the increasing economic growth contributed to the formation of a fairer income distribution (Fosu, 2008: 566).

In their study in which Fassil and Mukti used the data set of 16 African countries, they indicated that economic growth had a decreasing effect on fighting against poverty, and also, poverty decreased more in the countries with high levels of economic development. They emphasized that poverty reduction would be delayed in the countries with high inequality in income distribution. In conclusion, they emphasized that growth was an important instrument in fighting against poverty (Fassil and Mukti, 2009:1791).

Inequality and poverty, on the other hand, also affect the households' indebtedness level and consumption habits. Since the poor allocate their income for consumption rather than saving, decreases in national income also affect the level of consumption. In general, economic policies attempt to eliminate the decrease in consumption through financial markets. However, such a policy may lead to unsustainable debts for low and middle income households, especially in developing countries. The fact that credits continue to grow may cause that the real economy will be negatively affected and the possibility of crisis will increase (Kumhof and Ranciere, 2010: 22).

According to Ravallion (2014: 9), the problem of inequality can be assessed in several ways for the role of growth in fighting against poverty: "The first one is to determine to what extent the changes occurring in inequality during growth affect the poverty levels of economic growth. The second one is that inequality reduces growth elasticity in reducing poverty level. Although inequality is not increased during the period of economic growth, it may mean lower growth in case of higher initial inequality level, and minor improvements in absolute poverty. When there is an increase in inequality levels, poverty may increase despite economic growth". In conclusion, economic growth can improve the average income of the poorest only when it acts with the policies that reduce income inequality.

Inequality that appears with poverty may prevent economic growth. Economic growth in the long term is the main determinant of the change in poverty. The main success of growth depends on how it has affected the income distribution. If average income increases occurring in a particular region or country are accompanied by a deterioration in income distribution, no reduction in poverty can be expected (Gasparini et al., 2014: 581).

In the study carried out by Ateş in 2005, the effect of continuous high exchange rate policies, that were implemented between the years 1983 and 2003 in Turkey, was analyzed within the scope of the "Immiserizing growth theory" of Bhagwati (1958), and the validity of this theory was tested by a "cointegration test". As a result of the analysis, it was concluded that the immiserizing growth occurred in Turkey, and it was observed that the dimensions of impoverishment were not very deep (Ateş, 2005: 143).

Tokatlıoğlu and Atan performed a cross-sectional analysis for Turkey using the data on income distribution of regions with different levels of development. According to the results obtained, they concluded that the Kuznets Curve for Turkey was not U-shaped but U-shaped (Tokatlıoğlu and Atan, 2007).

In the study carried out by Yıldız in 2009, it was concluded that there was no pro-poor growth during the period between 2003 and 2005 in Turkey, and that non-poor people benefited more from growth, which was revealed to be caused by the deterioration of income distribution despite the realization of growth. The income distribution was divided into 1 % shares and analyzed, and it was observed that the situation was worsened for the first 20 % of the income distribution (Yıldız, 2009: 100).

In the study carried out by Kabaş in 2009, it was argued that the growth that occurred in the periods during which inequality in income distribution decreased would provide more effective results in poverty reduction compared to the growth in the periods during which inequality in income distribution increased. While economic growth in which income distribution has become more fair has a direct effect on poverty reduction, economic growth has a higher effect on the reduction of poverty caused by reduced inequality in income distribution in addition to it along with the contribution of indirect positive effect. The fact that income distribution is fairer will increase the effect of economic growth in future periods on poverty reduction. In conclusion, if economic growth leads to an increase in inequality in income distribution, poverty will increase, however, if growth leads to an improvement in income distribution, there will also be a decrease in poverty (Kabaş, 2009: 306).

In their study in 2010, Kızılgöl Ayvaz and Demir performed the poverty analysis on Turkey using the data set of households' annual income and monthly consumption expenditures between the years 2002 and 2006. In the study, they determined that there was a decrease in the rates of poverty, which was calculated both according to consumption expenditure and income, as the age of the household head increased. Furthermore, they also concluded that illiterate household heads were more likely to fall into poverty compared to other educational levels (Kızılgöl Ayvaz and Demir, 2010: 28–29).

In the study carried out by Yardımcıoğlu in 2012, it was aimed to reveal the relationship between education expenditures and income distribution and economic growth. In the study, while no causality relationship was found from gini coefficient to economic growth in the short term, a one-way causality was found from growth to the gini coefficient (GDP→GİNİ). In the long term, a bi-directional causality relationship was found between growth and gini (GİNİ↔GDP). The hypothesis that "the increase in growth will make the income distribution fairer", which was one of the hypotheses of the study, was not confirmed according to short-term panel causality analysis, however, it was confirmed in the long term (Yardımcıoğlu, 2012: 274–275).

3 Econometric Method

The analyzes were performed by EViews 10, Stata 14.0, and Gauss 9.0 package programs, and in the study, panel data analysis, which combines time series and cross-sectional analysis, was applied as the econometric method. Since the data of the OECD countries in the relevant databases were incomplete, some countries could not be included in the analysis and 24 of a total of 34 OECD countries were analyzed.

3.1 Data and the Models Established

The definitions of the variables used in models and the expected values of signs are presented in Table 1.
The study will be analyzed within the scope of the models established below;

Model I : $HDI_{it}=\alpha_0 +\beta_1\ GINI_{it} + \beta_2\ GROWTH_{it} + \varepsilon_{it}$
Model II : $HDI_{it}=\alpha_0 +\beta_1\ GINI_{it} + \beta_2\ GROWTH_{it} + \beta_3\ UNEMPL_{it} + \varepsilon_{it}$
Model III :$HDI_{it}=\alpha_0 +\beta_1\ GINI_{it} + \beta_2\ INFR_{it} + \beta_3\ OPEN_{it} + \varepsilon_{it}$
Model IV : $HDI_{it}=\alpha_0 +\beta_1\ GROWTH_{it} + \beta_2\ ER_{it} + \beta_3\ TAX_{it} + \beta_4\ FDI_{it} + \varepsilon_{it}$
Model V : $HDI_{it}=\alpha_0 +\beta_1\ GINI_{it} + \beta_2\ GROWTH_{it} + \beta_3\ UNEMPL_{it} + \beta_4\ OPEN_{it} +\varepsilon_{it}$
Model VI : $HDI_{it}=\alpha_0 +\beta_1\ GINI_{it} + \beta_2\ GROWTH_{it} + \beta_3\ OPEN_{it} + \varepsilon_{it}$
Model VII : $HDI_{it}=\alpha_0 +\beta_1\ INFR_{it} + \beta_2\ TAX_{it} + \beta_3\ FDI_{it} + \varepsilon_{it}$

In these models, i=1,2,3...........24; N indicates the number of countries; t=1990,1991,,...........2015 indicates time periods (25 periods annually). N x T gives the total number of observations in the data set (600).

3.2 Descriptive Statistics in Level Values

Descriptive statistics for the level values of the dependent and independent variables used in the analysis between 1990 and 2015 are presented in Table 2.

When the descriptive statistics of the variables in Table 2 were examined, the averages of the GINI, HDI and GROWTH variables were 30.94, 0.86 and 2.42, respectively. In OECD countries, the share of foreign direct investments in GDP was 5 % on average, and the share of tax revenues was around 34 %. It appears that unemployment and inflation rates were 8 % and 2.7 % on average. When whether the series were normally distributed or not was analyzed by considering the Jargue-Bera, skew and kurtosis statistics, while HDI, ER and TAX variables were negatively skewed (oblique), other variables were positively skewed. When the kurtosis values of the series were analyzed, it was found out that the kurtosis of the series was more pointed compared to normal distribution since the kurtosis value of the variables other than TAX and ER variables was greater than 3. It can be stated that TAX and ER variables were kurtic compared to normal distribution. When Jargue-Bera (J&B) probability values were analyzed, the fact that probability values of all variables except ER were lower than critical value 0.05 indicated that all variables except ER were not normally distributed.

"If the sample is small or finite, consisting of 100 (hundred) or fewer observations, the normality assumption plays a vital role, and this assumption can be loosened if the sample is large enough (Gujarati and Porter, 2012: 99)". In this context, the variables in the models established with an average of 576

Table 1: *Dataset*

Name of Variable	Abbreviation of Variable	Description of Variable	Expected Signs
Human Development Index	**HDI**	The "human development index" consists of three sub-indices: life index, education index and income index, and provides information about the development levels of countries.	----
Income Distribution	**GINI**	It was taken as the Gini coefficient. This coefficient indicates the distribution of national income among individuals in a country.	(−)Negative
Growth Rate	**GROWTH**	It is the rate of increase in monetary value of final goods and services produced by a country in a year to the monetary value of goods and services produced in the previous year.	(+)Positive
Inflation Rate	**INFR**	It is the "consumer price index". It is the percentage change compared to the same period of the previous year.	(−)Negative
Unemployment Rate	**UNEMPL**	It is the rate of the individuals who want to find a job at a current wage level within a certain period of time in a country and cannot find a job for reasons other than themselves.	(−)Negative
Exchange Rate	**ER**	It is the rate of purchasing power parity to market exchange rate. This rate tells us how many dollars is required to buy a dollar worth of goods in the country compared to the USA.	(−)Negative
Trade Openness	**OPEN**	It shows the share of total exports and imports of a country in GDP within a year.	(+)Positive
Foreign Direct Investments	**FDI**	Foreign direct investments are net investment inflows that investors make to achieve a permanent management activity (10 % and more voting rights) for a business operating in another economy. The rate of net capital inflows to GDP was used.	(+)Positive
Tax Burden	**TAX**	It is the rate of total tax revenues to GDP.	(−)Negative

Source: 1. World Bank, World Development Indicators, databank.worldbank.org
2. OECD, OECDstat, https://stats.oecd.org/#
3. The Standardized World Income Inequality Databases Version 6.2
4. United Nations Development Program

Table 2: *Descriptive Statistics*

Variables	GINI	HDI	GROWTH	FDI	ER	INFR	OPEN	TAX	UNEMPL
Mean	30,948	0,857	2,426	5,122	1,026	2,734	80,000	34,635	7,792
Median	30,500	0,867	2,457	2,093	1,034	2,200	67,192	34,400	7,160
Maximum	51,200	0,949	25,557	252,308	1,627	45,000	410,172	49,000	27,470
Minimum	21,000	0,668	−9,132	-58,323	0,392	-4,500	19,736	17,300	1,780
Std, Dev	5,872	0,051	2,935	14,238	0,239	3,178	50,869	7,537	4,059
Skewness	1,253	−0,963	0,607	10,592	-0,077	5,949	3,188	-0,205	1,843
Kurtosis	5,210	3,895	10,898	170,392	2,675	64,755	16,090	2,181	7,979
Jarque-Bera	259,528	104,822	1484,434	661900,2	2,995	91960,8	4929,16	19,529	892,345
Probability	0,000	0,000	0,000	0,000	0,224	0,000	0,000	0,000	0,000
Total	17269,20	478,27	1353,721	2858,086	572,52	1525,80	44640,25	19326,6	4348,06
Tot. Error Square	19206,15	1,425	4796,887	112921,5	31,79	5626,88	1441332,	31644,3	9174,746
Observation	576	576	576	576	576	576	576	576	576

observations will be included in the analysis under the assumption that they are normally distributed.

3.3 Correlation Matrix between the Variables

The primary purpose of examining the correlation matrices between the variables is to determine whether there is a multicollinearity problem. Multicollinearity can be briefly expressed as a high correlation between independent variables. The second purpose of the correlation analysis is to provide information about the direction and degree of the relationship between the variables.

When Table 3 was analyzed, while there was a significant and inverse relationship between inequality in income distribution and human development level (−0.53) and between human development and growth (−0.21), there was a significant and positive relationship between inequality in income distribution and growth (0.18). On the other hand, high correlations were found between GINI-ER and GINI-TAX variables and HDI-INFR and HDI-ER. With respect to the meaning of these results as a pretest, it can be concluded that the value of the GINI index, which shows the inequality in income distribution, increases, namely, the inequality in income distribution increases, in other words, the poor cannot get enough share from the growth as the economic growth increases. The negative correlation between growth and human development index also supports this argument.

Table 3: *Pairwise Correlations*

Variable	GINI	HDI	GROWTH	FDI	ER	INFR	OPEN	TAX	UNEMPL
GINI	1.000								
HDI	-0.5315*	1.000							
GROWTH	0.1793*	-0.2092*	1.000						
FDI	-0.0719	0.1381*	0.0701	1.000					
ER	-0.6942*	0.6120*	-0.2477*	0.0683	1.000				
INFR	0.4156*	-0.6598*	0.0788	−0.0612	−0.4191*	1.000			
OPEN	-0.3192*	0.2627*	0.1044*	0.5037*	0.2257*	−0.1489*	1.000		
TAX	-0.7494*	0.4117*	-0.2668*	0.0237	0.5610*	−0.3480*	0.1647*	1.000	
UNEMPL	0.1766*	-0.1948*	-0.1688*	−0.0911*	−0.2287*	−0.0022	−0.2250*	0.0695	1.000

*: indicates that the coefficient is significant at the level of 5 %.

3.4 Cross-Sectional Dependence Test

While there is a cross-sectional dependence (CSD), to perform analysis without considering this dependence significantly affects the results to be obtained (Breusch and Pagan, 1980; Pesaran et al., 2008). "Cross-sectional dependence means that a positive or negative shock experienced in any country also affects other countries. The methods used to test the cross-sectional dependence in panel data series are Pesaran (2004) CD_{LM} test, Breusch-Pagan (1980) CD_{LM1} test and Pesaran (2004) CD_{LM2} test. CD_{LM1} test, CD_{LM2} test and CD_{LM} test are the estimators that test whether there is a cross-sectional dependence in cases of T>N, T=N and T<N, respectively (Yıldırım, Mercan and Kostakoğlu, 2013; Çınar and Özçalık, 2014). In this regard, 25 years (T) and 24 countries (N) covering the 1990–2015 period in the study provided the necessary conditions to perform the CD_{LM1} T>N test. The hypotheses established to determine whether there was dependence between cross sections in the series"

H_0: There is no cross-sectional dependence.
H_a: There is a cross-sectional dependence.

According to the results in Table 4, since all probability values of the series were less than the critical value of 0.05, H_0 hypothesis was rejected. In other words, it can be said that there was a cross-sectional dependence, which means that the shock that will occur in one or several of these countries also affects other countries. In this case, the second generation unit root tests that take into account the cross-sectional dependence should be applied in the panel data analysis. Since the USA was taken as a Benchmark country while calculating

Table 4: *Cross-Sectional Dependence Tests Pesaran (2004) CD Test*

Variable	Cross Section	Period	Sample	CD – Test Statistics	CD – Test Probability
GINI	24	25	558	5.90	0.000
HDI	24	25	558	80.49	0.000
GROWTH	24	25	558	40.17	0.000
UNEMPL	24	25	558	9.33	0.000
INFR	24	25	558	41.19	0.000
TAX	24	25	558	6.41	0.000
OPEN	24	25	558	47.11	0.000
FDI	24	25	558	17.62	0.000
ER	24	25	558	-	-

the Exchange Rate variable, the cross-sectional dependence test of this variable could not be run.

3.5 Panel Unit Root Test Results

Macroeconomic time series are frequently devoid of stationarity by their nature. The variances, covariances and averages of non-stationary time series may change over time. Therefore, a regression to be established between non-stationary series will give an unreal, spurious correlation. However, the regression to be established between series with the same degree of stationarity may not give misleading results (Küçükaksoy and Çifçi, 2014: 113). When the differences of non-stationary time series at level values are taken at an appropriate level, they can be made stationary. According to Granger and Newbold, an econometric analysis to be performed with the series that are devoid of stationarity will not be reliable. Therefore, the series to be used in the models should be made stationary before starting the regression analysis. In particular, the unit root tests of the series should be performed and stability should be ensured in order to avoid spurious regression.

Pesaran (2007) CIPS unit root test, which is the second generation unit root test, was applied since there was a cross-sectional dependence between the variables to be used in the models. In the CIPS test, the null hypothesis indicates that the series are I(1).

Since dependence was found between the units in the study, Pesaran (2007) CIPS unit root test considering this situation was applied and the results are summarized in Tables 5 and 6 According to the CIPS test results, the null

Table 5: *Pesaran CIPS Test Results*

VARIABLES	Lag	At level			
		Detrending		Trending	
		Zt-bar		p-value	
GINI	0	1.323	0.907	4.395	1.000
	1	−2.168	0.015	-0.117	0.453
HDI	0	−1.626	0.052	-0.522	0.301
	1	−2.887	0.002	-3.418	0.000
GROWTH	0	−8.534	0.000	-5.819	0.000
	1	−4.584	0.000	-2.135	0.016
INFR	0	−7.063	0.000	-3.827	0.000
	1	−5.086	0.000	-2.228	0.013
UNEMPL	0	0.337	0.632	0.105	0.542
	1	−1.198	0.115	-1.277	0.101
ER	0	−0.750	0.227	-1.885	0.030
	1	−2.455	0.007	-4.330	0.000
TAX	0	0.192	0.576	0.753	0.774
	1	1.197	0.884	1.863	0.969
FDI	0	−6.864	0.000	-4.946	0.000
	1	−1.981	0.024	0.599	0.725
OPEN	0	−0.539	0.295	2.139	0.984
	1	−1.915	0.028	0.663	0.746

Ho: CIPS test: Series I(1).

hypothesis can be rejected for INFR and GROWTH variables. Therefore, INFR and GROWTH variables were set as I(0). In the variables other than this variable, the null hypothesis could not be rejected and it was observed that the series were I(1).

When the differences of the series without stationarity are taken, their averages, variances and covariances do not change over time, so they become stationary. Thus, the series get rid of the effect of permanent shocks which lead to the presence of the unit root. If the series become stationary when their first differences are taken, these series are called first-order integrated series (Çifçi, 2016: 98). In this context, when the first differences of the human development index (HDI), (GINI) coefficient, unemployment rates (UNEMPL), exchange rates (ER), trade openness (OPEN), foreign direct investments (FDI) and tax burden (TAX) series, that were non-stationary at the level value, were taken, it

Table 6: *Pesaran CIPS Test Results in the First Differences*

VARIABLES	Lag	1st Differences			
		Detrending		Trending	
		Zt-bar		p-value	
ΔGINI	0	−4.065	0.000	-3.201	0.001
	1	−2.748	0.003	-1.759	0.039
ΔHDI	0	−11.795	0.000	-8.805	0.000
	1	−6.302	0.000	-3.349	0.000
ΔUNEMPL	0	−9.070	0.000	-6.145	0.000
	1	−4.968	0.000	-1.898	0.029
ΔER	0	−10.205	0.000	-7.835	0.000
	1	−7.458	0.000	-4.531	0.000
ΔTAX	0	−14.742	0.000	-13.160	0.000
	1	−7.513	0.000	-5.915	0.000
ΔFDI	0	−18.498	0.000	-16.802	0.000
	1	−11.275	0.000	-8.834	0.000
ΔOPEN	0	−7.520	0.000	-5.151	0.000
	1	−4.616	0.000	-1.235	0.100

Ho: CIPS test: Series I(1).

was determined that they became stationary, excluding consumer price index (INFR) and economic growth (GROWTH).

3.6 Panel Data Analysis Results

While performing the panel data analysis, F test, Hausman test and Breusch-Pagan LM test were first applied to test which of the pool, fixed effects, and random effects models would be more appropriate to use. Selection will be made among the estimators according to the results of these tests. How to make this selection is explained in Table 7.

3.7 F Test-Chow Test

It is necessary to perform F-test to decide whether the efficient estimation model would be fixed effects model (FEM) or pooled least squares model (classic model PLSM), which is also expressed as a classic model. "If the data do not differ according to the units, the classic model is suitable" (Tatoğlu, 2013: 164). This test is also called as the Chow test (Baltagi, 2005:13). The hypotheses related to this test:

Table 7: *Determination of the Model*

Fixed Effects (F test or Wald test)	Random Effects (BreuschPagan LM test)	Model needed to be selected
"If H_0 is not rejected There are no fixed effects"	"If H_0 is not rejected There are no random effects"	"Data can be pooled. Pooled LS"
"If H_0 is rejected There are fixed effects"	"If H_0 is not rejected There are no random effects"	"Fixed Effects Model"
"If H_0 is not rejected There are no fixed effects"	"If H_0 is rejected There are random effects"	"Random Effects Model"
"If H_0 is rejected There are fixed effects"	"If H_0 is rejected There are random effects"	"Fixed or Random Effects model according to Hausman test result"

Source: Özer and Kılınç, 2014: 85.

Table 8: *F Test-Chow Test Statistics Results*

Dependent Variable HDI	Model 1	Model 2	Model 3	Model 4	Model 5	Model 6	Model 7
F statistics	1.65**	1.59**	1.57**	1.61**	2.04***	2.09***	1.72**
Model Preference **(PLSM/FEM)**	**FEM**	**FEM**	**FEM**	**FEM**	**FEM**	**FEM**	**FEM**

"*significant at the level of 0.01; ** significant at the level of 0.05; * significant at the level of 0.10"**

H_0: Classic Model (PLSM)
H_a: Fixed effects model (FEM)

According to Table 8 H_0 hypothesis was rejected since F probability values were below the critical value of 0.01 in the 5th and 6th models, where the dependent variable was HDI, and were below the critical value of 0.05 in other models, it can be said that the classic model (PLSM) was not suitable, so the fixed effects model (FEM) would be preferred to the classic model (PLSM) in all models established.

3.8 Breusch-Pagan Lagrange Multiplier Test

The Breusch-Pagan Lagrange Multiplier (LM) test based on the residuals of the classic model was performed to be able to make a selection between the Random

Table 9: *Breusch-Pagan Lagrange Multiplier Test statistics Results*

Dependent Variable HDI	Model 1	Model 2	Model 3	Model 4	Model 5	Model 6	Model 7
Breush-Pagan	3.16**	2.57*	2.21*	3.11**	6.40***	67.23***	2.58**
Model Preference (PLSM/REM)	**REM**	**REM**	**REM**	**REM**	**REM**	**REM**	**REM**

"*significant at the level of 0.01; ** significant at the level of 0.05; * significant at the level of 0.10"**

Effects model (REM) and the classic model (PLSM). Accordingly, the hypotheses to be tested (Tatoğlu, 2013:173);

$\mathbf{H_0}$: Classic model (PLSM)
$\mathbf{H_a}$: Random effects model (REM)

According to the results of the Breusch-Pagan Lagrange Multiplier (LM) test in Table 9, since the probability values in all models where the dependent variable was HDI were less than the critical value of 0.05 determined in the study, H_0 hypothesis was rejected for all models and therefore it was understood that the classic model was not suitable and the random effects model (REM) would be suitable. Both F test and Breusch-Pagan test statistical values were found to be significant in all models established. Therefore, Hausman test statistics was examined to determine which of the FEM and REM estimators produced effective results in these models.

3.9 Hausman Test

The difference between the random effects model estimators and the fixed effects model estimators should be statistically analyzed. The Hausman test statistics is used to determine which of the models, random effects model or fixed effects model, will be preferred. Accordingly, the hypotheses established;

$\mathbf{H_0}$: Random effects model (REM)
$\mathbf{H_a}$: Fixed effects model (FEM)

According to Hausman test results related to the models established in Table 10, the REM estimator produced more efficient results in the 2nd, 5th and 6th models since it was insignificant, and FEM estimator produced more efficient results in other models since the test statistics were significant.

Table 10: Hausman Test Statistics Results

Dependent Variable HDI	Model 1	Model 2	Model 3	Model 4	Model 5	Model 6	Model 7
Hausman Statistics	5.75*	5.67	7.53*	15.17***	1.35	1.76	6.25*
Model Preference (FEM/REM)	FEM	**REM**	FEM	FEM	**REM**	**REM**	FEM

"*significant at the level of 0.01; ** significant at the level of 0.05; * significant at the level of 0.10"**

3.10 Basic Diagnostic Tests

Basic diagnostic tests were performed test whether the results obtained from the estimators were reliable and the results are presented in Table 11.

While the Modified Wald test revealed that there was heteroscedasticity problem in the models where the FEM estimator gave efficient results, Bhargava et al., and Baltagi-Wu autocorrelation tests (since it is less than 2) showed a high correlation between the successive values of the error terms.

Hypotheses;

H_0: Unit variance is equal to the panel average.
H_a: Unit variance is not equal to the panel average.

H_0 hypothesis was rejected for 4 (four) models according to the results of Modified Wald test in the models where dependent variable was HDI and that was estimated by the fixed effects method. In other words, it can be said that there was heteroscedasticity problem in these series.

Furthermore, whether there was an autocorrelation problem for these models estimated by the fixed effects model was tested by Bhargava et al. and Baltagi-Wu LBI Test.

Hypotheses:

H_0: There is no first-order autocorrelation.
H_a: There is a first-order autocorrelation.

in the models with the hypotheses above where the dependent variable was HDI and that was estimated by the fixed effects method, according to the Bhargava et al. and Baltagi-Wu LBI Test results, the null hypothesis stating that there is no autocorrelation, which is the basic hypothesis, was not rejected since the test statistics values for 4 models were close to 2. Therefore, it can be said that there was

Table 11: *Testing of Deviations from Basic Assumptions in the Fixed Effects Models*

Dependent Variable HDI	Tests	Model 1	Model 3	Model 4	Model 7
Heteroscedasticity Test	**Modified Wald Test**	χ^2=(24):646.7 Probability:0.00	χ^2=(24): 728.7 Probability:0.00	χ^2=(24):490.1 Probability:0.00	χ^2=(24):818.7 Probability:0.00
Autocorrelation Tests	**Bahargava, Franzini and Narendranathan's Durbin-Watson Test**	DW = 1.613	DW = 1.537	DW = 1.592	DW = 1.540
	Baltagi-Wu's Locally Best Invariant Test (BW-LBİ)	LBI = 1.703	LBI = 1.604	LBI = 1.679	LBI = 1.606

Table 12: *Testing of Deviations from Basic Assumptions in the Random Effects Models*

Dependent Variable HDI	Tests	Model 2	Model 5	Model 6
Heteroscedasticity test	**Levene, Brown and Forsythe Heteroscedasticity Test**	$W_{0=}$ 1.5431570 Pr > F = 0.051	$W_{0=}$ 1.5606315 Pr > F = 0.473	$W_{0=}$ 1. .4656422 Pr > F = 0.075
		$W_{50=}$ 1.4485528 Pr > F = 0.048	$W_{50=}$ 1.3819508 Pr > F = 0.111	$W_{50=}$ 1.2943144 Pr > F = 0.163
		$W_{10=}$ 1.5094437 Pr > F = 0.608	$W_{10=}$ 1.4424721 Pr > F = 0.084	$W_{10=}$ 1.3503953 Pr > F = 0.128
Autocorrelation Tests	**Bahargava, Franzini and Narendranathan's Durbin-Watson Test**	**DW** = 1.632	**DW** = 1.592	**DW** = 1.677
	Baltagi-Wu's Locally Best Invariant Test (BW-LBİ)	**LBI** =1.721	**LBI** =1.679	**LBI** =1.753

heteroscedasticity problem in 4 (four) models with fixed-effect HDI, and there was no autocorrelation problem.

In the models where the random effects estimator produced efficient results, heteroscedasticity was tested by Levene, Brown and Forsythe Heteroscedasticity Test, autocorrelation was tested by Bhargava et al., and Baltagi-Wu autocorrelation tests.

Hypotheses;

H_0: Constant variance
H_a: Heteroscedasticity

in the models with the hypotheses above where the dependent variable was HDI and that was estimated by the random effects method, when Levene, Brown and Forsythe Heteroscedasticity Test results were analyzed, null hypotheses were rejected for all 3 (three) models. In other words, there was heteroscedasticity problem in the models, indicating that variance varied from observation to observation. The heteroscedasticity and autocorrelation problems were present in most of the models established in the study. Therefore, Driscoll-Kraay (1998) estimator, which gives resistant estimators in such cases, was used to overcome these problems ((Arık, Akay and Zanbak, 2014:105).

3.11 Empirical Results

According to the results of F, Breush-Pagan and Hausman tests performed to test which models were valid in testing the models where the dependent variable was HDI, the random effects estimator gave more accurate results in the 2nd, 5th and 6th models while the fixed effects estimator gave more accurate results in other models.

Basic diagnostic tests were performed test whether the results obtained from the estimators were reliable and the results are presented in Tables 11 and 12. While the Modified Wald test revealed that there was heteroscedasticity problem in the models where the FEM estimator gave efficient results, the statistics of the Bhargava et al., and Baltagi-Wu autocorrelation tests indicated that there was no autocorrelation problem in the models. Therefore, the models were re-tested using resistant standard errors. According to Annex 1 including the estimates made using resistant standard errors, GROWTH and OPEN variables had a positive and significant effect on HDI. However, it is understood that this effect was at very low levels. If it is interpreted from another perspective, it can be said that poverty rates would decrease even at very low levels as economic growth rates of OECD countries increased. Furthermore, it was observed that the human development index also increased as trade openness increased.

4 Conclusion and Evaluation

When the problem of poverty is examined in the historical process, it is one of the most important issues on the agendas of both policymakers and policy practitioners. These problems are among the main common problems for which all countries, whether they are developed or developing, seek solutions although their scope and content are not the same. With respect to the basic question for which the study looked for answer, it was attempted to determine whether the growth occurring in the countries within OECD, that also include the developed and developing countries, was an immiserizing growth or pro-poor growth. Accordingly, 7 (seven) models were established with 8 (eight) different independent variables, that were considered to be effective on poverty, using the annual data of the periods 1990–2015 for 24 OECD countries, and it was attempted to determine the relationship between them by using the "panel data analysis method".

The analyzes were primarily started by testing the cross-sectional dependence of the variables in the models established. According to the results obtained from the tests, it was concluded that there was cross-sectional dependence. Therefore,

Pesaran (2007) CIPS unit root test, which is the second generation unit root test that takes into account cross-sectional dependence, was performed in testing the stationarity of series. In this context, when the first differences of the human development index (HDI), (GINI) coefficient, unemployment rates (UNEMPL), exchange rates (ER), trade openness (OPEN), foreign direct investments (FDI) and tax burden (TAX) series, that were non-stationary at the level value, were taken, it was determined that they became stationary, excluding consumer price index (INFR) and economic growth (GROWTH).

Then, "Hausman test", "F test" and "Breusch-Pagan LM tests" were performed to test which of the pool, random effects and fixed effects models would be more appropriate. Basic diagnostic tests were performed to test the reliability of the results obtained from the estimators were reliable, and as a result of these tests, since there were heteroscedasticity and autocorrelation problems in most of the models established, the "Driscoll-Kraay (1998)" estimator, which gives resistant estimators in such cases, was used.

As a result of the tests performed, there was a positive relationship between economic growth and human development index, which means that as economic growth increased, development levels of OECD countries increased, in other words, poverty decreased. Furthermore, it was observed that the human development index increased as trade openness increased. As a result of the analyzes performed, increasing the production volume and income level of the economies is not enough by itself but it is an essential factor to reduce poverty. It can be said that the basic condition for countries to get rid of both poverty and the problem of inequality of income is a radical transformation in economic and social structures. Since these problems are basically partition problems, resource transfer is required between the classes to overcome this problem. Within the existing system, it seems possible that these problems are not entirely resolved but are likely to be improved. It can be said that neo-liberal policies, which have been applied in many countries especially since the 1980s, are the main reason for the increase in poverty and inequality in the world. Fighting against the problem of poverty and inequality is closely associated with the factors such as unequal distribution of resources, lack of control over production resources, and limited participation in both political and economic decision-making processes. The improvement of income distribution is possible primarily by ensuring the redistribution of wealth held by certain segments, and secondly, by realizing a more balanced distribution of income with increasing economic growth. It is not possible to reduce poverty in national income growth without considering the inequality in income distribution. In terms of poverty, the point to be considered in economic growth is that it covers all social classes fairly from the blessings of growth.

Today's world practice has made technology race one of the most important elements of the world system and has given it continuity, and the future of the countries is determined in this race. In today's world where technology has developed rapidly, customs walls have disappeared as much as possible, which is globalized according to some people and which globalizes according to some people, while the changes in consumption patterns cause the perception of need to be led to different dimensions, on the other hand, millions of people continue to die every year due to both hunger and poverty and the diseases caused by them. The plans, programs and targets created for the solution of these problems, both on a country basis and across countries, are unlikely to be successful in cases where the participation of all stakeholders is not ensured and there is no consensus on them. However, in countries and international organizations where democracy and participation have been established by all institutions and rules, it is possible to solve all economic and social problems for the benefit of not only a class or a country, but also for large groups. An approach that takes the solution of poverty and inequality problems to forefront should include the economic programs, policies and targets for improving the situation of the poor. It is necessary to prevent a certain section from getting richer, to prioritize public interests, and to ensure that the large groups of people, who realize most of the production, get more share from income. The solution of the poverty problem is too vital to be left to the mercy of global organizations, it can be said that the human-oriented economic and social structure, which places its own people at the center and cares about public interests, will be a solution to many problems, not just poverty and inequality.

In conclusion, although the question of whether the growth in OECD countries, which constitute the starting point of the study, is poor-oriented or impoverishing was answered to be poor-oriented in terms of the direction of coefficients, it can be said that it remained at very low levels in terms of its effect. In other words, it can be concluded that this situation called "neutral growth" is available in the literature. Furthermore, it should not be forgotten that these results are valid for OECD countries, and in future studies, it can be suggested that they will be analyzed by comparing them with groups of countries with different development scales.

References

Aktan, C. C. (2002). Niçin Bazı Milletler Zengin, Bazıları Yoksul?. Yoksullukla Mücadele Stratejileri, Hak- İş Konfederasyonu Yayını, Ankara.

Arık, A., Akay, Ö. & Zanbak, A. (2014). Doğrudan Yabancı Yatırımları Belirleyen Faktörler: Yükselen Piyasalar Örneği. Anadolu Üniversitesi Sosyal Bilimler Dergisi, 14(2), 97–110.

Ateş, İ. (2005). Türkiye Dış Ticaretinde Gelişmeler ve Yoksullaştıran Büyüme (1993–2003). Adnan Menderes Üniversitesi, S.B.E., İktisat Anabilim Dalı, Aydın..

Baltagi, B. H. (2005). Econometric Analysis of Panel Data. 3rd edition. West Sussex: Wiley.

Bhanojirao, V. V. (1991). Human Development Report 1990: Review and Assessment. World Development, 19 (10), 1451–1460.

Bourguignon, F. (2004). The Poverty-Growth-Inequality Triangle. New Delhi, India: Indian Council for Research on International Economic Relations.

Breusch, T. S. & Pagan, A. R. (1980). The Lagrange Multiplier Test and Its Applications to Modelspecification Tests in Econometrics. Review of Economic Studies, 47(1), 239–53.

Çifçi, İ. (2016). Balassa-Samuelson Hipotezi: Türkiye ve Dış Ticaret Ortakları Uygulaması. Dumlupınar Üniversitesi S.B.E., İktisat Anabilim Dalı Yüksek Lisans Tezi, Kütahya.

Dollar, D. & Kraay A. (2004). Growth Is Good for the Poor. In A. Shorrocks & R. Van Der Hoeven (Eds.), Growth, Inequality and Poverty". New York: Oxford University Press.

Driscoll, J. & Kraay A. C. (1998). Consistent Covariance Matrix Estimation with Spatially Dependent Data. Review of Economics and Statistics, 80(4):549–560.

Fassil, F. & Mukti P. U. (2009). Poverty Reduction, Economic Growth and Inequality in Africa", Applied Economics Letters, 16 (18), 1791–1794.

.

Fisher, E. & Giancarlo R. R. (2013). Desempeno Macroeconomico. Desigualdad, Productividad Pobreza en America Latina y Panama. FES Panamâ-No 1, 1–17.

Fosu, A. K. (2008). Inequality and the Growth–Poverty Nexus: Specification Empirics Using African Data. Applied Economics Letters, 15(7), 563–566.

Gasparini, L., Cicowiez, M. & Sosa, W. (2014). Pobreza Desigualdad en America Latina: Conceptos. Herramientas Aplicaciones. Buenos Aires: Temas Grupo Editorial.

Gujarati, D. N. & Porter, D. C. (2012).Temel Ekonometri (Basic Econometrics). Çeviri Editörleri: Ümit Şenesen ve Gülay Günlük Şenesen. Literatür Yayıncılık. İstanbul.

Heltberg, R. (2004). The Growth Elasticity of Poverty. In A. Shorrocks & R. Van Der Hoeven (Eds.), Growth, Inequality and Poverty. New York: Oxford University Press.

Ianchovichina, E., Lundstrom, S. & Garrido, L. (2009). What Is Inclusive Growth. http://siteresources.worldbank.org/EXTPREMNET/Resources/WhatIsIG.pdf?resourceurlname=WhatIsIG.pdf

Kabaş, T. (2009). Gelişmekte Olan Ülkelerde Yoksulluğun Nedenleri Ve Yoksullukla Mücadele Yolları. Çukurova Üniversitesi S.B.E. Doktora Tezi, Adana.

Kakwani, N. (2001). Pro-poor Growth and Policies. Asian Development Bank Annual Meeting Seminars. Honolulu, 1–24.

Kılıç, R. & Çetinkaya, Ş. (2012). Türkiye'de Gelir Dağılımı Adaleti ve Yoksullukla Mücadelede Bir Model Önerisi. Dumlupınar Üniversitesi Sosyal Bilimler Dergisi, 34, 93–114.

Kızılgöl Ayvaz, Ö. & Demir, Ç. (2010). Türkiye'de Yoksulluğun Boyutuna İlişkin Ekonometrik Analizler. İşletme ve Ekonomi Araştırmaları Dergisi, 1(1), 21–32.

Kumhofve, M. & Ranciere, R. (2010). Inequality, Leverage and Crises. International Monetary Fund Working Paper 268, 3–37.

Küçükaksoy, İ. & Çifçi, İ. (2014). Dış Ticaret Hadlerinin Dış Ticaret Dengesine Etkisi: Harberger-Laursen-Metzler Hipotezinin Türkiye Uygulaması. Optimum Ekonomi ve Yönetim Bilimleri Dergisi, 1(2),103–129.

Küçükaksoy, İ. & Şen, A. (2011). Küresel Dünyanın Karanlık Yüzü: Yoksulluk ve Açlık. Detay Yayıncılık, Ankara.

McGillivray, M. (1991). The Human Development Index: Yet Another Redundant Composite Development Indicator. World Development, 19(10), 1461–1468.

Özer, M. & Kılınç, E. C. (2014). Teknolojik Gelişme ve Ekonomik Büyüme: OECD Ülkeleri Üzerine Bir Uygulama. TİSK Akademi, 9 (17), 70–92.

Pesaran, M. H. (2004). General Diagnostic Tests for Cross Section Dependence in Panels. Cambridge Working Papers in Economics, 435.

Pesaran, H. M. (2007). A Simple Panel Unit Root Test in the Presence of Cross Section Dependence. Journal of Applied Econometrics, 22(2), 265–312.

Pesaran, M. H., Ullah, A. & Yamagata, T. (2008). A Bias-Adjusted LM Test of Error Cross-Section Independence. Econometrics Journal, 11(1), 105–127.

Ravallion, M. (2004). Pro-poor Growth: A Primer. Research Working Paper No. WPS3242. Washington, DC: World Bank.

Ravallion, M. (2014). Income Inequality in the Developing World. Science 344(6186), 851–855.

Ravallion, M. & Chen, S.(2003). Measuring Pro-poor Growth. Economics Letters, 78(1), 93–99.

Son, H. H. ve Kakwani, N.(2003). Pro-poor Growth: Concepts and Measurement with Country Case Studies. The Pakistan Development Review, 42(4), 417–444.

Tatoğlu, F. Y. (2013). İleri Panel Veri Analizi İstanbul: Beta.

Tokatlıoğlu, İ. ve Atan, M. (2007). Türkiye'de Bölgeler Arası Gelişmişlik Düzeyi ve Gelir Dağılımı Eşitsizliği: Kuznets Eğrisi Geçerli Mi?. Ekonomik Yaklaşım Dergisi, 18(65), 25–58.

Ünver, M. ve Koyuncu, J. (2016). The Impact of Poverty on Corruption. Journal of Economics Library, 3(4), 632–642.

Yardımcıoğlu, F. (2012). Eğitim Harcamaları, Ekonomik Büyüme ve Gelir Dağılımı İlişkisi. Sakarya Üniversitesi S.B.E., İktisat Anabilim Dalı Yüksek Lisans Tezi. Sakarya.

Yıldırım, K., Mercan, M. ve Kostakoğlu, S. (2013). Satın Alma Gücü Paritesinin Geçerliliğinin Test Edilmesi: Zaman Serisi ve Panel Veri Analizi. Eskişehir Osmangazi Üniversitesi İktisadi ve İdari Bilimler Dergisi, 8(3) , 75–96.

Yıldız, F.(2009). Yoksul Yanlısı Büyüme: 2003–2005 Türkiye İncelemesi. İstanbul Teknik Üniversitesi S.B.E. İktisat Anabilim Dalı Yüksek Lisans Tezi. İstanbul. https://oxfamapps.org/media/press_release/poor-worse-off-as-billionaire-fortunes-rise-2-5-billion-a-day/ 20/01/2018.

Tufan Sarıtaş

The Effect of Political Globalization on Economic Growth in Turkey: An Empirical Approach[1]

1 Introduction

Economic relations, which are enhanced by the developments in transportation and communication technologies, have brought cultures to interact with each other and also developed a global control mechanism in the international political arena. Therefore, today countries are unable to act independently and have to comply with international political norms and obligations. Because, non-compliance with international rules often brings some economic, political and even military sanctions on countries.

Considering this process, political globalization; world markets, it can be defined as destroying national political structures or beginning to replace them (Beck, 2009: 169). In addition; Depending on the developments in transportation and communication technologies, it can also be defined as the loss of the political borders in order to be included in the global arena (Şahin, 2010: 32).

The nation-state; commodity trade, computer data streams, nationalism currents, terrorist attacks, military operations, global institutions, satellite communications, diplomacy, capital flows, migration, environmental pollution, etc. are affected and react to these effects. For example; The state, which wants to benefit from capital flows, is often unable to prepare policies independent of global markets and has to share its will with transnational institutions, regional organizations or local governments by sacrificing full sovereignty. But, of course, this does not mean that the nation-state is completely ineffective. In this context, policy makers can implement measures that will make their economies more attractive to global investments. In addition, nation-states; They can also be considered effective in functions such as migration, education, infrastructure and population planning (Steger, 2013: 91–92).

---

1 This study was produced from Dr. Tufan Sarıtaş's doctoral dissertation "Analysis of the Relationship Between Economic, Social and Political Globalization Process and Economic Growth in Turkey".

According to Lucas, who emphasized the relationship between globalization and growth; Thanks to globalization, the efficiency of resource allocation is ensured and growth is positively affected in countries that make the best use of international factor fluidity (Yay, 2009: 3). Also Dreher (2006: 1092) believes that globalization positively affects economic growth.

In a study belonging to Dollar (1992), it was concluded that the export figures of the open economies are at high levels and the growth in the national economies is positively affected due to some export-related positive externalities. Rivera-Batiz and Romer (1990); When the benefits of globalization are analyzed within the scope of the neo-classical growth model, the benefit from globalization is low; however, when an evaluation is made within the scope of internal growth theories with the same data, they assume that the positive effect of globalization on growth is at much higher levels.

Looking at the studies examining the relationship between globalization and growth today, it is seen that the growth models used are mostly formed within the context of internal growth models (Çiftçi & Aykaç, 2011). In this context, growth and globalization have been associated with various theories proposed by economists such as Romer, Grossman, Helpman, Aghion, Howitt. As mentioned before, in internal growth models; technology, human capital, R&D studies, etc. are considered as the main drivers of growth. Therefore, this situation caused the internal growth models to gain weight among the growth models. In the literature, in addition to verbal discussions, a number of empirical studies that have attracted attention recently have been observed. A summary of the empirical literature can be presented as follows:

When we look at the empirical literature summary, it is seen that there is a meaningful relationship between political globalization and growth in the studies of Dreher (2006) and Potrafke (2010). On the other hand Chang et al. (2011), Doğan & Can (2016), Hayaloğlu et al. (2015) and Leitao (2012)'s studies have identified a positive relationship between growth and political globalization.

In the study, firstly information will be given about the data and methods to be used. Then, research findings will be reported and interpreted.

2 Data and Methodology

In this study, the period of 1970–2013 in Turkey; The relationship between political globalization and growth has been investigated using the ARDL Boundary Test method and Granger Causality Test was applied in the context of Toda-Yamamoto Approach. Variables used in this context; GDP6 (annual percentage growth in GDP), GFCF1 (gross fixed capital formation as a percentage of GDP),

Table 1: *Literature Summary*

Author	Period / Countries	Globalization Index	Empirical Results
Dreher (2006)	1970–2002 123 Countries	KOF Index	* Positive relationship between general, economic, social globalization and economic growth. * The relationship between political globalization and economic growth is meaningless.
Potrafke (2010)	1951–2006 21 OECD Countries	KOF, Potrafke and Bjonskov Index	* The relationship between political, social, general globalization and economic growth is meaningless. * Positive relationship between general globalization and economic growth.
Chang et al. (2011)	1990–2006 OECD Countries and Transition Economies	KOF Index	* Positive relationship between general, economic, social, political globalization and economic growth.
Leitao (2012)	1995–2008 Europen Union	KOF Index	* Positive relationship between economic, social, political, general globalization and economic growth.
Hayaloğlu, Kalaycı & Artan (2015)	1995–2011 91 Countries	KOF Index	* In the high, middle and low income country group; positive relationship between general, economic, social, political globalization and economic growth. * In the low income country group; negative relationship between general, economic, social globalization and economic growth.
Doğan & Can (2016)	1970–2012 South Korea	KOF Index	* Positive relationship between economic, social, political globalization and economic growth.

KOFPG (KOF Political Globalization Index), HC (Human Capital Index). The HC variable is from Penn World Table; The KOFPG variable was obtained from the Zurich Institute of Technology, and the remainder from the World Bank (WDI). In the established model, GFCF1 variable represents physical capital and HC variable represents human capital.

As known; Possible long-term relationships between series are tested by cointegration tests. However, as a constraint, the vast majority of cointegration tests require series to be integrated to the same degree. In the ARDL model, series does not have to be of the same degree. It is sufficient that the series are not integrated at two or higher degrees. It also allows the series to be available in different delay lengths. In addition to this; It also offers some privileges such as the ability to estimate short and long term parameters simultaneously (Pesaran et al., 2001).

Model 1 established to implement the ARDL Border Test Approach is as follows:

$$\begin{aligned} \Delta GDP6_t = &\beta_0 + \sum_{i=1}^{p} \beta_i \Delta GDP6_{t-i} + \sum_{i=0}^{q} \alpha_i \Delta KOFAG_{t-i} \\ &+ \sum_{i=0}^{r} \delta_i \Delta GFCF1_{t-i} + \sum_{i=0}^{m} \lambda_i \Delta HC_{t-i} + \theta_0 GDP6_{t-1} \\ &+ \theta_1 KOFAG_{t-1} + \theta_2 GFCF1_{t-1} + \theta_3 HC_{t-1} + \varepsilon_t \end{aligned}$$

For the model 1 we have installed, the error correction model is as follows:

$$\begin{aligned} GDP6_t = \beta_0 &+ \sum_{i=1}^{p} \beta_i \Delta GDP6_{t-i} + \sum_{i=0}^{q} \alpha_i \Delta KOFAG_{t-i} + \sum_{i=0}^{r} \delta_i \Delta GFCF1_{t-i} \\ &+ \sum_{i=0}^{m} \lambda_i \Delta HC_{t-i} + \varphi ECM_{t-1} + \varepsilon_t \end{aligned}$$

In addition to ARDL Border Test Approach in the study; Granger Causality Test with Toda-Yamamoto Approach was applied to determine the existence and direction of possible causality relationship between the series.

Table 2: *KPSS Stationarity Test Results*

Variable	Model	Test Statistic	Critical Value		
			%1	%5	%10
GDP6	Constant	*0.0513*	*0.7390*	*0.4630*	*0.3470*
	Constant, Linear Tr.	*0.0444*	*0.2160*	*0.1460*	*0.1190*
KOFPG	Constant	*0.7873*	*0.7390*	*0.4630*	*0.3470*
	Constant, Linear Tr.	*0.0999*	*0.2160*	*0.1460*	*0.1190*
ΔKOFPG	Constant	*0.1173*	*0.7390*	*0.4630*	*0.3470*
	Constant, Linear Tr.	*0.1123*	*0.2160*	*0.1460*	*0.1190*
GFCF1	Constant	*0.3617*	*0.7390*	*0.4630*	*0.3470*
	Constant, Linear Tr.	*0.1531*	*0.2160*	*0.1460*	*0.1190*
ΔGFCF1	Constant	*0.1175*	*0.7390*	*0.4630*	*0.3470*
	Constant, Linear Tr.	*0.0611*	*0.2160*	*0.1460*	*0.1190*
HC	Constant	*0.8342*	*0.7390*	*0.4630*	*0.3470*
	Constant, Linear Tr.	*0.0944*	*0.2160*	*0.1460*	*0.1190*
ΔHC	Constant	*0.0866*	*0.7390*	*0.4630*	*0.3470*
	Constant, Linear Tr.	*0.0798*	*0.2160*	*0.1460*	*0.1190*

3 Empirical Results

Whether the series are stationary series or not was examined by using Kwiatkowski-Phillips-Schmidt-Shin Test (KPSS). In KPSS Test, series are stationary in H_0, not stationary in H_1. KPSS Unit Root Test results for the level and first difference values of the series are reported in Table 2.

According to the KPSS unit root test, we can test whether co-integration exists by applying the ARDL boundary test approach to these series since none of our series are 2 and above integrated, and they are stationary in I (0) or I (1).

In the model (Model-1); It was observed that the most suitable model was ARDL (5,5,5,6) using the Schwarz criterion among 2058 different ARDL models estimated by giving a maximum of 6 delays for each series. In addition, the results of the boundary test related to the questioning of cointegration between GDP6, KOFPG, GFCF1, HC series are shown in Table 3. It is understood that there is a cointegration relationship between the variables. Because the F statistic value is greater than the upper limit values, I(1).

Table 4 shows the long-term results of the ARDL Model established for Model-1, where the GDP6 series is a dependent variable. The long-term coefficient of the KOFPG variable is 0.4370. It is seen that the probability value of this coefficient is statistically significant. This confirms that there is a long-term

Table 3: *ARDL Bound Test Estimation Results for Model-1*

F-Statistic 8.3516	Critical Value	
Significance	$I(0)$ ***Bound***	$I(1)$ ***Bound***
10 %	*3.47*	*4.45*
5 %	*4.01*	*5.07*
2.5 %	*4.52*	*5.62*
1 %	*5.17*	*6.36*

Table 4: *Long Term Coefficients of ARDL (5,5,5,6) Model for Model-1*

Dependent Variable: *GDP6*			
Variables	***Coefficient***	***t-Statistic***	***Prob.***
KOFPG	*0.4370*	*3.9822*	*0.0018*
GFCF1	*−0.7634*	*−3.5942*	*0.0037*
HC	*162.5259*	*4.1835*	*0.0013*
C	*−200.9355*	*−4.2211*	*0.0012*
@TREND	*−4.2111*	*−4.2829*	*0.0011*

relationship. In other words, there is a long-term positive relationship between the growth represented by GDP6 and political globalization (KOFPG).

In addition, as seen in Table 5, the ECM coefficient takes the negative value as desired and is statistically significant at 1 %.

Diagnostic Tests Results

Diagnostic Tests	**Test Value (Prob.)**
Breusch-Godfrey Serial Correlation LM Test	*17.4089 (0.0002)**
Heteroskedasticity Test: Breusch-Pagan-Godfrey	*2.2983 (1.0000)**
Ramsey RESET Test	*2.4145 (0.1395)**
Jarque-Bera Test	*2.9809 (0.2252)**

Notes: * The diagnostic test results at %1 significance level indicate that there is no problem in the model in terms of heteroscedasticity, normality, and model specification error. However, according to the LM Test results, there is an auto-correlation problem.

Table 5: Error Correction Estimation (ECM) Results of ARDL (5,5,5,6) Model for Model-1

	Dependent Variable: *GDP6*		
	Coefficient	***t-Statistic***	***Prob.***
$\Delta GDP6_{t-1}$	*0.2685*	*0.7103*	*0.4911*
$\Delta GDP6_{t-2}$	*−0.1808*	*−0.5161*	*0.6151*
$\Delta GDP6_{t-3}$	*−0.2026*	*−0.7540*	*0.4654*
$\Delta GDP6_{t-4}$	*−0.2118*	*−1.6951*	*0.1158*
$\Delta KOFPG$	*−0.5192*	*−2.0648*	*0.0612*
$\Delta KOFPG_{t-1}$	*−0.6602*	*−2.8023*	*0.0160*
$\Delta KOFPG_{t-2}$	*0.1324*	*0.5092*	*0.6198*
$\Delta KOFPG_{t-3}$	*−0.1362*	*−0.5714*	*0.5783*
$\Delta KOFPG_{t-4}$	*−0.6336*	*−2.7326*	*0.0182*
$\Delta GFCF1$	*1.1461*	*4.6435*	*0.0006*
$\Delta GFCF1_{t-2}$	*1.3877*	*2.9691*	*0.0117*
$\Delta GFCF1_{t-2}$	*1.2670*	*2.5956*	*0.0234*
$\Delta GFCF1_{t-3}$	*−0.0365*	*−0.0862*	*0.9327*
$\Delta GFCF1_{t-4}$	*0.5490*	*1.9042*	*0.0811*
ΔHC	*249.7801*	*3.2710*	*0.0067*
ΔHC_{t-1}	*129.6820*	*1.1628*	*0.2675*
ΔHC_{t-2}	*36.8618*	*0.2833*	*0.7817*
ΔHC_{t-3}	*173.3195*	*1.4266*	*0.1792*
ΔHC_{t-4}	*−71.9047*	*−0.5129*	*0.6173*
ΔHC_{t-5}	*−304.7615*	*−2.3898*	*0.0341*
$\Delta TREND$	*−9.7577*	*−4.4063*	*0.0009*
ECM_{t-1}	*−2.3171*	*−4.9277*	*0.0003*

$$ECM = GDP6 - \begin{pmatrix} 0.4371KOFPG - 0.7635GFCF1+ \\ 162.5260HC - 200.9355 - 4.2112@TREND \end{pmatrix}$$

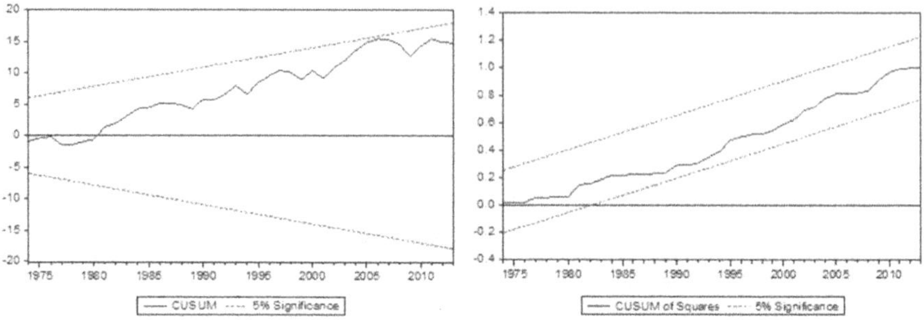

Figure 1: *Cusum and Cusum of Sqauares Test Result for Model-1*

Also, as seen below, it is understood that the model is stable according to Cusum and Cusum of Squares Test results.

After that, Granger Causality Test with Toda-Yamamoto Approach were applied to determine the causality relationship between the series. Since the GDP6 series I (0) and KOFPG, GFCF, HC series I (1), the maximum degree of integration for the series was found to be 1 (one). Schwarz criterion = 8.5307 for 1 lagged (P = 1) model of the unconstrained VAR models estimated by the level values of the series; Since Schwarz criterion = 8.5236 for 2 delayed (P = 2) model and Schwarz criterion = 9.4200 for 3 delayed (P = 3) model, the most suitable delayed model was found to be 2 (P = 2) delayed model according to Schwarz criterion. Then the VAR (p = 2 dmax = 1) model, namely VAR (3), is estimated and the VAR Granger Causality / Block Externality Test results are obtained and reported below. According to the test results; The following relationships were determined between the variables;

(a) A causality relationship at 10 % significance level from KOFPG to GDP6 and GFCF1.
(b) A causality relationship at 5 % significance level from GFCF1 to KOFPG.
(c) A causality relationship at 5 % significance level from HC to KOFPG and GFCF1.
(d) A causality relationship at 10 % significance level from GDP6 to HC.

4 Conclusion

In this study is discussed in Turkey for the period 1970–2013, political globalization, the impact on growth were examined. The existence of a possible relationship between variables; It was researched using the ARDL Boundary

Table 6: *VAR Granger Causality/Block Exogeneity Wald Tests for Model-1*

Dependent Variable: *GDP6*			
Excluded	***Chi-sq***	***df***	***Prob.***
KOFPG	*6.9302*	*3*	*0.0742*
GFCF1	*4.0071*	*3*	*0.2607*
HC	*0.8418*	*3*	*0.8394*
Tümü	*12.3884*	*9*	*0.1923*
Dependent Variable: *KOFPG*			
Excluded	***Chi-sq***	***df***	***Prob.***
GDP6	*2.6515*	*3*	*0.4485*
GFCF1	*9.1275*	*3*	*0.0276*
HC	*9.7119*	*3*	*0.0212*
Tümü	*27.4385*	*9*	*0.0012*
Dependent Variable: *GFCF1*			
Excluded	***Chi-sq***	***df***	***Prob.***
GDP6	*3.7316*	*3*	*0.2919*
KOFPG	*7.2831*	*3*	*0.0634*
HC	*11.1151*	*3*	*0.0111*
Tümü	*18.3692*	*9*	*0.0311*
Dependent Variable: *HC*			
Excluded	***Chi-sq***	***df***	***Prob.***
GDP6	*6.7667*	*3*	*0.0797*
KOFPG	*4.0118*	*3*	*0.2602*
GFCF1	*4.5537*	*3*	*0.2075*
Tümü	*8.9312*	*9*	*0.4436*

Test and Granger Causality Test with Toda-Yamamoto Approach. In the established model, the growth represented by the annual percentage growth rate in GDP has been accepted as the dependent variable. The independent variables are; representing political globalization, the KOF Political Globalization Index (KOFPG) is the gross fixed capital formation (GFCF1) and the Human Capital Index (HC) representing human capital as a percentage of GDP.

According to the empirical findings obtained as a result of the study; ARDL Border Test shows that political globalization positively affects growth in the long run. However, tests such as Heteroskedasticity (Breusch-Pagan-Godfrey) Test, Ramsey RESET Test, Jarque-Bera Test, Cusum Test and Cusum of Squares Test, which are the diagnostic tests applied for ARDL Border Test, show that the model is significant; The Breusch-Godfrey Serial Correlation LM Test result shows that the model has an auto-correlation problem. In addition, the results of Granger Causality Test with Toda-Yamamoto Approach show that political globalization is the cause of growth.

References

Beck,U. (2009). "Küreselleşme Nedir?", Kudret Bülbül (Ed.), (Trans. Kudret Bülbül); Küreselleşme Temel Metinler, Nobel Yayınları, Ankara, 169–174.

Chang, C.P., Lee, C.C. & Hsieh, M.C. (2011). "Globalization, Real Output and Multiple Structural Breaks", Global Economic Review, 40(4), 421–444.

Çiftçi, C. ve Aykaç, G. (2011). "İçsel Büyüme Modelleri ve Küreselleşme Sürecinde Gelişmekte Olan Ülkelerin Konumları", Sosyoekonomi Dergisi, 14(14), 160–181.

Doğan, B. & Can, M. (2016). "Küreselleşmenin Büyümeye Etkisi: Güney Kore Örnekleminde Eş-bütünleşme Analizi", Çankırı Karatekin Üniversitesi İktisadi ve İdari Bilimler Fakültesi Dergisi, 6 (1), 1–24.

Dollar, D. (1992). "Outward – Oriented Developing Economies Really Do Grow More Rapidly Evidence from 95LCDs: 1976–1985", Economic Development and Culturel Change, 40(3), 523–544.

Dreher, A. (2006). "Does Globalization Affect Growth? Evidence from a New Index of Globalization", Applied Econımics, 38(10), 1091–1110.

Hayaloğlu, P., Kalaycı, C. & Artan, S. (2015). "Küreselleşme Farklı Gelir Grubundaki Ülkelerde Ekonomik Büyümeyi Nasıl Etkilemektedir?", Osmangazi Üniversitesi İİBF Dergisi, 10(1), 119–152.

Leitao, N. C. (2012). "Economic Growth, Globalization and Trade", Management Research and Practise, 4(3), 18–24.

Pesaran M.H., Shin Y. & Smith R. (2001). "Bounds Testing Approaches to the Analysis of Level Relationship", Journal of Applied Econometrics, 16(3), 289–326.

Potrafke, N. (2010). "Political Cycles and Economic Performance in OECD Countries: Empirical Evidence from 1951–2006", Public Choise, 150(1–2), 155–179.

Rivera Batiz, Luis A. & Romer, Paul M. (1990). Economic Integration and Endogenous Growth (Working Paper No: 3528), The National Bureau of Economic Research.

Steger, Manfred B. (2013). Küreselleşme (Trans. Abdullah Ersoy), Dost Kitabevi, Ankara.

Şahin, K. (2010). "Küreselleşme ve Yeniden Yapılanan Ulus-Devlet", Murat Ercan (Ed.); Küreselleşme ve Türkiye'ye Etkileri, 1. Basım, Nobel Yayınları, Ankara, 27–38.

Yay, T. (2009). "Küreselleşme Karşısında Piyasa ve Devlet", Ekonomi Bilimleri Dergisi, 1(1), 1–11.

Yüksel Okşak

The Relationship between Poverty and Islam: Panel Analysis

1 Introduction

The fact that individuals do not have necessary resources and income to sustain their lives has become one of the main problems of the world. The word poor is used for people who can not meet their basic needs such as eating, drinking, and shelter. Poverty is a social and economic event felt by a certain part of the world societies. Although poverty is accepted as a social phenomenon, one of the main factors triggering poverty is undoubtedly economic factors.

The increase of the income of the person/household is directly related to the increase or decrease of the poverty when we look at the generally accepted evaluations. For this reason, people try to increase or diversify their economic resources in order not to be at the poverty or hunger line. However, the effort and desire to increase the income of the individual is not realized for every individual. In this case, people accept their poverty and internalize this situation. Individuals who accept that the poverty levels are permanent can move towards religion and religious values in order to legitimize their situation and make themselves feel more comfortable psychologically. Because in the basic teachings of many religions, there are suggestions for believers to act without a greed and to content himself/herself with less.

Religious beliefs also affect the consumption habits of individuals.

When we look at monotheistic religions including Islam, they express the necessity of saving and spending in line with basic needs. (1) the phenomenon of globalization, (2) the capitalist economic model being the dominant model on the earth, and (3) the adoption of a consumption-centered lifestyle lead to increase spending and cause societies to become impoverished rapidly.

Considering the concept of poverty and the protection of the needy according to religion, there is no serious and important difference in the views of religions. In the Quran and in the Bible of Lukas, there are verses referring to the concepts of poverty and destitution. With his words of "My God! I take refuge in you from the poverty", Prophet Muhammad explains that poverty is a difficult situation. Poverty discourses of both religions refer to material and moral situations. As can be seen from the examples given in two different religions, poverty is among the religious discourses. Islam religion advises that economic order, discipline and systems should be within the boundaries of Islam in order to avoid poverty. According to Islam, people don't incline to religion as a result of their poverty. The Islamic principle and teachings preach that people don't experience poverty with their orientation towards religion.

Salleh (2014: 243) evaluated the concept of poverty in Islam not only with material needs but also with its spiritual dimensions. However, Islam does not recommend impoverishment. On the contrary, it supports owning property but sharing it fairly. It has several mechanisms to prevent poverty. The healthy implementation of mechanisms brought by Islam such as zakat and charity will regulate economic life and contribute to the elimination of the unfair income distribution (Ali and Hatta, 2014: 62).

In addition, the concept of interest in Islam is considered haram. Therefore, a certain mass is not included in the financial system, which affects the economy. Therefore, poverty increases and prevents development on a country basis. These problems are tried to be overcome with methods such as traditional micro financing (Bahçe and Gümüş, 2016: 12–13).

Although this research addresses the relationship between poverty and the religion of Islam, it is important to examine the concept of poverty and its relationship with other science and disciplines. Based on this idea, poverty varies and varies depending on multi-stakeholder factors.

2 Poverty

Failure of individuals or households to meet their basic needs is defined as "poverty". When we evaluate the processes of world societies in a wide range, the poor people are not marginalized by the societies. On the contrary, especially when we consider the religious issue, it was accepted as an occasion to gain the appreciation and consent of divine might. Contrary to this understanding, some thoughts argue that poverty indicators negatively affect the image of a country (See: Mbonda, 2004).

The World Bank has succeeded with the policies it pursued and focused on especially the poor in developing countries (Arabacı, 2019: 124). Focusing on neo-liberal policies, the World Bank accepted poverty as an internal issue and shifted its attention to this area after 1990 (Şenses, 2002: 39–41) as such one of the goals of the World Bank is to increase the income of the poor living in every country around the world by 40 % (https://www.worldbank.org/en/who-we-are).

One of the most important points of poverty is undoubtedly the measurement of poverty level. Countries use different measurement methods to determine the poverty levels of their own country. In economic science, parameters such as average human life, education level, health and gross national income per capita are taken as basis to determine the poverty line.

In classical fiqh literature, quorum criteria are used to determine the poverty line. It is controversial in the doctrine whether the debt and essential need factors should be taken into account in determining the quorum (Korkut, 2019: 65).

The concept of relative poverty can be explained by the fact that the welfare level of individuals or households cannot reach the level of social welfare. In other words, relative poverty can be defined as poverty between the hunger line and general average well-being. Absolute poverty is the level of consumption required for individuals to sustain their lives only physically.

3 Literatur Review

Poverty has been at the focal points of different sciences and disciplines. The number of studies in this area has also had an important place in the world literature.

Adam Smith explained the emergence of poverty in the following way: the migration from the village to the city emerged as a result of the need for intense workforce in rapidly progressing industrial conditions. Thus, the living standards of the working class formed and the poverty increased accordingly (Turanlı, 2000: 21). This has led to the realization that the concept of poverty is not only personal but also a situation (problem) affecting countries and their policies.

Thomas Malthus and John Stuart Mill, one of members of the classical economics schools of thought, criticized the aid to the poor (Barber, 1999: 41). Unlike classical economists, Pigou, one of the Neo-Classical economists, states that cash aids from the rich to the poor are small for capital owners, but it is welfare increasing for the poor (Uyanık, 2017). In Keynesian economics, the thesis that poverty reduction will be overcome by taxation methods has been advocated. It was emphasized that the taxes collected by the state should be according to the richness level of citizens (Altıok, 2009). Marxist thought with a socialist approach argues that income inequality lies under poverty and this situation would disappear with the understanding of equality (Sallan and Gül, 1997: 13).

In their study on Bangladesh, Sohag et al. (2015) point out that the inclusion of zakat revenues to the system and distributing them to the needy will both reduce poverty and contribute to the delivery of zakat to the right people. Roni and Tarmidi (2015) evaluates e-zakat method while Abdullah et al. (2013) discuss the socio-economic evaluation of zakat in Pakistan.

According to Dwi (2015: 289), who analyzed various Islamic perspectives and thoughts on the impact of globalization on poverty reduction, today's world is under the influence of the superpowers. For example, using the dollar as the official currency for international transactions makes the dollar dominant in international transactions. As a result, the debt of developing countries keeps increasing due to the rising price of the dollar. Increasing debt value in developing countries causes the government to reduce social subsidies. Thus, economic troubles are increasingly felt for poor people. This makes it difficult to alleviate poverty.

Ahmad (1991: 105) emphasizes that Islam supports human dignity that suffers from the existence of poverty. Ahmad, who deals with the problem of poverty through Islamic approach, philosophy, private teachings and institutions, emphasizes that the special attention should be given to Prophet Muhammed's advice about taking care of the poor, feeding hungry people, and taking charitable acts. According to Abdelrahman (2018: 333), the current world statistical data reveals that the Muslim world often suffers from underdevelopment and poverty.

Okumuş (2011: 3) examines poverty in the light of the Qur'an and Sunnah in his study.

With the impact of globalization, international interaction is gaining momentum. Industrialization, which increased with the Second World War, created gaps between countries. With industrialization, poverty increased on an individual basis and cities started to fill with homeless people (Yenen and Fight, 2015: 95–98).

Poverty is also subject of many empirical studies. Some researchers analyzed the impact of Information and Communication Technologies (Koyuncu Yalcinkaya and Yılmaz, 2018)., banking crises (Yalcinkaya Koyuncu and Okşak, 2019), imports from China (Koyuncu and Yilmaz, 2010), and private forest ownership (Koyuncu and Yilmaz, 2013) on poverty, while some researchers investigated the effect of poverty on corruption (Koyuncu and Unver, 2016) and female labor force participation (Koyuncu and Özen, 2017a).

As can be seen, poverty has an important place in economics. Poverty can't be related only to the purchasing power of individuals. It should be noted that income isn't only way which makes individuals happy. Because income increase is not enough criteria for the elimination of poverty which is seen as a social and economic problem (Doğan and Tatlı, 2014: 14).

4 Relationship between Poverty and Islam

Most of the Muslim countries classified as low- or middle-income groups suffer from poverty and face serious difficulties in economic development. International development reports link the economic problems of Muslim countries to similar factors in other developing countries.

While determining the conditions of the people to be given zakat in the Quran, expressions in the definition of poverty are encountered. In Arabic, the word "poor" originates from the word "fakr", which means human with broken back. The person who could not meet his basic or essential needs was metaphorized with the person whose spine was broken (Beşer, 2016: 36).

When the studies on the relationship between poverty and Islam are examined, it is possible to say from the Islamic perspective that the concept of the poor and poverty is mainly treated as spiritual and material poverty. The concept of spiritual poverty is outside the main focus of this study. However, differences in the perception of the concept of spiritual poverty lead to a different understanding of material poverty on Islamic societies. Therefore, this issue can be seen as one of the parameters underlying the high poverty level of the majority of Islamic countries.

In the empirical part of this study, the model created in the light of the data obtained from the WDI to test the hypothesis of "the poverty increases as the rate of adopting Islam increases in societies that adopt the religion of Islam". Claiming that the relationship between a divine religion and poverty can't be of course clearly illuminated by an empirical study. But still, considering this analysis and seeking answers to the following questions will perhaps shed on future studies: Does adopting Islam really increase poverty? If the answer is yes, what is the reason behind the increase in poverty as the rate of adoption of Islam increases in the societies that adopt Islam, while view of Islam on income distribution, the poor and the poverty is clearly revealed in the Qur'an.

Khan and Ullah (2015: 26) addresses the issue of revising the concept of the poor. They proposes poor categories that takes Islamic principles into consideration (Table 1) and makes measurement suggestions for these categories.

Khan and Ullah (2015: 33–34) offers four categories of the poor: extreme poor, ultra poor, poor, non-poor. The extremely poor group is made up of people who cannot participate in physical economic activities due to physical or mental disability or old age and poor health. Therefore, these people cannot engage in economic activities. For such a group of people, it is necessary to provide credit facilities and ensure that credit is guaranteed when it is defaulted. The situation is the same in the ultra poor group. People belonging to this group have approximately the same characteristics as the extremely poor class. Therefore, they need the same relief package as the very poor group. People representing this group cannot effectively carry out economic activity. This group of people needs credit. The third category consists of the poor class. This class is in a better situation than the previous two classes. People in this group need loans and other opportunities for self-employment activities. They can carry out their economic activities and repay their loans within their terms. Despite their self-employment activities, the group needs other incentives such as subsidies, free access to education, health, clean water and shelter, etc. The last group of people is the non-poor group. In order to carry out effective economic activities, they require almost the same measures as the previous group.

In the Islamic context, the concept of poverty differs from the concept of poverty in capitalism. Poverty is a pure economic concept that does not affect the social class and social values of people in Islam. If the distribution tools of Islamic economics based on equality and justice regarding poverty are examined, the Islamic economic system may be a better system for the poor and marginalized classes.

5 Data and Metodology

This part of the study examines how poverty is affected in a society that adopts the religion of Islam with panel data analysis. To analyze how poverty is affected by the religion of Islam using the unbalanced panel dataset, the following multi-time fixed effect models are estimated:

$$X34_{it} = (\beta_1 + \tau_t) + \beta_2 X19_{it} + \beta_3 X59_{it} + \beta_4 X56_{it} + \beta_5 X63_{it} + \beta_6 X68_{it} + u_{it} \quad (1)$$

$$X35_{it} = (\beta_1 + \tau_t) + \beta_2 X19_{it} + \beta_3 X59_{it} + \beta_4 X56_{it} + \beta_5 X63_{it} + \beta_6 X68_{it} + u_{it} \quad (2)$$

$$X36_{it} = (\beta_1 + \tau_t) + \beta_2 X19_{it} + \beta_3 X59_{it} + \beta_4 X56_{it} + \beta_5 X63_{it} + \beta_6 X68_{it} + u_{it} \quad (3)$$

and also the following multi-time random effect model is estimated:

$$(-1 * X4)_{it} = \beta_1 + \beta_2 X19_{it} + \beta_3 X59_{it} + \beta_4 X56_{it} + \beta_5 X63_{it} + \beta_6 X68_{it} + (\tau_t + u_{it}) \quad (4)$$

it sub-index in the above models is the observation value of the i.th country regarding the relevant variable in t year; β_1 is the constant of the model; τ_t is the time-specific effect, which affects all countries in the same way but varies from time to time; u_{it} represents the error term of the regression model. The dependent and independent variables used in the model are described in Table 1 below.

Table 1: *Definitions and Sources of Variables*

x4	Human Development Index (HDI)	(WDI)World Bank
x34	(Headcount) poverty indicator, Percentage of people below the poverty line	(WDI) World Bank
x35	(Pov. Gap) poverty indicator, Poverty gap. Measures average distance below poverty line	(WDI) World Bank
x36	(Watts index) poverty indicator, It is the average of proportionate poverty gaps in the population, measured by proportioning the average of the poverty line in proportion to income, by counting the poor in the poverty line.	(WDI) World Bank
x19	Islam	(WDI) World Bank
x59	KBDMG(National Income Per Person)	(WDI) World Bank
x56	GDP Deflator	(WDI) World Bank
x63	Health Expenditures	(WDI) World Bank
x68	Public Education Expenditures	(WDI) World Bank

6 Estimation Results

Estimation results of multiple regression model are reported in Table 2 above. According to Hausman Test statistics, among the four models used in the analysis, it is seen that the Random Effect Model (REM) is selected in Model 4 and the Fixed Effect Model (FEM) in Models 1,2 and 3. In Model 1, the variables x19, x59, x56 and x68 are statistically significant, while the x63 variable is statistically insignificant. In Model 2, the variables x19, x59, x56 and x68 are statistically significant, while the x63 variable is statistically insignificant. In Model 3, the variables x19, x59, x56 and x68 are statistically significant, while the x63 variable is statistically insignificant. In Model 4, the variables x19, x59 and x68 are statistically significant, while variables x63 and x56 are statistically insignificant.

Table 2: *Estimation Results*

	Model 1	Model 2	Model 3	Model 4
Bağımlı Değişken	**x34**	**x35**	**x36**	**x4**
Sabit	13,445540	4,451331	6,353682	-0,613714
P-değeri	*0,0000*	*0,0000*	*0,0000*	*0,0000*
x19	7,776155	1,761712	2,152789	0,103456
P-değeri	*0,0000*	*0,0046*	*0,0273*	*0,0000*
x59	-0,000131	-0,000048	-0,000070	-0,000006
P-değeri	*0,0000*	*0,0001*	*0,0003*	*0,0000*
x56	0,003200	0,001920	0,003125	0,000010
P-değeri	*0,0287*	*0,0018*	*0,0012*	*0,2914*
x63	-0,189859	-0,005203	-0,030730	0,000384
P-değeri	*0,5187*	*0,9664*	*0,8742*	*0,7772*
x68	-0,893773	-0,339716	-0,432249	-0,006012
P-değeri	*0,0159*	*0,0292*	*0,0768*	*0,0009*
Gözlem Sayısı	680	680	680	1651
Hausman Test İst.	18,8941	21,9204	20,5481	5,1045
Hausman Testi P-değeri	0,0020	0,0005	0,0010	0,4033
Seçilen Model	**FEM**	**FEM**	**FEM**	**REM**

7 Conclusion

As a result of panel analyzes carried out by using four different poverty indicators, it has been observed that poverty increases as the rate of adopting Islam increases in the societies that adopt Islam. This finding preserves statistically significant validity for four out of four different poverty indicators in multiple regression models. As a result of this study, it is possible to say that religion plays an important role on poverty.

Güner (2002: 109–112) explains in detail the negative effects of poverty on belief, morality and life, the world of thought, the family order, the stability of the social order. Koyuncu and Özen (2017b) scrutinized the effect of religion on female labor force participation. These details will not be discussed here, as this will distract the empirical study you are reading. Islam does not reveal poverty as a target, a missed element. Poverty appears as a problem in Islam and requires a solution. Wealth, on the other hand, is not a prohibited phenomenon in Islam, provided that Islamic rules are followed. It is possible to propose justifications such as interest on which global economic system based is banned in Islam and alternative models based on Islam cannot become widespread. However, although the data emphasizes that as the rate of adoption of Islam increases, poverty increases, a multidisciplinary study is required to determine the underlying causes.

References

Abdelrahman, A. (2018). Islam and the Challenge of Economic Development in the Muslim World: Review and Evaluation of Secular Arguments. Intellectual Discourse, 26, 333–355.

Abdullah, M., Niaz, A. & Imran, S. R. (2013). The Role of Zakat Improving the Economic Status of Beneficiaries in Khyber Pakhtunkhwa. Journal of Managerial Sciences, 7(2), 243–253.

Ahmad, Z. (1991). Islam, Poverty and İncome Distribution. Leicester, UK: The Islamic Foundation.

Ali, I. & Hatta, Z. A. (2014). Zakat as a Poverty Reduction Mechanism Among the Muslim Community: Case Study of Bangladesh, Malaysia and Indonesia. Asian Social Work and Policy Review, 8(1), 59–70.

Altıok, M. (2009). Keynes ve Keynesci Kuramda Kriz ve İktisat Politikası Tartışmaları. Toplum ve Demokrasi, 3(6–7), 75–102.

Arabacı, Y. R. (2019). Dünya Bankasının Yeni Uluslararası Yoksulluk Sınırları ve Küresel Yoksulluğun Yeniden Değerlendirilmesi. Journal of Social Security, 9(1), 123–140.

Bahçe, A. B. & Gümüş, Ö. (2016), Kamu Maliyesi Açısından İslamiyette Yoksulluğun Görünümü ve İslami Mikrofinansın Kullanılabilirliği, Sosyal ve Beşeri Bilimleri Dergisi, 8(1), 1–18.

Barber, W. J. (1999). İktisadi Düşünce Tarihi. Şule Yayınları, 3. Baskı, İstanbul.

Beşer, F. (2016). İslam'da Zenginlik ve Fakirlik, Nun Yayıncılık, 3. Baskı, İstanbul.

Doğan, E. M. & Tatlı, H. (2014). İnsani Gelişme ve İnsani Yoksulluk Bağlamında Türkiye'nin Dünyadaki Yeri. Atatürk Üniversitesi İ.İ.B.F. Dergisi, 28(1), 99–124.

Dwi, S. (2015). Islam, Globalization, and Poverty Alleviation. Al-Iqtishad: Jurnal Ilmu Ekonomi Syariah, 5(2), 289–310, https://doi.org/10.15408/aiq.v5i2.2123.

Güner, O. (2002) Erdem Ve Esaret Arasında Yoksulluk -İslam Geleneğinde Yoksulluk Söyleminin İzdüşümleri-. [s. l.]: Abdülkadir OKUMUŞLAR. ISBN 2630–5550. Disponível em: http://search.ebscohost.com/login.aspx?direct=true&db=ir00559a&AN=tuda.article.436740&lang=tr&site=eds-live. Acesso em: 3 abr. 2020.

https://www.worldbank.org/en/who-we-are (18.03.2020).

Khan, Z. & Ullah, K. (2015). Conceptualizing Poverty in Capitalism and Islam. Al-Idah 31(2), 26–36.

Korkut, R. (2019). İslam İktisat Düşüncesinde Yoksulluk Problemi. Dokuz Eylül Üniversitesi İlahiyat Fakültesi Dergisi, 50, 61–97.

Koyuncu, C. & Özen, E. (2017a). Religious, Ethnic, Linguistic and Cultural Diversity and Female Labor Force Participation. Journal of Economics Bibliography, 4(1), 87–93.

Koyuncu, C. & Özen, E. (2017b). Yoksulluğun Kadın İşgücü Katılımına Etkisinin Ampirik Analizi, International Balkan and Near Eastern Social Sciences Conference Series, 28–29 Ekim, Ohrid/Republic of Macedonia, 189–196.

Koyuncu, C. & Yılmaz, R. (2010). China's Export Surge and World Poverty, Transformation in Business and Economics, 9, No.2 (20), 86–94.

Koyuncu, C. & Yılmaz, R. (2013). Impact of Private Forest Ownership on Deforestation and Poverty. Quality&Quantity, 47(3), 1657–1664, DOI: 10.1007/s11135-011-9618-7.

Koyuncu, J. Y. & Okşak, Y. (2019). The Impact of Banking Crises on Poverty: Panel Evidence. In R. Rasim Yilmaz & G. Löschnigg (Eds.), Studies on Balkan and Near Eastern Social Sciences, Vol. 3, pp. 255–262. Peter Lang Publishing, ISBN 978-3-631-78289-7.

Koyuncu, J. Y. & Ünver, M. (2016). The Impact of Poverty on Corruption. Journal of Economics Library, 3(4), 632–642.

Koyuncu, Y. J. & Yılmaz, R. (2018). The Contribution of ICT to Poverty Reduction: A Panel Data Evidence, Social Sciences Research Journal, 7(4), 63–75.

Mbonda, E. M. (2004). Poverty as a Violation of Human Rights: Towards a Right Non-Poverty. International Social Science Journal, 56(180), 277–288.

Okumuş, E. (2011). Bir Sosyal Eşitsizlik Örneği Olarak Yoksulluğun Dinî Meşrûlaştırımı. Şarkiyat, 5, 3–14.

Roni, R. A. & Tarmidi, M. (2015). An Exploratory Study of e-Zakat Usage Among Malaysian Academician, Proceedings of the Fourth Asia-Pasific Conference on Global Business, Economics, Finance and Social Sciences (AP15 Malaysia Conference), Malaysia. ISBN-978-1-63415-9.

Sallan G. S. & Gül, H. (1997). Yoksulluk ve Yoksulluk Sorununa Yaklaşımlar, Mülkiyeliler Birliği Dergisi, 21(199), 3–21.

Salleh M. S. (2014). İslam İktisadi Kavramlarına Yeniden Bakış: Yoksulluk Örneği. İslam İktisadını Yeniden Düşünmek, (Editörler: Taha Eğri, Oğuz Karasu, Necmettin Kızılkaya), İGİAD Yayınları, İkinci Basım, İstanbul, 243–263.

Sohag, K., Mahmud, K. T., Alam, F., & Samargandi, N. (2015). Can Zakat System Alleviate Rural Poverty in Bangladesh? A Propensity Score Matching Approach. Journal of Poverty, 19(3), 261–277.

Şenses, F. (2002). Küreselleşmenin Öteki Yüzü: Yoksulluk, İkinci Baskı. İstanbul: İletişim Yayınları, 39–41.

Turanlı, R. (2000). İktisadi Düşünce Tarihi. Bilim Teknik Yayınevi, 3. Baskı, İstanbul.

Uyanık, Y. (2017). Gelir Dağılımı Teorileri: Gelir Dağılımı ve Yoksulluk Kavram-Teori-Uygulama, Editörler: Özdemir, Çağlar, İslamoğlu, Emel, Seçkin Yayıncılık, Ankara.

Yenen, İ. P. & Fight, P. (2015). Yoksullukla Mücadele Araci Olarak Din, 9, 95–107.

Ebru Gül Yılmaz

The Effect of TFP, Patent Applications and ICT Exports on Per Capita Income in OECD Countries

1 Introduction

In all economies increasing the welfare of households is one of the most important concern of all governments. As a beginning point of the common definition of economy; 'meeting the unlimited needs of people with limited resources', the fact that using limited resources in the most efficient way is possible with technology is the main reason why technology has become so important. The technological improvement in most of the sectors and all over the world is considerable especially for the last two decades. The part of the mentioned developments, mostly in the field of information and communication technologies (ICT), has been one of the most important factor in the rapid spread of technological developments in other fields worldwide. On the other hand, in economics literature one of the most important and attractive subject for economists is GDP per capita differences among countries. Why some countries have growth problem while others are growing sustainably? Can technology levels of countries cause these differences? Although the empirical analysis of the paper is restricted with OECD countries we want share the selected countries trend analysis in terms of the paper's all variables. At Figure 1 and Table 1 we can follow the acceleration of Korea and China in terms of GDP per Capita. Did technological improvements force this acceleration? At the end of the empirical analysis we will get the result of this question specific to OECD Counties.

In the literature there are researches which analysis TFP and ICT Exports separately; Fagerberg and Bart Verspagen (1997) employed tests to examine the nexus between technology, growth and unemployment for 64 European countries using data from 1980 to 1990. Research and development (R&D) expenses are used as technology indicator. The finding of the paper revealed the differences across regions in terms of GDP Per capita growth may explained by technology. Zagorchev et al. (2011) examined dynamic relationship across GDP and ICT for 86 countries using data from 1991 to 2006 with panel cointegration analysis and DOLS-Dynamic Ordinary Least Squares. Number of personal computers, mobile phone subscribers and internet users are identified as the indicators of

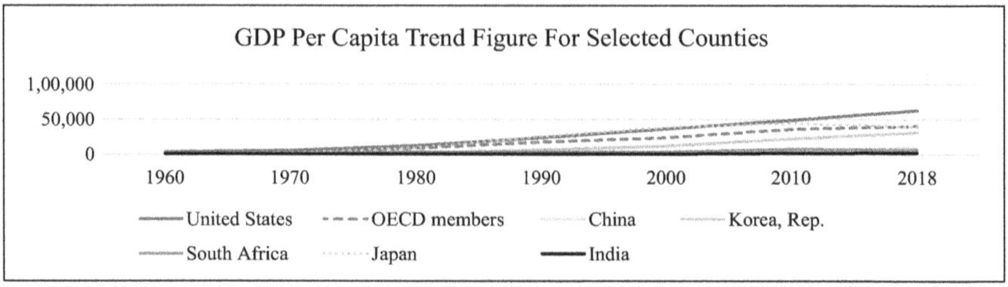

Figure 1: *GDP Per Capita Trend Figure for Selected Counties*
Resource: (https://data.worldbank.org/indicator/NY.GDP.PCAP.CD)

ICT. As a conclusion, researchers has found out that there is a long-run relationship among GDP Per Capita, financial system development and ICT network indicators. Falk (2007), has investigated impact of R&D expenditures to GDP on GDP per working age population by using GMM-Generalized Method of Moments estimator and revealed that R&D expenses to GDP has a strong positive effect on GDP Per Capita. Islam et al. (2006) have researched the role of TFP on China's growth by using dual approach and concluded that TFP growth rate has an important role in China's growth. In this paper, the total factor productivity, number of patent applications and the share of high-technology exports in total exports are determined as technology indicators, and model is set with all these three factors and that differentiates the paper in the literature.

In order to see the whole picture, it will be useful to shed light to both dependent and independent variables:

1.1 GDP Per Capita

Although recently GDP Per Capita is not a unique and adequate indicator for welfare by itself, it is used for many years as an important demonstrator by governments with other indicators such as human development index-HDI. All governments make calculations on GDP Per Capita and target to increase the ratio. As it can be followed from Figure 1 and Table 1 after second world war between 1960 and 2018 world's GDP Per Capita has raised from $453 to $11.313 with an 2399 % increase. OECD countries has an average approximately 4 times greater than worlds average as of 2018. But the remarkable acceleration has been realized especially by Korea Rep. by a 19723 % increase by the years between 1960 and 2018. Without making any technical analysis we can easily tell that technological improvements have an important role in Korea's economic boom. Naturally, there are also many scientific researches which explains that Korea's

Table 1: *GDP Per Capita between 1960 and 2018 for Selected Countries*

Country Name	1960	1970	1980	1990	2000	2010	2018	Change Between 1960–2018
World	453	805	2.536	4.290	5.493	9.541	11.313	2399 %
United States	3.007	5.234	12.575	23.889	36.335	48.467	62.795	1988 %
OECD members	1.354	2.667	8.899	17.513	23.664	35.986	40.410	2884 %
China	90	113	195	318	959	4.550	9.771	10815 %
Korea, Rep.	158	279	1.704	6.516	11.948	22.087	31.363	19723 %
South Africa	443	835	2.906	3.140	3.032	7.329	6.374	1339 %
Japan	479	2.038	9.465	25.359	38.532	44.508	39.290	8103 %
India	82	112	267	368	443	1.358	2.010	2346 %

Resource: (https://data.worldbank.org/indicator/NY.GDP.PCAP.CD)

economic development adventure is a process that extends from imitation to innovation (Atay, 2012: 252)

1.2 Technology Indicators

The main motivation for his paper is to provide new insights into the effects of technology on per capita income by taking technology with three different indicators. And also we consider that getting the research period as 2000–2017 which is last three rapid technological improvements decade, will provide a up to date point of view.

In the literature most of the researches defined technology with just one indicator. One of the primary contribution of this study to the literature is taking three variables which reflect different aspects of technology; TFP, patent numbers, ICT Exports/Total Exports as technology indicator.

1.2.1 Total Factor Productivity

One of the technology indicators is Toral Factor Productivity which is first mentioned by Robert M. Solow at 1957. Solow (1957) explained Total Factor Productivity with his research named 'Technical Change and Aggregate Production Function'

$$Q = f(K, L; t) \tag{1}$$

In the function 'K'; capital, 'L': labor and t' technical change which identifies any shift in aggregate production function. Then he defined the special form of neutral technical change which means marginal rates of substitution is untouched but there is decrease or increase in outputs (Solow, 1957: 312):

$$Q = AF(K,L)$$

$$\frac{\Delta Y}{Y} = \alpha \frac{\Delta K}{\mathrm{K}} + (1-\alpha)\frac{\Delta L}{\mathrm{L}} + \frac{\Delta A}{\mathrm{A}}$$

Denotations of components of equation are as follows:

$\Delta Y/Y$ = Change in Output, $\alpha\left(\frac{\Delta Y}{Y}\right)$ = Contribution of capital to change in output, (1-α) $\frac{\Delta L}{\mathrm{L}}$ = Contribution of labor to change in output, $\frac{\Delta A}{\mathrm{A}}$ = Change in Total Factor Productivity. Hence output, labor and capital variables are

Table 2: *Change in Patent Applications for the Selected Countries (2000–2018)*

Sütun1	2000	2005	2010	2015	2018	Change 2000–2018%
World	823.135	965.494	1.160.899	1.864.186	2.294.847	179 %
OECD	752.138	813.267	789.036	831.044	823.487	9 %
China	25.346	93.485	293.066	968.252	1.393.815	5399 %
Korea Republic	72.831	122.188	131.805	167.275	162.561	123 %
Japan	384.201	367.960	290.081	258.839	253.630	−34 %
South Africa	895	1.003	821	889	657	−27 %
India	2.206	4.721	8.853	12.579	16.289	638 %

Resource: (https://data.worldbank.org/indicator/IP.PAT.RESD)

measurable directly, TFP is measured indirectly and is the unexplained part of the change in the output via inputs. TFP is called as Solow Residual (Mankiw, 2010: 281).

1.2.2 Patent Numbers

Technology which was mentioned as one of the components of economic growth by Solow in 1957 is so important because of its effect on increasing efficiency in production. Mishkin (2018) determined three major promoting factor for efficiency; infrastructural construction, increase in human capital, incentives for research and development (R&D). Patent numbers, tax incentives and governmental R&D expenses were mentioned as components of incentives for R&D. Patent, contributes to the development of technology by securing the intellectual property rights of the patent inventor by encouraging research and development activities (Mishkin, 2018: 182).

Patent numbers can also directly be accepted as indicator of technological improvement by its definition: the official legal right to make or sell an invention for a particular number of years (Cambridge Dictionary https://dictionary.cambridge.org/dictionary/english/patent)

As of 2018 total number of patent applications is 2,3 million and increase in the numbers in between 2000 and 2018 is 179 %. OECD countries which has 91 % of world's total number of patent application at 2000, has 36 % of all by 2018 (Table 2). As it can be followed from Table 2, China has 5399 % improvement in terms of patent applications and by 2018 it has 61 % of whole world.

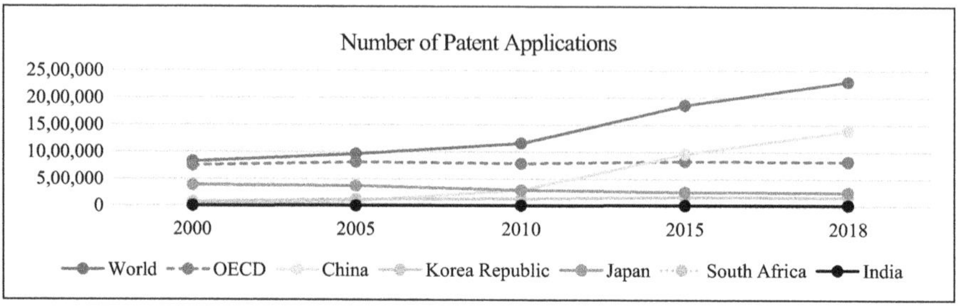

Figure 2: *Number of Patent Applications for the Selected Countries*
Resource: https://data.worldbank.org/indicator/IP.PAT.RESD

1.2.3 ICT Export of Goods/Total Exports

As the chosen third indicator of technology; information and communication technologies (ICT) export of goods to total exports, it is included computers and peripheral equipment, communication equipment, consumer electronic equipment, electronic components, and other information and technology goods as ICT goods. The idea behind getting ICT exports/Total exports ratio as an technology indicator is the theory of Hecksher-Ohlin which states that a country which is capital-abundant will export the capital-intensive good. Likewise, the country which is labor-abundant will export the labor-intensive good. Each country exports that good which it produces relatively better than the other country. In this model a country's advantage in production arises solely from its relative factor abundance (Suranovic, 2010: 60). With the main idea of Hecksher-Ohlin Theory it is assumed that counties which have the higher rate of ICT Export/Total Exports have comparative advantage about producing ICT goods.

In terms of improvement in computer technology, we can say that macroeconomic effects of computer revolution became visible especially after 1990s. Before that period; at 1980s the share of the computer sector investments was just 6 % of the whole investments excluding mortgage investments. At 2004 the share increased to 24 % (Mankiw, 2010: 267) And the latest data as of 2010 for USA is 32 % (OECD, 2020). One of the main reasons why the effects of computer technologies on the economy can not be felt in the early period is that the share of ICT investments in total investments gradually increases and it takes time for companies to use this technology (Mankiw, 2010: 267).

Table 3: *Change in ICT Exports/Total Exports Applications for the Selected Countries (2000–2017)*

Country Name	2000	2005	2010	2015	2017	Change 2000–2017
China	18	31	29	27	27	52,8 %
Korea, Rep.	34	30	21	22	25	−28,3 %
OECD members	14	11	8	7	7	−49,2 %
World	15	13	12	11	12	−22,0 %

Resource: (https://data.worldbank.org/indicator/TX.VAL.ICTG.ZS.UN)

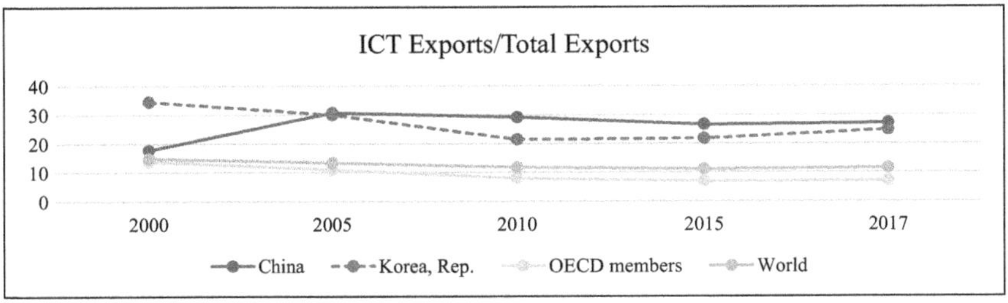

Figure 3: *ICT Exports/Total Exports for the Selected Countries*
Resource: (https://data.worldbank.org/indicator/TX.VAL.ICTG.ZS.UN)

The ratio of ICT Exports/Total Exports has a downward tendency for years between 2000 and 2017; it decreased to 12 % from 15 %. The same tendency is also valid for OECD countries (Table 3). But as we also can follow from Table 3 China's ICT Export/Total Export Ratio has increased from 18 %-2000 to 27 %-2017 which means as of 2017 nearly one third f exports are for ICT goods.

2 Data

The paper uses the annual panel data covering 2000–2017 on 33 countries which were selected within 36 OECD countries based on data availability. The countires that are included in the research are Australia, Austria, Belgium, Canada, Chile, Checz Republic, Denmark, Estonia, Finland, France, Germany, Greece, Hungary, Iceland, Israel, Japan, Latvia, Lithuania, Luxembourg, Mexico, Netherland, New Zealand, Norway, Poland, Portugal, Republic of Korea, Slovakia, Spain, Sweden, Switzerland, Turkey, United Kingdom, United States.

Table 4: *Data Details*

Abbrevation	Data	Sources
GDP	GDP Per Capita	World Bank
TFP	Total Factor Productivity	Penn World Table
PatentAppl.	Patent Applications	Worldbank
ICTExp.	ICT Exports/Total Exports	Worldbank

3 Empirical Model

In the study, it is aimed to analyze the relationship between GDP Per Capita and Total Factor Productivity, number of patent applications and ICT Exports/Total Exports ratio. The model created for this purpose is as follows:

$$GDPPerCapitait= \alpha it + \beta 1iTFPit + \beta 2PatentAppl.it + \beta 3ICTExpit + \mathcal{E}it$$

The aim is to examine the long-term co-integration relationship between the variables specified in model 1, and to determine the direction and severity of the relationship with the proper estimator in case of detection of the relationship.

The hypotheses to be tested in the study are as follows:

Hypothesis I: There is a long run relationship between GDP Per Capita and Total Factor Productivity

Hypothesis II: There is a long run relationship between GDP Per Capita and Number of Patent Applications

Hypothesis III: There is a long run relationship between GDP Per Capita and ICT Exports/Total Exports Ratio

3.1 Cross Border Dependency

Before determining a method for panel cointegration, it is a necessity to determine if there is cross-section dependency in the panel. In the globalizing world, the potential of an economic shock to be experienced in a large country with a large volume of trade, make other countries also affected by this due to the intensive transfer of goods and services between countries.

It is known that Pesaran CD test implies better results compared to Breusch and Pagan if N>T (Tatoğlu, 2018: 240). In the study N-Number of panels which is 33 is greater than T-time series which is 17. So Pesaran (2004) CD test is applied

Table 5: *Results of Cross Border Dependancy*

Test	Statistics	P-Value
CD-PDOLS Estimator	19.72	0.0000
CD-MG Estimator	46.34	0.0000

Table 6: *CADF Unit Root Test*

	Level		First Difference	
Değişken	t-bar	P-Value	t-bar	P-Value
GDPPerCapita	−1.882	0.196	−2.176	0.006
TFP	−1.760	0.433	−2.652	0.000
ICTExports/Total Exports	−2.322	0.000	−2.643	0.000
PatentNumber	−1.446	0.945	−2.849	0.000

*** % 1, ** %5 ve * %10 significant levels

to analyze cross border dependency and it is concluded that there is corelation between panel units.

3.2 Unit Root Analysis

Since the cross-section dependency was detected, the necessity of continuing the research by applying both the unit root and panel cointegration tests from the second generation groups. There are two groups of tests in panel unit root tests; While the first generation tests assume that there is no correlation between the units, the second generation tests assume that there is a correlation between the series (Tatoğlu, 2018: 22). Pesaran (2007), which is named as Cross Section Augmented Dickey Fuller (CADF), which is one of the second generation unit root tests, can also be used in cases where it is N <T or N> T (Pesaran, 2007: 266–267). Unit root detection in the CADF test includes the delayed cross-section averages of the model used in the ADF-Augmented Dickey Fuller test.

According to the CADF Unit root test (Table 6), it was determined that the series are not stationary since the t-bar value at the level is smaller than the critical value determined at the 5 % confidence level in all units of the panel. As a result of the test repeated with the first degree differences, it is seen that all variables become stagnant.

Table 7: *Westerlund Cointegration Results*

Test İst.	Value	Z-Value	P-Value	Robust P Value-100	Robust P Value-200	Robust P Value-400
Gt	−2.669	−5384	0.000	0.010	0.000	0.000
Ga	−6.668	1.051	0.853	0.020	0.010	0.010
Pt	−14.176	−5.045	0.000	0.010	0.000	0.003
Pa	−6.853	−2.349	0.009	0.010	0.020	0.010

3.3 Homogeneity Test

Swammy Test for homogenity applied and the results of the test is as follows;

Test of parameter constancy: chi2(96) = 9707.37 Prob > chi2 = 0.0000

The result of cross-section dependency and homogeneity test routed us to apply second generation and heteregenous cointegration test and apply second generation heteregenous panel estimator.

3.4 Cointegration Test

The Westerlund Cointegration test, which includes 4 cointegration tests (Ga & Gt-more reliable for homogenous group statistics, Pa & Pt-more reliable for heteregenous group statistics) and based on error correction model was applied to determine the presence of long-term relationship between variables, and bootstrap version was used for the presence of correlation between units

According to all four test results including bootsraps, it is concluded that there is a long-rung relationship between GDP Per Capita and TFV, ICT Exports and Total Exports and Patent Numbers. Thus all three hypothesis of the paper has been accepted. In order to clarify the strength of the nexus between dependent and independent variables, we apply heterogeneous PDOLS-Panel Dynamic Ordinary Least Squares Estimator.

3.5 Heterogeneous PDOLS Estimator

Pedroni's PDOLS (Group Mean Average)

Number of Panel Units:33
Number of Observations 561

Acccording to the t- statistics value for 95 % confidence interval is greater than 1.96 so all three independent variables are statistically significant. In the long run every 1 % increase in Total Factor Productivity causes 0.77 % increase in GDP

Table 8: *Heterogeneous PDOLS Estimator Results*

Variables	Beta	t-statistics
lTFP	.7712	16.77
lPatent#	.029	3.946
lICT	.1637	7.617

Per Capita, 1 % increase in patent numbers causes 0.029 % increase in GDP Per Capita and 1 % increase in ICT Exports to Total Exports Ratio causes 0.16 % increase in GDP Per Capita. Total Factor Productivity has the highest effect out of other two technology indicators but it should be taken into consideration that TFV includes not just technological improvement but also other can't measurable factors such as education. Patent number applications seems to have minor effect on GDP per capita.

4 Conclusion

Technology is a crucial phenomenon with its' both positive and negative aspects for the last half of the 20th century. Mostly all countries included technological improvement to their national development plan with the increasing efficiency property of technology idea behind. The rule of the game especially after second world war was, growth of economies, with the most important globalization tool which serves this purpose. While main purpose was growth, technology has become the most important propulsive force for both globalization and growth itself. As an indicator of technological improvement, the number of patent applications which was 823 k at the end of 2000 has increased to 2,3 million at the end of 2018 worldwide which is 179 % improvement. On the other hand, we observe that while OECD countries loose share, especially China and Korea Rep. has gained share in terms of patent number applications. China's share in the world has increased from 3 %-2000 to 61 %-2018. Parallel to patent number application numbers GDP Per Capita of China has increased from \$195 to \$ 9.771 which makes a increase of 4910 %. On the contrary for the same periods OECD Countries per capita income has increased by 354 %.

Most of the economists has made researches on the effect of technology on macro-economic indicators. And have found out that technological improvements make positive effects on macro-economic indicators. In this section it is also concluded that in the long-run technology has a positive effect on GDP Per capita. In detail; In the long run every 1 % increase in Total Factor

Productivity causes 0.77 % increase in GDP Per Capita, 1 % increase in patent numbers causes 0.029 % increase in GDP Per Capita and 1 % increase in ICT Exports to Total Exports Ratio causes 0.16 % increase in GDP Per Capita.

On the other hand, especially for the last decade many researchers study on the negative externalities; such as global warming, climate change of technology. One of the most important studies addressing the impact of technology on the environment is the Environmental Kuznet Curve study of Grossman and Krueger (1991). According to the Environmental Kuznet Curve, as countries have to consume more natural resources at the beginning of their development period, parallel to the increase in total greenhouse gas consumption, the effect of technology on environment will be negative. After a certain increase in the level of income, transition from industrialization to information society and increase in the awareness level about environmental issues, there occurs a decrease in environmental pollution.

The question for the next research must be what is the net of technology? At the bottom line did humanity gain more or loose more out of technology?

References

Atay, E. (2012). Krizden İnovasyona: Güney Kore Örneği. Dumlupınar Üniversitesi Sosyal Bilimler Dergisi, 239–254.

Fagerberg, J., & Bart Verspagen, M. C. (1997). Technology, Growth and Unemployment across European Regions. Regional Studies, 457–466.

Falk, M. (2007). R&D Spending in the High-tech Sector and Economic Growth. Research in Economics, 140–147.

Grossman, G. M., & Krueger, A. B. (1991) Environmental Impacts of a North American Free Trade Agreement, National Bureau of Economic Research Working Paper 3914 NBER, Cambridge, MA.

Islam, N., Dar, E., & Sakamato, H. (2006). Role of TFP in China's Growth. Asian Economic Journal, 127–159.

Mankiw, N. G. (2010). Makro Ekonomi. Ankara: Efil Yayınevi.

Mishkin, F. S. (2018). Makro Ekonomi Politika ve Uygulama. Ankara: Nobel Akademik Yayıncılık.

Peseran, H. M. (2004). General Diagnostic Tests for Cross Section Dependence in Panels. Discussion Paper, No. 1240 August, p. 5. https://doi.org/10.17863/CAM.5113.

Pesaran, H. M. (2007). A Simple Panel Unit Root Test in The Presence of Cross-Section Dependence. Journal of Applied Econometrics, 22(2), 265–312.

Solow, R. M. (1957). Technical Change and Aggregate Production Function. The Review of Economics and Statistics, 39(3), 312–320.

Suranovic, S. M. (2010). International Trade Theory and Policy. Boston: Flat World Knowledge.

Tatoğlu, F. Y. (2018). Panel Zaman Serileri Analizi. İstanbul: Beta Yayıncılık.

Zagorchev, A., Vasconcellos, G., & Bae, Y. (2011). The Long-run Relation among Financial Development, Technology and GDP: A Panel Cointegration Study. Applied Financial Economics, 1021–1034.

https://data.oecd.org/ict/ict-investment.htm (18.03.2020)

https://dictionary.cambridge.org/dictionary/english/patent

https://dictionary.cambridge.org/dictionary/english/patent

https://data.worldbank.org/indicator/TX.VAL.ICTG.ZS.UN

https://data.worldbank.org/indicator/IP.PAT.RESD

https://data.worldbank.org/indicator/NY.GDP.PCAP.CD

https://data.oecd.org/ict/ict-investment.htm (18.03.2020)

https://dictionary.cambridge.org/dictionary/english/patent

https://dictionary.cambridge.org/dictionary/english/patent

https://data.worldbank.org/indicator/TX.VAL.ICTG.ZS.UN

https://data.worldbank.org/indicator/IP.PAT.RESD

https://data.worldbank.org/indicator/NY.GDP.PCAP.CD

Figen Taşkın

İstanbul Mukataas between 1550 and 1605 in the Ottoman Empire[1]

1 Introduction

In the study, it was aimed to examine tax farming, which is an important issue in terms of Ottoman economic, financial and social history, through İstanbul mukataas. Only two of the mukataas given to tax farming, which was considered important to meet the cash needs of the Ottoman Empire and to operate the tax sources, were examined.

Due to the difficulties in investigating the mukataas and tax farming at large spatial and time dimension, İstanbul was selected as the settlement unit in the empire and the second half of the 16th century was selected as the period. Since İstanbul was the capital city and also located on significant trade routes, it was assumed that mukataas may yield more profits and therefore would be more demanded by tax-farmers. In the study, the boundaries of İstanbul covered the city walls region, which is called "Nefs-i İstanbul", and Bilâd-ı Selâse (three district: Üsküdar, Galata and Eyüp) qadi regions.

The period between the years 1550 and 1605 also covers the period during which inflation was experienced rapidly, especially after the 1570s.[2] It was possible to find interesting answers, since the period we discussed covered the periods before, during and after high inflation. In this period, it can also be observed how inflation affected the government's policy to give mukataas to tax farmers and how it was reflected in tax farming charges. It is also possible to find an answer to the question "How was the change of tax-farmers in the changing environment?".

---

1 This study was carried out by Figen Taşkın (1992) by shortening from the study entitled Tax-farmers and İstanbul Mukataas in the Ottoman Empire (1550–1605) (Unpublished Master's Thesis, Istanbul University, Institute of Social Sciences).

2 BARKAN, Ö. L. Indicates that inflation was observed after the second half of the 16th century ("Türkiye'de Fiyat Hareketleri, Belleten, v. 341 no.136, page 561). BRAUDEL, indicates that rapid inflation occurred in Mediterranean countries including the Ottoman Empire after the 1570s (Mediterranean and Mediterranean World, c. 1, Eren yayıncılık. İst. 1989, p. 346)

İstanbul mukataas were mostly examined through mukataa registers in the "Maliyeden Müdevver Classifications", the reason for which was that there were few or no registers complying with the time and space limits of the subject in other classifications.

One of the most important terms commonly used in the study was mukataa. Mukataa refers to a source of revenues entered into the central national treasury. In a sense, it is the source of revenues used to meet the central and especially cash expenditures of the government. There are also mukataas that are partially used to cover in-kind expenditures. For instance, while İstanbul barrel stave mukataa was given to tax farming for 9 years starting from Gurre-i Recep 1013 (13 November 1604), 30.000 barrel staves were stipulated to be given to the Imperial Dockyard (Tersane-i Amire) each year (MM 9821. p. 40).

The subject of mukataas is "...the right of disposition on a real business such as mine, saltworks, mint, fishery or the collection of some duties and taxes, such as customs and ispençe (tax on non-Muslims)..." (Sahillioğlu, H. 1963: 146).

The geographical borders and source of revenues of mukataa are definite. There could be more than one source of revenues within a mukataa unit. These sources of revenues did not have to be in the same geographic region. Ahyolu memlahası and İstanbul and Varna warehouse mutakaas can be shows as examples for it (Taşkın, 1992: 22) What was important was which mutakaas were taken by the tax-farmer.

The Ottoman Empire applied the timar system and tax farming method in taxation and tax collection between the years of 1550–1605. Each of these financial methods was aimed at meeting different financial needs of the state. "Timar system", that existed since the foundation of the Ottoman Empire[3], was the financial method that was used in the collection of taxes in different regions as the financial basis of the local military and administrative organization of the state. It became a significant mainstay for the Ottoman State, that could not establish a central administrative and financial system.

A civil servant was appointed from the center for the determination and collection of taxes in certain dirlik (fief) lands (there were three types of dirlik consisting of timar (small fief), zeamet (middle fief) and has (large fief), according to their income). This civil servant also had military obligations such as protecting the area and going with his soldiers he was responsible for feeding

3 BELDICINEAU, N. documents that the timar system was recognized as an institution since the beginning of the Ottoman Empire (Timar in the Ottoman Empire from the 14th century to the 16th century, Teori yayınları, Ankara 1985). C5

when called for military expedition. He did not send the taxes he collected to the center but he used them to fulfill such obligations. Through this system, the state also formed its local military power, which was the basis of central army, along with its administrative and financial system.

The start date of "tax farming", which was intended to complete the timar system, was approximately after Fatih Sultan Mehmet conquered İstanbul (Ahmed Aşıkı, 1332: 142). However, Suleiman the Magnificent started to use ulufeli eminler (trustees with ulufe [salaries]) in the administration of mukataas since 1538, and thus, ulufeli eminler were employed in the majority of mukatas in 1544 (AKDAĞ, M. 1974: 288). After the second half of the 16th century, its field of application became widespread in an inflationary environment.

In tax farming, as a rule, mukataa was hired to a private person who guaranteed to give the highest amount in a given period and who could provide surety. Mukataas that were not subject to bargaining and were given for a certain amount were also included in the scope of tax farming.[4] It was observed that "Hass-ı Hümayun (land owned by the Ottoman crown)" was also given to tax farming, which was one of the sources of revenue of the Hazine-i Amire (Imperial Treasury), although it did not bear the name mukataa. With the coffee tax of Istanbul and its surroundings, the fact that the mukataas of the lands of Rumeli and Anatolian provinces were given to tax farming from February 8, 1596 is an example (MM 399, p.42).

The state asked qadis to carry out studies to make sure that tax farming charges could be paid by the person who collected tax farming and his guarantors. The statement "... mezkur mültezim Mehmed'i ve 50.000 akçenin zararına vereceği küfelasın ve müzekkilerin ehl-i vukuftan dikkat ve ihtimamıyle teftiş edib göresin... " (p. 82) in the tezkire (collection of biographies) written to the qadi of İstanbul for İstanbul un kapanı mukataa in the Maliyeden Müdevver Classification register no.233 is the best example of asking qadis to investigate the claim for tax farming. However, after the investigation was found to be positive, charter was given for tax farming. In the same source, there is a statement that the document would be given if the investigation would be positive. The statement is as follows" ...malın edasına kadir oldukları malumumuz olduktan

4 The register no. 5954 in the Maliyeden Müdevver Classification includes a record regarding giving the mukataa to tax farming over a fixed amount determined by the state. The statement in the record is as follows "...Nefs-i İstanbul ve Anadolu ve Tokat ve Amasya ve Sivas ve Merzifon ve Kayseri ve Nefs-i Ankarave Trabzon ve Kefe ermenilerinin resm-i murahhasa mukataası sene-i 998 Ramazanı gurresinden ber vech-i maktu' her sene kırk iki bin iki yüz kırk akçe teslim eylemek... ".

sonra mültezimi ve küfelasının ve müzekkilerin sakin oldukları mahallerin ve kudretlerin ve mültezimin şartını ve iltizamın sebt-i sicil edib suret-i sicil imzalayıb Dergah-ı Mualla'ya götürtesin ve yazıb bildiresiniz ki Hazine-i Amire defterine kayd olunub berat-ı hümayun için mültezime tezkire verile." (p. 82).

The most important point underlying the tax farming was that the state obtained some of the mukataa's revenue in advance. The person who claimed for tax farming had to deposit a part of the tax farming charges as a down payment to the Hazine-i Amire (Imperial Treasury) while taking over the mukataa. The register no. MM 624 includes a document regarding how much down payment could be. The statement in the document is as follows: "ber vech-i peşini Hazine-i Amire'ye dört yük ve beş bin iki yüz yirmi akçe teslim edib altı yıla varınca yirmi yedi yük akçe, iltizam edib . . . " (p.74).

The possibility of two conditions was important for the state to meet its ever-increasing need for cash money after the second half of the 16th century. The first condition was that the demand for mukataa and parallelly tax farming charges should be increasing, and the second condition was the presence of people who could afford to collect tax farming in society.

Another term used in the documents is bond. While bonds have various meanings, it is the name given to the period of giving mukataa to tax farming in the Ottoman financial literature. Bond also refers to savings for mukataa within the period mentioned (Sahillioğlu, H. 1963: 146).

A bond period is usually 3 lunar years (Akdağ: 288). We see that the bond period is 1 year as a practice (Akdağ: 288). The tax farming procedure was not limited to a time of bond period. There were agreements in which the tax farming period was 6, 9 and 12 years (Sahillioğlu, H. 1963: 146). However, the expression of these periods in the form of 2, 3 and 4 bonds indicates that the rule that the tax farming procedure was limited to a bond was valid. The record on taking İstanbul slaughterhouse mukataa and its surroundings to tax farming for 3 bonds (that is, 9 years) since Gurre-i Safer 998 (30 November 1589) can be shown as an example (MM 7101, varak 9).

When a suitor was taken into tax farming while mukataa was on someone else, tax farming was not interrupted and the bond period would continue in the presence of the state. In other words, the bond period of the suitor would be as before, he would have taken the tax farming for the remaining period. which was the reason why bond periods of different people who took the same mukataa would occasionally coincide. The statements "Mahmiyye-i İstanbul'da pençik mukataasını sene-i 995 Zilhiccesinin yirmi altısında vaki olan Nevruz'un on sekizinden üç tahvile . . .Simon nam-ı yahudi iltizam edib . . . Mehmed nam kimesne Divan-ı Ali'ye gelib mukataa-ı mezbureye ibtida-i tarihden iltizam sabıka mucebince... iltizamı ve kabul edib..." (part 4) in the record in the register no. MM 3902 can be shown as example for it. A new bond period would be given to the suitor if he wished in a certain time of the bond period, so 4, 5-year tax farming periods appeared. According to the record in the register no.D.İSM 25365, it was possible "...hala dokuz yüz seksen yedi Şevvali gurresinden bakiyye kalan bir seneye üç sene dahi ilhak olunub iltizam-ı sabıka üzere dört yıla ... mukataa inayet buyrulursa..." (p. 2).

The term bond was also used in another way. The collection, the transaction of which was completed, was recorded in the account book under the title of "an tahvil" (Sahillioğlu, H., 1988: 13). It shows the amounts paid by the tax-farmer in installments from tax farming charges. The register no. 3802 in the Maliyeden Müdevver Classifications includes the records on bond transactions of tax-farmers.

According to the definition of Abdurrahman Vefik, tax-farmer is "...iltizam eden, üzerine lazım add eyleyen, üstüne alan, deruhde eden, hazinenin malını taahhüd eyleyen iltizamcı"dır (Abdurrahman Vefik, 1328: 266). Briefly, it is the person who takes mukataa to tax farming. In other words, tax-farmer is the person who takes tax farming for a certain price for a bond period and covers the profit or loss arising from the operation of the mukataa. In a sense, tax-farmers are contractors who are engaged in the works of the government.

The person who takes mukataa to tax farming "...has to pay an amount of two per thousand (0.2 %) of the total tax farming charges to the bailiff who came from Istanbul for this job every year by the name rüsum-ı bevvaban and rüsum-ı çavuşan in response to the salaries of kapucular and çavuşlar...also has to pay a fee called resm-i berat akçesi to the department of finance" along with the tax farming charges he has committed to pay (Akdağ, 1974: 289).

Tax-farmers required that conditions involving some issues, such as the protection of the revenues of mukataa, increasing taxes, and the employment of the people he wanted in the administration of the mukataa, should be included in the tax farming agreement. The tax farming agreement regarding Doors of Istanbul, Edirnekapı, Vize and Kırkkilise bac-ı pay-ı ağnam mukataas included the condition for the protection of the revenues of the mukataa. This condition was formulated in the way that when groups of herdsmen and butcher sold sheep, lambs and beef without paying tax and without the permission of the tax-farmer, an amount of money as much as the bac amount was confiscated from them for the state, and it was deducted from the debt of the tax-farmer (MM 9821, p.56).

An example for increasing the revenue of the mukataa in the tax farming agreement can be shown from the register no. MM 3902. There is a condition to increase taxes in the tax farming agreement made for Istanbul, Galata,

Thessaloniki, Bursa, Edirne and its surroundings, Jews, Armenians and kafirin kesim-i üsera mukataa. While 80 akçe was taken from unbelieving servants and non-muslim concubines of the Jewish, non-muslim and dhimmi groups residing in the region, it was stipulated to take 160 akçe in the bond period starting from twenty seventh of 997 Recebi (MM 3902, part 3).

There are many documents regarding the fact that the tax-farmer stipulated the employment of the people he wanted for the administration of the mukataa in the tax farming agreement. In one of them, the person who took Istanbul customs and environmental mukataa to tax farming stipulated in the tax farming agreement that all clerks and other janitors should be those he desired (D. İSM 25365, 1.parça. p. 3).

While the tax-farmer had the conditions he wanted included in the tax farming agreement, the state also had the authority to terminate tax farming before the bond period was over. A suitor who committed to pay higher tax farming charges could give mukataa to tax farming. The tax-farmer also had no the right to demand compensation for the damage incurred by the interruption of the tax farming. However, he stipulated in the tax farming agreement that the down payment he paid while entering tax farming would be returned to him by the new tax farmer. There are many documents including the condition regarding the refunding of the down payment given by the tax farmer at the beginning of tax farming. The person who took İstanbul pençik mukataa to tax farming stipulated in the tax farming agreement that when someone else asked for the mukataa, mukataa should not be given to anyone else giving the whole six yük akçe down payment to him (MM 3902, part 4).

TRUSTEESHIP: The principle of "trusteeship", that was used when the tax farming method was not applied, is the administration of mukataa by a civil servant and the collection of revenues. The fact that no one desired for the tax farming of mutakaa could be a reason for the application of trusteeship (Sahillioğlu, 1963: 147). In the register no. 3902 in the Maliyeden Müdevver Classifications, there is a document explaining why the Istanbul Jewish beytülmal mukataa was given to trusteeship. The statement in the document is as follows "...sene-i 987 tarihinde iltizamda iken mahsul gösterilmemekle cevab vermedikleri sebebinden bu ana değin iltizam ile kimesne taleb olmayub ber vech-i emanet verilmişdi..." (MM 3902, part 35).

Although the state left the collection or saving of the mukataa revenues to the tax-farmers, "...assigns a trustee by itself to check its accounts" (İnalcık, 1954: 19). Furthermore, the trustee had the administrative responsibility of mukataa.

If the trustee wanted to gain profit from the collection of revenues of the mukataa, he could take mukataa to tax farming by appropriating his salaries to tax farming charges (Sahillioğlu, 1963: 147; Akdağ, 1974: 290). These people were called "ber vech-i iltizam emini" or "emin-i mültezim". The statement "İstanbul'da vaki olan un kapanına ber vech-i iltizam emini olan Hafiz" in a document in the register no. 233 in the Maliyeden Müdevver Classifications can be shown as an example. The statement in the register no. MM 619 in which the term emin-i mültezim was used is as follows "... mukataa-ı memleha-ı Ahyolu ve anbar-ı memleha der İstanbul ve Varna der uhde-i Mihal emin-i mültezim.." (p. 6). He would take responsibility for profit or loss as the tax-farmer. Even though his mukataas lost, they would have to pay tax farming charges they committed, just like the tax-farmers.

2 İstanbul Mukataas (1550–1605)

Although the settlement area where mukataas were present was limited to "Nefs-i İstanbul", and Bilad-ı Selase (Üsküdar, Galata and Eyüp qadis), it will be observed that it also covers other places. The reason for this was that mukataas could spread to other regions other than İstanbul and Bilad-ı selase.

The total number of mukataas engaged in tax farming in Istanbul between the years 1550 and 1605 appears to be 37. In tax farming transactions of them, it was generally examined how much their income was. "Debt" and "bond" records do not provide much information about the content of the mukataa, they showed which mukataas were they.

In some of mukataas' tax farming dates, the names of the months are called "şemsi". This is because "... the names of the months of the solar year were used in the tax farming tenders, which were mostly held during the solar year,, while giving mukataas to tax-farmers, and also each time, these months were expressed with the year of the hegira, the month of the year they encountered..." (Sahillioğlu, 1988: 417).

1. İhtisab and ihzariye mukataa of Boğazkesen castle

The narh (fixed price) policy was valid in the trade within the boundaries of the Ottoman Empire. The prices of the goods produced and sold in accordance with the narh policy would be determined by the state according to their quality and variety. They were inspected by "muhtesib" coming after the "grand vizier" and "qadi" within the ihtisab institution. He would punish the tradesmen who did not apply the narh and produced bad goods, and he also collected a tax called "ihtisab tax". " This tax was collected since... it was stamped in cities and towns and in fairgrounds and market districts with the titles such as stamp, mizan, evzan and ekyal ve yevmiye-i dekkakin, bac-ı pazar …" (Ergin, 1338: 362). Stamp tax was collected from the "…manufacturers of the goods and the goods from the mine, horseshoes, copper, trays, jewelry or other gold and silver articles…" (Kazıcı, 1987:170). Yevmiye-i dekkakin was the tax collected every day from shop owners selling daily necessities (Kazıcı, 1987: 158). Bac-ı pazar would be known as " purchase and sale tax in the Ottoman city market…" (Kazıcı, 1987: 175). "Mizan tax" was the tax collected from weighing of the silk yarn, "evzan" and "ekyal" were the tax collected from weighing instruments.

Amounts of ihtisab tax during the reign of Suleiman the Magnificent

1. 1 akçe of 40 akçe of leather, honey, oil and similar goods sold by Muslims and unbelievers coming from the provinces was taken;
2. 2 akçe was taken from fabric, cloth, yarn, çuka, linen, pink, tin, lead and all such goods;
3. 1 akçe was taken from early grown yemiş yükü, and 2 akçe was taken from bol yemiş yükü;
4. When bir eşek yükü odun entered the castle, 1 wood was taken as the tax of the porter;
5. A total of 4 akçe, 2 akçe from the purchaser and 2 akçe from the seller when the cattle was sold, was taken;
6. A total of 4 akçe, 2 akçe from the purchaser and 2 akçe from the seller, was taken for the weighing instrument on which the cattle was weighed;
7. 1 akçe was taken for two sheep when the sheep from the provinces was slaughtered and sold. 1 akçe was taken for four sheep if the local butcher slaughtered it;
8. 130 akçe was taken from a shipload;
9. 4 akçe was taken from a trolley of onions, and 8 akçe was taken from rice and fish;
10. A total of 4 akçe, 2 akçe from the purchaser and 2 akçe from the seller, was taken the prisoner was sold;
11. Tax was collected at the rate of 2 % of the value of all goods coming from Eflak, Frank, Dubrovnik and other places;
12. 1 wood was taken from a trolley of woods;
13. 10 pieces of akçe were taken from bir fıçu suçu (means wine in Old Turkish) coming to the city;
14. 1 akçe was taken per pig fed for slaughtering;
15. 1 akçe was taken from the load of all grain varieties and two sheep coming for sale;

16. No tax was collected from the sheep that came up to six weeks after the kefere küfrü (Perhiz-i kebir and the big festival after it), but, 1 akçe from the sheep coming after that and 2 akçe from the cattle were taken;
17. 2 akçe from a cattle hide and 1 akçe from pigskin were taken,
18. 6 akçe was taken from each load of salt, cheese and honey;
19. 1 akçe was taken from 15-akçe oil bag;
20. 12 akçe was taken from each pastav (In the old Istanbul and Galata dellaliye code, it was declared that it was customary for each pastav to have 50 archine.), 2 akçe was taken from the sewed çuka kaftan;
21. 12 akçe was taken from a load of olive oil;
22. 6 akçe from a load of dry fish and 4 akçe from a load of wet fish were taken
23. 1 akçe was taken from a load of ice;
24. 4 akçe was taken from a load of linen;
25. 1 akçe was taken from dyed and white kaftanlık aba;
26. 6 akçe was taken from a load of iron, but, no akçe was taken from the iron required for mining (Ergin, 1338: 366–368).

Another tax collected by muhtesib, "ihzariye" is a term used about money received in response to the muhzır sent or the travel expenses given to the bailiff (Pakalın, 1946: 45). İhzariye fee ". . .was taken from the plaintiff. . .in the courts.. and from the libellee in administrative invitations" (Pakalın, 1946: 45). While there is no document regarding the amount of ihzariye fee, Mustafa Akdağ calculated that a 2 % fee was charged in personal actions (p. 101).

Mukataa was first taken to tax farming by committing 10,000 akçe tax farming charges for 3 years starting from Gurre-i Şevval 976 (19 March 1569). As required by per diem deduction, the state gave it to tax farming on condition that 3,333 akçe would be paid annually. Although the tax-farmer had no debt after 1-year tax farming, another suitor took tax farming for 3 years from Gurre-i Şevval 977 (9 March 1570). He increased the tax farming charge by 1,000 akçe (MM 166. varak 6, 4).

After a long time, tax farming was provided by committing an amount of 13,000 akçe for 3 years after Gurre-i Şaban 986 (22 October 1578) (MM 312, p.11, 28). A few months later, it was given to another suitor for 13,000 akçe in 3 installments for 3 years, without showing a reason, after Gurre-i Şevval 986 (1 December 1578) (MM5640, p.9).

Tax farming was provided for 13,000 akçe with its rüsum for 3 years from Gurre-i Şevval 989 (29 October 158l). However, there is a record indicating that 8.666, the amount that needed be paid in 2 years, was not paid (MM 6148, p. 130. MM 1838, p. 33).

Tax farming was provided for 13,000 akçe for 3 years from Gurre-i Ramazan 991 (8 September 1583). This tax farming was started by deducting the tax farming of previous tax-farmers who did not pay their debts. The government asked this debt to be covered by the new recipients of tax farming. However, it was also stated that it would be deducted from the installments of the last year (MM 6148, p. 130).

Tax farming was provided for 15,000 akçe for 3 years from Gurre-i Şevval 995 (24 August 1587). The tax-farmer requested that his salaries would be deducted from his debth while taking the mukataa. After this bond, he also wanted to take tax farming for 6 year from Gurre-i Şevval 998 (24 July 1590). The tax farming charge promised to be given was 30,000 akçe. Again he showed his salaries in return for his debt. He noted that 4 people from Boğazkesen residents would be guarantors in return for property damage (MM 9820, p. 32).

After a long time, tax farming charges increased significantly, and after 25 Şaban 1008 (3 March 1600), tax farming was provided since it was committed to pay 36,000 akçe for 6 years (MM 9820, p. 4).

After all these tax farming transactions, tax farming charges increased significantly. However, it is observed that the real value of the amount committed for the purchase of the tax farming on 24 August 1587 after inflation decreased significantly, as seen in Table 1.

2. bac-ı pay-ı ağnam mukataa of Edirnekapı, Doors of Istanbul and its surroundings

The tax that the state received from the sale of sheep (animals, including lamb, beef and pork, the meat of which is utilized) to butchers was called "bac-ı pay-ı ağnam" (Greenwood, 1988: 43). The animals listed other than the sheep are mentioned among the income sources of bac-ı pay-ı ağnam mukataa in the documents used (MM 9821, p. 56). The region of the mukataa subject to this tax is Edirnekapı[5], Doors of Istanbul and its surroundings. It is observed that "surrounding" was Vize and Kırkkilise in the tax farming agreement starting from 13 Şevval 987 (4 December 1579) (MM 1838, p. 26. MM 6209, p. 42). In the next records, surrounding is written clearly.

5 Edirne Kapısı selected as "Bab-ı Edirne" in the records is one of the ten big gates on the land that lies between Yedikule and Ayvansaray around the castle, which remained from Byzantine, which surrounded the city of Istanbul . . ." (KOÇU, R. E., İstanbul Ansiklopedisi, c. 9, Koçu yayınları, İst. 1967, p. 4922)

Table 1: *Tax Farming Periods and Tax Farming Charges of the İhtisab and İhzariye Mukataa of Boğazkesen castle*

Tax Farming Period (christian era)	Tax Farming Charge (akçe)	Tax Farming Charge per year (akçe)	Index	Real value compared to 1489/ 1490 prices (akçe)	Index
3 years from 19 March 1569	10,000	3,333	100		
3 years from 9 March 1570	11,000	3,666	110		
3 years from 22 October 1578	13,000	4,333	130		
3 years from 1 December 1578	13,000	4,333	130		
3 years from 29 October 1581	13,000	4,333	130		
3 years from 8 September 1583	13,000	4,333	130		
3 years from 24 August 1587	15,000	5,000	150	1,569,858	
3 years from 24 July 1590	30,000	10,000	300		
3 years from 3 March 1600	36,000	12,000	360		

(*) The indices in Ö. Lütfi Barkan's article entitled "Price Movements in Turkey in second half of the 16th century" (Belleten, c. 34, no. 136, TTK. Ankara 1970, p.569) were used to show to what extent the inflation rate in this table and other tables affected the tax farming charges.

While bac was not collected from sefer sheep, the sheep brought by herdsmen was subject to tax. In a document, it is observed that the butchers in İstanbul demanded that bac would not be taken by considering the sheep bought by herdsmen as sefer sheep. In the same document, tax-farmers also reported to the department of finance that the tax farming charge would be increased by 40,000 akçe in case of collecting bac from sefer sheep (MM 1838, p. 26. MM 6209, p. 42).

The revenues of mukataas and the rules for meeting the meat need of Istanbul are listed as follows:

1. Taking 1 akçe from two sheep coming to the door with hujjat, 1 akçe from Haymana sheep coming from Eflak, Boğdan, Rumeli and Karaman, 1 akçe from sheep and lamb, 2 akçe from cattle and 5 akçe from pig that were sold

and sacrificed in Vize and Kırkkilise sanjaks; taking bac by law from the lamb and ewe sheep suitable for slaughtering brought to Kalyoz[6] and sold;
2. Arresting those who secretly bring and sell sheep, lambs and cattle without giving bac and putting their financial asset into account of tax-farmer
3. Not selling in any place other than Edirnekapı Tokat[7]. Arresting the seller, if sold;
4. The çavuş who came to Istanbul to ask for cereals would not buy sheep;
5. Not distributing the sheep coming to door without the order of "Koyun Emini"[8];
6. If the group of herdsmen and butchers sold sheep, lamb and beef without giving bac, taking the amount sold on behalf of the state and deducting it from the account of the tax-farmer;
7. Not passing through the sheep from another place other than Edirnekapı.

The first tax farming record was that tax farming was provided with a tax farming charge of 1,331,870 akçe for 3 years from Gurre-i Zilhicce 969 (2 August 1562) (MM 166, varak 14). 1,350,000 akçe was proposed for 3-year tax farming starting from Gurre-i Zilhicce 972 (30 June 1565) (MM 166, varak 15). In the record on tax farming agreement that started from 13 Şevval 987 (4 December 1579), it is observed that there was 290. 000 akçe "kesir" (deficit that arises if the expected crop is not obtained) in two slaughterhouses. It shows that during this period, slaughterhouses were the sources of income for this mukataa. The tax farming charge for 3-year bonds was 1,300,000 akçe (MM 1838. p. 26. MM 6209. p. 42).

A charge of 1,300,000 akçe was committed for tax farming for 3 years from 17 Zilkade 990 (4 December 1580). There was a condition that the kesir remaining from the previous tax farming should be paid in fabric and çuka and then tax farming should be started. After the place of residence and fortune of those who provided surety while tax-farmer was taking tax farming were investigated by qadis and made into registers, they were sent to Asitane-i Amire (MM 5640, p. 2. MM 6209, p. 42–43). There is a provision sent to various qadis related to sending the desired sheep until 3 Cemaziyelahir 993 (3 June 1585) (Altınay, A. Refik, 1953: 98-99). This provision shows that the fact that the sheep was not sent on

6 The place where animals are brought and their sales tax are collected (GREENWOOD, A, İstanbul's meat. . ., p. 45).
7 Here is also the place where animals are brought and the sales tax is collected (GREENWOOD, A, A.g. e., p. 45).
8 Koyun emini, is the person who is engaged in selling and slaughtering the sheep (See. GREENWOOD, A, a.g.e., p. 45, 46).

time was a factor that reduces the return of the mukataa and therefore the tax farming charges. In this period, in other words between the years 1580 and 1583, 651,109 sheep sent by celepkeşan yielded an income of 325,554 akçe.

3 Conclusion

The method of giving mukataas to tax farming started after the conquest of Istanbul in the period of Fatih Sultan Mehmet. Nevertheless, there was an increase in giving mukataas to tax farming in the reign of Suleiman the Magnificent during which cash need increased more. It was determined that there were thirty seven mukataas in and around Istanbul between the years 1550 and 1605 discussed. By examining the records of these mukataas, the meanings of the terms mukataa, tax farming, trusteeship, tax-farmer and bonds were revealed.

In the Ottoman economic and social history literature, there are studies considering tax-farmers as the people who rob the public and even free riders. The fallaciousness of this was not detected in the study, but the logic of tax-farmer in robbing the people and the state was understood. The right of tax-farmer to hold the mukataa that he purchased by tender for a certain period of time was not protected against the state's authority to terminate the unilateral tax farming agreement. Therefore, it assumed that the tax-farmer may have unjustly benefited from the revenues of the mukataa in order to maximize his profits as much as he could hold.

It was observed from the tax farming records that the tax farming provided a certain income to the state. The state was able to increase the tax farming charges in the period during which inflation increased. The reason why the state terminated the contract of the previous tax-farmer in the face of another suitor's increasing the tax farming charge despite the existing tax farming agreement was an effort to increase its own profit.

References

A. Başbakanlık Osmanlı Arşivi Belgeleri, İstanbul (BOA)

Maliyeden Müdevver Tasnifi (MM), Defterdarlık İstanbul Mukataası Tasnifi.

B. Secondary Sources

Akdağ, Mustafa. Türkiye'nin İktisadi ve İçtimai Tarihi, 2. Basımı, 2. cilt. Cem yayınevi, İst. 1974. s. 288.

Ahmed Aşıki, Aşık Paşazade Tarihi. Maarif-i Umumiye Nezaret-i Celilesi yayını. Matbaa-ı Amire. İst. 1332

Ahmet Vefik, Abdurrahman. Tekalif-i Kavaidi, c.l, Dersaadet, 1328

Altınay, Ahmet Refik, On Altıncı Asırda İstanbul Hayatı (1553–1591), 2. Basım, İstanbul Devlet Basımevi, İstanbul. 1935.

Barkan, Ö. Lütfi, "Price Movements in Turkey in second half of the 16th century", Belleten, c. 34, no. 136, TTK. Ankara. 1970.

Beldicineau, N. 14. yüzyıldan 16. yüzyıla Osmanlı Devleti'nde Tımar, Teori yayınları, Ankara, 1985.

Ergin, Osman Nuri. Mecelle-i Umur-u Belediye. c.1. Matbaa-ı Amire, İst. 1338.

Greenwood, Antony, İstanbul's meat provisioning, a study of the celebkeşan system, doktora tezi, Chicago, Illinois 1988.

İnalcık, Halil, Hicri 835 tarihli Suret-i Defter-i Sancak-i Arnavid, Türk Tarih Kurumu yayını, Ankara. 1954.

Kazici, Ziya, Osmanlılarda İhtisab Müessesesi (Ekonomik, Dini ve Sosyal Hayat). Kültür Basın Yayın Birliği, İst. 1987.

Koçu, R. E., İstanbul Ansiklopedisi, c. 9, Koçu yayınları, İstanbul. 1967.

Pakalin, M. Zeki, Osmanlı Tarih Deyimleri ve Terimleri Sözlüğü, c. 2, Milli Eğitim Basımevi, İstanbul. 1946.

Sahillioğlu, H. "Bir mültezim zimem defterine göre Darphane Mukataası". İ. Ü. İktisat Fak. Mecmuası, c. 2. sayı 1–2, İst. 1963.

Sahillioğlu, H., Türk İktisat Tarihi yüksek lisans ders notları. İst. 1988.

Sahillioğlu, H. "1524–1525 Osmanlı Bütçesi", Ö. L. Barkan'a Armağan, İ. Ü. İktisat Fak. Mecmuası, c. 41, sayı 1–2, İst. 1988 pp. 415–449.

Taşkın, Figen, Tax-farmers and İstanbul Mukataas in the Ottoman Empire (1550–1605), Unpublished Master's Thesis, Istanbul University, Institute of Social Sciences, 1992.

Selami Erdoğan & Fikret Karakoç

Britain as the Source of the Parliamentary Government System[1]

1 Introduction

The classification of government systems is a classification made by considering the mutual relations of the legislative, executive and judicial powers that are accepted as basic organs. Roughly, these systems are divided into two, based on the union of powers and those based on separation of powers. Systems based on the union of powers have largely lost their validity. There are three government systems that are widely adopted today, all based on separation of powers. These systems are; the parliamentary system is the presidential system and the semi-presidential system.

While the presidential system is based on the principle of separation of hard powers, the parliamentary system is based on the principle of separation of soft powers. The semi-presidential system, another government system, is; It emerged in France as a system that is a mixture of the two. It has been successfully applied in France since 1958. The presidential system is known as the USA-originated government system. It is regarded as a system successfully implemented in this country. The homeland of the parliamentary government model is England. In this study, the parliamentary system that has been successfully applied in England for many years; conceptual framework, historical background, general characteristics and example of England as a model country will be examined.

2 Conceptual Framework and Historical Background of the Parliamentary System

As one of the oldest systems, we see a parliamentary system. Conceptually Parliamentarism; It is the general name of the system where governments are responsible for the legislature consisting of representatives of the people. Before the theory of separation of powers, it is seen that all power in England belongs to

1 This study is derived from the master's thesis prepared and presented by Fikret Karakoç under supervision of Selami Erdoğan at Kutahya Dumlupinar University, Institute of Social Sciences, Department of Public Administration Thesis was name as "Presidential System in Turkey Debate in the Context of Political Stability"

the monarch or the king. However, with the formation of this system over time, a period began in which the distribution of power changed, the powers of the king was limited, and the parliament was formed. The relationship between parliament and the king is increasingly established on solid grounds.

Today, the parliamentary government system can be defined as follows. There is in the parliamentary government "there is a politically irresponsible head of state, the separation of Powers between the executive and the legislature is soft, a representative regime in which the legal relationship between the bodies is based on equality and balance" (Fendoğlu, 2013: 573). As a result of this opinion, the system allows interaction between powers and brings the executive body to the fore. Since the system is based on soft separation, the legislative and executive organs appear to functionally and organically influence each other.

If we look at the historical background of the parliamentary system; it is understood that the parliamentary system emerged in England and later developed and changed. There are also important points that lie on the historical background of the parliamentary government system. The first of these points is the Magna Carta Declaration. The other is the Westminster model, on which the origin of the system is based (Arslan, 2001: 28–29).

In this context, the Magna Carta Declaration, which was first signed in England in 1215, stands out on the basis of the emergence and development of the parliamentary system in England (Yayla, 2014: 99). The basis of the declaration is the changing management approach between the king and the people. This change caused some of the king's powers to be restricted and the existence of rights granted to citizens. In this case, the management approach that changed with the Magna Carta Declaration in the 13th century has become the basis of the parliamentary system. In addition, the following are based on the parliamentary system that has survived to the present day. Political techniques, protection of freedom of citizens, restriction of state forces ect. On the other hand, constitutional movements have emerged as a factor strengthening this system (Şıvgın, 1997: 92).

In the process of emergence and development of the parliamentary system, the king's powers are limited and an advisory board is increasingly developing (Bitkin, 2018: 20). Thus, it was encountered that the participants were determined democratically and started to take the form of consultation meetings over time. These consultation meetings have turned into places of speech, which meant parliament and where speeches were held. In other words, these places have become platforms for explaining political ideas and thoughts. Thus, it is thought that this situation led to the emergence of the concept of parliament. Thus, it is thought that this situation led to the emergence of the concept of parliament. The parliamentary system is a system that has been formed for centuries and which has been created on the presenter of democratic awareness of the society. In other words, this system is a natural system, not fictionalized.

Another point on the historical background of the parliamentary system; It is the Westminster model that was born and developed in England as the origin of the system (Lijphart, 2006: 21). The Westminster model, which is the origin of parliamentarism, is essentially an English model. It is also a model in which the executive is strong and the legislature (House of Commons and House of Lords) is weak. The adoption of the Westminster model, on the other hand, affected the fiction of the parliamentary system and the position of the state among the powers. Thus, it can be said that this system has developed within the framework of the Magna Carta Declaration and the Westminster model. In addition, the researches show that the modern parliamentary system is a system emerging in countries with old state tradition. This feature points out that the basis of the system is the result of the influence of historical, cultural and social events.

However, the concepts of parliament and parliamentarism refer to an egalitarian and legal boundary regime. This government model appears to have emerged in countries with some traditional and royal elements. On the other hand, apart from the historical effect, the important effect of the parliamentary system came from the geographical features of the country. The parliamentary system is a UK-born system. However, this system has developed over time, has spread and has been exposed to differences. There are two countries where differences are most noticeable in the implementation of the system. These two countries are England and Germany. While the parliamentary system implemented in the UK is in a monarchy and central political structure, the parliamentary system implemented in Germany is in a republican and federal structure (Arslan, 2001: 28). The reasons that reveal this difference are cultural, traditional, geographical and historical influences. In this case, it affects the management understanding of countries to a large extent as well as democratic conditions. However, although there are differences in the implementation of the parliamentary system of countries, there are certain points that are accepted as the general features of the system.

3 General Features of the Parliamentary System

The system based on the soft forces separation among the forms of government organization is the parliamentary system (Yayla, 2014: 71). The parliamentary system is a representative management system. In accordance with the principles of separation of powers, the country's administration has been softly divided into three bodies as legislative, executive and judicial powers (Arslan, 2001: 28). the parliamentary system is based on cooperation between these three forces. In this case, there is no sharp mention of organic and functional separation among powers in parliamentary systems. From this perspective, the general features of parliamentary systems are as follows.

In parliamentary systems, the executive body generally has two heads. This is marked by two-headed execution. It is a system based first on the President and secondly on the Prime Minister and the Council of Ministers (Gözler, 2004: 100). Also, execution in this system; in the hands of the council of ministers and the politically irresponsible head of state (Hardalaç, 2016: 27–28). In addition, the executive body is made up of members of the ruling party, with the exception of special governments. Thus, the head of government elected from the parliament naturally from the ruling party. However, the head of state was not held politically responsible. Its existence is described as the survivability or symbol of the state.

Another point that stands out as part of the executive body in parliamentary systems is the Council of Ministers. Members of the Council of Ministers are individually and collectively responsible to parliament. In this context, ministers are personally liable to the parliament in case of a setback or failure to ensure the order and measures taken by their ministries (Güvenç, 2015: 13–14). In addition, the collective responsibility of ministers is based on their co-operation as a government. As the government acts as a whole, any responsibility imposed on the government includes ministers in this responsibility.

Another feature that draws attention in parliamentary systems is that the legislature is a council consisting of representatives elected by the people. However, in parliamentary systems, the number of councils can vary from country to country. Although there may be changes in the number of these councils, the legislative power generally has three main tasks. These; expressed as making laws, supervising the government and accepting the state budget (Hardalaç, 2016: 43). It is understood from this point that the heart of parliamentary systems is parliament. The fact that it gives the system its name supports this situation.

On the other hand, when evaluated in terms of separation of powers, legislative and executive powers are defined as two separate powers in parliamentary systems. However, in parliamentary systems, although legislation and executive are two different bodies, they are actually allowed to act in cooperation (Gözler, 2004: 100). This functional union is at the core of the functioning of the parliamentary system. In this context, considering that the executive leaves the legislature in the parliamentary systems and that the executive body is responsible to the legislative body, the legislative and executive must act in cooperation.

Similarly, another point of co-operation is that the prime minister, who is the head of the executive body, is also in the parliament. That is, the prime minister is also a deputy. Therefore, the Prime Minister emerges as the strongest man in the system, since he is involved in both executive and legislative terms. The prime minister's position is an important point in the parliamentary system. In fact, some authors have called the system "prime minister system" because of this feature (Yayla, 2014: 71). The Prime Minister can steer legislation as the head of the ruling party in the legislature. It also has the power to oppose or support certain decisions. On the other hand, the prime minister shares the executive duty with the council of ministers and chairs the council of ministers. While the Prime Minister shares political responsibility with the council of ministers in the executive body, he can also act with his party in the legislature.

Another factor to be addressed in parliamentary systems is the judicial body. It is seen that the judiciary draws attention as the most independent body in the system. In other words, the superiority and independence of the judiciary are accepted. The overall separation of the superiority and independence of the judiciary applies to forms of government based on separation of powers. However, this is the reason why it draws attention in the parliamentary systems because it is the organ that has the sharpest boundaries in the relationship between the three organs of the state. But in England, where the parliamentary system emerged, the judiciary seems to have not been placed on a solid written basis (Lijphart, 2006: 29). This shows that there may be differences in the judiciary in terms of the applications of the parliamentary system.

Political parties emerge as another important element of the parliamentary system. A strong political party in the state plays an important role in the functioning of the parliamentary system. The reason for this is that in parliamentary systems, the executive power comes out of the legislature. This situation causes strong political parties to come to the fore and address the executive. In some cases, strong political parties prevent the executive. A strong political party can gain the support of the people and gain the majority in the legislature or resist the mobility of the executive with the power it has. In this case, the parliamentary system needs particularly strong and disciplined parties (Yayla, 2014: 71). This requirement is an important detail for the functioning of the system and democracy.

On the other hand, if we look at the countries where the parliamentary system is applied, we see the following countries. the countries where the parliamentary system is implemented are mainly England, Germany, Italy, Switzerland, Sweden, Belgium, Spain, Japan, Denmark, Israel, Estonia, Croatia, Serbia, Netherlands, Luxembourg and Norway (Gözler, 2004: 100). Of these, the UK is where the parliamentary system first appeared. Moreover, it is a country that stands out as a prototype. For this reason, the example of England as the model country of the parliamentary system will be considered in the continuation of the study.

4 As a Prototype of the Parliamentary System: The Case of Britain

England, which is located on the European continent and has a natural sheltered position, is the place where the parliamentary system emerged due to the historical reasons. For this reason, Britain was considered as the model country for the implementation of the parliamentary system. First of all, it is necessary to take a look at the social, economic and religious existence of England. England is a country devoted to social classes and strong in civil society. In addition, state and non-state organizations have a solid foundation in the UK. Economically, Britain has adopted liberal economic policies. The fact that a large element such as industrialization lies in the historical background of the country also contributed to the economic development of the country. The phenomenon of religion in England is based on the national church. Due to the concept of the national church, it is understood that there is an official religion in England. In this context, even if these factors affect the political system in the UK, the main effective factor is the historical basis.

Considering the historical dimension of the British parliamentary system, the first thing that draws attention is the fact that the parliamentary phenomenon in England dates back to the 13th century. Magna Carta, signed in 1215 in the history of England, is the world's first written constitutional document. This document is called 'Great Edict' (Şaylan, 1981: 38). One of the most important works in the historical background of the parliamentary system, Magna Carta is a UK based document. To put it more clearly, Magna Carta is a product of the struggle between the king and the aristocracy in British history. This struggle laid the foundations for today's representative government, democracy and many civil rights (Roskin, 2012: 24). In addition, this process, which started with the 1215 Magna Carta Declaration, continued with key documents that limited the monarchy, such as the 1689 Bill of Right and 1707 Act of Union, Habeas Corpus Act and formed important parts of the British constitution (Yayla, 2014: 104). The British parliamentary system is based on all these declarations and laws.

On the other hand, when we look at the history of England, the Revolution of 1688, in other words, the Glorious Revolution is a revolution that has shaped the British constitutional monarchy significantly and without the use of weapons (Yayla, 2014: 102). The background of the 1689 Declaration of Rights, signed after this revolution, has implications. The Bill of Rights was signed in 1689 as a result of this effect. With this document, the legislative power was entirely in the hands of parliament and any interference by the king was blocked (Aydın, 2017: 76–77). The system continued to evolve by building on these foundations.

On the other hand, in general, there is a law that states that political institutions are within certain limits in many countries and is at the top of the legal norms hierarchy. This law is considered as a constitution. But there is no written legal basis in the UK which is described as a constitution (Gürbüz, 1987: 61). However, despite the existence of a constitutional document in the UK, the parliamentary system has been shaped according to laws, jurisprudence, constitutional traditions and customs (Örgün, 1999: 62).

In this context, the fact that the British parliamentary system is a model country is based on the parliament in England and the historical and functional situation of this parliament. In this case, the existence of a peculiar relationship between parliament and the UK emerges. This is because Britain is the first country to establish a parliament for the first time in history, bringing together representatives elected by the people and empowering them to resolve economic, social and legal issues through free discussion and lawmaking (Güngör, 2004: 53). In this framework, the legislature in England attracts attention. In the British parliamentary system, the legislature has a two-chamber structure. One of these assemblies is composed of people who are entitled to be there because of their traditional aristocratic ties, while other members are composed of parliamentarians elected by the people (Yayla, 2014: 105). Based on traditional aristocratic ties, the assembly is the Lord's House. The assembly elected by the people is called as House of Commons.

In the British parliamentary system, the legislative power is mainly used by the House of Commons. In England, the House of Commons is the lower house of legislation. This council consists of 650 members. In addition, members of this council can be elected from the age of 21 for a five-year term (Yayla, 2014: 105). The House of Commons is the institution that makes the most important decisions for the legislative power. In addition, the House of Commons is an assembly formed by the people. In this context, the existence of the House of Commons is formed with a majoritarian principle in the British political system, and is based on the rule of law and sovereignty.

The other wing that makes up the legislature in England is the House of Lords. The first thing that attracts attention in the House of Lords, the upper house, is that the number of members is variable. The members forming this assembly are as follows; lords who are political party representatives, independent lords, lords who come with the inheritance system, judge lords and clergymen

(Laski, 2015: 111–138). As can be understood from the name of this council, the members of this council bear the title of Lord. In addition, the number of members of the House of Lords is about 800 members. In addition to the number of 800 members, there is room for 35 members who are on leave or who may be banned from sitting in the parliament for any reason. In this case, the number of members of the House of Lords can reach up to 835. On the other hand, the distribution of the members of the House of Lords is as follows; 617 members are noble ones, 92 members are appointed by inheritance, 75 members are appointed by political party administrations, 15 members are brought to work by the votes of the House of Lords, and 26 members are Spiritual Lords, consisting of high-level priests (Roskin, 2012: 49–50).

In this framework, the House of Lords is considered a legal part of the British parliamentary system. However, they are not chosen by the public (Arslan, 2001: 35). In return, the House of Commons, selected by the people, undertook many activities on behalf of the legislature. In contrast, the House of Lords has been given the right and authority to veto laws (Yıldız, 2015: 46). They are the two institutions that make up the legislative structure of England. That is, the two important parts of the system are the House of Commons, which effectively fulfills the legislative function, and the House of Lords who have the power to veto legislative procedures.

On the other hand, another outstanding task of the House of Lords is the duty of judging. The Lord, who is in the House of Lords and is a judge, has been given the authority to carry out judicial and judicial activities (Örgün, 1999: 63). Moreover, these judge lords draw attention as the highest authority of the judicial body. In addition, there are no courts in which the administrative lawsuits are filed due to the lack of public and private law in the British parliamentary system. There is only one understanding of law in terms of judgment. Moreover, considering that there is no constitution in England, it is understood that there is no constitutional court. In this framework, the House of Lords has been empowered as a decision-maker based on the country's traditions and jurisprudence in order to find solutions to constitutional problems and congestions in England (Lijphart, 2006: 29).

In England, the president is the king or queen. In the UK, the president is determined by inheritance, provided that it complies with the rules set out in legal documents such as Bill Of Rights and Act Of Settlement of 1701. In the British parliamentary system, most of the duties of the president, in other words the king or queen, are symbolic. These tasks are as follows; It can be expressed as representing the state, chairing the council of ministers, appointing some higher-level authorities, vetoing the law, to file and annualment case against the law, appointing judicial bodies and proposing a law in parliament (Özbudun, 1968: 61–62). In fact, kingdom or queenship as head of state in England is an honorary duty with a lot of symbolic power but no real political power. The King or Queen do not actually exercise these powers (Roskin, 2012: 37–38). Obviously, the king or queen imposes its existence within the political structure. However, they never rule the system.

5 Conclusion

Britain's adoption of the parliamentary government system has historically been the result of socio-political events. It is possible to say that two factors play an important role in the emergence and implementation of this system. The first of these is Magna Carta, dated 1215, which is accepted as the first constitutional document in the world. The powers of the British king with this document are limited. All power is no longer in one person. There is a situation where powers are shared. In the following period, it is seen that parliament is getting stronger in British history. The second factor is the Westminster model. This model is a model that strengthens execution.

Britain is regarded as a country that has successfully implemented the parliamentary government model for many years. It can be said that this model is generally successful in countries with a long-established state tradition. We can evaluate Germany in this category. In this context, there are many different state structures in the countries that implement the parliamentary government system. While England has a unitary state structure, Germany has a federal state structure.

There are important factors behind Britain's successful implementation of this government model. England is an economically strong country that first realized its industrialization. Again, there is a strong civil society tradition in the UK. Another advantage of England is; this country is located in a protected and safe geography. In addition, the country has a strong constitutional tradition, even if it is not a written constitution in the UK. Roughly, documents like Bill of Rights, Habeas Corpus Act, Act of Union. Thanks to all this, the parliamentary government system has been successfully implemented in the UK.

References

Arslan, R. (2001). Siyasi Sistem Önerisi Türkiye Tipi Başkanlık Sistemi. İstanbul: Livane.

Aydın, R. (2017). Hükümet Sistemleri ve Siyasi Partiler: Başkanlık, Yarı-Başkanlık ve Parlamenter Sistemler. Gazi University, Institute of Social Sciences, Ankara.

Bitkin, S. (2018). 1980'den Günümüze Hükümet Sistemleri Tartışmaları. Karabük University, Institute of Social Sciences, Karabük.

Fendoğlu, H. T. (2013). "Başkanlık Sisteminin Türkiye'de Uygulanabilirliği". New Turkey Journal, 9(51), 567–586.

Gözler, K. (2004). Anayasa Hukukuna Giriş. Bursa: Ekin.

Güngör, E. (2004). Türkiye'de Parlamenter Sisteme Getirilen Eleştiriler Işığında Başkanlık Sistemi Senaryolarının Değerlendirilmesi. Dokuz Eylül University, Institute of Social Sciences, İzmir.

Gürbüz, Y. (1987). Karşılaştırmalı Siyasal Sistemler. İstanbul: Beta.

Güvenç, İ. (2015). Türkiye'de Başkanlık Sisteminin Uygulanabilirliği. İstanbul University, Institute of Social Sciences, İstanbul.

Hardalaç, M. (2016). Parlamenter Yapı Karşısında Başkanlık Sistemi. İstanbul: Lord.

Laski, H. J. (2015). Parliamentary Goverment in England. London and New York: Routledge.

Lijphart, A. (2006). Demokrasi Motifleri (G. Ayas ve U. U. Bulsun, Trans.). İstanbul: Salyangoz.

Örgün, F. (1999). Dar Gelen Gömlek Başkanlık Sistemi, İstanbul: Bilge.

Özbudun, E. (1968). İngiltere'de Parlemanto Egemenliği Teorisi. Journal of Ankara Law Faculty, 25(1), 59–79.

Roskin M. G. (2012). Çağdaş Devlet Sistemleri Siyaset, Coğrafya, Kültür (B. Seçilmişoğlu, Trans.). Ankara: Adres.

Şaylan. G. (1981). Çağdaş Devlet Sistemleri. Ankara: Sevinç.

Şıvgın, H. (1997). Türkiye İçin Umut Krizden Çıkış - Yeniden Yapılanma ve Başkanlık Sistemi. Ankara: Gaye.

Yayla, A. (2014). Karşılaştırmalı Siyasal Sistemler. Ankara: Liberte.

Yıldız, A. (2015). Başkanlık Sisteminin Türkiye'de Uygulanabilirliği Üzerine Bir İnceleme. Niğde University, Institute of Social Sciences, Niğde.

Serdar Ögel & Rıza Aşıkoğlu

The Examination of Effects of 2001 Financial Crises on Manufacturing Sector Through Financial Ratios Analysis[1]

1 Introduction

The developments occurred in different areas in the world have paved the way for changes in economic structures. For instance, together with the increase of globalization phenomena, national and international markets have been much more integrated and this integration has made national economies more open to several global risks (Delice, 2003). Furthermore, in developing world, new approaches occurred particularly in economics and politics have caused appearance of complex financial problems and increase in solution seeking to them. These economic facts which are mostly described as financial crisis are accepted as one of the most important cases that influence the nations' economies negatively. In fact, increase in globalization removes the financial borders among countries and so it provides free movement of capital among countries. Nevertheless, it also gives way to spread of crises from one country to another and this makes economies affect each other in a negative manner. Thus, economic crises in the world that we live have started to be regarded as phenomena which create more complex and more destructive effects on several parts in the society.

Several economic crises that dramatically influenced the world have been experienced, so far. For instance, Great Depression in 1929; economic crises which were experienced in Latin American countries in 1970s and 1980s as a result of unstability and unsuccessful programs performed by governments; financial crisis experienced in Mexico in 1994; crises oberved in East Asia in 1997 and followingly observed in Russia in 1998; and global economic crises that were experienced all over the world in 2008, are most outstanding crises that the world saw (Çakmak, 2007). Turkey was also effected by either the financial crises occurred in the world or financial crises occurred depending upon its

1 This study is derived from doctoral thesis titled "The Examination of Effects of 2001 Financial Crises on Manufacturing Sector Through Financial Ratios Analysis" written by Serdar ÖGEL under the supervision of Prof.Dr. Rıza Aşıkoğlu in Afyon Kocatepe University, Institute of Social Sciences.

own internal dynamics. In this context, one of the most well-known crisis in the history of Turkey is the financial crises occurred in 2001. 2001 financial crisis of Turkey has created numerous negative effects on economic, social and financial areas, and so it has made way for substantial loss in economic structure of the country. For that reason, understanding the effects of the 2001 financial crises is still important nowadays, as well.

Initiated by the importance of understanding the effects of the 2001 crisis of Turkey, this study attempts to examine and demonstrate the financial effects of crises on firms on the basis of 2001 financial crisis. In the direction of this aim, to better understand the effects of crisis, manufacturing firms which were directly influenced by 2001 crisis are included into the study. Here, it is important to signify that at the crisis period, the name of Turkish stock exchange was Istanbul Stock Exchange (ISE). In order not to cause any confusion, instead of its former name ISE, its current name BIST is going to be used in throughout the study. In this context, all firms operating in manufacturing sector and traded at formerly named Istanbul Stock Exchange (ISE) in crisis period and currently named Borsa Istanbul (BIST) are subject of study. However, although all firms whose shares were publicly traded at manufacturing sector of BIST are selected as population of the study, only the data of 72 manufacturing firms were reached for pre-crisis and post-crisis period that covers the six years from 1998 to 2003. For that reason, financial ratio analysis was performed initially by using financial data of 72 manufacturing firms that covers the given time period. In order to better evaluate the effects of crisis on manufacturing sector, calculated financial ratios are also analyzed with paired sample t-test. In this way, whether there is a significant differences between pre-crisis and post-crisis periods of the firms in terms of financial ratios are tested in the study.

2 The Effects of 2001 Crisis on Turkish Economy

Regardless of whether it is developed or developing economy, many economies in the world have been exposed to effects of economic and financial crises. Turkish economy, which is regarded as developing economy, have experienced the effects of a great deal of global crises. Nevertheless, Turkish economy has not only been exposed to the effects of global crises but also experienced the crises which arisen from problems in its own economic and financial systems. The economic crisis experienced in 2001 is accepted as one of the most well-known crises in Turkey which can be given an example to this type of crisis.

In order to understand the 2001 crisis, understanding the economic environment which leads to 2001 crisis is significant. For that reason, it is useful to discuss economic conditions before the crisis, and to know what kind of factos pave the way for the crisis. When it comes to the beginning of 2000s, decay of financing balance of public; increase in debt stock originating from high real interest rate; rising tendency of inflation and continuation of recession in the economy have made a new, medium-term and extensive stabilization program, necessary. However, the main lacks of this program were its openness to speculative behaviours due to fixed exchange rate regime and its dependency on passive position of Central Bank (Voyvoda and Yeldan, 2002; Mangir, 2006).

In November 2000, due to increase in current accounts deficit and together with the increasing foreign exchange demand as a result of market disequilibrium originating from sudden foreign exchange demand of foreign investors, exchange rates have also showed an increase (Mangir, 2006). Under these circumstances, the crisis, which has started in banking sector on 22 November 2000, has become twin crisis by also turning into foreign exchange crisis on 19 February 2001 because of high open position of foreign exchange. Together with the 21 February 2001 crisis, IMF program that dated from 9 December 1999 completely has been removed; the Central Bank of Turkey has lost six billion dollars reserve; and overnight interest rates have gone beyond 6000 % in interbank market, and they have averagely actualized at 4000s %. In parallel with these developments, exchange has been floated (Karaçor, 2006). Thus, the crisis process, which would be referred as 2001 financial crisis in the later years, has started.

The Turkish economy has been substantially affected from the 2001 February crisis, negatively. The effects of this economic crisis can be ordered as given below through several economic and financial indicators (Ögel, 2005):

- While gross national product (GNP) was 200 billion dollars in 2000; it has decreased to 145 billion dollars in 2001. As a result of this negative effect, the Turkish economy has shrinked at the rate of 9,5 %. Additionally, per capita income has decreased from 2,965$ to 2,123$.
- Whereas, average borrowing interest rate of treasury was 38.20 % and the inflation rate was 33.47 % in 2000, average borrowing interest rate of treasury and inflation rate have increased to 100 % and 53.64 %, respectively, in 2001.
- In 2001, the number of banks operating actively in the sector was 61. Nevertheless, after crisis, 12 of the these banks were either liquidated or transferred and so the number of banks has decreased from 61 to 49.
- In 2001, 1.363.000 people had to quit their jobs.
- While balance of payment deficit was 2.9 billion dollars in 2000, it has increased to 12.9 billion dollars by rising more than 4 times.

- Together with the use of floating exchange rate system in 2001; exports have increased from 27.7 billion dollars to 31.3 billion dollars. On the other hand, imports have decreased from 54.4 billion dollars to 41.3 billion dollars. Hence, while the export/import coverage ratio was approximately 50.9 % in 2000, this ratio has raised to 75.78 % in 2001.Together with the use of floating exchange rate system in 2001; exports have increased from 27.7 billion dollars to 31.3 billion dollars. On the other hand, imports have decreased from 54.4 billion dollars to 41.3 billion dollars. Hence, while the export/import coverage ratio was approximately 50.9 %9 % in 2000, this ratio has raised to 75.78 %78 % in 2001 (T.R. Prime Ministry Undersecretariat of Foreign Trade, 2006).

  These developments occurred in 2001 crisis have caused huge negativities in terms of economy. So, individuals, firms, institutions and state have been substantially affected negatively. The decrease in per capita income in consequence of shrinkage in GNP has negatively influenced the purchasing power of individuals and this has paved the way for shrinkage in households' demand. In addition, the increase in interest rate and uncertainities in the country have increased the risk level that the firms had to take.

Since the real interest rates have ranged up to high levels in 2001 financial crisis, the profitability of firms have got on top of interest burden. Accordingly, this has caused to decrease in their capitals, and dramatic increase in their borrowing needs, inherently. When it is looked at the financial expenses to total revenues ratio of 500 big industrial enterprises in 1995, the ratio was 5.4 %, but it was 7.7 % in 1999; 4.3 % in 2000; and 8.1 % in 2001 (Mutluer, 2002).

The increase in interests from 1980s to nowadays has made the non-operating income of entreprises more than the yield of real economy, and so the firms have increasingly invested their savings to non-operating activities. As a result of this, the decrease has been observed in the share of fixed capital investments (Gürbüz, 1998). One of the other important factors which weakened the strength of the firms in our country against crises was their efforts to maintain their operations with short term liabilities by working with insufficient shareholder's equity. So, the financial structure of private firms was not strong enough and even the share of average shareholder's equity of the big firms was one-third of total liabilities. Additionally, the remarkable part of the shareholder's equity in these firms has consisted of revaluation funds.

The slowness of turnover rates of the firms is also regarded as one the other factors which have weakened the financial structure of the firms. Since, the collection ability of the firms has decreased due to decrease in turnover rates, their liability requirements have increased. This case affected their profitability, negatively. The firms have enhanced their profits by increasing their profit margins instead of increasing their productivity and efficiency in resource utilization. In other words, they have obtained profits by doing increase in price. The continuous increase in the prices have made the turnover rates of the firms slowing down, and so it has limited the increase in their sales. Thus, maintaining profitability through increase in turnover rates but a lower profit margin have been ignored (Birgili and Tunahan, 2002). At this point, the results of the crises mentioned above and the findings of the study have similarities.

The structural problems of the economies make the relationship between capital movements and economic stability more meaningful. In this respect, foreign investors' exits, which have started at the end of the 1999, have triggered and increased effects of the crises experienced in 2000 and 2001. At the same time, foreign investors' interests, which have started to re-increase in 2000, have brought boom in financial markets and economic recovery in its wake (Ögel, 2005).

3 Data Set and Methodology

As stated before, ratio analysis is performed initially by using financial data of 72 manufacturing firms traded at BIST. So, through the ratio analysis, it is tried to be detected in which aspects the crisis influenced the firms, financially. Additionally, pre-crisis and post-crisis periods of the manufacturing firms are compared with respect to their financial conditions. Hence, the study also attempts to examine that whether there is a significant differences between pre-crisis and post-crisis periods of manufacturing firms in terms of their financial ratios. In order to perform the comparison of two different periods, paired sample t-test is used in the study. While the t-test is performed, financial ratios of given manufacturing firms calculated for three years before crisis (1998, 1999, 2000) and three years after crisis including the crisis year (2001, 2002, 2003) were compared with each other. The financial ratios used in t-test and their average values according to years are given in Table 1. The results of t-tests performed on the basis of given financial ratios are displayed in Table 2.

As a result of the paired sample t-tests which is performed to indicate whether there is a significant difference between pre-crisis and post-crisis period with respect to financial ratios, it is found that:

- in terms of ***Current Ratio***, there is not a statistically significant difference between pre-crisis and post-crisis periods ($t(215)=-0{,}90921$, $p > 0.05$).

Table 1: *The Average of Financial Ratios of Manufaturing Firms for 1997–2003*

	Current Ratio: Current Assetst/ Short-term Liabilities	**Acid-Test Ratio: (Current Assests-Inventories)/ Current Liabilities**	**Cash Ratio: (Cash and Cash Equivalents)/ Current Liabilities**	**Trade Receivables/ Current Assets**	**Net Working Capital/ Total assets**	**Total Debt/ Total Assets**	**Equity/ Total assets**	**Short Term Debt / Total Assets**	**Long Term Deb t/ Total Assets**	**Inventory Turnover Ratio**
1998	1,8300	1,19765133	0,20102	0,4050919	0,20667573	0,51587731	0,48412	0,40416	0,11171024	5,08238
1999	1,6362	1,07846681	0,16999	0,41604619	0,16398297	0,58185616	0,41814	0,45807	0,12378408	5,32068
2000	1,5637	1,00801203	0,12183	0,43129772	0,14309290	0,58542238	0,41457	0,46455	0,12086360	5,41067
2001	1,5430	1,00799799	0,18681	0,4245523	0,06397903	0,72106785	0,27893	0,55827	0,16278907	5,85181
2002	1,6480	1,06634888	0,20380	0,4052211	0,09096983	0,69841852	0,29905	0,50728	0,19113829	5,08145
2003	2,0867	1,37304614	0,36098	0,40509782	0,16608925	0,60708348	0,39377	0,40512	0,20195664	5,79428
		Accounts Receivables Turnover Ratio	**Days' Collections in Accounts Receivables**	**Equity Turnover Ratio**	**Net Working Capital Turnover Ratio:** Net Sales/ Net Working Capital	**Total Assets Turnover Ratio:** Net Sales /Total Assets	**Return on Equity:** Net Profit / Shraholder's Equity	**Earnings before Tax/ Equity**	**Net Profit/ Total Assets**	**Earnings before Tax / Total Assets**
1998		6,98752736	85,6339	2,89988	9,21245754	1,12308	0,11053299	0,18345908	0,06903541	0,148881
1999		5,65783721	94,9819	2,78865	6,97099173	1,10827	0,05515727	0,11085361	0,00767013	0,110941
2000		5,31506456	92,7359	3,36543	6,48092808	1,10770	0,23974261	-0,09143430	-0,00448895	0,063342
2001		6,58241961	93,8022	5,45203	-2,2895745	1,16346	-0,6762096	-0,64326855	-0,11856425	0,118831
2002		8,99357569	87,9105	1,69604	5,70341889	1,12429	0,21428463	0,25178830	-0,00647875	0,096151
2003		10,6016375	83,4885	2,49722	7,79035713	1,15423	0,30092707	0,32247262	0,02696993	0,036311

Table 2: *Paired Sample T-Test Results of Given Manufacturing Firms*

	Pre-Crisis	**Post-Crisis**	***d***	***t***	**Sig (two-tailed)**	***s^d***	**N**
Current Ratio	1,676687	1,75928	−0,08259	−0,90921	0,364257	1,33508	216
Acid–Test Ratio	1,09471	1,149131	−0,05442	−0,7664	0,444279	1,043606	216
Cash Ratio	0,16428	0,25053	−0,08625	−2,10965	**0,036046**	0,600859	216
Trade Receivables/ Current Assets	0,417479	0,411624	0,005855	0,541521	0,588709	0,1589	216
Net Working Capital / Total Assets	0,171251	0,107013	0,064238	2,246244	**0,025705**	0,420299	216
Total Debt / Total Assets	0,561052	0,675523	−0,11447	−3,11565	**0,002086**	0,539978	216
Equity/ Total Assets	0,438943	0,323917	0,115029	3,128239	**0,002002**	0,540424	216
Long Term Debt / Total Assets	0,44226	0,490223	−0,06651	−3,00643	**0,002958**	0,325125	216
Short Term Debt / Total Assets	0,118786	0,185295	−0,04796	−1,8291	0,06877	0,385374	216
Inventory Turnover Ratio	5,271243	5,575847	−0,30461	−1,38992	0,16599	3,220883	216
Accounts Receivables Turnover Ratio	5,98681	8,725878	−2,73907	−1,53843	0,125414	26,16686	216
Days' Collections in Accounts Receivables	91,1172	88,4004	2,716809	0,868843	0,385902	45,95626	216
Equity Turnover Ratio	3,017987	3,215097	−0,19711	−0,18972	0,84971	15,26954	216
Net Working Capital Turnover Ratio	7,554792	3,734734	3,820059	1,040581	0,299239	53,9537	216
Total Assets Turnover Ratio	1,113017	1,147327	−0,03431	−0,91976	0,358729	0,54822	216
Net Profit / Equity	0,135144	−0,05367	0,063912	0,19745	0,843662	4,757239	216
Earnings before Tax/ Equity	0,067626	−0,023	0,090629	0,28025	0,779555	4,752775	216
Net Profit / Total Assets	0,024072	−0,03269	0,056763	2,549108	**0,011497**	0,32727	216
Earnings before Tax/ Total Assets	0,107722	0,083765	0,023957	2,31136	**0,02176**	0,152334	216

- in terms of ***Acid Test Ratio***, there is not a statistically significant difference between pre-crisis and post-crisis periods ($t(215)= -0{,}7664$, $p > 0.05$).
- in terms of ***Trade Receivables/Current Assets Ratio***, there is not a statistically significant difference between pre-crisis and post-crisis periods ($t(215)= 0{,}541521$, $p > 0.05$).

- in terms of ***Short Term Debt/ Total Assets Ratio***, there is not a statistically significant difference between pre-crisis and post-crisis periods ($t(215)= -1{,}8291$, $p > 0.05$).
- in terms of ***Inventory Turnover Ratio***, there is not a statistically significant difference between pre-crisis and post-crisis periods ($t(215)= -1{,}38992$, $p > 0.05$).
- in terms of ***Accounts Receivables Turnover Ratio***, there is not a statistically significant difference between pre-crisis and post-crisis periods ($t(215)= -1{,}53843$, $p > 0.05$).
- in terms of ***Days' Collections in Accounts Receivables***, there is not a statistically significant difference between pre-crisis and post-crisis periods ($t(215)= 0{,}868843$, $p > 0.05$).
- in terms of ***Equity Turnover Ratio***, there is not a statistically significant difference between pre-crisis and post-crisis periods ($t(215)= -0{,}18972$, $p > 0.05$).
- in terms of ***Net Working Capital Turnover Ratio***, there is not a statistically significant difference between pre-crisis and post-crisis periods ($t(215)= 1{,}040581$, $p > 0.05$).
- in terms of ***Total Assets Turnover Ratio***, there is not a statistically significant difference between pre-crisis and post-crisis periods ($t(215)= -0{,}91976$, $p > 0.05$).
- in terms of ***Net Profit / Equity Ratio***, there is not a statistically significant difference between pre-crisis and post-crisis periods ($t(215)= 0{,}19745$, $p > 0.05$).
- in terms of ***Earnings before Tax / Equity Ratio***, there is not a statistically significant difference between pre-crisis and post-crisis periods ($t(215)= 0{,}28025$, $p > 0.05$).

- On the other hand, it is found that;

- in terms of ***Cash Ratio***, there is a statistically significant difference between pre-crisis and post-crisis periods ($t(215)= -2{,}10965$, $p < 0.05$).
- in terms of ***Net Working Capital / Total Assets Ratio***, there is a statistically significant difference between pre-crisis and post-crisis periods ($t(215)= 2{,}246244$, $p < 0.05$).
- in terms of ***Total Debt / Total Assets Ratio***, there is statistically significant difference between pre-crisis and post-crisis periods ($t(215)= -3{,}11565$, $p < 0.05$).
- in terms of ***Equity/ Total Assets Ratio***, there is a statistically significant difference between pre-crisis and post-crisis periods ($t(215)= 3{,}128239$, $p < 0.05$).

- in terms of ***Long Term Debt / Total Assets Ratio***, there is a statistically significant difference between pre-crisis and post-crisis periods ($t(215)= -3{,}00643$, $p < 0.05$).
- in terms of ***Net Profit / Total Assets Ratio***, there is a statistically significant difference between pre-crisis and post-crisis periods ($t(215)= 2{,}549108$, $p < 0.05$).
- in terms of ***Earnings before Tax/ Total Assets Ratio***, there is a statistically significant difference between pre-crisis and post-crisis periods ($t(215)= 2{,}31136$, $p < 0.05$).

4 Conclusion

Crises should be accepted as an economic fact which continues to appear in different forms. For that reason, understanding the effects of crises on firms is significant in terms of business owners and partners, investors and decision makers in the economy. In this respect, this study tries to reach a conclusion by examining financial statements of the firms, and in fact it tries to demonstrate in which aspects the crisis more influenced the firms, negatively.

As a result of the analyzes, it is seen that financial indebtedness ratio of manufacturing firms traded at BIST has been negative in post-crisis period, when it is compared to pre-crisis period. The share of liabilities has increased in financing of total assets of the firms in post-crisis period with respect to pre-crisis period, and so the share of their equities has declined. The decrease of the share of equity in total assets and the increase in use of liabilities to finance assets have confronted firms with a problem of more risky financing options. Thus, this has also paved the way for increase of financing expenses.

In crises periods, in which the uncertainties particularly increase and the money inherently becomes much more valuable, firms have great difficulty in finding long-term and low interest liabilities. This enforces the firms to find short-term and high cost liabilities. So, firms are more likely to be vulnerable against the effects of crises. When the cash ratio of manufacturing firms are examined, it is seen that they have had more cash in post-crisis period when it is compared to pre-crisis period. This can also be explained with firms' motives to act in a cautious way in uncertainity environment created by crisis.

The decrease in share of net working capital in total assets is also explained with the necessity of the firms to use short-term liabilities, intensively in post-crisis period. When the net profit to total assets ratio is checked, it is seen that there is a statistically significant difference between pre-crisis and post-crisis periods. So, it is concluded that the profits of the firms have decreased and even turned into loss. The decrease in profits of the firms is also indicated that the crisis has negatively influenced profitability of the manufacturing firms.

In conclusion, it can be readily said that particularly financial structure of the firms are influenced by the economic conditions originating from the crisis. In the light of this fact, the firms, which have poor financial structures, are the ones which are more likely to be affected by the crises. For that reason, the firms, which intensively use liabilities in their growth opportunities, should always pay attention to the reality of crisis. As well as the firms, investors should also take this into consideration, when they invest in the stocks of these types of firms; because particularly in crises period, the stocks of the firms with a poor financial structures are more likely to be influenced by the effects of crisis, negatively.

References

Birgili, E., & Tunahan, H. (2002). Döviz Krizlerinde İşletme Sermayesi Davranışı. In VI. International Conference In Economics.

Çakmak, U. (2007). Kriz Modelleri Çerçevesinde Türkiye 2001 Finansal Krizinin Değerlendirilmesi. Gazi Üniversitesi İktisadi ve İdari Bilimler Fakültesi Dergisi, 9(1), 81–101.

Delice, G. (2003). Finansal Krizler: Teorik Ve Tarihsel Bir Perspektif. Erciyes Üniversitesi İktisadi ve İdari Bilimler Fakültesi Dergisi, 20, 57–81

Gürbüz, B. (1998). 1988–95 Yılları Arası Türkiye"nin Birikim Sürecinde Devlet Finansal Kurumlar ve Çalışanlar. İktisat İşletme ve Finans, 13(152), 56–70.

Karaçor, Z. (2006). Öğrenen Ekonomi Türkiye: Kasım 2000-Şubat 2001 Krizinin Öğrettikleri. Selçuk Üniversitesi Sosyal Bilimler Enstitüsü Dergisi, (16), 379–391.

Mangir, F. (2006). Finansal Deregülasyonun (1989–2001) Türkiye Ekonomisi Üzerine Etkileri: Kasım 2000 Ve Şubat 2001 Krizleri. Selçuk Üniversitesi Sosyal Bilimler Enstitüsü Dergisi, (16), 459–472.

Mutluer, M. K. (2002). Türkiye'nin 500 Büyük Sanayi Kuruluşu 2001, İstanbul Sanayi Odası Dergisi, 437, 1-224.

Ögel, S. (2005). "2001 Krizinin İmalat Sanayi Üzerindeki Etkilerinin Oran Analizi Yoluyla Belirlenmesi" Afyon Kocatepe Üniversitesi, Sosyal Bilimler Enstitüsü, Yayınlanmamış Doktora Tezi, 1–232.

Voyvoda, E., & Yeldan, E. (2002). Türkiye Ekonomisi İçin Kriz Sonrası Alternatif Uyum Stratejileri. İktisat İşletme ve Finans Dergisi, 17(200), 18–28.

Safiye Süreyya Bengül & Mediha Mine Çelikkol

The Impact of Perceived Financial Risks on Customers' Purchasing Decisions, Satisfaction and Loyalty in Online Shopping Processes

1 Introduction

The incredible rise in internet-based commerce in recent years and the expectation that this rise will continue in the future have made customers a focal point in the online market. In order to provide online shopping opportunities to customers, to maintain loyalty, and accordingly to increase sales, companies of different sizes in different sectors build up web sites. Web sites have evolved into a personal structure that not only provides the product but also monitors and stores customer data in order to expedite decision-making and purchasing through developing technologies. The basis of this transformation is that despite the unpredictability of online shopping, customers are encouraged to buy. However, some uncertainties perceived by the customer in this shopping environment may disturb the purchasing process and hinder this process.

Uncertainty is expressed as risk as to whether the customer's decision to buy during the purchase process will lead him to the conclusion he has targeted. The concept of risk perception was introduced in the marketing literature by Bauer (1960), who evaluated customer behavior within the scope of risk theory. Bauer (1960), argues that the result of a customer's purchase action cannot always be predicted and that it includes objective and subjective risks that can sometimes lead to undesirable situations, and he focuses on subjective (perceived) risk in his study. According to Bauer, customers can perceive risks not only in the pre-decision process but also in the post-decision process.

The risk perceived by the customer during a purchase process is significant in terms of influencing purchase behavior. At this point, another critical matter is the quality and quantity of perceived risk. Cox and Rich (1964) in their study, considered the most accessible and relevant shopping process in the 1960s; the process of Teleshopping. The findings of the study reveal that the quality of the risk perceived by the customer, the degree of risk and the way of dealing with the perceived risk are essential determinants of the decision to purchase by telephone.

Cox (1967) emphasized the necessity of understanding the presence of perceived risk. Cox states that customers may be inadequate or unwilling to express that the situation they encounter is risky, but for the intentions of buying, they perceive it in some way and undertake the risk. The magnitude of the potential loss as a result of the purchase behavior and the certainty of the individual's feeling that the consequence will be negative, determines the degree of perceived risk. This two-factor risk structure can be reduced to a tolerable level by actions that reduce the magnitude of loss and the certainty of the loss.

2 Perceived Risk Types

Studies are focusing on specific types or components of the perceived risk in the literature. Jacoby and Kaplan (1972) discussed the basic structure of risk components of about twelve different products and identified five types of risk that are classified as financial, performance, physical, psychological, and social. Brooker (1984) included the risk of loss of time as an extra element to the five risk components identified by Jacoby and Kaplan. By the 1990s, the risks perceived by customers were differentiated by the impact of the internet, which interconnected enterprise and personal networks worldwide. Traditionally perceived risk types in online shopping have been added; resource risk, privacy risk, and post-sales risk (Cöddü et al., 2017).

Performance risk is also termed as a functional risk. It includes the belief that the customer will not get the benefit he desires at the end of the purchase process, and that the product or service that is subject to the purchase will not show the performance he demands (Jarvenpaa et al., 1999). Physical risk refers to the perception that a product or service may be hazardous to health or safety when it is not operating correctly (Roselius, 1971; Garner, 1986). A physical risk in online shopping includes the concern of encountering physical damage as a result of the customer's purchase action. Psychological risk refers to the potential loss of self-confidence (ego loss) caused by frustration in achieving a purchase intention (Zheng et al., 2012). It includes the negative mood caused by unsuccessful purchases made by customers in the online shopping environment and the possibility of tension that they may encounter (Hassan et al., 2006). Social risk refers to the adverse impact of other individuals on the consumer's perceptions of online shopping. In the case of a purchase of a product or service, it can be defined as the probability of loss of status in the society with which the customer is associated (Zheng et al., 2012). The risk of time loss refers to the perceived risk associated with conditions that may cause time loss during the online shopping process. The perceived resource risk is the risk that the customer perceives as the reliability and expertise of the company he/she will be online shopping with. Privacy risk refers to the risk which the customer perceives in the case that private information is lost during the online shopping process. Delivery risk is the perceived risk of failure to deliver the product on the promised date at the end of the online shopping process, a long time for delivery, delivery of a damaged product to the customer, the loss of the product in the delivery process and misdelivery (Iconaru, 2012).

One of the most effective risk types on customers' online buying decisions is financial risk. It refers to the possibility of purchase causing a loss of money (Tsiakis, 2012). The main subject of the study is the financial risk perceived during the online shopping process, which has potential effects on customers' purchasing decisions, satisfaction and loyalty, which is taken into consideration under the main heading.

3 Perceived Financial Risks in Online Shopping

Perceived financial risk is defined as the potential financial resource loss or the possibility of exposure to financial losses occurring from online shopping. Financial risk can be expressed as the product whose purchase is not worth the compensation (Roselius, 1971). In online shopping, the inability to measure performance and compliance with expectations of the product before its purchase increases the perceived financial risk. Also, the payment method used to pay the price of the product purchased and the resulting costs are efficient on the financial risk perceived by the customers.

Misappropriation of the financial information (card number, etc.) used in payment and leaking this information to third parties are the customers' main concerns when paying. Specifications of financial and non-financial information that may reveal the incorrect or unintended use of information disturb customers and preferring not to shop online because they fear that it will be stolen or used without their consent. Therefore, they have a high level of financial risk perception at this stage (Hong and Yi, 2012).

3.1 Components of Perceived Financial Risk

Financial risk reflects the customer's concern that the product or service purchased will not achieve the best monetary gain for him. The sources of this concern are the potential losses arising from the method of online payment and the possibility that the costs incurred during the purchase process cannot compare with the benefit obtained.

3.1.1 Purchase Cost

Products and services ranging from non-durable to durable consumption goods, from daily journals to consultation in the business world are subject to commerce in this environment. Kiang and Chi (2001) express that online shopping customers perceive lower financial risks in products such as books, music and clothing. According to Ye (2004), products can be sold at higher prices in online shopping, and extra charges can be made for delivery and payment. This situation increases the purchase cost and therefore the occurrence of financial loss. When the subject product is technologically developed and the unit price rises, the perceived degree of financial risk increases. In particular, if there are significant differences in financial, social and psychological factors among customers, there are discrepancies in the degree of perceived risk. Customers in an advanced social network can take greater financial risks with the impact of this network (Bhatnagar et al., 2000; Sims and Xu, 2012).

3.1.2 Payment Method

Financial risk represents the fear of monetary losses arising from online shopping; if customers pay online, it is related to the acquisition of financial information, the stealing of credit card numbers, and the fear of being attacked by bank accounts. In order to increase online commerce, companies must assure the customer that their web sites do not carry this risk; therefore, there is no possibility of financial loss (Arshad et al., 2015).

Iconaru (2012) found that online customers stopped shopping because of the possibility of suffering from financial damage if they used a credit card during the payment phase. The individuals surveyed declared that they preferred to make payments using alternative methods such as cash, money transfer or PayPal as possible and that they relied more on the internet banking platform than on the e-commerce platform. In a study, it is emphasized that customers think that small businesses do not have enough financial resources to keep their e-commerce platforms safe and to find a payment system guaranteed by companies other than the merchants to be more secure. Customers who prefer to transact with well-known vendors against financial risk generally only receive a low-limit credit card that they use in online transactions.

Financial risk plays a vital role in making decisions when shopping online and adversely affects purchasing behavior. Studies reveal that suspicion of credit card fraud is one of the most disturbing issues in online shopping. These studies focus on the relationship between financial risk and online shopping behavior and emphasize the importance of confidence. If retailers focus on financial risk and give the customer confidence in paying, they will be able to sell their products online more easily (Bhatti et al., 2018).

4 The Impact of Perceived Financial Risk on Customer Behavior in Online Shopping

In the online shopping process, the financial risks that customers perceive and the methods of payment that they use or have to use, influence their behavior in this process. By continuing to influence not only a one-off purchase but also recurring purchase decisions, they lead to shifts in the customer's satisfaction in and loyalty to the seller company and its web site.

4.1 The Effect of Perceived Financial Risk on the Customer Purchasing Decision

The most common method of payment in online shopping is by credit card. In online shopping, payment by credit card affects customers' confidence in the payment system. Because of the nature of the internet, easier access to personal information has increased the risk of intruders and made it easier for the acquisition of personal information. On the one hand, customers avoid shopping online because of being exposed to an intrusion of their personal information, and on the other hand, it is due to the risk of others getting the passwords of their credit cards and performing some transactions using their cards (Keser, 2000). If customers do not believe their data will remain confidential and that payment is secure, they will not use the internet for shopping (McCole et al., 2010). If online customers' credit card numbers and personal information are guaranteed and this assurance is stated on a web site, only then will customers decide to purchase (Salisbury et al., 2001).

In addition to the reservations of online shoppers about providing identity and credit card information in payment processes, there are also doubts about whether the e-commerce business really exists, whether the product purchased will be the same as the image on the web site, and whether the product will meet expectations. Other factors that impact customers' online purchase decisions are their doubts about whether or not product delivery will be made after payment and whether they can benefit from after-sales services (Bhatnagar et al., 2000). Such suspicions that customers experience about purchasing behavior can be reflected in their behavior and can negatively affect future purchasing decisions (Soutar and Sweeney, 2003; Koller and Salzberger, 2008).

4.2 Impact of Perceived Financial Risk on the Customer Satisfaction

Customer satisfaction is defined as the positive result of comparing the expectations of customers before purchasing a product with the value of the product after purchasing (Oliver, 1980; Zeithaml et al., 1990). Customer satisfaction is the perception of satisfactoriness in the form of a pleasurable loyalty provided by the fulfillment of an item of merchandise or service (Oliver, 1997). Satisfaction is the happiness generated by these positive emotions in the customers, and the customer who achieves this happiness will be willing to buy from the same business again in his/her next selection (Ladhari and Leclerc, 2013).

E-satisfaction is defined as the departure of customers from the stores where the electronic commerce has been conducted and the future thinking of using this online shopping environment again (Bayram and Şahbaz, 2017). In online shopping processes, a web site that provides the customer with what he/she wants ensures customer satisfaction (Mitra and Fay, 2010). Factors affecting customer satisfaction in traditional markets include quality, delivery speed, delivery reliability, elasticity, values, competitiveness, product mix, customer service, price, reliability, professionalism, employee behavior, technology, suppliers, costs and perceived risks (Zhang et al., 2012; Bitner and Hubbert, 1994; Dick and Basu, 1994; Jones, 1996; Zeithaml et al., 1990); those affecting e-customer satisfaction, include accessibility of the web site, emendation of errors, site reliability, flexibility, communication, and feedbacks (Tontini, 2016). Especially in online shopping, reducing the risks perceived by customers will increase e-satisfaction (Chen et al., 2011). Online shopping sites need to follow and support all processes until the product is delivered to the customer in order to provide customer satisfaction. As a result, the level of satisfaction of the e-customer will increase, and a customer who is pleased with the product or service he/she purchased will make another selection from the same web site; in short, loyalty will be provided (Ladhari and Leclerc, 2013).

4.3 The Effect of Perceived Financial Risk on the Customer Loyalty

Customer loyalty is the commitment made by the customer to purchase preferred products or services consistently in the future, and this commitment maintains repetitive purchasing behavior against all situational factors and marketing efforts that fuel brand change and enable the customer to spend more time on the web site (Oliver, 1999; Jeon, 2009). E-loyalty is the repeated purchasing behavior of the customer as a result of the positive attitude towards the e-retailer (Srinivasan et al., 2002). E-loyalty is the desire of the customer to maintain a future relationship consistently. It enables the customer to choose the business web site as the first choice among alternatives, to revisit the site and to show the behavior of buying online products by developing positive feelings and assurance towards the business (Toufaily et al., 2013). If the customer purchases again from the same vendor, this indicates a potentially loyal customer, which is directly associated with customer satisfaction and loyalty (Jaiswal et al., 2010).

Among the pioneers of e-loyalty, confidence and satisfaction are of great significance. In particular, there is a stronger relationship between e-satisfaction and e-loyalty on online shopping sites compared to conventional purchasing channels. Therefore, online customers have more levels of loyalty to the internet retailers that they like (Horppu et al., 2008). Because loyal customers prefer a web site, they trust and are satisfied with it when choosing from alternative web sites during online shopping. At the same time, as long as the web site perseveres with its business life, it will be the invariable preference of the loyal customer (Audrain-Pontevia et al., 2013). Every time the customer wants to purchase a product, the web site he/she is loyal to is always the first preference. Even if the customer finds a competing web site that offers the same benefit, or a web site that offers a lower price, he/she does not change his/her preferred site (Toufaily et al., 2013). E-loyalty encourages the customer to stay longer on the web site, to participate more in the assertive world of marketing and to purchase products from the site that he/she is satisfied with, even if the product is at a lower price on another web site (Hou, 2005).

Brand loyalty is one of the critical factors that reduce perceived risk (Mitchell and Greatorex, 1993) because customers tend to reduce uncertainty and risk by repurchasing the brands they are satisfied with. When repurchasing the same brand, customers are loyal to avoid errors and risks rather than to obtain more benefits (Mitchell, 1999). Therefore, customer loyalty reduces perceived risk if the customer detects a high level of differentiation between brands, the perceived risk increases. It is asserted that this situation triggers loyalty to reduce perceived risk (Chaudhuri, 1998). If the customer is satisfied with the brand that he/she bought the first time, it is anticipated that loyalty will occur in order to avoid risk. In other words, customers buy the same brand over and over again to avoid the risk of trying a new brand (Demir, 2011).

5 Conclusion

There are more types of risk perceived by customers in online shopping than those perceived in traditional shopping. Reducing the risks perceived by customers in online shopping processes leads to ensuring that the e-commerce business is reliable and credible, that the customers are positive towards the store and that the intention to shop from that store is revealed and also repeated. Customers' confidence and their positive attitudes in e-commerce businesses affect results, such as satisfaction and loyalty, by increasing the company's care of customers (Badrinarayanan et al., 2014).

The fact that it is not possible to test the products offered on web sites before the purchase results in increased financial and performance risk perceptions in customers. The degree of perceived financial risk increases with uncertainty about the vendor and its representative web site. This situation prevents the customer from having confidence in the web site and its products thus increasing the risk perception and adversely affecting the repurchase intention, loyalty and satisfaction (Gefen, 2000; Lim, 2003; Evanschitzky et al., 2004; Kim et al., 2008). The perceived financial risk level may increase when low prices are combined with; high discount rates and uncertainty about the seller. When the perception is added that the method used in the payment phase is far from secure, the purchase is renounced. The risks perceived by customers for the assurance of financial security and privacy assessed within the framework of site security are a fundamental prerequisite in the online shopping processes, and the perceived quality of service has a substantial impact on e-satisfaction and e-loyalty (Szymanski and Hise, 2000; Wolfinbarger and Gilly, 2003). However, customers ' interaction with e-store executives on the internet, payment processes and risk perceptions related to transaction activity, which are defined as ensuring order follow-up, are effective on e-satisfaction and e-loyalty (Loiacono, 2000). Online shopping sites need to increase their confidence in the site by producing solutions for the risks they perceive in order to influence their customers' satisfaction and loyalty positively (Kuo and Wu, 2012). In online shopping, if payment is required by credit card; SSL Certificate and 3D secure integration in particular, such as PayPal, and security-approved payment system options should be available on the web site for trading. When proceedings to the payment page, these security applications in the field where credit card information is given are essential to eliminate the perceived financial risk.

References

Arshad, A., Zafar, M., Fatima, I. & Khan, S. K. (2015). The Impact of Perceived Risk on Online Buying Behavior. International Journal of New Technology and Research (IJNTR), 1(8), 13–18.

Audrain-Pontevia, A. F., N'Goala, G. & Poncin, I. (2013). A Good Deal Online: The Impacts of Acquisition and Transaction Value on E-Satisfaction and E-Loyalty. Journal of Retailing and Consumer Services, 20, 445–452.

Badrinarayanan, V., Becerra, E. P. & Madhavaram, S. (2014). Influence of Congruity in Store-attribute Dimensions and Self-Image on Purchase Intentions in Online Stores of Multichannel Retailers. Journal of Retailing and Consumer Services, 21, 1013–1020.

Bauer, R. A. (1960). Consumer Behavior as Risk-Taking. In R. S. Hancock (Ed.), Dynamic Marketing for a Changing World (pp. 389–398). Chicago: American Marketing Association.

Bayram, A. T. & Şahbaz, P. (2017). E-Hizmet Uygulamalarında Kalite Algısı, Memnuniyet ve Sadakat Tutumlarının Demografik Özelliklere Göre İncelenmesi: Seyahat Acentaları Müşterileri Örneği. Journal of Tourism and Gastronomy Studies, 5(1), 60–75.

Bhatnagar, A., Mısra, S. & Rao, R. (2000). On Risk, Convenience and Internet Shopping Behavior. Communications of the ACM, 48(2), 98–105.

Bhatti, A., Saad, S. & Gbadebo S. M. (2018). The Effect of Financial Risk and Convenience Risk on Online Shopping Behavior with the Moderating Role of Trust. International Journal of Academic Management Science Research (IJAMSR), 2(8), 38–42.

Bitner, M. J. & Hubbert, A. R. (1994). Encounter Satisfaction Versus Overall Satisfaction Versus Quality. Service Quality: New Directions in Theory and Practice, 34, 72–94.

Brooker, G. (1984). An Assessment of an Expanded Measure of Perceived Risk. Advances in Consumer Research, 11, 439–441.

Chaudhuri, A. (1998). Product Class Effects on Brand Loyalty. The Journal of Marketing and Management, 8(2), 60–77.

Chen, J., Hui, E. C. M. & Wang, Z. (2011). Perceived Risk, Anticipated Regret and Post-Purchase Experience in the Real Estate Market: The Case of China. Housing Studies, 26(3), 385–402.

Cöddü, M. B., Çabuk, S. & Tanrıkulu, C. (2017). İnternetten Alışverişte Tüketiciler Tarafından Algılanan Riskin Etkileri ve Cinsiyet Farklılıkları Açısından İncelenmesi. Uluslararası Sosyal Araştırmalar Dergisi, 10(52), 982–994.

Cox, D. F. (1967). Risk Handling in Consumer Behavior – an İntensive Study of Two Cases. In D. F. Cox (Ed.), Risk-Taking and İnformation-Handling in Consumer Behavior (pp. 34–81). Boston: Harvard University Press.

Cox, D. F. & Rich, S. U. (1964). Perceived Risk and Consumer Decision-Making-the Case of Telephone Shopping. Journal of Marketing Research, 1(4), 32–39.

Dick, A.S. & Basu, K. (1994). Customer Loyalty: Toward an Integrated Conceptual Framework. Journal of the Academy of Marketing Science, 22(2), 99–113.

Demir, M. Ö. (2011). Risk Algısının Marka Sadakatine Etkisi: Cep Telefonları Kategorisinde Bir Uygulama. Ege Akademik Bakış- Ege Academic Review, 11(2), 267–276

Evanschitzky, H., Iyer, G. R., Hesse, J. & Ahlert, D. (2004). E-Satisfaction: A Reexamination. Journal of Retailing, 80(3), 239–247.

Garner, S. J. (1986). Perceived Risk and Information Sources in Services Purchasing. The Mid-Atlantic Journal of Business, 24(2), 49–58.

Gefen, D. (2000). E-Commerce. The Role of the Familiarity and Trust. The International Journal of Management Science, 28, 725–737.

Hassan, A. M., Kunz, M. B., Pearson A.W. & Mohamed, F. A. (2006). Conceptualization and Measurement of Perceived Risk in Online Shopping. Marketing Management Journal, 16(1), 138–147.

Hong, Z. & Yi, L. (2012). Research on the Influence of Perceived Risk in Consumer Online Purchasing Decision. Physics Procedia, 24, 1304–1310.

Horppu, M., Kuivalainen, O., Tarkiainen, A. & Ellonen, H. K. (2008). Online Satisfaction, Trust and Loyalty, and the Impact of the Offline Parent Brand. Journal of Product & Brand Management, 17(6), 403–413.

Hou, Y. (2005). Service Quality of Online Apparel Retailers and Its Impact on Customer Satisfaction, Customer Trust and Customer Loyalty. Greensboro: UMI Company.

Iconaru, C. (2012). Perceived Risk When Buying Online: Evidence from a Semi-Structured Interview. Economics Series, 22(2), 63–73.

Jaiswal, A. K., Niraj, R. & Venugopal, P. (2010). Context-General and Contextspecific Determinants of Online Satisfaction and Loyalty for Commerce and Content Sites. Journal of Interactive Marketing, 24(3), 222–238.

Jacoby, J. & Kaplan, L. B. (1972). The Components of Perceived Risk. In M. Venkatesan (Ed.), SV – Proceedings of the Third Annual Conference of the Association for Consumer Research (pp. 382–393). Chicago, IL: Association for Consumer Research.

Jarvenpaa, S. L., Tractinsky N. & Saarinen L. (1999). Consumer Trust in an Internet Store: A Cross-Cultural Validation. Journal of Computer-Mediated Communication, 5(2). https://doi.org/10.1111/j.1083-6101.1999.tb00337.x

Jeon, M. (2009). Impact of Perceived Website Service Quality on Customer E-Loyalty on a Lodging Website. Graduate Theses and Dissertations, Iowa State University.

Jones, T. O. (1996). Why Satisfied Customers Defect. Journal of Management in Engineering, 12(6), 5–13.

Keser, A. (2000). Rekabetin Değişen Yüzü: Elektronik Ticaret. İŞ, GÜÇ Endüstri İlişkileri ve İnsan Kaynakları Dergisi, 2(1). http://www.isguc.org/?p=article&id=86&cilt=2&sayi=1&yil=2000.

Kiang, M. Y., & Chi, R. T. (2001). A Framework for Analyzing the Potential Benefits of Internet Marketing. Journal of Electronic Commerce Research, 2(4), 157–163.

Kim, D. J., Ferrin, D. L. & Rao, H. R. (2008). A Trust-Based Consumer Decision-Making Model in Electronic Commerce: The Role of Trust, Perceived Risk, and Their Antecedents. Decision Support Systems, 44(2), 544–564.

Koller, M. & Salzberger, T. (2008). Cognitive Dissonance in Retail Versus E-Commerce: First Findings and Implications. Proceedings of Australian and New Zealand Marketing Academy Conference, Australian and New Zealand Marketing Academy: Australia, pp. 1–8.

Kuo, Y. F. & Wu, C. M. (2012). Satisfaction and Post-purchase Intentions with Service Recovery of Online Shopping Websites: Perspectives on Perceived Justice and Emotions. International Journal of Information Management, 32(2), 127–138.

Ladhari, R. & Leclerc, A. (2013). Building Loyalty with Online Financial Services Customers: Is There a Gender Difference?. Journal of Retailing and Consumer Services, 20(6), 560–569.

Lim, N. (2003). Consumers' Perceived Risk: Souces Versus Consequences. Electronic Commerce Research and Applications, 2, 216–228.

Loiacono, E. T. (2000). WebQual: A Web Site Quality Instrument. Doctoral dissertation. Athens – Georgia: University of Georgia.

McCole, P., Ramsey, E. & Williams J. (2010). Trust Considerations on Attitudes Towards Online Purchasing: The Moderating Effect of Privacy and Security Concerns. Journal of Business Research, 63, 1018–1024.

Mitchell, V. M. (1999). Consumer Perceived Risk: Conceptualizations and Models. European Journal of Marketing, 33(1/2), 163–195.

Mitchell, V. M. & Greatorex, M. (1993). Risk Perception and Reduction in the Purchase of Consumer Services. Service Industries Journal, 13(4), 179–200.

Mitra, D. & Fay, S. (2010). Managing Service Expectations in Online Markets: A Signaling Theory of E-tailer Pricing and Empirical Tests. Journal of Retailing, 86, 184–199.

Oliver, R. L. (1980). A Cognitive Model of the Antecedents and Consequences of Satisfaction Decisions. Journal of Marketing Research, 17(4), 460–469.

Oliver, R. L. (1997). Satisfaction: A Behavioral Perspective on the Consumer. New York: Irwin/McGraw Hill.

Oliver, R. L. (1999). Whence Consumer Loyalty?. Journal of Marketing, 63, 33–44.

Roselius, R. (1971). Consumer Rankings of Risk Reduction Methods. Journal of Marketing, 35(1), 56–61.

Salisbury, D., Pearson, R. A., Pearson, A. W. & Miller, D.W. (2001). Perceived Security and World Wide Web Purchase Intention. Industrial Management and Data Systems, 101(4), 165–177.

Sims, J. & Xu, L. (2012). Perceived Risk of Online Shopping: Differences Between the UK and China. UK Academy for Information Systems Conference Proceedings 25. https://aisel.aisnet.org/ukais2012/25.

Soutar, G. N. & Sweeney, J. C. (2003). Are There Cognitive Dissonance Segments?. Australian Journal of Management, 28(3), 227–249.

Srinivasan, S. S., Anderson, R. & Ponnavolu, K. (2002). Customer Loyalty in E-Commerce: An Exploration of Its Antecedents and Consequences. Journal of Retailing, 78(2), 41–50.

Szymanski, D. M. & Hise, R. T. (2000), E-Satisfaction: An İnitial Examination. Journal of Retailing, 76(3), 309–322.

Tontini, G. (2016). Identifying Opportunities for Improvement in Online Shopping Sites. Journal of Retailing and Consumer Services, 31, 228–238.

Toufaily, E., Richard, L. & Perrien, J. (2013). Customer Loyalty to Commercial Web Site: Descriptive Meta Analysis of the Empirical Literature and Proposal of an Integrative Model. Journal of Business Research, 66 (9), 1436–1447.

Tsiakis, T. (2012). Consumers' Issues and Concerns of Perceived Risk of Information Security in Online Framework. The Marketing Strategies. Procedia-Social and Behavioral Sciences, 62, 1265–1270.

Wolfinbarger, M. & Gilly, M. C. (2003). eTailQ: Dimensionalizing, Measuring and Predicting Etail Quality. Journal of Retailing, 79(3), 183–198.

Ye, N. (2004). Dimensions of Consumer's Perceived Risk in Online Shopping. Journal of Electronic Science and Technology of China, 2(3), 177–182.

Zeithaml, V. A., Parasuraman, A. & Berry, L. L. (1990). Delivering Quality Service: Balancing Customer Perceptions and Expectations. New York: Free Press.

Zhang, L., Tan, W., Xu, Y. & Tan, G. (2012). Dimensions of Consumers' Perceived Risk and Their Influences on Online Consumers' Purchasing Behavior. Communications in Information Science and Management Engineering, 2(7), 8–14.

Zheng, L., Favier, M., Huang, P. & Coat, F. (2012). Chinese Consumer Perceived Risk and Risk Relievers in E-Shopping for Clothing. Journal of Electronic Commerce Research, 13(3), 255–274.

Yusuf Kaya & Mehmet Utku

Integrated Reporting and Its Application in Turkish Banking Sector

1 Introduction

The approach of sustainable development, which came up towards the end of the 20th century, focused on the sustainability of the economic and social development of societies. At this point, global economic crises, rapid population growth, environmental problems, limited natural resources, epidemic diseases, economic and social structure make it necessary to evaluate the environment in a holistic way. Sustainability of the global socio-economic structure is closely related to both private and public institutions and organizations act with corporate social responsibility awareness and integration with the society. Today, organizations are asked to be responsible and transparent to their employees, shareholders, stakeholders and the whole society. In this case, the need to identify and report the social, environmental and economic impacts of the organizations' activities has arisen and a new reporting approach based on integrated thinking has emerged due to the inadequate traditional reports containing financial information. This new understanding, which envisages the provision of all financial and non-financial information about the organization, is "Integrated Reporting".

Integrated reporting is a holistic and integrated representation of company performance in terms of both financial and sustainability (Eccles and Armbres ter,2011:14). The integrated report reports the organization's data on efficiency and performance for a more sustainable global economy. The integrated report reveals the created value by offering a holistic perspective to all stakeholders of the organization.

The International Integrated Reporting Council (IIRC) was established in 2010 in order to develop integrated reporting activities, guide organizations that want to prepare integrated reports and establish international standards in reporting. The council has given integrated reporting a global institutional structure. In this context, the "International Integrated Reporting Framework" (International IR Framework) was published by IIRC in 2013, which includes guidelines and content elements to be taken as basis in integrated reporting. In Turkey, it has entered into an integrated reporting process for the first time in 2011. Since 2011, important steps have been taken to expand integrated reporting, various organizations have been established and co-operation agreements have been signed with IIRC. Even there is no legal requirement about issuing integrated report in Turkey, there are 14 organization that engage integrating reporting as of 2019.

The aim of this study is to analyze the integrated reporting activities in the Turkish banking sector in terms of content in line with the International Integrated Reporting Framework by explaining the concept of integrated reporting. For this purpose, in the second part of the study, basic information about integrated reporting is given. In the third section, the international development process of integrated reporting and developments in Turkey are mentioned. In the fourth section, the International Integrated Reporting Framework is examined. In the fifth part of the study, the reports of banks that prepared integrated reports in the Turkish banking sector in 2019 were analyzed in terms of content items in line with the framework published by IIRC. In the last part, the conclusions reached within the scope of the research are presented and suggestions are made.

2 Integrated Reporting Concept

Integrated report; It is a short and concise explanation of how an organization's strategy, corporate management, performance and expectations from the future will create added value for the organization's external environment in the short, medium and long term (IIRC, 2013: 7).

Integrated reporting is a reporting method that requires an integrated mindset based on society, aims to consolidate existing financial and non-financial reporting practices and also defines the future strategies of the institution in the reports (Borsa Istanbul Sustainability Bulletin, 2014: 38). In addition to financial data, the report also includes social, environmental and institutional information.

The main idea of integrated reporting is to build a sustainable society. For this reason, integrated reporting is expected to help businesses take sustainable risk into consideration, adopt sustainable activities and create a sustainable society (Hoque 2017: 242). Integrated reporting is more focused on the future, unlike traditional reporting. While traditional reporting focuses on the past results of an organization, integrated reporting provides comprehensive information on the future value generation of organizations (Gökten, 2016: 745). The integrated report reflects the future value, risks and opportunities and strategy of the organization with a forward-looking perspective (Aras and Sarıoğlu, 2015: 44). Accordingly, with the integrated reporting, it is aimed to change from the approach of generating information for shareholders in the short term to the idea of producing information that includes all stakeholders in the long term, that is, to the integrated opinion.

The main purpose of an integrated report is to explain to parties that provide financial capital how an organization will create value over time. Integrated reporting takes a more unified and effective approach to corporate reporting and aims to improve the quality of information provided to parties that provide financial capital to distribute capital more effectively and productively (IIRC, 2013, 4). In this context, with integrated reporting, shareholders will be able to analyze the organization's ability to create sustainable value.

According to the integrated reporting framework published by the international integrated reporting council, Integrated reporting pursues the following objectives:

- To increase the quality of the information provided to parties that provide financial capital in order to distribute capital more effectively and productively.
- Introduce a more unified and effective approach to corporate reporting that includes different reporting paths and includes all factors that materially affect an organization's ability to create value over time.
- To strengthen the elements of accountability and manageability for the broad base of capital and to understand their interdependence.
- Supporting integrated thinking, decision making and action elements that focus on creating value in the short, medium and long term.

3 Development Process of Integrated Reporting and Integrated Reporting in Turkey

King reports prepared to reduce the distrust of institutions in South Africa were effective in the emergence of integrated reporting. In 1994, Nelson Mandela appointed Mervyn King to promote transparency and information sharing. Reports of King I in 1994, King II in 2002 and King III in 2009 were published. The results of the social, environmental and financial responsibilities of the companies were reported. After the King Reports, it was made compulsory for all companies quoted on the stock exchange in the South Africa to publish integrated reports for the first time in 2010, and to explain the reason for those who did not (ERTA, 2020).

With the establishment of the International Integrated Reporting Council (IIRC) in 2010, studies on integrated reporting have gained a global corporate structure. IIRC has announced its long-term vision as "a world where integrated reporting is used as the corporate reporting norm in the public and private sectors, and an integrated thinking structure is applied in common corporate practices". IIRC has determined the mission of preparing an internationally accepted integrated reporting framework that will guide companies in their integrated report preparation (IIRC, 2013: 2). IIRC published the "Integrated Reporting International Framework" (International IR Framework), which will be based on integrated reporting that was put into final form in line with the opinions of industry representatives and academicians from many countries including Turkey, in December 2013.

South Africa, which is a leader in integrated reporting, is followed by the Netherlands, Brazil, Australia, Finland, Switzerland, Spain, USA, Sweden, Canada, Germany and the UK. Finland and Australia are the countries with the most integrated reporting in the public sphere (Aras and Sarioglu, 2015: 76).

Turkey was entered into the process of integrated reporting by the studies carried out by Corporate Governance Association of Turkey (TKYD) and Sustainable Development Association (SKD) in 2011. Within this period, TKYD was the contact point of IIRC in Turkey.

Turkey Integrated Reporting Network (ERTA) was established in 2011 on the purpose of making adopted integrated reporting and giving guidance to the companies. By 2017, Borsa Istanbul became the first European stock exchange to prepare an integrated report by signing a co-operation agreement between Borsa Istanbul and IIRC to disseminate integrated reporting. As of 2019, there are 14 organizations in Turkey that provide integrated reporting. Finally, the report Vakifbank integrated 2019 integrated annual report published in Turkey was the first public bank. Finally, Vakifbank is the first public bank that published integrated annual report in Turkey in 2019.

4 International Integrated Reporting Framework

Since its establishment, IIRC has aimed to guide companies in preparing integrated reports. The International Integrated Reporting Framework was published in December 2013, following a two-year cooperation process in line with the opinions of industry and NGO representatives, accounting experts and academicians of many countries worldwide. The framework has been translated into 11 different languages and has been used worldwide.

The purpose of this framework, put forward by IIRC, is to set out the elements and guidelines that regulate the content of an integrated report and explain the concepts that form the basis of these principles. The framework defines the information to be included in the integrated report and sets out the principles for how to prepare integrated reports.

Table 1: *Integrated Reporting Framework Guidelines and Content Elements.* Source: *(IIRC, 2013)*

Guiding Principles	Content Elements
1. Strategic focus and future orientation	1. Organizational overview and external environment
2. Connectivity of information	2. Governance
3. Stakeholder relationships	3. Business model
4. Materiality	4. Risks and opportunities
5. Conciseness	5. Strategy and resource allocation
6. Reliability and completeness	6. Performance
7. Consistency and comparability	7. Outlook
	8. Basis of preparation and presentation

The framework does not include a standard format for integrated reporting but includes guidelines and content elements to guide organizations in the preparation and submission of the report. For this reason, the organizations will make a report in accordance with their own structures, taking into account certain principles. The guidelines provide information about the content of the integrated report and show how the information is presented. An integrated report should also include eight content items and questions and answers related to those items. The content of the integrated report is determined according to the conditions encountered by the relevant institution. For this reason, the content items are presented in the framework in the form of questions, not as a list of specific topics. Table 1 shows what guidelines and content items are.

This principle and the basis of the elements that form the integrated report are based on three main components. These are value creation, capital elements and process of creating value.

Creating value forms the basis of integrated thinking and integrated reporting. The value created by an organization over time is the changes and transformations that occur on capital elements as a result of the activities of the organization (IIRC, 2013: 10).

Capital items cover all the resources an organization uses to carry out its activities and achieve success. In this framework, capital items are classified as financial capital, manufactured capital, intellectual capital, human resources, social capital, relational capital and natural capital. However, organizations can categorize capital items differently in their integrated reports for their own purposes. Because capital items are not equally applicable to every organization (IIRC: 2013: 11).

The process of creating value is a process that shows how an organization creates value through its business model. The business model takes inputs from capital elements and converts them into outputs through business activities. These outputs create value for the organization, stakeholders, society and the environment in the short, medium and long term (EY & IIRC, 2013: 1). The integrated report should reveal to what extent and how the capital elements used by the organization create value in business processes and all factors affecting this value.

5 Integrated Reporting in Turkish Banking Sector

In this part of the study, the 2019 Integrated Activity reports prepared by Vakifbank, Garanti BBVA and Turkiye Sınai ve Kalkinma Bank (TSKB) were analyzed in terms of content.

5.1 Purpose and Method of Research

Operating in Turkey, besides Garanti BBVA, Turkiye Sinai ve Kalkinma Bank (TSKB) and Vakifbank, also Is Bankasi published Integrated Report in 2018 but Is Bankasi has not published the Integrated Report of 2019 yet. Therefore Garanti BBVA and Turkiye Sinai ve Kalkinma Bank (TSKB) that has published Integrated Report for last 3 years and Vakifbank, published Integrated Report in 2019 first time, are included in this study. The purpose of the study is to determine the extent to which the Integrated Reports prepared by banks correspond in terms of content with the International Integrated Reporting Framework.

The 2019 Integrated Annual Reports published by three banks in the study were analyzed through document review in terms of 8 content items in the Integrated Reporting Framework.

These content items are determined as "Corporate Overview and External Environment, Corporate Management, Business Model, Risk and Opportunities, Strategy and Resource Transfer, Performance, Overview, Preparation and Presentation Basis".

5.2 Corporate Overview and External Environment:

In the Corporate Overview and External Environment section, which is the first of the content elements, the promotion of the institution, mission, vision, basic fields of activity, ethical principles and values, and the situation in the sector should be introduced to stakeholders. In addition, external environmental factors such as technological, legal, commercial, social and environmental factors affecting the creation of value in the short-medium and long term should be addressed.

In its 2019 Integrated Report of 544 pages, Garanti BBVA stated that it has prepared a report in compliance with IIRC, and that the report consists of six main sections in accordance with the GRI Standards. The partnership structure of the institution is shown on page 21. Accordingly, the bank's shareholders and shares consist of 49.85 % BBVA, 44.65 % Corporate Investors, 1.7 % Individual Investors and 3.8 % unidentified investors. Banking activities are defined under three main headings and market shares in the sector are shown on page 22. The capital elements of the bank are grouped in five main groups;

- **Financial Capital:** $ 54 billion was provided to the economy through cash and non-cash loans. The market value of the bank has increased to $ 7.9 Billion.
- **Digital & Intellectual Capital:** Through digital channels, the bank's sales increased to 46 % of its total sales.
- **Human Capital:** Garanti BBVA, providing job opportunities to 18.784 people, with 40 % of middle and senior female employee ratio in Turkey is the only company in the Bloomberg position within the Gender Equality Index.
- **Relationship Capital:** The bank working to satisfy customer expectations achieved the highest recommendation score among private banks.
- **Natural & Social Capital:** It contributed approximately $ 4 million to community investment programs.

TKSB 2019 Integrated Annual Report consists of 245 pages. It was stated that the report was prepared in accordance with the International Integrated Reporting Framework proposed by IIRC and the GRI reporting guide published by GRI (TKSB Integrated Report, 2019; 2).On the 4th page of the report, the general view of the institution was introduced to the readers. Accordingly, the bank serves with 359 people as of the end of 2019. Partnership structure; Turkey Is Bank group 50.9 %, 40.7 % public and other investors and 8.4 % Vakiflar Bank. The mission, vision and values of the institution are also reflected on the same page. The capital elements of the Bank and its value creation model are reflected on the 5th page of the report. Accordingly, the capital items used by the bank to create value are classified into five main groups;

- **Financial Capital:** The Bank stated that it created 17.8 % capital adequacy ratio, 16.1 % equity profitability and 4.2 % interest net margin in 2019.
- **Human Capital:** The ratio of female employees in the entire bank was 54 %, and the ratio of female employees among middle and senior executives was 49 %. Participation rate in the employee satisfaction survey was 87 %.

- **Natural Capital:** 14, 4 million tons of annual contribution was made to CO2 emission reduction. The sustainable loan portfolio ratio was 74 %.
- **Intellectual Capital:** The Bank carried out 61 consultancy projects and prepared sustainability reports in 2019.
- **Social Capital:** Participation in working groups on international platforms, increasing the rate of female employment, increasing employment through APEX loans.

Vakifbank briefly touched on its history and its shareholding structure in its Integrated Activity report, which was prepared for the first time in 2019. Accordingly, 25.22 % shares of the bank are open to the public and the remaining shares are in public and bank funds and foundations. The vision, mission and basic principles of the bank are mentioned in the report (Vakifbank Integrated Report, 2019). The bank's main values are; widespread access to finance, sustainable development, innovative approach and capacity building. In the value creation model, the capital elements used by the bank to achieve value outcomes are as follows;

- **Financial Capital:** The Bank adopts a strong capital structure and sustainable growth approach.
- **Produced Capital:** It is one of the banks with the highest number of branches and ATMs in the sector.
- **Intellectual Capital:** Digital transformation is aimed by investing in information technologies.
- **Human Capital:** Equality of women and men, low employee turnover, and high hours of internal training are provided.
- **Social and Relational Capital:** The bank, which carries out social responsibility projects in various fields, also strives to increase customer satisfaction.
- **Natural Capital:** Financial support is provided to renewable energy projects.

5.3 Corporate Management and Business Model

In the reporting of the Corporate Governance and business model, it is expected that the business' ability to create value in the short, medium and long term, leadership structure of the enterprise, wage and incentive policies, organization and business model will be transferred to the users.

In the Garanti BBVA 2019 Integrated report, the organizational structure, committees and policies of the bank were explained. The Bank has gathered its strategic priorities under three headings and identified them as differentiation in the eyes of their customers, the keys of superior success and elements that will enable them to realize strategies. Although the business model of the bank is shown as inputs, risks and created values, business activities are not included in this scheme.

In line with its mission and business plan, TKSB supports projects for Turkey's development through three basic services; development banking, investment banking and consulting. The organizational structure and committees of the bank are not included in the report.

In addition to its medium and long-term goals, Vakifbank touched on the bank's organizational structure and committees. Bank sustainability has positioned at the center of the business model. It was emphasized that the priority is qualified personnel for the implementation of the business model. In the report, the business model is defined as explicitly explaining how it will achieve its goals in an external environment that includes economic conditions, technological changes, social problems and environmental challenges, and how it creates value for the economy, society and environment in the face of risks and opportunities posed by the external environment. The business model is not schematically defined. However, the concept of creating value for stakeholders is emphasized in the business model.

5.4 Risks and Opportunities, Strategy and Resource Transfer

Possible risks and opportunities that institutions may face must be included in the content of the integrated reports. In addition, the goals of the institution, the strategies and resources it will implement to achieve these goals should be included.

The Garanti BBVA 2019 Integrated Report explains that the bank's goal is sustainable growth by creating value for all its stakeholders. It has determined its strategic priorities as competition, customer expectations, sustainability and data. Possible risks and opportunities are grouped in five groups. These five groups; business environment, society, economy, environment and technology have been determined (Garanti BBVA Integrated Report, 2019).

TKSB explained the risk policies of the bank in detail in the 2019 Integrated report. In the strategic plan of the bank, who are the stakeholders were identified and primary and secondary priorities were determined. Effective risk management is also a primary priority for the bank. Analysis of external factors in the strategic plan can also be seen in detail in the report. The issue of risk and opportunities is not addressed in a separate title in the report. Possible risks and opportunities are mentioned within the capital components.

Vakifbank schematically demonstrated the impact of risks and opportunities on outputs within the value creation model. A section is reserved for risk management in the report. In this section, the risks faced by the bank are explained and how risk measurements are performed is shown. Accordingly, the bank has risks such as market risk, interest rate risk, liquidity risk, operational risks, nominal risk, credit risk, country risk. These risks are measured by the value-at-risk method that is developed continuously. Although the source structure of the bank is mentioned in the report, it is not mentioned what the targets are.

5.5 Performance, Overview, Preparation and Presentation Basis

Garanti BBVA provides a lot of data on the financial performance of the bank in the 2019 Integrated Annual Report. The extent to which the targets in the period were reached was explained to the users by making a table. The evaluation of goals and achievements together, presenting qualitative and quantitative data together provided convenience for the reader. Possible uncertainties, estimates and potential impacts are presented in the report when creating the corporate strategy for the general opinion section. According to the report, uncertainties experienced at home and abroad caused the investment appetite in 2019 to be low. While preparing the integrated annual report, Garanti BBVA took into consideration the issues requested by the stakeholders and also addressed important issues for the bank.

TSKB has devoted a large part to the financial performance of the bank in the report. Qualitative and quantitative data are presented here. Besides the 2019 financial data, the bank's 2020 projections are also included in the report. However, as with Garanti BBVA, the target achievement of the previous year has no values. The report also addressed the uncertainties that could affect key performance indicators. Possible effects of factors such as external environment and risk on the bank's performance were included. In the preparation of the report, the bank was based on the stakeholder analysis study it carried out in 2018. The perceptions and attitudes of the bank were measured, and the priorities were determined with the face-to-face interview technique, which was determined in the stakeholder analysis.

In 2019, Vakifbank announced its financial performance in an integrated annual report with qualitative and quantitative data. In the report, along with the 2019 data, the financial data for 2018 was also presented and the development of the bank was shown. However, 2019 target realization figures and 2020 predictions are not included in the report. The report also addressed the uncertainties experienced in 2019 and expected in the future. External environmental factors, risks and opportunities are also covered in this context. The Integrated Reporting Framework published by IIRC and Sustainability Accounting Standards Board Provisional Standard for Commercial Banks (SASB) were taken into consideration in the preparation of the report. As in TKSB, there is no information that stakeholder views were received.

6 Conclusion

Today, the development of communication opportunities and technology provides important facilities for the shareholders and the whole society in evaluating the business activities. In the context of the changing information need of the society, in this environment where financial data alone is not sufficient to evaluate the success and sustainability of the businesses, the reports to be prepared should also reflect the corporate governance understanding of the companies, their environmental awareness and social responsibility awareness. The reports, which will be prepared with this integrated mindset, give institutions the opportunity to provide a holistic and transparent information. Successful implementation of sustainable development strategies with integrated reporting will make a significant contribution to creating sustainable value for both institutions and the whole community and to creating permanent community welfare in a healthy environment.

Accordingly, with the study carried out on the banking sector, which is one of the important sectors of the Turkish economy, the reports of three banks that published the Integrated Annual Report in 2019 were analyzed in terms of content. Among these banks, Vakifbank prepared a report this year for the first time as a state-owned deposit bank. Garanti BBVA and TSKB have regularly published integrated reports for 3 years. When the reports are examined, it is determined that all three banks are preparing reports based on the IIRC Integrated Reporting Framework. Therefore, adhering to the guiding principles. However, it has been determined that the reports prepared by Garanti BBVA and Vakifbank are not sufficiently compliant with the principle of being short and concise, they are generally quite long and contain detailed information. TSKB also conducted stakeholder analysis, taking into account the priorities of the stakeholders, and prepared an Integrated Annual Report, taking into account the results of the analysis. The 2019 report of TSKB, which was selected among the best ones in 2017, offers more summary and explanatory information compared to other reports. In the coming years, it can be said that more Integrated Annual Reports will be prepared with the participation of other banks in the Turkish Banking sector. In order to better meet the information needs of the report user stakeholders, it would be beneficial for all banks to conduct stakeholder analysis, as in the case of TSKB. In addition, shorter and more concise preparation of Integrated Annual Reports will be more beneficial for stakeholders in terms of understandability. Integrated reporting in line with the information needs of the stakeholders of other banks operating in the sector will contribute significantly to the development of the sector.

References

Aras, G., & Sarioglu, G. U. (2015). Kurumsal Raporlamada Yeni Dönem: Entegre Raporlama, TÜSİAD Publications, 10–567.

Borsa Istanbul Sustainability Bulletin. (2014). https://www.borsaistanbul.com/docs/default-source/yayinlar/borsa-istanbul-2014-surdurulebilirlik-bulteni.pdf?sfvrsn=4

Eccles, R. G., & Armbrester K. (2011). Two Disruptive Ideas Combined: Integrated Reporting in the Cloud. IESE Insight, 8, 13–20.

Entegre Raporlama Turkiye Ağı (ERTA). http://www.entegreraporlamatr.org/tr/

EY & IIRC. Value Creation Background Paper. July 2013. https://integratedreporting.org/wp-content/uploads/2013/08/Background-Paper-Value-Creation.pdf

Garanti BBVA Integrated Report. (2019). https://www.garantibbvainvestorrelations.com/ en/images/entegre-faaliyet-raporu-2019/garanti-bbva-integrated-annual-report-2019.pdf

Gökten, S. (2016). Entegre Raporlama Yaklaşımı İçin Uygulamaya Yönelik Sistematik Bir Öneri. Muhasebe Bilim Dünyası Dergisi, 18(4), 741–765.

Hoque, M. E. (2017). Why Company Should Adopt Integrated Reporting?. International Journal of Economics and Financial Issues, 7(1), 241–248.

International Integrated Reporting Council (IIRC). (2013). The International Integrated Reporting Framework. https://integratedreporting.org/resource/international-ir-framework/

TKSB Integrated Report. (2019). http://www.tskb.com.tr/i/content/4202_1_Integrated%20 Report%202019.pdf

Vakifbank Integrated Report. (2019). https://www.vakifbank.com.tr/documents/finansal/14052020-Integrated%20Annual%20Report%202019.pdf

Derya Öztürk

Assessment of Consumer Preferences for Chain Coffee Shops Using AHP-Based TOPSIS Method

1 Introduction

In recent years, chain coffee shops have become alternative to homes and workplaces where people of all ages and social backgrounds spend significant portions of their time to socialize. Every day, coffee companies open up new stores where people can rest and meet friends or make new ones. Chain coffee shops also serve a great variety of drinks, ice cream, and chocolate, and pastries such as cookies, sandwiches, cakes, cakes, sweets, bagels etc. The chain coffee shops in Turkey are generally located on main streets, shopping malls, airports, and beaches (Bayındır and Öncel, 2019: 1808).

In recent years, local and foreign coffee companies have opened up numerous shops in Turkey. There are 61 coffee chain companies with multiple stores operating in Turkey. The great majority of those chain coffee shops are Turkish brands (85 %). Fifty-six percent of 1,580 stores in Turkey belong to Turkish brands. Four of the ten biggest chain coffee shops in Turkey are local companies, while three are American companies, and one is an Italian, one is a Finnish and one is a British company. The chain coffee shops with the most stores in Turkey are Starbucks, *Kahve Dünyası*, *Kahve Diyarı*, *Gönül Kahvesi*, *Kahve Deryası*, Gloria Jeans, Caffe Nero, *Kahve Durağı*, and Tchibo (www.dunya.com, 2020). Chain coffee shops that wish to maximize growth and revenue and have competitive advantage in the market focus on satisfying as many wants and needs of their customers as possible (Kadıoğlu, 2017:2). Chain coffee shops cater to different types of customers, and therefore, have different marketing policies. Chain coffee shops, each with a different marketing strategy, have different high-quality coffee choices, provide comfortable environments, adopt eco-friendly business practices, and use energy efficiently in order to increase customer satisfaction and brand loyalty (Kadıoğlu, 2017: 4).

2 Method

2.1 Analytical Hierarchy Process

The Analytical Hierarchy Process (AHP) is a multi-criteria decision-making method developed by Thomas L. Saaty (1977) to solve complex problems. The AHP makes pairwise comparisons of relative importance between hierarchy elements based on decision makers' opinions. The AHP is an easy-to-use method to solve numerous different decision problems because it integrates qualitative and quantitative criteria, involves multiple decision makers in the process, and allows the user to choose among many alternatives (Avcı and Çınaroğlu, 2018: 323). The following are the steps of the AHP:

Step 1. Constructing a Hierarchical Structure

First, an objective is determined, and then, a hierarchical structure is constructed to indicate the relationship between the main criteria, sub-criteria, and alternatives, all of which are necessary to achieve that objective (Yang and Lee, 1997: 246).

Step 2. Constructing Pairwise comparison Matrices

In pairwise comparisons, Saaty's 1–9 scale (1988) as shown in Table 1, is used to digitize subjective/objective qualitative data and to obtain pairwise comparison matrices. First, the main criteria, and then, the sub-criteria, if any, are pairwise compared.

Table 1: *Scale of Pairwise Comparisons.* Source: (Saaty, 1977)

Intensity of Importance	Definition	Explanation
1	Equally preferred	Two elements contribute equally to the object
3	Moderately preferred	One element is moderately preferred over another element
5	Strongly preferred	One element is strongly preferred over another element
7	Very strongly preferred	One element is very strongly preferred over another element
9	Extremely preferred	One element is extremely preferred over another element
2,4,6,8	Intermediate values	Intermediate values between the two adjacent judgments when compromise is needed

Step 3. Normalizing the Pairwise Comparison Matrix

The elements of each column are divided by the sum of that column.

Step 4. Deriving Weights

The rows are averaged. The consistency ratio (CR) is calculated to make sure that the weights are valid.

Step 5. Calculating the Consistency Ratio

A CR is calculated for each matrix to determine whether pairwise comparisons are consistent (Saaty, 1990: 13).

$$CR= CI/RI \tag{1}$$

where CI and RI are the consistency and random indices (RIs), respectively. Table 2 shows the RIs calculated based on different n values.

Table 2: *Random Consistency Index*

n	1	2	3	4	5	6	7	8	9	10	11	12	13	14	15
RI	0.00	0.00	0.58	0.90	1.12	1.24	1.32	1.41	1.45	1.49	1.51	1.53	1.56	1.57	1.59

CI indicates the deviation of λmax from n and is calculated using the equation $CI = (\lambda_{max} - n)/(n-1)$ (Ömürbek et al., 2014: 195).

λmax is the largest eigenvector value, and n is the number of columns.

CRs smaller than 0.1 indicate consistent pairwise comparison matrices (Chan et al., 2006: 641). This means that if CRs are smaller than 0.1, comparisons made by decision makers are consistent whereas if CRs are greater than 0.1, there are calculation errors or decision makers' responses to the comparison matrices are inconsistent. In that case, pairwise comparison matrices are reconstructed and are decided accordingly.

Afterwards, the priorities of the sub-criteria are multiplied by those of the main criteria to determine the general priorities, and thus the overall weights, of the criteria. The sum of these values is equal to 1.

2.2. TOPSIS Method

The Technique for Order Preference by Similarity to Ideal Solution (TOPSIS) developed by Hwang and Yoon (1981) is a multi-criteria decision analysis method used to determine positive and negative ideal solutions of decision-making problems in order to select the ideal alternative (Öztürk and Onurlubaş, 2019: 84). The main principle is that the ideal alternative should have the shortest distance to the positive-ideal solution and the farthest distance from the negative-ideal solution. It is used in different areas because it is free from complex mathematical expressions or algorithms, and easy to understand and interpret (Özdemir, 2015: 134). TOPSIS consists of six steps (Özcan et al., 2018: 5–7):

Step 1 – Constructing the decision matrix (A): Alternatives and criteria are listed on the rows and columns, respectively. Matrix A is an initial matrix generated by the decision-maker. The following is the decision matrix:

$$A_{ij} = \begin{bmatrix} a_{11} & a_{12} & \dots & a_{1n} \\ a_{21} & a_{22} & \dots & a_{2n} \\ \cdot & & & \cdot \\ \cdot & & & \cdot \\ \cdot & & & \cdot \\ a_{m1} & a_{m2} & \dots & a_{mn} \end{bmatrix} \tag{1}$$

where m is the number of decision-making alternatives and n is the number of evaluation criteria.

Step 2 – Constructing the standard decision matrix (R): The Standard Decision Matrix is calculated using the matrix A as in the equation below:

$$R_{ij} = \begin{bmatrix} r_{11} & r_{12} & \dots & r_{1n} \\ r_{21} & r_{22} & \dots & r_{2n} \\ \cdot & & & \cdot \\ \cdot & & & \cdot \\ \cdot & & & \cdot \\ r_{m1} & r_{m2} & \dots & r_{mn} \end{bmatrix} \tag{2}$$

$$r_{ij} = \frac{a_{ij}}{\sqrt{\sum_{k=1}^{m} a_{kj}^2}} \tag{3}$$

Step 3 -Constructing the weighted standard decision matrix (V): First, weight values (w_i) associated with the evaluation criteria are calculated.

$$\sum_{i=1}^{n} w_i = 1$$

$$V_{ij} = \begin{bmatrix} w_1 r_{11} & w_2 r_{12} & \dots & w_n r_{1n} \\ w_1 r_{21} & w_2 r_{22} & \dots & w_n r_{2n} \\ \cdot & & & \cdot \\ \cdot & & & \cdot \\ \cdot & & & \cdot \\ w_1 r_{m1} & w_2 r_{m2} & \dots & w_n r_{mn} \end{bmatrix} \tag{4}$$

Step 4 – Determining the positive (A^*) and negative (A^-) ideal solutions: The ideal solution set is calculated using the following equation:

$$A^* = \left\{ (\max_i v_{ij} \middle| j \in J), (\min_i v_{ij} | j \in J' \right\} \tag{5}$$

$$A^- = \left\{ (\min_i v_{ij} \middle| j \in J), (\max_i v_{ij} | j \in J' \right\} \tag{6}$$

$A^* = \{v_1^*, v_2^*, ..., v_n^*\}$ denotes the set calculated.
$A^- = \{v_1^-, v_2^-, ..., v_n^-\}$ denotes the set calculated.

Step 5 – Making Separation Measurements: Equation (6) and (7) are used to calculate the positive ideal separation (S_i^*) and negative ideal separation (S_i^-), respectively.

$$S_i^* = \sqrt{\sum_{j=1}^{n} (v_{ij} - v_j^*)^2} \tag{7}$$

$$S_i^- = \sqrt{\sum_{j=1}^{n} (v_{ij} - v_j^-)^2} \tag{8}$$

where the number of S_i^* and S_i^- is naturally equal to the number of alternatives.

Step 6 – Calculating the Relative Closeness to the Ideal Solution: The relative closeness to the ideal solution is calculated using the following equation:

$$C_i^* = \frac{S_i^-}{S_i^- + S_i^*} \tag{9}$$

where $0 \leq C_i^* \leq 1$, and $C_i^* = 1$ is the absolute closeness of the alternative to the ideal solution while $C_i^* = 0$ is the absolute closeness of the alternative to the negative ideal solution.

The values in the previous step are ranked in order of size to rank the alternatives in order of importance, according to which the ideal alternative is chosen.

3 An Application on Chain Coffee Shops Operating in Turkey

The aim of this study was to use the AHP and TOPSIS methods to determine the importance weights of criteria affecting consumer preferences for chain coffee shops and to rank the chain coffee shops based on those criteria. The study population consisted of all coffee consumers in the city of Samsun. The total number of customers of the coffee shops, and thus, the main mass, could not be numerically determined. The sample size was limited to 100 customers based on the implementation and time-cost constraints of the AHP method. Participants were randomly selected from the customers of the coffee shops in the city center. The sample included the customers of all chain coffee shops for data validity and reliability. A survey was conducted to determine the top chain coffee shops operating in Samsun. The names of the other coffee shops (alternatives) were kept confidential so that the survey results would not tarnish their reputation. While their real names were used in the survey, they were referred to as A, B and C in the study. Data were collected through face-to-face interviews using the questionnaire developed by Kadıoğlu (2017). Data were analyzed using Microsoft Excel 2013. The model developed for consumer preferences for chain coffee shops consisted of five main criteria and their sub-criteria (Table 3).

3.1 Determination of Weights of Evaluation Criteria Using AHP

Determining evaluation criteria weights is based on decision makers' knowledge and experience. Numerous subjective weighting methods have been developed to determine criteria weights. In this study, the AHP was the method of choice to determine the evaluation criteria weights of the chain coffee shops because it is a user-friendly method that allows the user to determine group decisions, simplify complex problems, and calculate the CRs of decision makers' judgments (Kuruüzüm and Atsan, 2001:93). Table 4 shows the comparison matrices, relative importance weights (RIWs), CRs, and final weight values of the main and sub-criteria. The geometric mean of participants' pairwise comparison results was calculated.

Table 3: *Criteria and Subcriteria*

Criteria	Subcriteria
Financial characteristics	Reasonable Price (RP)
	Offering Loyalty Programs (OLP)
	Offering Sales Promotion (OSP)
Product characteristics	Wide Range of Products (WROP)
	Serving Delicious Products (SDP)
	Serving Fresh Products (SFP)
	Serving Healthy/Eco-friendly Products (SHEP)
	Product Presentation Style (PPS)
Service characteristics	Staff Attitude towards Customers (SATC)
	Quick Service (QS)
	Providing the Right Service (PRS)
	Style of Service (SOS)
Shop/Setting Characteristics	Pleasing and Colorful Store Design (PACSD)
	Setting (Place of Product Consumed) Hygiene (S(POPC)H)
	Relaxing and Pleasant Ambient Music (RAPAM)
	Pleasing and Distinctive Ambient Fragrance (PADAF)
	Tidy and Clean Place for Product Preparation (TACPFPP)
Brand image	High Brand Awareness (HBA)
	Being Consumers' Favorite Brand (BCFB)
	Fair Trade (FT)
	Environmentally Friendly (EE)

Table 4: *Comparison of Main Criteria*

	Financial characteristics	Product characteristics	Service characteristics	Shop/Setting Characteristics	Brand image	RIWs
Financial characteristics	1.000	0.125	0.167	0.250	0.333	0.046
Product characteristics	8.000	1.000	1.400	1.840	1.640	0.337
Service characteristics	6.000	0.714	1.000	0.970	1.896	0.251
Shop/Setting Characteristics	4.000	0.543	1.031	1.000	1.650	0.216
Brand image	3.000	0.610	0.527	0.606	1.000	0.150
CR: 0.01						

CR: Consistency Ratio

The pairwise comparison result of the main criteria showed that "product characteristics" was the most important criterion (0.337), followed by "service characteristics" (0.251), "shop/setting characteristics" (0.216), "brand image" (0.150), and "financial characteristics" (0.046). The Pairwise comparison matrix had a CR of 0.01, indicating highly reliable evaluation (Table 4). Tables 5, 6, 7, 8, and 9 show the pairwise comparisons, RIWs, and CRs of the subcriteria.

Of the subcriteria of "financial characteristics," OSP had the highest weight (0.394), followed by RP (0.359) and OLP (0.247) (Table 5).

Table 5: *Comparison of Subcriteria of Financial Characteristics*

	RP	OLP	OSP	RIWs
RP	1.000	1.582	0.840	0.359
OLP	0.632	1.000	0.680	0.247
OSP	1.190	1.471	1.000	0.394
CR: 0.01				

CR: Consistency Ratio

Of the subcriteria of "product characteristics," SHEP had the highest weight (0.300), followed by PPS (0.214), SFP (0.205), SDP (0.145), and WROP (0.135) (Table 6).

Of the subcriteria of "service characteristics," SATC was the most important (0.334) (0.300), followed by PRS (0.316), SOS (0.185) and QS (0.165) (Table 7).

The subcriteria of "shop/setting characteristics" were ranked as TACPFPP (0.269), S(POPC)H (0.220), RAPAM (0.201), PADAF (0.187), and PACSD (0.122) (Table 8).

The subcriteria of "brand image" were ranked as EE (0.318). HBA (0.276), BCFB (0.243), and FT (0.163) (Table 9).

Table 6: Comparison of Subcriteria of Product Characteristics

	WROP	SDP	SFP	SHEP	PPS	RIWs
WROP	1.000	0.778	0.667	0.542	0.630	0.135
SDP	1.285	1.000	0.712	0.473	0.560	0.145
SFP	1.499	1.404	1.000	0.786	0.876	0.205
SHEP	1.845	2.114	1.272	1.000	1.894	0.300
PPS	1.587	1.786	1.142	0.528	1.000	0.214
CR: 0.01						

CR: Consistency Ratio

Table 7: *Comparison of Subcriteria of Service Characteristics*

	SATC	QS	PRS	SOS	RIWs
SATC	1.000d	2.356	1.130	1.463	0.334
QS	0.424	1.000	0.630	0.876	0.165
PRS	0.885	1.587	1.000	2.180	0.316
SOS	0.684	1.142	0.459	1.000	0.185
CR: 0.02					

CR: Consistency Ratio

Table 8: *Comparison of Subcriteria of Shop/Setting Characteristics*

	PACSD	S(POPC)H	RAPAM	PADAF	TACPFPP	RIWs
PACSD	1.000	0.520	0.651	0.827	0.345	0.122
S(POPC)H	1.923	1.000	1.043	1.112	0.884	0.220
RAPAM	1.536	0.959	1.000	1.120	0.756	0.201
PADAF	1.209	0.899	0.893	1.000	0.845	0.187
TACPFPP	2.899	1.131	1.323	1.183	1.000	0.269
CR: 0.03						

CR: Consistency Ratio

Table 9: *Comparison of Subcriteria of Brand Image*

	HBA	BCFB	FT	EE	RIWs
HBA	1.000	1.424	1.732	0.690	0.276
BCFB	0.702	1.000	1.910	0.743	0.243
FT	0.577	0.524	1.000	0.654	0.163
EE	1.449	1.346	1.529	1.000	0.318
CR: 0.02					

CR: Consistency Ratio

Table 10: *Matrix of Main and Subcriteria*

Criteria	Weights	Subcriteria	Weights	W
Financial characteristics	0.046	RP	0.359	0.017
		OLP	0.247	0.011
		OSP	0.394	0.018
Product characteristics	0.337	WROP	0.135	0.046
		SDP	0.145	0.049
		SFP	0.205	0.069
		SHEP	0.300	0.101
		PPS	0.214	0.072
Service characteristics	0.251	SATC	0.334	0.084
		QS	0.165	0.041
		PRS	0.316	0.079
		SOS	0.185	0.046
Shop/Setting Characteristics	0.216	PACSD	0.122	0.026
		S(POPC)H	0.220	0.048
		RAPAM	0.201	0.044
		PADAF	0.187	0.040
		TACPFPP	0.269	0.058
Brand image	0.150	HBA	0.276	0.041
		BCFB	0.243	0.036
		FT	0.163	0.024
		EE	0.318	0.048

In the last step of the AHD, the final weight (W) of each subcriterion was calculated by multiplying the weight values of the sub-criteria and criteria (Table 10).

The two most important criteria for participants were "serving healthy/eco-friendly products" and "staff attitude towards customers" whereas the least important criterion for them was "offering loyalty programs."

3.2 TOPSIS Procedure

TOPSIS was performed in six steps as follows:

Table 11: Decision Matrix

	RP	OLP	OSP	WROP	SDP	SFP	SHEP	PPS	SATC	QS	PRS	SOS
A	6.140	6.170	6.930	7.650	7.280	5.840	7.680	7.150	6.550	7.890	6.900	7.180
B	4.700	4.660	4.540	4.300	6.290	6.500	7.890	5.550	8.760	7.550	7.510	6.400
C	8.150	6.170	7.520	7.050	7.530	6.660	7.420	7.300	6.680	7.560	7.590	7.420

Step 1: Constructing the Decision Matrix: Table 11 shows the decision matrix based on the geometric mean of the scores (1–10) given by the decision makers for the alternatives.

PACSD	S(POPC)H	RAPAM	PADAF	TACPFPP	HBA	BCFB	FT	EE
8.250	7.210	5.430	7.560	6.770	7.210	7.960	6.070	6.750
7.200	5.650	7.340	6.200	5.670	5.480	5.310	6.000	7.880
8.210	8.234	6.230	7.670	7.210	7.310	7.730	6.920	7.360

Step 2 – Creating the Standard Decision Matrix (R): The TOPSIS method begins with the normalization of values in decision matrices. Each value in the columns was divided by the square root of the sum of the squares of all values in the column and reduced to a single denominator. Table 12 shows the standard decision matrix of the problem.

Table 12: *Standard Decision Matrix*

	RP	OLP	OSP	WROP	SDP	SFP	SHEP	PPS	SATC	QS	PRS	SOS
A	0.547	0.624	0.619	0.680	0.596	0.532	0.578	0.615	0.511	0.594	0.543	0.591
B	0.418	0.471	0.406	0.382	0.515	0.592	0.594	0.477	0.683	0.568	0.591	0.527
C	0.725	0.624	0.672	0.626	0.616	0.606	0.559	0.628	0.521	0.569	0.597	0.611

PACSD	S(POPC)H	RAPAM	PADAF	TACPFPP	HBA	BCFB	FT	EE
0.603	0.585	0.491	0.608	0.594	0.620	0.647	0.552	0.531
0.526	0.459	0.664	0.499	0.497	0.471	0.432	0.546	0.619
0.600	0.669	0.564	0.617	0.632	0.628	0.628	0.630	0.579

Step 3: Constructing the Weighted Standard Decision Matrix (V): The weighted decision matrix (Table 14) was generated by multiplying the standard decision matrix values with the weight coefficients of the AHP criteria (W) (Table 13).

Table 13: *Criterion Weight Values*

	RP	OLP	OSP	WROP	SDP	SFP	SHEP	PPS	SATC	QS	PRS	SOS
W	0.017	0.011	0.018	0.046	0.049	0.069	0.101	0.072	0.084	0.041	0.079	0.046

PACSD	S(POPC)H	RAPAM	PADAF	TACPFPP	HBA	BCFB	FT	EE
0.026	0.048	0.044	0.040	0.058	0.041	0.036	0.024	0.048

Table 14: *Weighted Decision Matrix*

	RP	OLP	OSP	WROP	SDP	SFP	SHEP	PPS	SATC	QS	PRS	SOS
A	0.009	0.007	0.011	0.031	0.029	0.037	0.058	0.044	0.043	0.025	0.043	0.027
B	0.007	0.005	0.007	0.017	0.025	0.041	0.060	0.034	0.057	0.024	0.047	0.024
C	0.012	0.007	0.012	0.029	0.030	0.042	0.057	0.045	0.044	0.024	0.047	0.028

PACSD	S(POPC)H	RAPAM	PADAF	TACPFPP	HBA	BCFB	FT	EE
0.016	0.028	0.021	0.025	0.035	0.026	0.024	0.014	0.025
0.014	0.022	0.029	0.020	0.029	0.020	0.016	0.013	0.030
0.016	0.032	0.025	0.025	0.037	0.026	0.023	0.015	0.028

Step 4: Determining the Positive (A^*) and Negative (A^-) Ideal Solutions: For the ideal solution from each column in the weighted decision matrix, ideal negative values are selected for the ideal negative solution to create ideal and negative ideal solution sets. Table 15 shows the positive and negative ideal solution sets. The criteria that were believed to affect participants' preferences for chain coffee shops were the benefit criteria, hence, criteria maximization. The highest and smallest values for benefit criteria are positive ideal and negative ideal solutions.

Table 15: *Positive and Negative Ideal Solution Sets*

	RP	OLP	OSP	WROP	SDP	SFP	SHEP	PPS	SATC	QS	PRS	SOS
A^*	0.012	0.007	0.012	0.031	0.030	0.042	0.060	0.045	0.057	0.025	0.047	0.028
A^-	0.007	0.005	0.007	0.017	0.025	0.037	0.057	0.034	0.043	0.024	0.043	0.024

PACSD	S(POPC)H	RAPAM	PADAF	TACPFPP	HBA	BCFB	FT	EE
0.016	0.032	0.029	0.025	0.037	0.026	0.024	0.015	0.030
0.014	0.022	0.021	0.020	0.029	0.020	0.016	0.013	0.025

Step 5: Calculating the Separation Measures: Positive ideal and negative ideal values were subtracted from the values in the column of each criterion, and distances from the positive and negative ideal solutions were determined (Tables 16 and 17).

Table 16: *Distance from Positive Ideal Solution*

	RP	OLP	OSP	WROP	SDP	SFP	SHEP	PPS
A	0.0000089	0.0000000	0.0000009	0.0000000	0.0000010	0.0000267	0.0000026	0.0000009
B	0.0000263	0.0000031	0.0000238	0.0001842	0.0000244	0.0000010	0.0000000	0.0001176
C	0.0000000	0.0000000	0.0000000	0.0000059	0.0000000	0.0000000	0.0000128	0.0000000

SATC	QS	PRS	SOS	PACSD	S(POPC)H	RAPAM	PADAF
0.0002086	0.0000000	0.0000184	0.0000008	0.0000000	0.0000157	0.0000565	0.0000001
0.0000000	0.0000011	0.0000002	0.0000151	0.0000041	0.0000998	0.0000000	0.0000228
0.0001848	0.0000011	0.0000000	0.0000000	0.0000000	0.0000000	0.0000191	0.0000000

TACPFPP	HBA	BCFB	FT	EE	TOTAL	SQUARE ROOT	S*
0.0000050	0.0000001	0.0000000	0.0000036	0.0000181	0.0003679	0.0191817	S1
0.0000617	0.0000425	0.0000618	0.0000042	0.0000000	0.0006939	0.0263411	S2
0.0000000	0.0000000	0.0000005	0.0000000	0.0000038	0.0002280	0.0150985	S3

Table 17: *Distance from Negative Ideal Solution*

1	RP	OLP	OSP	WROP	SDP	SFP	SHEP	PPS
A	0.0000046	0.0000031	0.0000153	0.0001842	0.0000156	0.0000000	0.0000039	0.0000983
B	0.0000000	0.0000000	0.0000000	0.0000000	0.0000000	0.0000173	0.0000128	0.0000000
C	0.0000263	0.0000031	0.0000238	0.0001241	0.0000244	0.0000267	0.0000000	0.0001176

SATC	QS	PRS	SOS	PACSD	S(POPC)H	RAPAM	PADAF
0.0000000	0.0000011	0.0000000	0.0000088	0.0000041	0.0000364	0.0000000	0.0000195
0.0002086	0.0000000	0.0000144	0.0000000	0.0000000	0.0000000	0.0000565	0.0000000
0.0000007	0.0000000	0.0000184	0.0000151	0.0000038	0.0000998	0.0000099	0.0000228

TACPFPP	HBA	BCFB	FT	EE	TOTAL	SQUARE ROOT	S^-
0.0000315	0.0000380	0.0000618	0.0000000	0.0000000	0.0003249	0.0180259	S1
0.0000000	0.0000000	0.0000000	0.0000000	0.0000181	0.0002387	0.0154496	S2
0.0000617	0.0000425	0.0000515	0.0000042	0.0000053	0.0003466	0.0186184	S3

Step 6: Calculating the Relative Closeness to the Ideal Solution (C^*): For each alternative value, the negative ideal solution value was divided by the sum of its own value and the positive ideal solution value of the same alternative (Table 18).

This study employed the TOPSIS method to determine the criteria affecting participants' preferences for chain coffee shops. According to the relative closeness to the ideal solution, "C" was the ideal chain coffee shop.

Table 18: *Relative Closeness to the Ideal Solution*

Chain Coffee Shop	C^*	Ranking
A	0.545	2
B	0.407	3
C	0.634	1

4 Conclusion

This study provides information about the criteria that affect people's preferences for chain coffee shops. The results show that the most important factor is "product characteristics," followed by "service characteristics," "shop/setting characteristics," "brand image," and "financial characteristics." The most important subcriteria of the criterion of "product characteristics" is healthy/eco-friendly products, which becomes increasingly important for consumers due to rapid advances in technology and population growth. How a product looks and is presented is as important as how healthy and ecological it is. For example, plated desserts and latte art make products appealing. Serving a wide range of delicious and fresh products is another criterion affecting participants' preferences for chain coffee shops.

"Service characteristics" is the second most important factor affecting participants' preferences for chain coffee shops. Warm welcome, smiling face, and sincerity make customers feel important, valued, and comfortable (Onurlubaş and Şener, 2016). Service sector employees' positive attitudes in particular make customers feel safe, which promotes brand reputation. Another important point of service characteristics is delivering the right product to the right customer. Receiving the wrong order is disappointing for most customers, and disappointed customers are less likely to visit the same shop again. Every chain coffee shop has its own marketing strategy, and hence, a different style of service. Some chain coffee shops are self-service, some are a-la-carte service, and some are semi self-service. Fast service is also another important criterion making participants more likely to visit the same coffee shop again.

Every step of service should promote customer satisfaction and loyalty to thrive in the developing coffee market. High-quality products, perfect service, organized and clean kitchen, eco-friendly branding, and sales promotion are of paramount importance. For example, cleanliness and nice smell appeal to customers. Consumers prefer coffee shops that use eco-friendly products and pay attention to recycling. Sales promotion, special offers, and discount coupons also affect consumers' preferences for chain coffee shops. TOPSIS results show that participants prefer the chain coffee shop "C" the most, followed by A and B. This indicates that chain coffee shops that take into account the importance criteria and the determined criteria to improve their service quality can gain a great competitive advantage. We, therefore, believe that the results of this study will be useful for chain coffee shops.

The greatest limitation of the study was that only the customers of three chain coffee shops could be included in the study because the TOPSIS method requires that customers purchase services of each company (alternatives as well) at least once. Future studies should include more chain coffee shops and comparatively use multi-criteria decision-making methods besides the TOPSIS method.

References

Avcı, T. ve Çınaroğlu, E. (2018). AHP Temelli TOPSIS Yaklaşımı ile Havayolu İşletmelerinin Finansal Performans Değerlemesi. *C.Ü. İktisadi ve İdari Bilimler Dergisi*, 19(1): 316–335.

Bayındır, B. ve Önçel, S. (2019). Üniversite Öğrencilerinin Kahve Dükkânlarını Tercih Etme Nedenleri: Anadolu Üniversitesi Örneği. *Journal of Tourism and Gastronomy Studies*, 7 (3): 1806–1820.

Chan, F. T. S., Chan, H. K., Lau, H. C. V. and Ip, R. W. L. (2006). An AHP Approach in Benchmarking Logistics Performance of the Postal Industry. *Benchmarking: An International Journal*, 13(6): 636–661.

Hwang, C. and Yoon, K. (1981) Multiple Attribute Decision Making Methods and Application. Springer, New York.

Kadıoğlu, G. (2017). Tüketicilerin Türkiye'deki Kahve Zincirlerini Tercihlerine Yönelik Bir Karar Destek Modeli, Yayımlamamış Yüksek Lisans Tezi, İstanbul Teknik Üniversitesi, İstanbul.

Kuruüzüm, A. ve Atsan, N. (2001). Analitik Hiyerarşi Yöntemi ve İşletmecilik Alanındaki Uygulamaları". *Akdeniz University Faculty of Economics & Administrative Sciences Faculty Journal*, 1(1): 83–105.

Onurlubaş, E. ve Şener, T. (2016). Markalı Ürün İle İlgili Tüketici Düşüncelerinin Belirlenmesi Üzerine Bir Araştırma. *Selçuk Üniversitesi Sosyal Bilimler Enstitüsü Dergisi*, (35): 325–341.

Ömürbek, N., Karaatlı, M. ve Yetim, T. (2014). Analitik Hiyerarşi Sürecine Sayalı TOPSIS ve VIKOR Yöntemleri ile ADIM Üniversitelerinin Değerlendirilmesi. Selçuk Üniversitesi Sosyal Bilimler Enstitüsü Dergisi, 32 (Dr. Mehmet YILDIZ Özel Sayısı), 189–207.

Özcan, B., Akman, G., Başlı, H. ve Gündüz, E. B. (2018). Çok Kriterli Karar Vermede AHP ve TOPSIS Yöntemleriyle Uçuş Noktası Seçimi. *Erciyes University Journal of Institue of Science and Technology*, 34(3): 1–13.

Özdemir, M. (2015). *Operasyonel, Yönetsel ve Stratejik Problemlerin Çözümünde Çok Kriterli Karar Verme Yöntemleri*, (Ed. Bahadır Fatih Yıldırım & Emrah Önder), Dora Basım Yayın Dağıtım, Bursa:133–146.

Öztürk, D. ve Onurlubaş, E. (2019). Havayolu Taşımacılığında Hizmet Kalitesinin AHP ve TOPSIS Yöntemleri ile Değerlendirilmesi. *Gümüşhane Üniversitesi Sosyal Bilimler Enstitüsü Elektronik Dergisi*, 10(Ek Sayı), 81–97.

Saaty, T. L. (1977). A Scaling Method for Priorities in Hierarchical Structures. *Journal of Mathematical Psychology*, 15: 234–281.

Saaty, T. L. (1990). How to Make a Decision: The Analytic Hierarchy Process. *European Journal of Operational Research*, 48: 9–26.

Yang, J. and Lee, H. (1997). An AHP Decision Model for Facility Location Selection. *Facilities*, 15(9–10): 241–254.

https://www.dunya.com/sektorler/kahvede-kiran-kirana-rekabet-var-sekiz-yabanci-yarisina-hakim-yerliler-yukseliyor-haberi-424239

Yavuz Selim Düger

Investigation of Contemporary Leadership Styles within the Framework of Social Exchange Theory

1 Introduction

Researchers have long been on various seek to solve organizational problems and eliminate organizational conflicts. Many theories emerged as a result of the researches, particularly in the field of social psychology, to well manage and motivate employees; social exchange theory, social learning theory, attribution theory, role theory, leader exchange theory, upward influence, etc. The common purpose of these theories is to realize the attitudes and behaviors of the employees in the organization and to manage them effectively.

Organizational behavior consists of the individual's attitudes and behaviors that affect organizational outcomes. Companies desire to improve the employees' attitudes and behaviors displayed in the organization so as to be accomplished and profitable. In order to develop the attitudes and behaviors of the employees, it is initially necessary to define and clarify the source of these attitudes and behaviors (Aydın, 2017:548). In this sense, social exchange theory is significant in terms of defining the source of the employees' attitudes and behaviors. The fact that social exchange theory deals with the relations between the employee and the leader makes this concept significant in terms of organizational behavior. As yet, social exchange theory's impacts on many outcomes of organizational behavior have been studied in the literature; organizational citizenship behavior (Cohen et al., 2012:705; Ahmadi et al., 2010:107), organizational commitment (Yiğit, 2016:47), organizational justice (Chen, 2010:1090; Cropanzano and Rupp, 2008:92), perceived organizational support (Ahmadi et al., 2010:107; Settoon et al., 1996: 219), psychological contract (Seçkin and Çoban, 2018:7), task performance (Bal Taştan, 2014:42), leadership (Liden et al., 1997:47), etc. The researches indicated that social exchange theory is quite powerful in explaining the source of organizational behavior.

The basis of the theory of social exchange, which allows defining employees' behavior in the workplace, is based on anthropology, social psychology, and sociology. Social exchange theory, which is described as conditional interactions depending on the actions among people, generally occurs within the framework of mutual obligation (Cropanzano and Mitchell, 2005:875).

Leaders who formalized the behavior of employees in organizations and participate in the process of social exchange representing on behalf of the company are significant elements. Recently, many factors such as technological development, culture change, generational and gender change in the workforce, etc. have also caused changes in management approach. Newly emerging contemporary leadership styles, such as ethical, transformational, servant, relational, etc. are focused on meeting the needs of organizations and increasing the performance by effectively managing a qualified workforce. Leader behaviors that various emerging newly lead to changes in mutual expectations, obligations, and acquisitions in the process of social exchange. In fact, leaders impact the quality of social exchange depending on the adopted leadership behaviors. In this study, it is aimed to reveal how social exchange takes place depending on the leadership styles. In other words, it is aimed to reveal the growing impacts of new leadership styles depending on the theory of social exchange. Accordingly, leader-member exchange, ethical leadership, and transformational leadership styles are examined within the framework of social exchange theory.

2 Theoretical Framework

Leaders, who formalized organizational behavior, build organizational culture, being role models for employees and have the power to motivate employees with their behavior, play an active role in the social exchange process. Moreover, leaders who represent the enterprise in the social exchange process, deliver the expectations from them and could increase their performance by establishing well relationships with the employees. Leaders can interact with their employees at different levels by undertaking different behavioral roles. In this section, social exchange theory, leader-member exchange, ethical leadership, and transformational leadership were examined within the framework of social change theory.

2.1 Social Exchange Theory

From Smith' study (1759) to the study of Blau (1964) many researchers contributed to the theory of social exchange. However, Blau (1964) shaped the current form of social exchange theory defining as "social interactions in the exchange process". According to Blau (1964), social exchange is voluntary activities that emerge with motivation as a result of the gains that the employees expect to receive during the exchange process.

Social exchange theory focuses on the benefit and disadvantages to be achieved depending on the degree of fulfillment of one's obligations. Social exchange theory is different from economic exchange. The benefit provided in the face of its economic exchange has a definite value, it is also known in advance of when it will take place. On the contrary, in social change, the benefit to be provided is not complete and exact, and the time is not exactly clear. It is not guaranteed to achieve the expected gain as a result of mutual interaction in social exchange theory so trust gains importance. Besides, employees expect a fair reward depending on how much contributed to the company. Regardless, employees expect a fair reward depending on how much contributed to the company. However, when employees cannot achieve a fair and balanced gain, dissatisfaction and psychological tension occur between the parties (Aydın, 2017:549). As a result of social exchange, an imbalance occurs when the employee thinks that he has fulfilled his obligations, but he has not received expected gains. Likewise, when the leader thinks that he/she has fulfilled his/her obligations, but it has not received expected effort from employees an imbalance occurs. However, if both the employee and the leader think that the obligations are met at a high level, the exchange relationship is well balanced. In this case, the employee indicates high performance and effort, gets high acquisitions. However, if both the employee and the leader fulfill their obligations at a low level, the exchange relationship is poorly balanced. In this case, the employee indicated a limited effort and receives a limited acquisition from the organization (Shore and Barksdale, 1998:732–735).

Social exchange theory has a phenomenon characteristic that initiates, strengthens and maintains inter-individual relations in the process of exchange. Leaders and employees both desire to develop relationships between individuals and to become sustainable. However, the social exchange makes participants social and makes participation constant to enable social interaction to be stable. Moreover, the strength of social exchange varies depending on the degree of mutual expectations of the participants (Lynch et al., 1999:467–470).

2.2 Leader-Member Exchange and Social Exchange Theory

Researches in the literature reveal that 90 % of the leaders interact in different ways with each employee and only 10 % indicated the same kind of interaction with all employees (Liden et al., 1997:48). Leader-member exchange differs from other leadership approaches at this point (Baş et al., 2010:1014). The interaction that leaders develop with employees is based on material value or emotional support, besides it is psychological or mental. Leader-member exchange is divided into two groups; in-group and out-group. The employee of the in-group who has a high level of interaction exhibits extra-role behavior. In return, the employee expects financial or intangible rewards. The employee of the out-group who has a low level of interaction does not go beyond job descriptions. Mutual expectations are low in the low level of Exchange (Liden et al., 1997:48).

Leader-member exchange is based on role theory. Role theory reveals the effect of the roles that the individual has undertaken in patterning the behavior of the individual. Employees have a role while meeting their tasks within the organization. Besides, leaders have expectations to fulfill this role from employees. The leader assesses the employees according to the degree of fulfillment of the roles and expectations, determines both financial and behavioral rewards in return (Çiftçi, 2019:169). In other words, the employee initially takes a role within the organization and then depending on the level of fulfilling the role, and performance of the employee, the quality of the relationship with the leader is patterned. A permanent and high-quality relationship is developed with the leader if employees meet the expectations with their performance (Yıldız, 2018:482).

The occurring of a high-quality leader-member exchange depends on the theory of social change. This process will be much faster, especially in cases where mutual trust and justice are built (Liden et al., 1997:50). In other words, leaders influence employees' efforts and desires with their behavioral, social or financial support, and determine their contribution levels to the organization as a result. As a result of the positive behaviors of the leader, it is assumed that the employees will act with a sense of gratefulness and will exhibit extra-role behavior for the organization (Çiftçi, 2019:169).

2.3 Ethical Leadership and Social Exchange Theory

Brown et al. (2005) defined ethical leadership as "*demonstrating normative appropriate behavior through personal actions and interpersonal relationships and promoting followers of such behavior through bi-directional communication, empowerment and decision making*". Ethical leaders who care about their employees are honest, trustworthy and fair decision-makers. Ethical leaders deliver ethical codes to everyone within the organization and encourage employees to observe ethical rules (Hassan et al., 2013:134; Brown and Trevino, 2006:596). Leaders act as role models to other employees by displaying ethical behavior inside and outside of the organization (Hansen, 2011:41). In other words, ethical leadership unlike other leadership styles generally focuses more on the moral and ethical behavior of the individual and enables these behaviors to spread among the employees (Kalyar et al., 2019:64–65; Brown and Trevino, 2006:596).

Ethical leadership is a highly effective leadership style in terms of social exchange theory. In social exchange, trust is extremely important for mutual exchange to happen in a high way. Since the trust in the ethical leadership style comes to the fore, it ensures a high level of exchange (Mayer et al., 2009:4). Employees have trust in their leaders, as the ethical leader has a high moral and is thought to have an honest and fair decision-making personality who tries to do the right thing. The employees' sense of the high-level of trust in the leaders makes a catalyst effect on the development of strong social exchange relations between the parties (Brown and Trevino, 2006:596–600). According to Hansen (2011), the strength of the relationship between ethical leadership and social change theory is closely related to individuals' sensitivity to moral rules, ethical decision-making, and social culture. Besides, the relationships developed by ethical leaders based on trust are directly related to the theory of social exchange as well as the leader-member exchange (Hansen, 2011:42).

In some studies, in the literature, it has been revealed that the leadership positively impact on affective commitment, job satisfaction, organizational citizenship behavior, employee voice behavior, and job performance as a result of the social exchange that comes up with ethical leadership behavior. Indeed, in return for ethical leaders' positive behaviors, employees will also exhibit positive attitudes and behaviors that is, it will ensure that employees exhibit positive organizational behavior (Lio et al., 2015:647; Hansen, 2011:45).

2.4 Transformational Leadership and Social Exchange Theory

Transformational leadership is a process in which prioritizes the request and expectations of the organization and transform values, needs, preferences, and wishes of employees. Transformational leadership based on the idea that motivates employees to perform beyond their job descriptions (Nohe and Hertel, 2017:1364). Horton (1985) defined the transformational leader as "*creating the motivation to meet the high-level needs of followers by providing working to achieve the vision that actively shapes the future*" (Çatı et al., 2017:75). Yammarino and Bass (1990) defined transformational leadership as "*the person who uses the business resources effectively within the organization, taking into account the needs and expectations of the employees, gathering the employees around a strong vision, and directing and advising them continuously*".

Transformational leaders motivate employees with a high expectation of performance. Besides, transformational leaders raise the consciousness and awareness of the importance of organizational goals among employees. According to Bass and Avolio (1990), transformational leadership behavior makes employees feel admiration, loyalty, and trust towards their leaders. And this allows employees to prioritize the interests and objectives of the organization beyond their interests or goals. Transformational leadership style, unlike some other leadership styles, give priority to social and psychological exchange with their employees rather than economic exchange (Zeinabadi, 2013:732).

When the transformational leadership style is analyzed with its sub-dimensions, the relationship with the theory of social exchange can be better understood. According to Bass and Avolio (1990), the sub-dimensions of transformational leadership; idealized influence, individualized consideration, inspirational motivation, and intellectual stimulation.

Idealized influence: The leader gives confidence, cares and respects employees. The leader encourages employees to act with a collective belief, value, and mission. Thus, leaders who exhibit ideal behaviors are imitated by their employees, that is, they become role models. The leader, who is appreciated for her ideal behavior, leads to a high level of social exchange, and in return, employees show respect and obey their leaders. Moreover, employees feel sense of admiration and loyalty to their leaders as a result of positive developments in employees' behavior (Çatı et al., 2017:75).

Individualized consideration: The leader recognizes his employees well and guides them to ensure their development. At this point, the leaders take care of the needs of the employees and support their personal development. Moreover, the leader encourages employees' development through coaching and mentoring. Thus, the leader ensures that employees are emotionally satisfied and motivated, and in return (social exchange) employee exhibits a maximum effort for the company as a person with high organizational citizenship.

Inspirational motivation: Leaders are visionary, passionate about working and optimistic about their employees. Leaders emotionally motivate their employees to achieve success through the vision they offer. Employees who motivated by their leaders rely on their leaders in the social exchange process, feel commitment and ready to fulfill high expectations (Taslak, 2008:127).

Intellectual stimulation: Leaders encourage innovation, creativity and problem-solving. Leaders also encourage and transform their employees from the old ways of thinking to acquire a new way of thinking. Leaders offer their employees an environment where they can use their skills and abilities, and as a result of social exchange, they exhibit innovative behaviors as extra-role behavior in employees.

The social exchange between leader and employee replace from lower-quality to higher-quality levels with transformational leadership behavior. In transformational leadership, there is an economic exchange when lower-quality exchange occurs between the parties, whereas when higher-quality exchange occurs, there is a psychological contract beyond the economic exchange (Zeinabadi, 2013:733).

3 Conclusion

In the past two decades, rapid change has forced businesses to change and to take part in the change. This change has become inevitable for businesses to compete and survive in the long-term. At this point, the significance of human resources becomes clear once again. The qualified workforce of businesses gives companies a great ability to compete. In recent years, the problem that has emerged is to manage them effectively beyond having a qualified workforce. Because the contribution of the qualified workforce that cannot be managed effectively will be very limited. Researchers have done various studies on leadership and different leadership styles have emerged with the occurrence of the significance of management. The purpose of the contemporary leadership styles is to increase efficiency and performance, thereby making a positive impact on affective commitment, job satisfaction, organizational citizenship behavior, employee voice behavior, etc.

Over the last two decades, technological development, participation of generation Y and women into business life particularly have had a major impact on the development of modern leadership behaviors. Contemporary leadership styles which emerging newly also significantly affected the quality of social exchange in organizations. However, contemporary leadership styles that give confidence to its employees, act fairly and equally, develops, understands and cares, integrate their goals with company goals, respond to performance, and use a variety of ways to motivate them in brief, have become much more effective with the theory of social exchange. Many research results in the literature are mentioned in the previous sections, with the intent of revealing the increasing effects of contemporary leadership styles with the social exchange theory. These studies indicate that an effective management approach can be achieved by adopting an employee-oriented perceptive. It appears that motivating factors of employees differ depending on their leadership behavior. And these motivating factors indicate that social and psychological reciprocity (social and psychological exchange) gain importance beyond the economic reciprocity (economic exchange). Besides, contemporary leadership styles reinforced by social exchange theory seem to have much more impact on organizational behavior.

It provides the output of many positive organizational behaviors in particular, such as organizational citizenship, organizational commitment, organizational justice, perceived organizational support, psychological contract, affective commitment, job satisfaction, employee voice behavior, etc.

References

Ahmadi, P., Forouzandeh, S. & Kahreh, M. S. (2010). The Relationship between OCB and Social Exchange Constructs, European Journal of Economics. Finance and Administrative Sciences, Issue 19, 107–119.

Aydın, E. (2017). Social Exchange in the Context of Culture: A Theoretical Study. International Journal of Economic and Administrative Studies, UIK Special Issue, 547–562.

Bal Taştan, S. (2014). The Impact of Employee-Organization Relationship on Individuals' Behavioral Outcomes of Task-Related Performance. Contextual Performance and Intention to Turnover: An Evaluation with Social Exchange Theory. International Journal of Business and Management Studies, 6(1), 42–53.

Bass, B. & Avolio, B. (1990). Transformational Leadership Development: Manual for the Multifactor Leadership Questionnaire. Palo Alto, CA: Consulting Psychologists Press.

Baş, T., Keskin, N. & Mert, İ. S. (2010). Leader Member Exchange (LMX) Model and Validity and Reliability of Its Instrument in Turkish. Ege Academic Review, 10(3), 1013–1039.

Blau, P. (1964). Exchange and Power in Social Life. New York: Wiley.

Brown, M. E. & Trevino, L. K. (2006). Ethical Leadership: A Review and Future Directions. The Leadership Quarterly, 17, 595–616.

Brown, M. E., Trevino, L. K. & Harrison, D. A. (2005). Ethical Leadership: A Social Learning Perspective for Construct Development and Testing. Organizational Behavior and Human Decision Processes, 97, 117–134.

Chen, H.-F. (2010). The Relationships of Organizational Justice, Social Exchange, Psychological Contract, and Expatriate Adjustment: An Example of Taiwanese Business Expatriates. The International Journal of Human Resource Management, 21(7), 1090–1107.

Cohen, A., Ben-Tura, E. & Vashdi, D. (2012). The Relationship between Social Exchange Variables, OCB, and Performance: What Happens When You Consider Group Characteristics?. Personnel Review, 41(6), 705–731.

Cropanzano, R. & Mitchell, M. S. (2005). Social Exchange Theory: An Interdisciplinary Review. Journal of Management, 31(6), 874–900.

Cropanzano, R. & Rupp, D. E. (2008). Social Exchange Theory and Organizational Justice: Job Performance, Citizenship Behaviours, Multiple Foci, and a Historical Integration of Two Literatures. In S. W. Gilliland, D. P. Skarlicki, & D. D. Steiner (Eds.), Research in Social Issues in Management: Justice, Morality, and Social. Information Age Publishing: Greenwich, 63–99.

Çatı, P., Uludağ, G. & Kızıltoprak, A. (2017). The Effect on Customer Focus on the Interior Marketing Framework of the Transformational and Transactional Leadership Styles: Düzce University Example. Journal of Van Yüzüncü Yıl University Faculty of Economics and Administrative Sciences, 2(4), 71–106.

Çiftçi, D. Ö. (2019). Lider Üye Etkileşiminin İşe Adanmışlık Üzerindeki Etkisinde Psikolojik Güçlendirmenin Aracı Rolü. Business and Economics Research Journal, 10(1), 167–186.

Hansen, S. D. (2011). Ethical Leadership: A Multifoci Social Exchange Perspective. The Journal of Business Inquiry, 10(1), 41–55.

Hassan S., Mahsud R., Yukl G., & Prussia, G. E. (2013). Ethical and Empowering Leadership and Leader Effectiveness. Journal of Managerial Psychology, 28(2), 133–146.

Kalyar, M., Usta, A. & Shafique, I. (2019). When Ethical Leadership and LMX Are More Effective in Prompting Creativity: The Moderating Role of Psychological Capital. Baltic Journal of Management, 15(1), 61–80.

Liden, R. C., Sparrowe, R. T. & Wayne, S. J. (1997). Leader-Member Exchange Theory: The Past and Potential for the Future. Research in Personnel and Human Resources Management, 15, 47–119.

Loi, R., Lam, L., Ngo, H. & Cheong, S. (2015). Exchange Mechanisms between Ethical Leadership and Affective Commitment. Journal of Managerial Psychology, 30(6), 645–658.

Lynch, P. D., Eisenberger, R. & Armeli, S. (1999). Perceived Organizational Support: Inferior versus Superior Performance by Wary Employees. Journal of Applied Psychology, 84(4), 467–483.

Mayer, D. M., Kuenzi, M., Greenbaum, R., Bardes, M. & Salvador, R. B. (2009). How Low Does Ethical Leadership Flow? Test of a Trickle-down Model. Organizational Behavior and Human Decision Processes, 108(1), 1–13.

Nohe, C., & Hertel, G. (2017). Transformational Leadership and Organizational Citizenship Behavior: A Meta-analytic Test of Underlying Mechanisms. Frontiers in Psychology, 8, 1364.

Seçkin, Ş., & Çoban, R. (2018). A Research on Work Life Quality, Psychological Contract and Psychological Ownership Relationship in the Context of Social Exchange Theory. Comment Management Method International Management Journal of Economics and Philosophy, 6(1), 7–17.

Settoon, R. P., Bennett, N. & Liden, R. C. (1996). Social Exchange in Organizations: Perceived Organizational Support, Leader–Member Exchange, and Employee Reciprocity. Journal of Applied Psychology, 81(3), 219–227.

Shore, L. M. & Barksdale, K. (1998). Examining Degree of Balance and Level of Obligation in the Employment Relationship: A Social Exchange Approach. Journal of Organizational Behavior, 19, 731–744.

Taslak, S. (2008). An Ethical Evaluation of Transactional and Transformatioanal Leadership on Task Conflict. Journal of Erciyes University Faculty of Economics and Administrative Sciences, 31, 121–144.

Yammarino, F. J., & Bass, B. M. (1990). Transformational Leadership and Multiple Levels of Analysis. Human Relations, 43(10), 975–995.

Yıldız, S. M. (2018). An Empirical Analysis of the Leader–Member Exchange and Employee Turnover Intentions Mediated by Mobbing: Evidence from Sport Organisations. Economic Research-Ekonomska Istraživanja, 31(1), 480–497.

Yiğit, İ. (2016). The Effect of Organizational Commitment on the Social Exchange and Organizational Socialization: A Study in Research and Practice Hospital of Kocaeli University. KAUJEASF, 7(12), 25–50.

Zeinabadi, H. R. (2013). Social Exchange Outcomes of Transformational Leadership: Comparing Male and Female Principals of Public Primary Schools in Iran. International Journal of Educational Management, 27(7), 730–743.

Fulya Mısırdalı Yangil

Manager-Free Management: Holacracy

1 Introduction

Peter Drucker stated in his book Management Challenges for 21st Century "These days we often hear the expression that the end of the hierarchy has come. It is obvious that this expression is nonsense. It is obligation that every institution has a final authority" (1999: 18). Drucker expresses the necessity of having a hierarchy or manager with this sentence. However, this reality suggested by Drucker has started to lose its validness in today's business world. Hence, as of 2007, a new discourse called Holacracy was at the top of the agenda. Holacracy refers to an organization in which there are not any managers or that is manager-free.

Even if the approaches to management science change in every period, the features of management have not changed in books and scientific researches. The first of these feature is hierarchy. This feature is described as an environment where some people are in higher ranks while some other people are in lower ranks. In the changing theories of management science the basic situation is the manager's approach to his subordinates and their direction when they leading them.

The 21st century is a century in which the basic assumptions suggested in the past centuries are challenged once again. Realities of this century do not coincide with those of the past period and it causes the past realities to be questioned. As a matter of fact, discourses and practices such as lean organization, teamwork, team spirit, and self-governing organizations have formed the basis for questions such as "What would happen if hierarchy did not exist today" and "Should there be managers", and presented approaches that would ultimately suggest their removal.

2 The Conceptual Framework of the Holacracy

In most of the studies conducted on the field of business, it is stated that the world, having started to reshape since the beginning of this century, is quite risky for businesses. Many circumstances such as economic recession, acts of terrorism, global disease risks, changes in people's lifestyle, migrations, the speed of technology and its impact show the intensity of the level of environmental uncertainty and change. While this uncertainty and change affects the number of risks businesses face and how they could manage them. In such a chaotic environment, it is not possible for businesses to achieve and maintain a competitive advantage through practices used in the past. It is seen difficult for organizations that have complex business relations to maintain their competitive advantages especially in this period. In their book titled "The Future of Management", Hamel and Breen described companies such as Kodak, Sony, General Motors, Sun Microsystems as dinosaurs since they could not recreate their themselves, and questioned the cause of aging outbreak. They expressed the reason as the accelerating rate of change and emphasized the importance of changing as fast as the rate of change (2007: 54). In short, it is important for businesses to use their financial and non-financial resources faster and more rationally in this period. Because emperors of today's business world are not businesses with the greatest and the most resources, but they are businesses that are smarter, faster, and that could see new opportunities as well as finding and integrating new business methods into their companies in a rapid fashion (Velinov et al., 2018: 330).

Originally a software developer, Brian Robertson introduced the concept of holacracy into the literature in 2007. Holacracy aims to eliminate the slowness caused by bureaucracy in organizational changes. The concept is derived from the word "holos" in Greek that could be translated as "whole". Holos was first put forth by Arthur Koestler, and contemporary philosopher Ken Wilber enriched the content of this concept as constant development and expansion (Krasulja et al., 2016: 189).

Holacracy, as a concept destroying hierarchy that is the basis of management science, has mostly attracted attention from businesses. It attracts attention that academic studies in this context are limited. Holacracy is the manager-free management in which the power is taken from the manager and redistributed into teams. Robertson explains the concept of Holacracy as follows (https://infoloji.com/ast-ust-iliskisinin-olmadigi-bir-yonetim-sekli-holakrasi/):

> *"Holacracy is a different way of managing an organization. Normally, the hierarchy is sought in an organization in order provide order and unity, and we expect managers to provide this. There are different mechanisms to achieve this in holacracy. We are now talking about a governance system in which all team members interact and think about who should do what, rather than a system in which managers lead the flow. There are a series of rules that determine what kind of autonomy you will have instead of managers deciding on what people should do. Within these rules, you can make your own decisions on issues that make sense to you."*

According to Robertson's explanation, even though the manager is not at the basis of holacracy, there are some rules established in order to ensure the continuity of the organization. These rules are alternatives used in order to provide

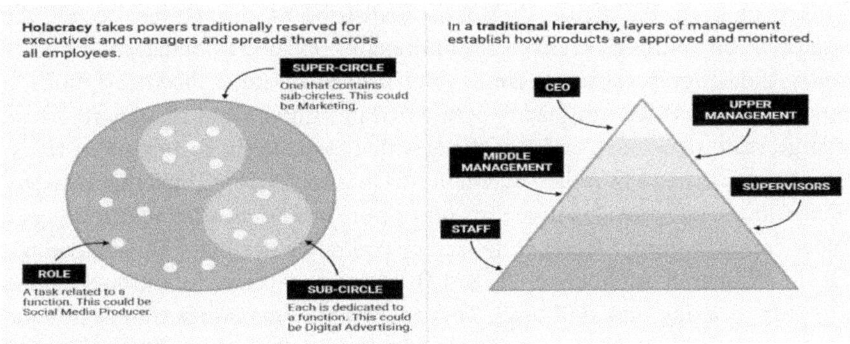

Figure 1: *Holacracy in place of hierarchy.* Source: Gouveia (2016)

supervision without a manager. While the rules set in holacracy provide freedom in employees' behavior, the basis of this freedom lies at the recognition of duties and responsibilities by individuals and teams. Therefore, the scope of authority in employees and teams is drawn. Organizations should have the ability to renew themselves continuously and without any trauma in this period. This situation may be likened to autonomous systems of the human body. For example, when one starts running on the treadmill, the heart automatically increases the amount of blood transferred to muscles. Words such as automatic, sudden, and reflex define radical changes in organizations and contain the automatic process conducted by organizations to make radical changes before crises may occur (Gary & Breen, 2007: 55). In this context, holacracy can also be considered as integrating the automatic process in the human body's functioning system into the organization. In short, it is like the cell function, in which the body automatically acts in order to solve the problem even without signals from the brain when an abnormal condition is felt in the body (Kolkitchaiwan, 2018: 336).

In holacracy, there is a structure composed of teams called "circles" in which individuals have more than one role. These circles design and control themselves within the framework of guidelines or principles. This structure provides an explanation for how roles should be defined, assigned, what these roles should be, and how these circles interact, rather than just telling people how to fulfill their duties. Briefly, a broad explanation is provided on how the circles should be formed and operated (Bernstein et al., 2016). In this context, holacracy offers a management framework that radically changes some practices such as top-down hierarchy and the need for management (Van De Kamp, 2014: 13). Figure 1 shows the difference between hierarchy and holacracy.

According to the figure, holacracy redistributes the powers to all the employees by taking these powers traditionally allocated to managers. In other words, holacracy presents dynamic roles instead of static job descriptions, a decentralized authority instead of authorized positions, rapid repetition instead of large-scale structures, and key changes that provide the formation of transparent rules instead of policy adaptation (Gouveia, 2016). Thus, this management framework provides urgency and responsiveness in time and space as a leader-free structure. Moreover, holacracy promotes flexibility and individualization (Kumar & Mukherjee, 2018: 12). Holacracy allows to regroup around a deeper meaning and skill level. This enables the increasing complexity and uncertainty to be used more skillfully in today's business world. In this way, holacracy prepares the ground for the highest potential to emerge (Robertson, 2007:6).

2.1 Basic Dynamics and Characteristics of Holacracy

Kolkitchaiwan (2018: 337) tackled the rules of holacracy that are different from traditionally managed organizations as (i) A constitution that sets game rules and redistributes authority, (ii) Structuring, organizing, and defining roles and scopes of authority in humans, (iii) A unique decision-making process in order to update roles and powers, and (iv) The process providing synchronization of teams and working together. In this context, holacracy is a new social technique. There are four points that are effective in the functioning of this social technique, and the system is based on these points. These are (Robertson, 2007: 7):

- Organizational Structure: The holacracy replaces the hierarchy with a fractal "holarchy" of self-organizing circles, and renders the organization's structure more organic. Figure 2 shows the link between hierarchy and holacracy. According to the figure each circle is connected to lower circles by a bi-directional connection, with one member of the circle becoming a member of the other circle. Thus, a bi-directional information flow and fast feedback loops are formed. Each circle sets the roles required to achieve its goal and manages itself by assigning members to these roles.

The contrast of the holacracy to the existing hierarchical order results in the elimination of titles within the organization. Within an organizational structure dominated by holacracy, roles are defined with explicit purposes only at the point where they contribute to the aims of the organization and the circle. A role is retrieved when it does not contribute to the process anymore.

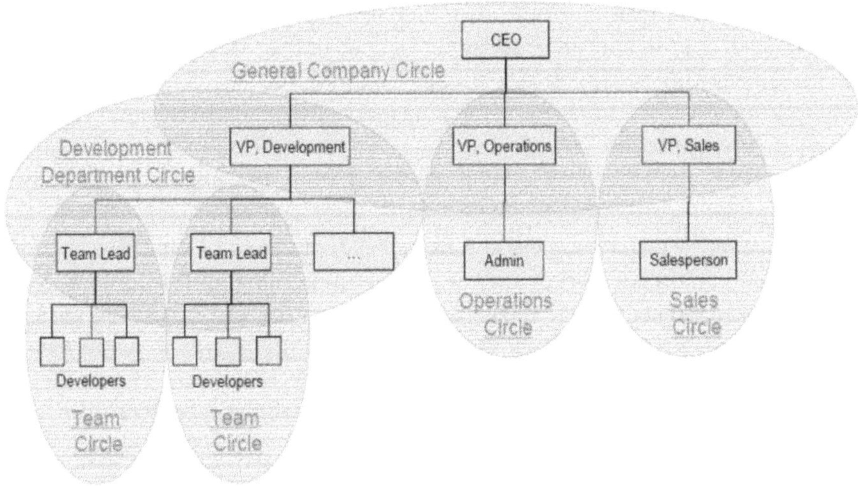

Figure 2: *From Hierarchy to Holacracy.* Source: Robertson (2007: 11)

Therefore, roles serve a specific purpose and contain responsibility and authority (Van De Kamp, 2014: 17).

- Organizational Control: Holacracy increases organizational agility by improving the methods we use to control organizational activities. It helps to make decisions in a rapid and progressive fashion with maximum information, thereby enabling the organization to constantly adjust itself as new information is acquired. Holacracy encourages the individual to take individual action using his/her best judgment, to take the ownership of the impact, and then to help the organization learn from experience.
- Key Practices: The key practices of holacracy include regular environmental meetings for both governance and operations. Governance meetings help define how to work together and also facilitate assignment process by setting the roles required to achieve the circle's aim. Operational meetings help to get duties done and facilitate the planning and executing of daily duties of the circle in an effective fashion. In addition to these key practices, holacracy includes additional practices or "modules" that address many private organizational processes, from recruitment to budgeting and to project management.
- Shared Language and Meaning: Holacracy creates a union of culturally shared language and meaning that facilitates communication by injecting strong intellectual models and concepts into organizational culture.

The general characteristics of the holacracy system can be listed as follows: The system can be applied in every sector and organization. More than 300 companies are using this system. It sets simpler rules for the organization. With the implementation of this system, some managers have started to lose their jobs. There are ways in which powers could be taken from the employee who cannot self-discipline, and the individual is removed from the organization. While holacracy enables organization employees to better use and evaluate their ideas, it is important to include an idea if anyone inside the organization have a good idea on reducing costs, improving products, or increasing profits. It has a "lead link" role that is accountable to the board of directors, and it runs the system (Sarıoğlu Uğur, 2017: 215–216; Robertson, 2015).

2.2 Concerns About Holacracy and Organizational Benefits

There are many new models tested in management. However, most of these models are forgotten within a few years. The most valid model among these models is holacracy (http://liberteryen.org/2018/06/holakrasi-ve-anayasasi/). The very young nature of the holacracy causes the system to have undiscovered aspects. This situation causes concerns in managers about the possible difficulties during implementation (Krasulja et al., 2016: 192). These concerns are:

- The idea suggesting that the holacracy system will cause anarchic tendencies when put into practice is prevalent. In other words, it can be said that there are disagreements on whether the chaotic environment will arise within the organization while fighting the chaotic environment (Krasulja et al., 2016: 192).
- Hierarchical structures create certainty and clarity in organizations. However, it is also thought that holacracy does not provide this certainty and clarity. In addition, the superiority of hierarchies in ensuring the coordination of many people with different roles is not overlooked (Gary & Breen, 2007: 73).
- It is possible for a good manager to make faster decisions in the hierarchy. This causes the idea suggesting that it could provide more savings to be prevalent (http://liberteryen.org/2018/06/holakrasi-ve-anayasasi/).
- Hierarchy is an encouraging system since it provides the opportunity to rise as well as providing built-in order. Lack of a clear hierarchy can cause problems in performance evaluation and rewarding (Meinert, 2016).
- In addition, there may be tasks within the organization that nobody likes to do. In this case, the question on who will carry out these tasks is among the criticisms towards holacracy (Meinert, 2016).

Based on the organizations where holacracy is applied, against these concerns, its benefits for the organization are as follows:

- The lack of management layer means less approval in decision-making. Therefore, decisions can be made faster as well as providing fast responses to new opportunities and threats (Yugendhar & Ali, 2017: 168).
- The extent to which holacracy is acceptable is based on the implementation process and the adaptability of organization members. Holacracy can be effective when organization members value autonomy, commitment, risk-taking and creativity. Combining holacracy with these traits in employees may sustain and revive an entrepreneurial culture (Kumar & Mukherjee, 2018: 12).
- Holacracy can create an organizational learning process (Kolkitchaiwan, 2018: 343).
- Holacracy disciplines the meetings within the organization, which renders meetings more productive.
- The fact that too much management causes less freedom in people reduces their passion for their work. Therefore, holacracy may also increase people's passion by eliminating management oversight. This created passion encourages people to do more than what is expected and required (Gary & Breen, 2007: 72–73).
- Holacracy ensures better and more frequent communication among employees. In this way, holacracy allows for the more adoption of organizational goals and better understanding of daily operational problems (Yugandhar & Ali, 2017: 168).
- Holacracy is a more systematic management than hierarchical management. Holacracy has roles that make many critical decisions in difficult times when employees need to be very productive, which makes the system successful.

However, there are success factors that should be considered in creating organizational benefit via holacracy. The leading success factor is leaders' dedication to building a strong culture where holacracy can be applied. In addition, as in every management model, high level support is an important success factor also in holacracy. In this direction, training and participation at all leadership levels are required for the formation of strong culture. Other success criteria are as follows: the adaptation of the culture to be formed with organizational strategy, comprehensive communication, feedback system informing employees on the impacts of the culture, customer and supplier evaluations that could be filled out rapidly by employees, the authority to make decisions and suggestions affecting basic organizational activities of employees, prioritization of customer services for everyone, forming an enjoyable working environment with social activities, and the improvement of the organizational process in order to create an organization learning with success (Kolkitchaiwan, 2018: 341–342).

3 Conclusion

The world order in which tomorrow is foreseeable in the management of organizations has been replaced by dynamic and chaotic environments. This forces academicians working in the management field to develop new and different perspectives for practitioners. The construction of the future which has a high predictability and low level of uncertainty and the construction of the future including uncertain and different risks have different ways and methods. Holacracy has been proposed as a management system that could enable the organization to act in a rapid and flexible manner in these dynamic and chaotic environments.

Holacracy is considered as an opposite of the hierarchical structure in organizations in the literature. The hierarchical structure is the most important unchanging feature in the entire historical process of management to date -the period before its scientific definition may also be included-. It is worth noting that there is always a manager or a decision-maker even though hierarchical steps are reduced. With holacracy, it is observed that managers, authorities, and titles have been removed and that authority has been redistributed into the organization.

This feature of holacracy may be expressed as a basic feature that enables employees to exhibit their knowledge, skills and abilities. The system of holacracy is based on guidelines and principles, and individuals and circles working accordingly can shape their own framework of authority and responsibility. There is no role that is not needed. Therefore, it eliminates the loss of time created by the bureaucracy and also increases the adaptation skill of the organization.

In light of all these explanations, it is thought that holacracy may be considered as a popular management system in the future. However, it is primarily necessary to form its theoretical framework, to study it with applied academic studies, and to eliminate concerns/worries about the concept.

References

Bernstein, E., Bunch, J., Canner, N. & Lee, M. (2016). Beyond the holacracy hype: too much of good thing?. Harvard Business Review, Vol. 94 No. 7. https://hbr.org/2016/07/beyond-the-holacracy-hype.

Drucker, P. (1999). 21. Yüzyıl İçin Yönetim Yaklaşımları, Çev:, Ankara: İş bankası Yayınları.

Gary, H. & Breen, B. (2007). Yönetimin Geleceği. (Çev: Fezal Gülfidan). İstanbul: Mess Yayınları.

Gouveia, L. B. (2016). Holacracy as an alternative to organisations govarnance. https://bdigital.ufp.pt/bitstream/10284/5649/1/holocracy2016.pdf.

Kolkitchaiwan, P. (2018). "Holacracy"- new flexible management systemfor 2020. Journal of Pacific Institute of Management Science, 4(1), 334–345.

Krasulja, N., Radojevic, I., & Janjusic, D. (2016). Holacracy- the new management system. International Scientific Conference the priority Directions of National Economy Development, Faculty of Economics, Universtity of Nis, 13-October-2016. 187–196.

Kumar, V. S. & Mukherjee, S. (2018). Holacracy- the future of orgazing? The case of Zappos. Human Resource Management International Digest, 26(7), 12–15.

Meinert, D. (2016). Is it time to tear up organizational chart? Why workplace hierarchies aren't all bad. HR Magazine, 61(2), https://www.shrm.org/hr-today/news/hr-magazine/0316/pages/is-it-time-to-tear-up-the-organizational-chart.aspx.

Robertson, B. (2007). Organization at the leading edge: ıntroducing holacracy. 26.02.2020) http://gbds.us/clientuploads/downloads/Holacracy.pdf.

Robertson, B. (2015). Yöneticisiz Yönetim Çok Daha Başarılı, Capital Dergisi, 2015/9, (26.02..2020), https://www.capital.com.tr/yonetim/yeni-trendler/yoneticisiz-yonetim-cok-daha-basarili.

Sarıoğlu Uğur, S. (2017). Yönetimde yeni bir örgütsel davranış modeli: Holakrasi. Akademik Sosyal Araştırmalar Dergisi, 5(59), 211–218.

Van De Kamp, P. (2014). Holacracy- a radical approach to organizational design. In Hans Dekkers, Wil Leeuwis, & Ivan Plantevin (Eds.), Elements of the software development process – Influences on project success and failure (pp. 13–26). Amsterdam, North Holland, Netherlands: University of Amsterdam.

Velinov, E., Vassilev, V., & Denisov, I. (2018). Holacracy and obliquity: contingency management approaches in organizing companies. Problems and Perspectives in Management, 16(1), 330–335.

Yugendhar, A., & Ali, S. M. (2017). Evaluation of implementing holacracy, a comprehensive study on Zappos. International Journal of Engineering and Management Research, 7(5), 163–171.

https://infoloji.com/ast-ust-iliskisinin-olmadigi-bir-yonetim-sekli-holakrasi/

Mehmet Cıranoğlu

Management of After Sales Services in the Durable Household Goods Market: Determinations and Suggestions

1 Introduction

In the economic environment, where competition increases rapidly, the care of businesses to create value increases with the same speed. This means that businesses increase their efforts to satisfy their customers not only with the product itself, but also with the services provided beyond the product.

These efforts may be developing new methods in pre-sales marketing strategies, as well as investing in new technology in production, R&D or product development investment, or providing more effective after-sales services. The targeted competitive advantage may vary according to the unique characteristics of each sector. This advantage can be achieved in some sectors only with technology investment and in some sectors with elements such as qualified employees or a new business model. Especially for durable household goods, the quality of after-sales services is an important competitive area (Keaveney, 1995: 74).

Durable household goods are the first product group that comes to mind about after-sales services due to services provided without the desire of the consumer. Satisfaction with this service is one of the important reasons that push the consumer to buy the same brand again (Beneke et al., 2013: 221). The content of this situation, which is expressed as 'perceived value' in the studies (Zeithaml, 1988: 3), includes issues such as product functionality, quality of after-sales services (Petrick, 2004: 31).

In our study, in the light of the information obtained in the literature, various determinations have been made regarding what kind of disruptions are experienced in after-sales services in the white goods and furniture sectors especially in Turkey's market. In line with these determinations, suggestions were made regarding what kind of steps should be taken to manage this process correctly. It is thought that researching this issue, which is considered important in terms of contributing to the advantage that businesses can achieve in the market, will be a guide for businesses.

In this context, in the first part of the study, the basic concepts of the subject were tried to be explained in line with the literature review, and then the results and suggestions of the interviews conducted within the scope of the research were included.

2 Perceived Value

The concept of perceived value, which emerged in the studies in the field of service marketing in the 90s and which has been done many studies, is an increasingly important issue in the manufacturing sector (Sinha & DeSarbo, 1998: 13).

Zeithaml (1988: 5), who is one of the authors who dealt with the subject first and studies on it, defines the perceived value as a perceptual concept that emerges by comparing the difference between produced and purchased. Beneke et al. (2013: 221) refer to it as "a comprehensive assessment of a particular good or service in the mind". Monroe, on the other hand, defined the value as a concept that expresses the exchange between the payments and sacrifices (trade off) they make for the products and the benefit or quality they receive from the customers according to their own perceptions (Woodruff, 1997: 144). Similarly, Dumond stated that customer value requires a trade-off between what customers give up (price, sacrifice etc.) and achieve in order to use or obtain any product or service (quality, benefit etc.) (Ramsay, 2005: 550). According to Sweeney et al. (1999: 81), perceived value is the balance between price and quality.

As can be seen from these definitions, consumers take into account the benefits they have gained against the cost they incur. From this point of view, it can be interpreted that any cost increase (negative) or benefit increase (positive) that may occur after purchasing will increase or decrease the value perception of the consumer (Şimşek & Noyan, 2009: 129).

Considering that the common point emphasized in these definitions and evaluations is 'benefit', the benefit dimension of the value concept should be mentioned:

Benefit is a concept that can be defined based on the needs of the consumer. Park et al. (1986: 138) distinguished consumer needs functionally and symbolically. Functional needs are associated with searching for products to solve certain consumption problems. Symbolic needs are related to the desire of products and brands that meet their inner needs such as self-definition, role position, group membership or enrichment of self. Therefore, this classification for needs leads us to the classification for benefit.

Functional benefit reflects the inherent advantages of product or service consumption and is generally related to the properties of the product (Keller, 1993: 2). In other words, functional benefit is related to lower level of needs. The functional benefit meets the individual's functional or objective needs, such as warranty (Chaudhuri & Holbrook, 2001: 82). Symbolic benefit reflects the external advantages of product or service consumption (Keller, 1993: 2). Symbolic benefit refers to non-product attributes and relates to social acceptance or personal expression and self-esteem needs. For this reason, consumers can value the prestige, privilege or fashion appropriateness of a product that suits their own selves (Solomon, 1983: 321). Symbolic benefit is especially important for visible products (Aaker & Keller, 1990: 27).

As it turns out, the perceived cost being below the perceived benefit means a high perceived value (Dursun & Çerçi, 2015: 4). As emphasized in the literature, businesses that want to increase their market share should increase the value perceived by the consumers about the product, brand or company (Petrick, 2004; Sweeney & Soutar, 2001; Sweeney et al., 1999; Sinha & DeSarbo, 1998; Parasuraman, 1997). One of the most valid ways to achieve this is to distinguish both its products and themselves from their competitors by creating values that increase the benefit of the product, reduce its cost or strengthen complementary services such as after-sales services.

3 After Sales Services

Although there are different classifications and naming in the literature, it can be stated that the product has 3 dimensions. In the first classification made by Kotler (1998: 446), the first and most important dimension is the core benefit dimension that answers the question of what the customer really buys. The second dimension, the actual product dimension, includes characteristics such as product specifications, packaging, quality, design and brand name. And finally, the largest dimension of the product that Levitt calls enriched product, Grönroos calls supporting product (Ravald & Grönroos, 1996:29), and Kotler calls augmented product includes additional services/benefits such as delivery time, installation, warranty, and after-sales services (Kotler, 1998:446).
Based on this classification, after-sales services are handled in an augmented product dimension, and according to Levitt, it is a process that needs to be carefully organized as an element of modern competition. Because now, competition will be among other things that add value to the product, not just what businesses produce. Only in this way, businesses will have the opportunity to enrich their presentations and make them more preferable (Tek, 1999: 341).

After-sales services are activities that involve efforts such as installation, repair, maintenance, improvement, warranty, usage, provision of spare parts, training of the consumer and dealing with complaints in order to ensure the continuation of the sales after the completion of the sales process (Özgören, 2014: 2).

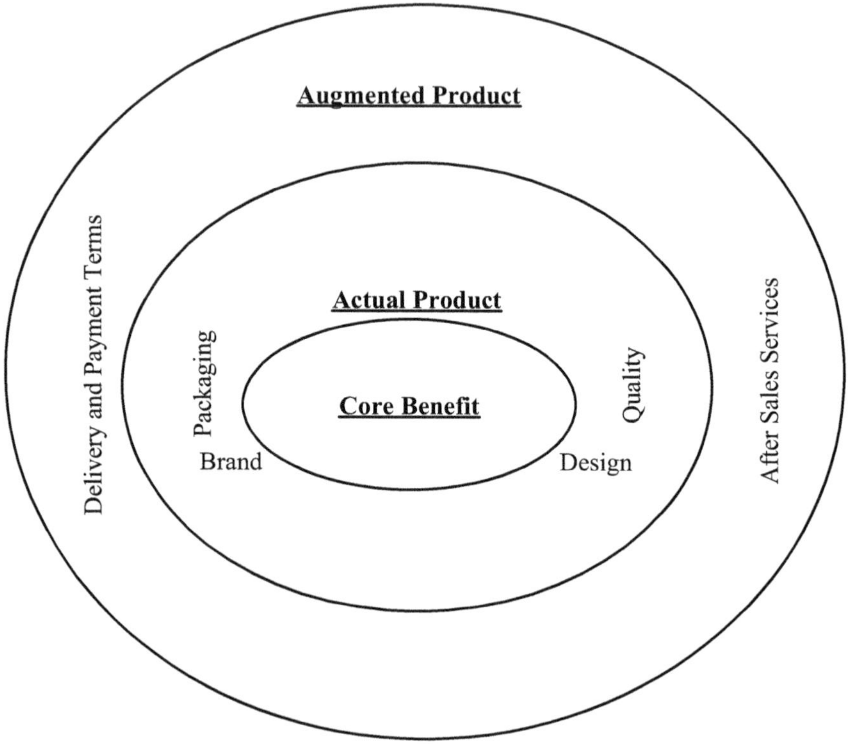

Fig. 1: The Levels of Product (Kotler, 1998: 446)

Especially in markets covering durable household goods such as furniture and white goods, consumers are disadvantaged in terms of seeking rights against producers and dealers. They are incompatible with the seller in terms of knowledge, experience and economics. Therefore, this situation causes the producers of goods and services (strong side) to impose on the consumers (weak side) and even make them accept the conditions they set unilaterally. Apart from the economic side of after-sales services, there is also a meaning in this unbalanced relationship to maintain balance in favor of the consumer (Koral, 2011: 24).

Economically, improving the quality of after-sales service is very important for businesses that want to gain competitive advantage. In other words, in today's competitive conditions, a product perceived well by consumers should be beyond well-produced (Barnes, 1993: 45). Businesses that want to achieve this should have an integrated sales and service process logic to increase their sales. In this logic, they try to make the quality of the services that complement the products visible to consumers (Parasuraman, 1997: 156). It can be said that the most common sectors are furniture and white goods sectors as a complementary process that provides competitive advantage among the products and sectors (Murthy et al., 2004: 110) where after-sales services are important as described above.

4 After Sales Services and Perceived Value Relationship

As explained above, after-sales services, which are perceived as complementary to the products within the renewed competitive conditions, are a factor that provides businesses with competitive advantage as much as the quality and price of the product. In the durable household goods sector, where the quality differences based on the concrete features of the product can be quickly closed, the consumers are increasingly conscious and tend to show loyalty once satisfied, it is not considered sufficient to offer functional products at an affordable price. Complementary services such as after-sales services that can increase the value of the product formed in the mind of the consumer and provide confidence to the consumer should also be provided (Sweeney & Soutar, 2001: 208).

As a result, the difference between the customer's pre-shopping and post-sales perceived performance emerges as customer satisfaction (Wouters, 2004: 583). One of the important areas that will be used to increase this difference positively and which needs high performance is after-sales services. Because the beliefs that consumers receive fast and timely services both for monetary and time savings increase the "perceived value" they create regarding the product (Keaveney, 1995: 74).

In this context, ways to increase the level of satisfaction of consumers from warranty, transportation and assembly services, which are considered as the most realized after-sales services (Türedi, 2010: 30), have been investigated. Interviews were made with sector representatives, considering the results obtained in Cıranoğlu's studies (2018, 2019), which investigated the relationship between after-sales services and customer satisfaction by using the PERVAL scale developed by Sweeney and Soutar (2001). The PERVAL scale is a scale prepared for durable household goods and consists of the sub-dimensions of Quality Value, Price Value, Emotional Value and Social Value. In Cıranoğlu's studies (2018, 2019), it was concluded that the level of satisfaction with after-sales services affects the perceived value, together with its sub-dimensions, separately, closely and strongly.

Below are the different studies using the PERVAL scale developed by Sweeney and Soutar (2001) apart from the studies of Cıranoğlu and some findings obtained from these studies:

In the research conducted by Naseema (2016), how the after-sales services provided in the white goods sector affect the consumer perceptions about the quality of the products. According to the findings obtained in the research, after-sales services contribute positively to the emotional ownership of the brand. At the end of the research, the importance of these services of the companies was emphasized.

In the research carried out by Oko and Onuoha (2013) on refrigerator consumers, it was also found that many brands increased their perceived value in quality dimension thanks to after-sales services.

In the studies of Choudhary et al. (2011) about durable household goods, it was observed that a quality and systematic after-sales services policy convinced consumers to pay extra for the price paid to the product. In addition, it has been found that these services make consumers feel strong socially because they own the product.

In their study that emphasizes the competition beyond the product in industrial products, Markeset and Kumar (2003) states that the perception of value desired to be created in consumers can be achieved by the services including after sales.

5 Determinations and Suggestions Regarding Management of After Sales Services

In this section, the results of the field research conducted by us in the light of previous studies on the subject are presented. Within the scope of the research, face-to-face interviews were held with enterprises operating in the furniture and white goods sector, with a focus on after-sales services. During the interviews conducted with 92 business officials operating in the producer and intermediary positions from the two sectors, using semi-structured interview forms[1], they were asked to evaluate the 'problems' and 'suggestions' regarding after-sales services. In the light of the findings and comments expressed in the interviews, the following suggestions/evaluations were made:

1. After-sales services are followed by sales or production units. This situation causes the said services to be perceived as an additional job and to disrupt

1 While preparing the interview form, the previous studies about the after sales services and the literature review were taken into consideration by the author.

the services. Therefore, it is beneficial to employ separate personnel for the after-sales service process. In addition, a separate department can be created according to the business capacity.

2. In the interviews, it was understood that the enterprises did not know the concept of augmented product. Therefore, it was observed that they did not fully grasp the competitive advantage provided by the after-sales services included in the concept of augmented products. Enterprises' efforts to get feedback (customer evaluations) related to after-sales processes may increase their awareness on this issue. Businesses with business capacity can also establish a call center consisting of one or more people.
3. Especially, it is determined that the enterprises that do not carry out the transportation business within their own organization experience more problems. It is seen that the carrier companies which are focused only on the transportation business without knowing the features of the product cause wrong perceptions both during the transportation of the product and in communication with the customers. It is considered to be an important issue for the transportation process to be incorporated or strictly monitored.
4. It is understood that the manufacturer companies are more advantageous in terms of warranty, but the companies that dealership experience various problems due to the problems arising from the parent company. It can be said that it is important for the companies that are in the sales part of the business to follow the contracts they have made with the main company regarding the warranty and the customer demands within the scope of the warranty.
5. It is understood that the most common problems, especially in the furniture sector, originate from installation. Confusing these problems with usage errors is a very common result. This means either customer dissatisfaction or extra cost, albeit small. Since both results are negative, it is necessary for businesses to eliminate these results. It is important for businesses to get instant feedback on installation and/or create a 'final check' process that includes the customer during the delivery stage.

References

Aaker, D.A. & Keller, K.L. (1990). Customer Evaluations of Brand Extensions. Journal of Marketing, 54(1), 27–41.

Barnes, J.G. (1993). New Technologies, New Markets, and Changing Marketing Practice. Irish Marketing Review; Dublin, 6, 44–52.

Beneke, J., Flynn, R., Greig, T. & Mukaiwa, M. (2013). The Influence of Perceived Product Quality, Relative Price and Risk on Customer Value and Willingness to Buy: A Study of Private Label Merchandise. Journal of Product and Brand Management, 22(3), 218–228. doi:10.1108/JPBM-02-2013-0262.

Chaudhuri, A. & Holbrook, M.B. (2001). The Chain of Effects from Brand Trust and Brand Affect to Brand Performance: The Role of Brand Loyalty. Journal of Marketing, 65(2), 81–93.

Choudhary, A.I., Akhter, S.A., Asif, M., Choudhry, R.M., Siddique, Z. & Mughal, A. (2011). Impact of After Sale Service Characteristics on Customer Satisfaction. Information Management and Business Review, 3(6), 360–365.

Cıranoğlu, M. (2018). Mobilya Sektöründe Satış Sonrası Hizmetlerin Ürünlerin Değer Algıları Üzerine Etkisi: Bursa İli İnegöl İlçesinde Bir Alan Araştırması, Mehmet Akif Ersoy Üniversitesi İktisadi ve İdari Bilimler Fakültesi Dergisi, 5(3), 783–796.

Cıranoğlu, M. (2019). Tüketicilerin Satış Sonrası Hizmetlerden Duydukları Memnuniyetin Satın Alınan Ürünün Algılanan Değerine Etkisi: Beyaz Eşya Ürünleri Üzerine Bir Araştırma. International Journal of Social Inquiry, 12(1), 65–98.

Dursun, Y. & Çerçi, M. (2015). Algılanan Sağlık Hizmeti Kalitesi, Algılanan Değer, Hasta Tatmini ve Davranışsal Niyet İlişkileri Üzerine Bir Araştırma. Erciyes Üniversitesi İktisadi ve İdari Bilimler Fakültesi Dergisi, (23), 1–16.

Keaveney, S.M. (1995). Customer Switching Behavior in Service Industries: An Exploratory Study. Journal of Marketing, 59(2), 71–82. doi:10.2307/1252074.

Keller, K.L. (1993). Conceptualizing, Measuring, and Managing Customer-Based Brand Equity. Journal of Marketing, 57(1), 1–22.

Koral, K. (2011). Satış Sonrası Hizmetlerin İşletmelerin Rekabet Gücü Üzerindeki Etkisi: Elektronik Eşya Sektörü. (Yayımlanmamış yüksek lisans). İstanbul Ticaret Üniversitesi SBE, İstanbul.

Kotler, P. (1998). Marketing Management. Prentice-Hall International Editions, New Jersey.

Markeset, T. & Kumar, U. (2003). Design and Development of Product Support and Maintenance Concepts for Industrial Systems. Journal of Quality in Maintenance Engineering, 9(4), 376–392.

Murthy, D.N.P., Solem, O. & Roren, T. (2004). Product Warranty Logistics: Issues and Challenges. European Journal of Operational Research, EURO Excellence in Practice Award 2001, 156(1), 110–126. doi:10.1016/S0377-2217(02)00912-8.

Naseema, C.M. (2016). Customers Attitude towards After Sales Services of White Goods. Asia Pacific Journal of Research, 1(43), 69–72.

Oko, A.N. & Onuoha, O.A. (2013). After-Sales Services and Customers' Perception of Quality: A Study of Refrigerator Users (Customers) in South East Nigeria. Business and Management Horizons, 1(2), 56–83.

Özgören, Ö.G.F. (2014). Satiş Sonrasi Hizmetin Müşteri Sadakatine Etkisi Ve Ericsson Örneği. Marmara Sosyal Araştırmalar Dergisi, (2), 1–23.

Parasuraman, A. (1997). Reflections on Gaining Competitive Advantage Through Customer Value. Journal of the Academy of Marketing Science, 25(2), 154–161.

Park, C.W., Jaworski, B.J., Macinnis, D.J. (1986). Strategic Brand Concept-Image Management. The Journal of Marketing, 50(4), 135–145.

Petrick, J.F. (2004). First Timers' and Repeaters' Perceived Value. Journal of Travel Research, 43(1), 29–38. doi:10.1177/0047287504265509.

Ramsay, J. (2005). The Real Meaning of Value in Trading Relationship. International Journal of Operation & Production Management, 25(6), 549–565.

Ravald, A. & Grönroos, C. (1996). The Value Concept and Relationship Marketing. European Journal of Marketing, 30(2), 19–30, https://doi.org/10.1108/03090569610106626.

Sinha, I.J. & DeSarbo, W.S. (1998). An Integrated Approach toward the Spatial Modeling of Perceived Customer Value. Journal of Marketing Research, 35(2), 236–249.

Solomon, M.R. (1983). The Role of Products as Social Stimuli: A Symbolic Interactionism Perspective. Journal of Customer Research, 10(3), 319–329.

Sweeney, J.C. & Soutar, G.N. (2001). Customer Perceived Value: The Development of a Multiple Item Scale. Journal of Retailing, 77(2), 203–220.

Sweeney, J.C., Soutar, G.N. & Johnson, L.W. (1999). The Role of Perceived Risk in the Quality-Value Relationship: A Study in a Retail Environment. Journal of Retailing, 75(1), 77–105. doi:10.1016/S0022-4359(99)80005-0.

Şimşek, G. & Noyan, T.F. (2009). Türkiye'de Cep Telefonu Cihazı Pazarında Marka Sadakati İçin Bir Model Denemesi. ODTÜ Gelişme Dergisi, 36(1), 121–159.

Tek, Ö.B. (1999). Pazarlama İlkeleri, Beta Basım A.Ş, İstanbul.

Türedi, H. (2010). Zonguldak İli Mobilya Sektöründe Satış Sonrası Hizmet Üzerine Bir Araştırma. (Yayımlanmamış yüksek lisans tezi). Bartın Üniversitesi FBE, Bartın.

Woodruff, R.B. (1997). Customer Value: The Next Source for Competitive Advantage. Journal of the Academy of Marketing Science, 25(2), 139–153.

Wouters, J.P.M. (2004). Customer Service Strategy Options: A Multiple Case Study in a B2B Setting. Industrial Marketing Management, 33(7), 583–592. doi:10.1016/j.indmarman.2003.12.003.

Zeithaml, V.A. (1988). Customer Perceptions of Price, Quality, and Value: A Means-End Model and Synthesis of Evidence. Journal of Marketing, 52(3), 2–22.

Münevver BAYAR

Relationship of Organizational Performance and Commitment Levels with Leadership and Power Sources

1 Introduction

Organizational performance has organizational psychology, organizational commitment, abilities of the individual and features that can be influenced by organizational leaders. Organizational commitment level includes variables such as organizational justice and organizational work performance. It can be said that job stress, job insecurity and employability, and the position of leaders are related to the organizational commitment of employees.

There are many loyalty models that are becoming widespread in the literature. The most common of these is the loyalty model of Meyer and Allen. Meyer and Allen's (1991) three-component participation model was created to claim that participation has three different components corresponding to different psychological situations.

In this study, the existence of a strong relationship between organizational performance, organizational commitment and leadership power resources was investigated. This process, which started with the understanding of the value of the individual factor in the success of the organizations, led to the understanding of the value of the emotions and behaviors of the human. As a result of the use of power resources, which management sees as a right granted to him, it is seen that it has a significant effect on employees to do their jobs more effectively and efficiently.

In this context, it can be interpreted that the organization members' efforts to feel the emotions they have to show besides not reflecting the emotions they really feel will decrease emotional exhaustion and desensitization, which will allow employees to increase their sense of success.

2 Conseptual Framework

2.1 Organizational Performance

The first development of the concept of performance originated from the contributions of authors such as McClelland, Boyatzis, Nordhaug. In order to achieve the desired level of performance, rational approaches should be adopted that emphasize the characteristics of individuals. This type of approach has been widely criticized, given the independence of context-related qualities, that the interpretive approach that already thinks of this dependency is seen as an alternative.

Boterf argues that performance can be seen as a result of three factors.

These ones:

- To have information about how and in which direction related resources will be used,
- Willingness to act expressing the motivation and participation of the individual;
- The capacity to act, expressing the existence of a context, the organization of work and the social conditions that make it possible and legitimate for individuals to embrace responsibilities.

This concept has more constructive features as it pays attention not only to qualifications and context, but also to the individual's social environment and the individual's tendency to act and participate in a particular context.

Basically, it can be defined as a series of tasks aimed at a common goal between different areas of a company. Organizational performance can be applied in a wide range of industrial and commercial activities, and all sectors of the company work together to achieve and measure the best results. In this model, all efforts are dedicated and reassigned to achieve a specific goal.

The first step to implement the organizational performance concept in a company is to specify what processes will be carried out in the medium or long term and the responsibilities of each sector of the company within an integrated program across all areas. Today it is imperative to present the details of the project very clearly, including opening up space for discussions by the whole team.

Another point to consider is that your team can produce results within the expertise of each professional, that is, demanding that the employee can produce is a consistent measure within the concept of organizational performance. It is necessary to establish indicators to measure the success of the program during and after the completion of the study and evaluate whether this is a positive experience and whether it can be implemented within the company.

The concept of evaluating performance and efficiency in organizations arises from positivist ideals in a scientific revolution that mathematics supports for the experiments and validations of operational processes. These ideas then influenced Management academicians, for example, classic Taylor and Fayol, which relied on measuring time and positioning calculations to seek better efficiency in operational activities.

Therefore, the initial efforts to measure performance and efficiency in structured forms date back to the 19th century, although under uncertain and decentralized goals in some areas or sectors. With the further structuring of the academic research field in management, some studies emerged directly on performance measurement in the 1950s.

Performance criteria need to be based on a strategy for the goals the organization wants to achieve. Considering the relationship between performance criteria and operationalization determined within the framework of the global strategy, performance evaluation takes an important place in the organization strategy. Within this concept, the performance evaluation system of the institutions is a way to ensure that managers have better management control over the organization and that the strategy determined by the activities of their organizations is compatible.

2.2 Organizational Commitment

Organizational commitment is a structure that strongly affects the organizational effectiveness and well-being of the individual. There are several ways to define and operate this structure. Although some authors see participation as a one-dimensional structure and others as multi-dimensional, there is a core core that characterizes and distinguishes commitment from other structures, according to Meyer and Herscovitch. There are two common points in loyalty definitions:

- It is an establishing, imposing and connecting power.
- Directs behavior

Meyer and Herscovitch (2001) define loyalty as "a force that connects an individual to a path of action related to one or more targets". According to the authors, the connection can be determined by an asset (for example, organization) and / or a behavior. However, when loyalty refers to a business, behavioral results are often implied. Similarly, when commitment refers to a mode of action, the entity to which the behavior is attached can usually be found. For example, in the case of Meyer and Allen's continued commitment, the link is with an organization, but this also refers to behavior (maintaining membership).

The authors of the general commitment model distinguish focus behavior from discretionary behavior. Focused behavior is the behavior that the person is connected through loyalty, optional behavior is any behavior that can be included in these terms at the discretion of the committed person, although it is not explicitly stated in the terms of loyalty. Research shows that commitment is associated with a large amount of organizational results. However, a continuous result is that emotional commitment is more closely associated with these results. However, it is difficult to explain why the relationships between emotional commitment and turnover are stronger than the relationship between continuity and turnover commitment. The structure is divided into three dimensions:

- Emotional commitment: employee emotional commitment to the organization, identification with the organization, participation with it;
- Commitment to attendance: the utilitarian dimension that refers to the awareness of costs associated with leaving the organization;
- Regulatory commitment: a sense of moral obligation to maintain one's relationship with the organization.

Meyer and Allen define emotional attachment as a "desire" component. An emotionally committed employee is identified by the organization's goals and wants to remain part of the organization. Attendance is the "need" component or the gain against job losses in an organization. In regulatory commitment, the individual accepts an organization because of the feelings of foresight, which is the last component of organizational commitment, and stays with it. For example, the organization may have invested resources in the training of an employee who feels a 'moral' obligation to stay in the organization to work and pay 'debt'. Regulatory participation of employees is high in cases where employers see examples of employers showing that they are dependent on employee well-being regularly. Meyer and Allen bases their research in this area on theoretical evidence rather than empirical evidence that can explain the lack of depth in this part of their work compared to others.

2.3 Leadership

Numerous leadership theories have emerged over the years, and according to the literature, there are five major leadership theories: features, behavior, power effect, situational and integrative theories. However, these theories are based on the claim that there is only one person in the leadership position. However, evidence has emerged that leadership can be shared.

According to Pearce and Conger, leadership can be defined as a dynamic and interactive process of influence, which is carried out by a group of individuals and the goal will be to achieve the expected results. The chances of success in this leadership style increase when leaders play different and complementary roles. In addition, leaders know how to work together, how to deal with the credit division, communicate effectively, deal with crises, allocate and re-allocate common tasks and decisions.

The leader manages or groups a group and includes industry, army, etc. It is a person who can be placed in context. There are several types of leaders (combat unit, work team, young group) that vary according to the characteristics of the group. The leader has the function of combining the elements of the group so they can achieve the goals of the group together. Leadership is about motivation because an effective leader knows how to motivate the elements of his group or team. New approaches on the subject argue that leadership is a behavior that can be implemented and developed. The skills of a leader include charisma, patience, respect, discipline and above all the ability to influence subordinates.

The concept of leadership is related to authority positions, people who are official leaders. In practice, however, a leader can be an informally prominent person, a reference that motivates and exemplifies others within a group. Especially in the organizational environment, the leader must be able to work together and thus reach the company's goals together. In fact, some people have more natural leadership skills, while others should develop them. In addition, the concept of leadership has evolved over the years. Thus, factors such as the economic scenario and rapid pace of the market have created new demands on the humanitarian aspect of professionals. Although much has been said about leadership and the importance of being a good leader, this concept is universally used as if there is only one model that everyone follows. Therefore, there are three leadership styles, each based on the personal and behavioral characteristics of the leader. Thus leadership can be autocratic, democratic or liberal, as we will see below.

- Autocratic leadership; In this concept of leadership, the leader makes his ideas and decisions basically without resorting to followers' opinions. He is also central and authoritarian.
  Democratic leadership; Democratic or participatory leadership is leadership that encourages the group's participation in decision-making. Therefore, it increases the self-esteem of the group by valuing the contribution of professional team members who possess the characteristics of this leadership concept.
- Liberal leadership; In this leadership model, it gives complete freedom to the leader group. It only participates in decisions when requested. Team members are free to run their projects.

After all, the leader plays an important role in the team. It is the person who guides the team members for the goals of the organization. In addition, it is very effective on the group / team's performance. The leader is the most important factor for the organization to reach its goals in the fastest way by establishing a mutual trust relationship with its team members.

2.4 Power Sources of Leader

Leadership in the organization is a key issue, as it is about success or failure with reaching the set goals. It is important to know how to distinguish between leader and boss, especially in the context of business or organization. Effective leaders steer success by using discipline, patience, commitment, respect and humility. Leaders use some power sources to steer groups. These power sources are described below.

2.4.1 Rewarding Power

Leaders use the reward system as a source of motivation within the organization. The main theme when dealing with motivation management is the design and implementation of reward systems. The motivational aspect of the rewards stems from the belief that, as with Taylor's scientific management, wage and additional payments will be the main source of motivation for motivation. According to Taylor, the selection of employees is made by the majority of workers based on the wage perspective, not the type of job or the content of the positions. Accordingly, people are affected only by salary, economic and social rewards.

According to Bergamini and Coda (1997), factors outside the worker such as security, wages, organizational policy, conditions of the work environment, interpersonal relations mobilize employees and enable them to fight to reach them.

2.4.1 Punishment and Compelling Power

Fear management is a motivational tool that can create side effects. When the employee feels constantly watched, creative processes are closed. In addition, because they are afraid of making mistakes and being punished and there is no communication, teamwork cannot take the initiative because it is not very good. When the leader often refers to punishing authority, employees tend to be more insensitive, although it is just a threat, and instead they leave the job and set aside quality. This method reveals what the manager intends to prevent.

2.4.2 *Legal Power*

It is the power that comes from the organizational hierarchy and comes from the status of the leader within the organization. It expresses the power and authority to influence the people around him due to the position of the person (Eraslan, 2004). The researchers stated that influencing efforts based on this power require oversight and that there is a suitable environment for it, otherwise the legal power source will decrease.

2.4.3 *Power of Expertise*

It is the power obtained by the acceptance of the knowledge, skill and expertise of the leader regarding his job by the audience.

2.4.4 *Charismatic Power*

According to members of the organization Charismatic leaders have a vision and since they are willing to face this vision and take risks, charismatic leaders are sensitive to both environmental constraints and their followers' needs and behave differently than ordinary ones. Charismatic leaders convey their high performance expectations and express their confidence in team members who can definitely reach them.

In general, the charismatic leader sacrifices himself to show courage and belief in his vision and engages in some unusual behavior. Charismatic leadership is associated with high performance and full satisfaction among leaders. Some experts argue that people can be trained to behave in a charismatic manner, so that they can enjoy the benefits of a charismatic leader. Charisma is appropriate even when followers' task adds an ideological component or the environment is involved in a certain uncertainty or tension. This is a reflection of the fact that the charismatic leader appears at certain times in politics, religion or war, or faces a crisis in the company's new life.

3 Relationship of Organizational Performance and Commitment Levels with Leadership and Power Sources

Leadership plays a key role in the results achieved by companies. In keeping with the rest of the business structure, a change in the leader can often save or deter a company. The complexity of the modern world requires leaders to have a variety of competencies that often show seemingly dissonance, and the successful leader is a cognitively complex person. The complexity of the markets, the increasing pace of business, and the need to adapt strategies or tactics constantly force leaders to play different leadership roles.

In cases where demands are high for a single leader, leadership teams are organized to ensure continued performance. Leaders' talent alone does not guarantee successful business performance. In order to maximize the influence of leadership, the rest of the business structure needs to trust the leader, which makes the impact of trust important. Charismatic, transformative or inspiring leadership are the names used for leaders who offer the task of fulfilling the task as a reward. The charismatic leader causes his followers to overcome their interests and work only to achieve the mission, cause and goal. In order to achieve this degree of commitment and success, leaders pay special attention to the needs and potentials of their followers.

Charismatic leaders deeply influence their followers' emotions, encourage them and inspire them to identify problems differently, give them their best ideas and present fresh ideas. Charismatic leadership consists of creating certain values and presenting new ideas. Standards set values and create tools to guide targeting efforts. The charismatic leader has the ability to encourage followers and ensure their past performances and personal interests and create a commitment about goals.

In addition, the reward power causes an additional source of motivation on the organization. Evidence of Abraham Maslow's theory shows that wages are a basic and sufficient requirement for employees to feed themselves and to accommodate themselves and their families satisfactorily. In order to motivate Maslow's employees, managers should deal with salary issues before providing incentives to increase self-esteem, create feelings of participation or growth opportunities for employees. Later, the American psychologist Herzberg classified salary (external rewards) as a hygiene factor in his two-way theory and was also used as a motivation factor for employees.

4 Conclusions

Looking at the causes of organizational performance is not only academic but also very practical and political. Because it should also be decided whether the proposed measures and recommendations address the root cause of the problems that arise. In order to reach the expected performance level in organizations, the historical scope of organizational changes and their central roles in the process of socio-economic change should be determined. The essential perspective in which changes in organizational performance are recorded is based on the limitation of organizational structures and relationships that were previously stable.

For this reason, in our study, organizational performance, organizational commitment, leadership and power sources of leaders are handled together.

Leadership is the art of dominating people, attracting followers, and positively influencing mentality and behavior. Leadership can come naturally when a person stands out in a leadership role, without necessarily having a leadership position. It is an unofficial type of leadership. When a leader is chosen by an organization and is in the position of authority, he takes official leadership. These leaders can organize their organizations using their charismatic powers.

In addition, leaders can motivate members of the organization with their reward powers. It has been found that the rewards motivate employees and this provides greater commitment to the cooperative to adapt to the goals and objectives suggested by their employees. Organizational commitment leads to continuity of action within an action process to separate it from structures such as motivation and attitudes, but it can also cause contradictory attitudes. According to Meyer and Herscovitch (2001), what distinguishes one commitment from another is the presumed mindset that it characterizes (e.g. emotional commitment, feeling connected, the belief of accepting a particular purpose). In this context, it can be said that the leader's reward and charismatic power affect his followers.

References

Aguinis, H. (2009). Performance management. Upper Saddle River, NJ: Pearson/ Prentice Hall.

Aslan, Ş. (2009). Karizmatik liderlik ve örgütsel vatandaşlık davranışı ilişkisi:"Kurumda çalışma yılı" ve "ücret" değişkenlerinin rolü. Uluslararası İnsan Bilimleri Dergisi, 6(1), 256–275.

Bergamini, C. W., & Coda, R. (1997). Psicodinâmica da vida organizacional: motivação e liderança. 2. ed., pp. 69–93, São Paulo: Atlas.

Burns, J. M. (2012). Leadership. Open Road Media.

Conger, J. A., & Pearce, C. L. (2003). A Landscape of Opportunities: Future Research on Shared Leadership. In C. L. Pearce & J. A. Conger (Eds.), Shared Leadership: Reframing the Hows and Whys of Leadership, pp. 285–303, Thousand Oaks, CA: Sage.

Eraslan, L. (2004). Liderlik olgusunun tarihsel evrimi, temel kavramlar ve yeni liderlik paradigmasının analizi. Milli Eğitim Dergisi, 162(01), 1–14.

Gruman, J. A., & Saks, A. M. (2011). Performance management and employee engagement. Human Resource Management Review, 21(2), 123–136.

Jaros, S. (2007). Meyer and Allen model of organizational commitment: Measurement issues. The Icfai Journal of Organizational Behavior, 6(4), 7–25.

Kaplan, R. S., & Norton, D. P. (1992). In Search of Excellence–der Maßstab muß neu definiert werden. Harvard Manager, 14(4), 37–46.

Le Boterf, G. (1998). Évaluer les compétences. Quels jugements? Quels critères? Quelles instances. Education permanente, 135(2), 143–151.

McClelland, D. C. (1971). Assessing human motivation. New York: General Learning Press

.

Meyer, J. & Allen, N. (1991). A three-component model conceptualization of organizational commitment. Human Resource Management Review, 1, 61–89.

Meyer, J. P., & Herscovitch, L. (2001). Commitment in the workplace: Toward a general model. Human Resource Management Review, 11(3), 299–326.

Nordhaug, O. (1993). Human capital in organizations: Competence, training, and learning. Oslo: Scandinavian University Press.

Pearce, C. L. (2004). The future of leadership: Combining vertical and shared leadership to transform knowledge work. Academy of Management Perspectives, 18(1), 47–57.

Sandberg, J. (2000). Understanding human competence at work: An interpretative approach. Academy of Management Journal, 43(1), 9–25.

Yağcı, K. (2007). Meyer-Allen örgütsel bağlılık modeli yaklaşımıyla otel işletmeleri işgörenlerinin örgütsel bağlılık düzeylerinin ölçülmesine yönelik bir araştırma, Dokuz Eylül Üniversitesi Sosyal Bilimler Enstitüsü Dergisi, 9(3), 114–129

Nuran Varışlı

Examination of Leadership Styles and Organisational Culture in Modern Management Systems

1 Introduction

Modern society has been facing huge socio-economic and political changes in the current time. The last 10 years have been marked with continuous changes that have been affecting countries and people all around the globe. Considering the consolidation of capitalism and the development of the consumer society in this scenario, adaptation of the organizations to a brand new competitive, dynamic and brutal context becomes a must.

In the modern society, changes to the production of goods and daily life has been achieved through technological innovation and socio-economic changes. In this sense, environment created by the current global and technological powers is based on change and complexity. Therefore, in the context of internationalization of the markets, organizational harmony becomes the critical success factor for the survival of the organizations in the competitive and turbulent environment of changes and innovations.

In this scenario of continuous changes and adaptations, it can be seen that leaders, as the driving force for the organizations during the adaptation perocess to new phenomena, are as important as ever for turning threats and market uncertainty into business opportunities. In this context, studies regarding organizational leadership have become an important and wide area of research over the last 10 years.

However, the view that states the fact that organizational leadership has a strong dependancy on organizational culture has been getting stronger in the scientific field. In this sense, our study examines the problems of leadership and organizational culture affecting leadership in modern management systems.

As such, studies regarding organizational leadership have also been examined not only due to the possible correlation between leaders but also due to the need for analyzing this structure together with organizational culture, which has a huge effect on creating strategies and organizational performance.

Organizational structures cease to represent the decisive aspect of human behavior, which is defined from a technical point of view, in exchange for an understanding that arises from different interpretations of their actors and the results of the dynamic and continuous negotiation processes between their interests. Therefore, organizational structures are modeled and even transformed, with negotiation processes between different political interests in mind. As for the perception of leadership styles, one of the main contributions of the study is, after the analysis of the research factor, the identification of 3 aspects that do not match those proven in the examples of the original study. This suggests that depending on the context, leadership styles can be perceived differently.

Organizational culture is a component that guides people on the best way to achieve goals within the company. As such, it represents a link that guides employees to realize their talents. This way of interpreting leadership involves not only subordinates but also the involvement of peers and superiors.

2 Conceptual Framework

2.1 Concept of Management

Management has been strongly influenced by philosophy since the ancient times. Confucius emphasized the importance of personal value and advocated for information based management. Greek philosopher Socrates presented his view of management as a personal skill separate from technical knowledge and experience. Plato, another Greek philosopher, has shown the democratic management of public enterprises in his work Republic.

Organization management is the planning of all actions that contribute to the full functioning of a system and lead to the realization of tasks, goals and general goals of an organization. It's nothing different than the management of a business, company or organization in order to reach goals and achieve positive and profitable results. The purpose of this type of management concept is to direct people and processes effectively, to encourage improvements, to create a collaborative and motivated environment, to be suitable for self-improvements and last of all, to achieve results. Such an organization, which is seen as a working model, is driven by a policy of values that affects all stages of processes in different areas of the organization[1].

Repetitive changes and advancement of technologies in today's organizational scenario make effective organization leadership more efficient and necessary. Therefore, it becomes possible to create operating methods and techniques that can guarantee the healthy adaptation, survival and competitiveness of a

1 Bolat, T., Seymen, O. A., Bolat, O. İ., & Erdem, B. (2009). Yönetim ve organizasyon.

company that wants to be relevant in the market. These guidelines should be in strategies such as[2]:

- Internal or external action planning;
- Human and material resource management;
- Creation of a hierarchical or horizontal structure;
- Determination of the scope of each employee;
- Development of career plans;
- Pricing rules;
- Organizational culture guides.

Organization management is the fraction responsible for defining effective and ambitious strategies for the growth and expansion of the organization's results. It is a way to target and leverage existing resources. These strategies should be in line with the company's mission and policies and take internal factors, such as strengths and weaknesses, and external factors, such as threats and opportunities, into account. Organizational culture, which is common in business context, represents a combination of values, beliefs, norms and rituals adopted by a company.

2.2 Modern Management System

Organization management is responsible for evaluating employee performance as well as supporting improvements, benefits and continuous development which will enable employees to be productive professionals and focus on results. Since an organization's greatest wealth is human capital (the value of every individual that contributes to the growth of the company), a good management knows how to invest in and qualify people. Therefore, it is extremely necessary to work on recruiting talented people as well as encouraging employees in the company. The concept of management aims to achieve the most satisfactory results possible. However, these can be only achieved when strategies and processes are in harmony[3]. The organization creates its own principles and values which are the result of interaction between people. For this reason, most managers and entrepreneurs prefer to get consultation to create an assessment and analyze the points needed to create an effective organizational management.

---

2 Christiansen, J. (2000). *Building the innovative organization: Management systems that encourage innovation*. Springer.

3 Barnard, C. I. (2003). *Organization and management: Selected papers* (Vol. 7). Psychology Press.

Various studies on trends in organization management have shown that traditional management practices can no longer respond to an organization's increased performance, product offer and service delivery. When an organizational system is considered from such a perspective, the "participation" factor is more valued because it enables people to gain more knowledge and commitment regarding basic or strategic issues[4]. This is the basis for defining rules and procedures in collective decision-making, where opportunities are created for the widest possible involvement of interested parties and their participation in everything that is essential to them, also known as the democratic problem in modern organizational management.

Participatory strategies have been highlighted in modern times as effective ways to manage conflicts and increase production and productivity rates. In addition, authors such as Mintzberg[5] and McLagan[6] acknowledge that participatory management practices often improve the distribution of business benefits and redistribute power in the organization. Its adoption entails legitimizing shared values and goals which are aimed at satisfying individual initiative and creativity aspirations. Modern organizations should have a leadership that can change at any time. In these times, where information spreads easily and new tools emerge in a very short time, a manager needs a "sensation" to adapt to change in their job.

2.3 Leadership and Leadership Styles

Leaders can be signs of the organization's success or failure, therefore leadership is a topic that encourages research to pursue ways to achieve effective leadership through its effects and characteristics, deserving attention from researches, academics and consultants. Various studies have been developed to identify different styles, competencies, skills and attitudes of leadership in the search for an ideal model for managers who easily adapt to different organizational cultures. It should be noted that, especially in retailing, there are very few theories or research that relate the leader's style to different organizational groups. Selecting

---

4 Boje, D. (1996). *Postmodern management and organization theory*. Sage.

5 Mintzberg, H. (2001). The yin and the yang of managing. *Organizational dynamics*, *29*(4), 306–306.

6 McLagan, P. A. (2000). Portfolio thinking. *Training & Development*, *54*(2), 44–46.

professionals is a complex and time-consuming process that requires thinking and planning[7].

Continuous improvements, the pursuit of excellence in terms of quality, increasing competitiveness, exceeding the expectations of its customers and wanting a continuous future among companies push organizations to be in larger processes. However, a concern among leaders is the leadership linked to the motivation factors of their employees[8].

Leaders are constantly considered active, as they are the people who mobilize their teams to do business, encourage fast learning and the adoption of new roles, relationships and values. The leader is responsible for the growth of the organization and based on this principle, it is important to emphasize the importance of investigating the relationship between the ideal profile of people in senior management positions and their attitudes at work.

Leadership is the ability to influence, persuade and motivate people to achieve common goals. It is a continuous selection process that allows the group to move in the same direction. It also means coordinating and influencing people positively.

Posner ve Kouzes[9] suggest one of the reasons why a leader exists is to show the importance of people in the organization, in other words, they suggest a strategy which needs to be constantly reviewed to achieve the results necessary to maintain the team's motivation.

The leader is seen as a catalyst for talent in the formation of new skills and guarantee of results in a highly competitive and globalized environment present today. Accordingly, the ability to influence people or groups is deliberate and involves power and authority in a psychological way by changing the way of the affected person. In short, the definition of leadership changes simultaneously according to each approach as a result of the focus given by each researcher. Due to the diversity of material currently present, there is a difficulty in establishing a concept in leadership theories that covers all of the approaches involved in this phenomenon.

---

7 Alkahtani, A. H., Abu-Jarad, I., Sulaiman, M., & Nikbin, D. (2011). The impact of personality and leadership styles on leading change capability of Malaysian managers. *Australian Journal of Business and Management Research*, *1*(2), 70.

8 Bencivenga, J. (2002). John Kotter on Leadership, Management and Change. *School Administrator*, *59*(2), 36–40.

9 Kouzes, J. M., & Posner, B. Z. (2011). *Credibility: How leaders gain and lose it, why people demand it* (Vol. 203). John Wiley & Sons.

Posner ve Kouzes (2011) point out what needs to be done to achieve extraordinary results in leadership[10]:

(1) Draw the way;
(2) Inspire a common vision;
(3) Challenge the process;
(4) Getting others to act;
(5) Stimulating emotions.

Individual competence is knowing how to act in a way that results in mobilization, integration, knowledge, resource and skill transfer which add value to the individual and organization. Leadership is the art of delegation and decentralization, namely the art of empowerment, a well-known art to clearly combine goals, specifications, and deadlines. However, to lead or coordinate a team, whether a born or a made leader, each of the leaders have their own style.

- Compelling; The leader says exactly what to do. The leader is critical and very difficult in criticism, it gives employees fear. It is used when the leader does not have much time and it is easier to do this than to discuss solutions.
- Sovereign; The leader has a competent and broad vision. It is the leader style who tries to involve people to follow their aspects. Requires a lot of time, experience, knowledge and preparation.
- Emotional; Seen when people are more important than tasks. The leader treats their employees well and of course is rewarded with loyalty and increased performance. Interest in people brings more harmony and closeness to the team. The important thing is that the compassionate boss can protect everything.
- Democratic; The leader who makes the most of his team from the decision and responsibility division. This style of leader creates high-performance collective environments. However, if the team is too young and inexperienced, extreme democracy tends to have harmful consequences.
- Modelers; The details of the instructions increase the quality levels of the products.
- Coaching; This leader spends time and effort to get to know their team so that they develop their team individually to get good results.

---

10 Kouzes, J. M., & Posner, B. Z. (2011). *Credibility: How leaders gain and lose it, why people demand it* (Vol. 203). John Wiley & Sons.

2.4 Organizational Culture

The theme of organizational culture is known as a subject of great importance with administrative studies, especially in organizational studies. Under different theoretical and methodological perspectives, authors such as Smircich[11] and Schein[12] have examined this phenomena which occurs in organizational environments in some of their works. Although it has been of interest by researchers for a long time, studies on organizational culture relate to the field of management, especially since this concept is objectively visualized.

Organizational culture refers to the deep structure of the organization, based on the values, beliefs and assumptions of company members. The meanings are provided by the socialization of the various group identities that come together in the workplace. Interactions, due to dependence on the system of individual actions and cognitions, produces a symbolic world that gives organizational culture a stable and fragile foundation at the same time[13].

Culture, personality, behavior and mentality, that is, the organizational culture, has a strong and growing effect on the recognition factor of companies and the performance of the organization. In this way, it personalizes the organization more compared to others. When it comes to organizational climate, it depicts the organizational environment based on the organization's value system, but tends to present this social environment in static terms as a set of fixed dimensions. Therefore, the climate is considered to be relatively temporary, subject to direct control, and is largely limited to aspects of the social environment, which are consciously percieved by the company's professionals. Climate expresses a situation and its connections to thoughts, emotions and organizational behavior.

Climate is temporary, subjective and often manipulated by those with power and influence. Business effectiveness depends on adapting cultural standards to the challenges the company faces at a particular time. All organizations have a purpose they have created, culture is an important factor in achieving this purpose. Organizational culture is a mechanism to standardize and predict people's behavior, as it is described as a set of values that people cultivate and believe. This reveals the importance of employees' roles in strengthening the organizational culture.

---

11 Smircich, L. (,jo). Concepts of culture and organizational analysis. In *The Anthropology of Organisations* (pp. 255–274). Routledge.

12 Schein, E. H. (1985). Defining organizational culture. *Classics of organization theory*, *3*(1), 490–502.

13 Schein, E. H. (2010). *Organizational culture and leadership* (Vol. 2). John Wiley & Sons.

First of all, it can be said that organizational culture consists of ethical and moral values, principles, beliefs, domestic and foreign policies, systems and organizational climate. These are the rules that all members of this organization adopt as guidelines and facilities to guide business and behavior. Organizational culture in an organization is a series of beliefs or habits developed by its managers, values and teachings built throughout the organization's management. Organizational culture is a set of unofficial rules through which employees are guided through their daily activities and thus achieve organizational goals. The culture of an organization can positively affect the fulfillment of these requirements[14].

The organization defines the reality that its members will experience through culture. In the case of an organization, organizational culture is a series of beliefs or habits developed by managers or employees throughout the organization's existence. These are the values and teachings that shape the company's management model. It is a meaning system shared by all members of an organization and it separates an organization from others. It represents the way of acting and thinking within the company and how it motivates employees, how it does business, how it treats customers or employees and what its managers think. Therefore, organizational culture is very important for organizations because it is the informal and unwritten rules that guides employees in their daily activities so they can achieve organizational goals. When an organization is strategically planned, this culture should be taken into consideration so as not to cause dissatisfaction among the employees.

3 Conclusion

Modern management systems have created increasingly integrated and flexible performances in the business environment with fierce competition and the search for corporate effectiveness. This scenario encourages initiatives to create strategies that consider a vision that focuses on the perfection of production processes and technical and administrative practices. On the side, there is an increasing need for people to develop and recover their skills based on deliberate actions, ethical and social responsibility assumptions. The emergence of innovative and integrated forms of organization management to deal with

14 Henri, J. F. (2006). Organizational culture and performance measurement systems. *Accounting, organizations and society*, *31*(1), 77–103.

environmental changes has played an important role in the discussions in the academic and business world.

In this context, the change in human behavior, especially at the level of behavior, becomes the central axis for new management technologies to provoke people for better awareness and commitment to performing collective actions and to justify provocative values. This is because such principles prevent the creation of a learning environment and participation of most employees in organizational practices. The specialized literature allows us to understand the existence of a direct and repetitive relationship between organizational learning.

Organizations are complex social systems that offer a different feature: sometimes they get surprising results and sometimes they fail. The versatile character offered by organizations implies the need for any researcher to interpret it as a series of events and comments that are partially subject to the characteristics and interests of the observer. Managing these authentic organic units is largely based on understanding the variety and its modification for richer models and these are tailored to suit any situations, emergence or custom.

As the central concepts in organizational theory, organizational culture and leadership are that undisputed important variables to be considered and there are scientific studies conducted by the modern society. Increasingly, organizational culture, which accepts itself as an indispensable component for the well-being of employees, ensures the growth and development of individuals. It also allows the creation of relatively consensual information about the meaning of the world and some form of power and validation of the adopted practices.

Interpreting organizations as cultural systems shows us that the organization is a result of a system of common meanings, allowing us to be interested in the symbolic sense of most company events. Thus, a value is given to the events expressed in it. In this way, it is clear that organizations go beyond physical boundaries, structures and available resources; they also represent structures that are equipped with a strong human and social component.

Leaders use their functions in a global and complex market surrounded by an atmosphere of uncertainty and constant change. Among the challenges in this context are the imperative of reducing followers' complexity and sense of doubt in order to create a positive vision for the future that everyone shares. Leaders need an increasing sense of cautiousness and a guiding vision in their ability to bring together and mobilize individual and organizational forces. In addition, they use their leadership roles in a business context that faces a crisis of legitimacy and trust that has been lost over a wide range of events over the years. In a global community with several stakeholders, long-term feasibility and success largely depends on the company's ability to act responsibly towards everyone involved, and hence its leadership. The leader then becomes the creator of relationships for employees, customers, business partners and everyone in the environment.

References

Alkahtani, A. H., Abu-Jarad, I., Sulaiman, M., & Nikbin, D. (2011). The impact of personality and leadership styles on leading change capability of Malaysian managers. Australian Journal of Business and Management Research, 1(2), 70.

Barnard, C. I. (2003). Organization and management: Selected papers (Vol. 7). Psychology Press, London.Bencivenga, J. (2002). John Kotter on leadership, management and change. School Administrator, 59(2), 36–40.

Boje, D. (1996). Postmodern management and organization theory. Sage. https://dx.doi.org/10.4135/9781483345390.Bolat, T., Seymen, O. A., Bolat, O. İ., & Erdem, B. (2009). Yönetim ve Organizasyon. Detay Yayıncılık, İstanbul.Christiansen, J. (2000). Building the innovative organization: Management systems that encourage innovation. Springer. https://dx.doi.org/10.1057/9780333977446Henri, J. F. (2006). Organizational culture and performance measurement systems. Accounting, Organizations and Society, 31(1), 77–103.

McLagan, P. A. (2000). Portfolio thinking. Training & Development, 54(2), 44–46.

Mintzberg, H. (2001). The yin and the yang of managing. Organizational Dynamics, 29(4), 306–306.

Posner, B. Z., & Kouzes, J. M. (2011). Credibility: How Leaders Gain and Lose It, Why People Demand It (Vol. 203). John Wiley & Sons, New Jersey.

Schein, E. H. (1985). Defining organizational culture. Classics of Organization Theory, 3(1), 490–502.

Schein, E. H. (2010). Organizational culture and leadership (Vol. 2). John Wiley & Sons, New Jersey.Smircich, L. (2017). Concepts of culture and organizational analysis. In The anthropology of organisations (pp. 255–274). Routledge, Abingdon.

Setenay Yağmur

Business Judgment Rule in Terms of Turkish Commercial Code

1 Introduction

The business judgment rule in Turkish law is not regulated by the lawmaker. However, in the justification of Article 369 of Turkish Commercial Code (TCC) where the obligation of care and loyalty of members of the executive board has been regulated, as a benchmark of being a prudent manager, it is accepted that *"business judgment"* can be delivered in line with corporate governance principles. According to this, in case necessary conditions are met, as the result of decisions of the executive board, even if the developments are in the opposite direction and the company has lost, dereliction will be out of question considering behaviors of member of executive board and manager and thus, they will not have any responsibilities.

2 Concept

2.1 Source of Business Judgment Rule in Terms of Turkish Law

Although the origins of the business judgment rule are based on common law, the principle has also influenced civil law. In Turkish law, this rule is not regulated as a clear provision. However, with the effect of both two legal systems, in the justification of article 369 of TCC, business judgment rule is mentioned considering the determination of benchmark of prudent manager in terms of care and loyalty obligation of members of executive board. So, the implementation of the business judgment rule in the Turkish legal system is mainly influenced by common and civil law systems since there is no clear provision in the Turkish legal system on the subject.

In the American legal system, in the cases raised against decisions delivered by the members of the executive board, business judgment rule is considered. Within the scope of the business judgment rule, courts evaluate the decision-making process, rather than the appropriateness of the decisions of the executive board (Akdağ Güney, 2016, p. 189; Bozkurt Yaşar, 2014a, p. 101). The emergence of the rule in US as a legal concept dates back to *"Percy v. Millaudon"* case of Lousiannan Supreme Court in 1829. In this case, briefly it was ruled out that only wrong decision of manager could not be interpreted as a requirement of his duty (Göktürk, 2011, p. 210).

The established jurisprudence in American law is that decisions on the management of the enterprise will not be the subject of litigation. A decision in accordance with business judgment rule has to be related with business management, focused on business improvement and commercial issues and all kinds of necessary information source has to be used while taking such decision, manager who takes such decision shall believe that it will be the most beneficial decision for company and decision shall not contradict the goodwill rule (Hacımahmutoğlu, 2014, p. 111; Kervankıran, 2007, p. 259; Pulaşlı, 2017, p. 482).

The backbone of the TCC is parallel to the German and Swiss legal systems. However, of course, there are some differences specific to Turkish law, or as a result of the differences between these systems, one of them is prioritized compared to the other.

With the code which was enacted in German law in 2005 and called UMAG *("Gesetz zur Unternehmensintegrität und Modernisierung des Anfechtungsrecht")*, significant convenience was provided to the shareholders regarding the internal responsibility of the board of directors. On the other hand, the business judgment rule in the American legal system was adopted in German law with the purpose of balancing the aforementioned convenience (Ayan, 2011, p. 68; Göktürk, 2011, p. 221; Kervankıran, 2007, p. 249; Pulaşlı, 2017, p. 475). Therefore, the business judgment rule is a legal regulation in the German legal system. According to § 93/1.2 titled *"Duty of the members of the board of directors to exercise skill and care, liability and responsibilities"* in Stock Corporation Act, *"No dereliction of duties shall be given in those instances in which the member of the management board, in taking an entrepreneurial decision, was within his rights to reasonably assume that he was acting on the basis of adequate information and in the best interests of the company."*

In the article 717 titled *"Duty of care and loyalty"* of Code of Obligations in the 1991 dated revision relevant to joint stock companies in the Swiss legal system, just like in Turkish legal system, business judgment rule is not regulated. However, the Swiss Federal Court has various decisions that involve business judgment rule (for the decisions of Swiss Federal Court relevant to subject, Pulaşlı, 2017, p. 476).

Turkish jurisdiction authorities have not explained which country's regulation would be mainly applied relevant to the implementation of the business judgment rule in the justification of TCC. On the other hand, it was clearly stated that the provision of the German Joint Stock Companies Act § 93 cannot be considered as a source. In the justification of article 369 of TCC, law maker explained this preference as follows: "*Contrary to what is defended in classical German school, performing for the best of the company and avoiding the issues for the loss of the company, shall not be considered as a measure of care duty. Because, it is necessary for the member of the board of directors to identify the risks arising from all the crises in the economy, changes in the market conditions and uncertainties and take the necessary precautions, otherwise he/she has to be held responsible.*" In addition, in German law, violation of managers' duty of care is only possible in the event of a gross fault. However, in Swiss and Turkish legal systems, since the principle of differentiated solidarity applies, responsibility may be in question even in the case of a slight fault (Pulaşlı, 2017, p. 479).

Since condition of gross fault is sought for the responsibility of the board member in American legal system (Hacımahmutoğlu, 2014, p. 121; Pulaşlı, 2017, p. 479), it is not appropriate for Turkish law to implement business judgment rule in this legal system as a whole (Pulaşlı, 2017, p. 479). Moreover, there are some cases in which the implementation of business judgment rule is limited in the American legal system. Such cases are *defensive decisions of the target company in unfriendly take overs* and *decisions of special litigation committee*. However, decisions of special litigation committee are not implemented in Turkish legal system (Pulaşlı, 2017, p. 480).

As a result, Swiss legal system shall primarily be taken into consideration in comparison with German and American systems considering the implementation business judgment rule in the Turkish legal system. Because the regulations of both Swiss and Turkish legal systems regarding the duties of the board members are parallel. In addition, in both legal systems, managers are expected to take all care duty in all conditions of the event (for a similar opinion, please refer Pulaşlı, 2017, p. 480).

2.2 Regulation in Turkish Law

The business judgment rule is not regulated by the lawmaker in Turkish law. On the other hand, in the justification of article 369 of TCC where care and loyalty duty of members of the board of directors are arranged, it is stated, "*prudent manager benchmark acknowledges that the board member can make a business judgment in accordance with corporate governance principles, and is based on the principle that the member should not be held responsible in the event that the risk arises from this. In accordance with the generally accepted principle, in case appropriate researches have been made, information is taken from the relevant parties and the decision is made on the board of directors, then it is not possible to mention dereliction even if the developments occurred in the opposite direction and the company has lost.*"

According to *Çamoğlu*, this new measure, which is included in the justification of 6102 numbered TCC, is fair and can respond better to the needs of company. Because the old regulation was strongly associated with management subject of the company. This opinion which expects the care of an individual who has more expertise in the decision making and behavior of the members within management subject, was bearing risks on issues such as protecting company assets, relations with affiliates, confidentiality (Poroy, Tekinalp and Çamoğlu, 2019, p. 421).

Managers of joint-stock company are not obliged to achieve a certain result as a requirement of the task they have undertaken. In other words, within the framework of a contractual relationship with the company, they are obliged not to perform a specific result, but to perform the task undertaken to them diligently and with the best effort (Göktürk, 2011, p. 208).

Since the task performed by the managers is related to commercial life, taking risk to a certain degree is inevitable. Because risk is an element that characterizes trade. Thus, undertaking the risk in company activities with the condition of following certain conditions, cannot be interpreted as violating care duty and thus they have faults. However, in undertaking the risk arising from commercial activities, it is necessary to set limits on which principles managers shall be discharged from their responsibilities. Business judgment is a basic rule used to set these limits (Akdağ Güney, 2016, p. 191; Göktürk, 2011, p. 208).

As a result, there is no obstacle to the implementation of the business judgment rule that is accepted in modern legal systems, in the Turkish legal system. In this context, the rule has importance especially in terms of liability cases. The business judgment rule enables managers to be more courageous when making business decisions, while on the other hand softens the benchmark of care for board members (Akdağ Güney, 2016, p. 193).

2.3 Benchmark of Prudent Manager

According to article 369 of TCC, members of the board of directors have to behave with diligence while performing company business. In addition, members of the board of directors and third parties in charge of management are obliged to observe the interests of the partnership in accordance with the rules of honesty while performing their duties.

With 6102 numbered TCC which entered in force in 2012, relevant to liabilities of members of board of directors, the criteria of "*foresight*" indicated in article 320 of previous 6762 numbered TCC was left and benchmark of *"prudent manager"* was adopted.

According to the explanation in the justification of TCC article 369, the term *"prudent manager"* plays a benchmark role in fault while on the other hand defines objective behavior on decisions and actions, but it does not cover the measure that is beyond the objective control of a manager and beyond objective expectations. So that, according to article 553/3 of TCC, *"No one can be held responsible for any violations or illegalities to the law or articles of association beyond control, this non-accountability cannot be invalidated on the grounds of custody and care duty."* Furthermore, due to the differentiated solidarity principle indicated in article 557 of 6102 dated TCC, the care shall be evaluated on the basis of individual.

The prudent manager benchmark is based on an objective criterion. In the justification of article 369 of TCC, law maker indicated that the care required by the members of the board of directors in similar enterprises should be taken as basis. According to the explanation of law maker on the new 6102 numbered TCC, it is seen that foresight criteria which was predicted on the article 320 of 6762 numbered previous TCC have intentionally not been mentioned on the new law, even it is stayed away from *"foresighted businessman"* criteria. At this point, it is mentioned that Court of Cassation has identified foresighted businessman hard or even extreme expectations, it is stated that implementing the same criteria to the members of the board may cause unfair results.

Members of the board of directors shall show all the care that a knowledgeable and conscious manager should show during his/her management. Lack of knowledge and insufficiency shall not release the manager from duties deriving from law and articles of association. The person lacking the necessary information for the management of a joint stock company is obliged to avoid taking such a task. Therefore, a board member cannot escape responsibility by claiming his/her lack of knowledge (Üçışık and Çelik, 2013, p. 489).

The lawmaker has adopted an objective benchmark based on the care shown by a prudent manager. Therefore, the relevant member or manager and the company he/she works with are not taken into consideration in determining the necessary care. In this case, the care taken by the relevant member or manager for his own business and the potentiality of the company he/she is working with are not considered. In terms of determining the care of a prudent manager, a member or manager working in a company of the same size and volume with the same type of work is taken into account (Ayhan, Çağlar and Özdamar, 2019, p. 321; Hacımahmutoğlu, 2015, p. 29; Kırca, Şehirali Çelik and Manavgat, 2013, p. 657).

According to the justification of article 369 of TCC, benchmark of a prudent manager, accepts that member of board of director may give business judgment in line with corporate governance principles and in cases where risk arises from these, it is based on the principle that member is being held responsible.

In accordance with the generally accepted rule, if the appropriate researches are made, information is taken from the relevant parties and the decision is made on the board of directors, even if the developments occur on the contrary and the company has lost, dereliction will be out of question. However, it is of course possible to aggravate the care duty of the member of the board of directors by contract.

3 Necessary Conditions to Implement Business Judgment Rule

3.1 Shall Be a Business Decision

A decision in accordance with business judgment rule has to be related with the business, consciously and formally correct. In addition, this decision should be objectively acceptable within the scope of the minimum demands that cause it (Pulaşlı, 2018, p. 1475–1476).

It is necessary for the board members to actively participate in the meetings, not only because it is a duty but also in terms of care duty. Therefore, a problem shall be carefully discussed in the board of directors and the formal conditions shall be strictly followed. In case the decision in the board of managers is taken with insufficient quorums or a member is not invited to the meeting, then the prudent behavior has not been fulfilled. Since participating the meeting is a right for every member of director of board as well actively participating to the formation of decisions is a right. Therefore, a member who is not taken to board meetings without a significant justification cannot benefit from the protection of business judgment rule (Pulaşlı, 2018, p. 1475–1476).

3.2 Members of the Board of Directors and Managers Shall Be Impartial and Independent, or Shall Not Be Under the Influence of the Third Party

In order for the members of the board of directors to benefit from the protection of the business judgment rule, they must behave exclusively impartial in making decisions. In other words, the personal or third party's interests shall not affect the decision-making, the decision completely shall be taken by independent members (Kırca, 2004, p. 94–95; Pulaşlı, 2018, p. 1478).

The company is an umbrella concept that protects everyone, directly or indirectly benefits from the company (Sulu, 2019, p. 72). Although this concept has not been defined by the legislator; the doctrine explains that the joint stock company maintains its legal and economic presence in the best possible way (Helvacı, Çamurcu and Türkyılmaz, 2017, p. 311).The compliance of the decision of the board of directors with the business judgment rule depends on the fact that priority has been attributed to the benefit of the company.

3.3 Necessary Studies Have to Be Fulfilled

In case they do not have adequate information, while having decisions, board of directors shall have necessary information from experts. The information requested at this point shall serve to the best performance of the member of the board of directors in accordance with the company's interests (Kırca, 2004, p. 93–94; Pulaşlı, 2018, p. 1479). In other words, being able to benefit from the business judgment rule depends on the fact that the information regarding the decision of the board of directors has been taken from the experts and at a sufficient level (Pulaşlı, 2018, p. 1479).

3.4 Members of the Board of Directors and Managers Must Have Good Faith

Board members and managers must have good faith while taking decisions in the board of directors (Bozkurt Yaşar, 2014b, p. 115; Pulaşlı, 2018, p. 1480). In other words, decisions that are found to be most suitable for the economic interests of the company shall be taken. At this point, the argument that the member of the board may perform the same transaction for himself, is not valid. In Swiss Law, Federal Court in its BGE 99 II 180 numbered decision, did not accept the argument appropriate relevant to member of the board of director invested the significant amount of company assets to a highly speculative share, also invested individually three times to the same share (Pulaşlı, 2018, p. 1480).

According to article 553/1 of TCC, "*Founders, members of the board of directors, managers and liquidators are responsible for the damage they have caused both to the company, the shareholders and the creditors of the company, in case they violate their obligations arising from the law and articles of association with fault.*" It is not possible for the managers and members of the board of directors to benefit from the "*business judgment rule*" in terms of compensation for losses that arise within the scope of the mentioned regulation. Since this principle applies to the lawful actions and transactions of the members of the board of directors and managers. Other acts and unfair actions that are contrary to the law, articles of association and internal directive, will not be evaluated within the scope of the business judgment rule (Pulaşlı, 2017, p. 475).

4 Conclusion

The business judgment rule is not regulated as a clear law provision in Turkish law. However, with the effect of modern legal systems, it is used to determine the criteria regarding the care duty of the members of the board of directors. The relationship between joint stock companies and their managers requires that managers not to perform a certain result, but to perform their duties carefully and with the best effort.

The undertaking of the risk, provided that certain conditions are followed in the company's activities, does not mean that the managers violate the duty of care and thus, they are considered as faulty. While undertaking the risks deriving from commercial activities, in case of acting as a prudent manager, one cannot mention about the liability. At this point, benchmark relevant to necessary care, is same with the amount expected from members of board of directors of similar enterprises.

Benchmark of prudent manager recognizes that member of board of directors may give business judgment rule in accordance with corporate governance principles. In cases where the risk derives from business judgment, the principle is that the manager cannot be held responsible.

According to the generally accepted rule, if appropriate researches are made, information is provided from the relevant parties and the decision is made by the board of directors, dereliction will be out of question even if the company has lost. However, it is possible to aggravate the care duty of the member of the board of directors by contract.

For this decision to be evaluated within the limits of business judgment rule, it has to be a management decision, members of board who take such decision have to be impartial, all necessary studies have to be performed before the decision and actions will be performed with good will.

References

Akdağ Güney, N. (2016). Anonim Şirket Yönetim Kurulu. İstanbul: Vedat Kitapçılık.

Ayan, Ö. (2011). "Anonim Şirket Yönetim Kurulu Üyelerinin ve Yönetimle Görevli üçüncü Kişilerin Özen ve Bağlılık Yükümlülüğü". Maltepe Üniversitesi Hukuk Fakültesi Dergisi, 1 (2), 63–89.

Ayhan, R., Çağlar, H., Özdamar, M. (2019). Şirketler Hukuku Genel Esaslar. Ankara: Yetkin Yayınları.

Bozkurt Yaşar, S. (2014a). "Amerikan Hukukunda Yönetim Kurulu Üyelerinin Sorumluluk Rejimi". Terazi Hukuk Dergisi, 9 (100), 99–116.

Bozkurt Yaşar, S. (2014b). Anonim Şirketlerde İşadamı Kararı İlkesinin (Business Judgment Rule) Uygulanması. Doktora Tezi, www.tez.yok.gov.tr, (351543).

Göktürk, K. (2011). "Amerika, Alman, İsviçre ve Türk Hukukunda İşadamı Kararı İlkesi". İnönü Üniversitesi Hukuk Fakültesi Dergisi, 2 (2), 207–247.

Hacımahmutoğlu, S. (2014). "The Business Judgment Rule: İşadamı Kararı mı Yoksa Ticari Muhakeme Kuralı mı?" BATİDER, 30 (4), 99–145.

Hacımahmutoğlu, S. (2015). "Anonim Ortaklığın Yönetim Kurulu Üyelerinin Özen Yükümlülüğü: Fonksiyonel Bir Yaklaşım". BATİDER, 31 (3), 23–56.

Helvacı, M., Çamurcu, E., Türkyılmaz, İ. (2017). "Özellikle Anonim Şirketler Açısından Şirket Menfaati Kavramı". Prof. Dr. Hamdi Yasaman'a Armağan, İstanbul: On İki Levha Yayıncılık

Kervankıran, E. (2007). "Alman Hukuku'nda Business Judgment Rule'nin Kodifikasyonu – Türk ve Amerikan Hukuku ile Karşılaştırmalı Bir Değerlendirme-". Prof. Dr. Hüseyin Ülgen'e Armağan, İstanbul: Vedat Kitapçılık.

Kırca, İ. (2004). "Anonim Şirket Yönetim Kurulu Kararlarında Takdir Yetkisi – Özen Borcu". BATİDER, 22 (3), 85–96.

Kırca İ., Şehirali Çelik F. H., Manavgat Ç. (2013). Anonim Şirketler Hukuku I. Ankara: Banka ve Ticaret Hukuku Araştırma Enstitüsü.

Poroy R., Tekinalp Ü., Çamoğlu E. (2019). Ortaklıklar Hukuku I. İstanbul: Vedat Kitapçılık.

Pulaşlı, H. (2017). Şirketler Hukuku Genel Esaslar. Ankara: Adalet Yayınevi.

Pulaşlı, H. (2018). Şirketler Hukuku Şerhi II. Ankara: Adalet Yayınevi.

Sulu, M. (2019). Anonim Ortaklıkta Şirket Menfaati Kavramı. İstanbul: On İki Levha Yayıncılık.

Üçışık, G., Çelik, A. (2013). Anonim Ortaklıklar Hukuku I. Ankara: Adalet Yayınevi.

Ramazan Durgut & Erkam Hasim Bulut

Contract of Carriage for Passenger, Luggage and Cargo by International Airline

1 Introduction

With the globalization of the world, the importance of international transportation has increased considerably. Due to the international dimension of the transportation process, the determination of the rules to be applied to the international transportation has significant importance in terms of legal security. For this reason, in the field of the international private law, the various arrangements have been made regarding transportation law from past to present and "*Convention for the Unification of Certain Rules for International Carriage, 1999 Montreal Convention*" (the Montreal Convention) (hereafter referred to as MC) is deemed as the most recent one. The most important success of MC was the consolidation of all the texts included in the previous Warsaw System in a single text, which provided clarification of the international law to be applied and eliminated the discussions about which text should be applied to a conflict that occurred during the Warsaw System period (Gogen, 2012).

The purpose of MC is not to set binding uniform rules with regard to each issue to be applied in international air carriage by eliminating the differences in the national regulations; if anything the purpose is to ensure a uniform application only in certain aspects. In general, we can list the issues that MC will find an application area as follows: (Hobe, von Ruckteschell, Heffernan, 2013).

- Carriage documentation,
- Property rights and liabilities,
- Auxiliary duties regarding with the cargo carriages,
- Form requirements.

Besides that, the national courts of the Contracting States will make *"lex fori"* evaluation on the matters not covered by MC, provided that they adhere to the general provisions set out in MC. For example, there are several articles in MC regulates that the court seized of the case applies *"lex fori"* while examining the followings:

i. to oblige the carrier with the whole or part of the court costs and of the other expenses of the litigation incurred by the plaintiff, (MC Art.22/6)

ii. questions of procedure (MC Art. 33/4)
iii. the method of calculating the prescription period (MC Art. 35/2)
iv. in case of joint liability, the notification procedure if the case is filed against only one defendant (MC Art. 45).

Although there is no specific definition for the contract of carriage in the Turkish Commercial Code (TCC) numbered 6102 and the MC, the elements that the air carriage contract must bear can be understood from the articles of TCC and MC. According to the Art.1 of MC, "*This Convention applies to all international carriage of persons, baggage or cargo performed by aircraft for reward.*" Besides, according to the Art.850/2, "*The carrier is obliged to take the goods to the destination and deliver it to the addressee, or to deliver the passenger to the destination, with a carriage contract, in return, in carriage of goods, the sender; in carriage of passenger, the passenger owes the carrier to pay the carriage fee.*" Although both of the regulations do not give a full definition of the contract of carriage, they draw a general framework. Generally, it is understood that, to mention a contract of carriage, there should be an agreement, a carriage service, a reward. Additionally, in the light of these definitions, it can be concluded that the carriage should be performed by an aircraft in terms of air carriage.

MC, which is included in Turkish law as a result of the law numbered 5866, applies directly provided that the required elements exist. In order for the Montreal Convention to apply to the matters relating to international air transport contracts, some elements are required. These elements can be listed as follows:

1. There should be a contract of carriage between the parties.
2. The contract should be regarding carriage of passenger, luggage or cargo.
3. The contract of carriage should have international characteristics.
4. The carriage should be performed for reward.
5. The carriage should be performed by an aircraft.

2 Conditions for the Implementation of Montreal Convention

2.1 Contract of Carriage

As it was mentioned above, the first condition required for the implementation of MC is, there should be a contract of carriage between the parties. In this sense, a party of the carriage contract is a carrier and the other party is a passenger or a cargo sender depends on the subject of the contract. The only requirement for the acquisition of the title of "the carrier party to the contract" is to make a commitment to carry and whether it is an aircraft operator or having the title of "merchant" is not important. However, it should not be forgotten that the administrative permits and licenses required for the performance of the carriage service should be obtained (Ortac, 2014).

When we look at the issue from the perspective of the counterparty of the contract, if there is a carriage of passenger and luggage, although the counterparty of the contract of carriage is usually the passenger itself, this is not compulsory (Drion, 1954; 57). The situation that the passenger is not the other party of the contract appears when the contract is concluded as a "contract for the benefit of the third party". In carriage contracts made as contracts for the benefit of third parties, the duty of fee is the obligation of the contracting party. The authority to claim the rights arising from the contract belongs to the passenger who is not a party to the contract (Can, 2011). If there is a cargo carriage, the counter party of the contract will be cargo sender.

In this contract, the carrier is obliged to provide carriage service against the contracting party. However, the commitment of the carrier to carry is not sufficient in terms of the contract being covered by MC, but it should also be committed that the carriage will be performed by air and the places of departure and destination should be decided in the carriage contract.

It should be stated that, there is no specific rule with regard to the form of the contract of carriage in MC. For this reason, it is accepted that there is no form requirement for the implementation of MC to the contracts of carriage. Therefore, the written or oral form is not determinative for effectiveness of the contract of carriage. Although the written form is not an effectiveness requirement in terms of carriage contracts, it provides an important ease proof for the contracting parties. In parallel, it should be emphasized that the form is not even a requirement for proof. Hence it is accepted in the doctrine (Tompkins, 2010) that the existence of the contract of carriage can be proven in other ways, for example, if the passenger ticket is lost in an airplane accident.

In this context, the legal nature of the flight booking should be examined. Practically, there are two ways in the flight booking: early reservation and definite reservation. In early reservation, the customer and the aviation company have not concluded a transportation contract yet, if anything, they have an intent to conclude a contract. It can be understood that, there is a precontract which obliges the parties to conclude a carriage contract in future. In early reservation, if the customer does not pay the carriage fee, the reservation will automatically be cancelled and the contractual relationship between the parties is terminated. When it comes to definite reservation, the customer pays the carriage fee and the final transportation contract is concluded between the parties. Hence, the definite reservation can be deemed as the conclusion of the carriage contract (Golcuklu, 2018).

Finally, as it aforementioned, there should be a contract of carriage between the parties in order for MC to apply to the relationship. So, it must be understood that MC does not apply to the discrepancies between the aviation company and its crew. Because there is not a contract of carriage between them, if anything there is an employment relationship (Canbolat, 2009).

2.2 Subject of the Contract

In terms of MC, the subject of the contract should be passenger, luggage or cargo carriage.

In terms of passenger carriage, the subject of the carriage contract is an alive person. The word of "passenger" is defined in the doctrine (Sozer, 1977; Ulgen, 1987) as the person who is on the aircraft in accordance with the contract of carriage with the carrier and is excluded from the crew. Since the acquisition of "passenger title" depends on the existence of a carriage contract concluded with the carrier, the passengers who sneak onto the aircraft without the will of the carrier (stowaway) are not considered as "passengers". Therefore, if a stowaway suffers any damage during the carriage, MC does not apply to the case (Uzun, 2012).

To make an explanation about the term of "luggage", initially, it is defined in the doctrine (Zeyneloglu, 1993) as "the items that the passenger carries with him except for the personal belongings". However, MC has made a distinction between checked and unchecked baggage, and according to MC Art.17/2, "*The carrier is liable for damage sustained in case of destruction or loss of, or of damage to, checked baggage upon condition only that the event which caused the destruction, loss or damage took place on board the aircraft or during any period within which the checked baggage was in the charge of the carrier*." On the other hand, the carrier is only responsible for the loss or damage of unchecked baggage, including personal belongings, in the event of a fault of himself or his servants and agents.

When it comes to cargo, the subject of a carriage contract of cargo is any material thing that can be carried. In this regard, the cargo does not necessarily have to be commercial item. So, the cargo might be alive or lifeless (Ozdemir, 1992).

2.3 International Characteristics

According to the Art.1 of MC, *"This Convention applies to all **international** carriage of persons, baggage or cargo performed by aircraft for reward."* It is obvious that this regulation reveals the rule that MC applies to the international carriages. But what should be understood from the term "international"? Art. 1/2 and 1/3 of MC regulate that what should be understood from the term "international" and explain which transports made outside the country borders have an international character. For a better understanding, it would be more appropriate to examine the regulation in question part by part. According to this;

"the expression international carriage means;

i. *any carriage in which, according to the agreement between the parties, the place of departure and the place of destination, whether or not there be a break in the carriage or a transhipment, are situated either within the territories of two States Parties. . ."*(Art. 1/2)

   According to this part, regardless of whether there is a determined stopping place or not, if both of the place of departure and the place of destination are situated within either of the territories of the two states which are parties to MC has an international characteristic.
ii. *". . .within the territory of a single State Party if there is an agreed stopping place within the territory of another State, even if that State is not a State Party."* (Art. 1/2)

   According to this part, if the contracting parties determined a stopping place that whether it is situated within a State Party or not, both of the place of departure and the place of destination are situated within the territory of just one State Party, this carriage is deemed as "international" within the scope of MC.
iii. *". . .Carriage between two points within the territory of a single State Party without an agreed stopping place within the territory of another State is not international carriage for the purposes of this Convention."* (Art. 1/2)

   It means, if the parties do not agree on a stopping place and both the place of departure and the place of destination are situated within the territory of the same State Party, this carriage cannot be deemed as "international" according to MC.
iv. *Carriage to be performed by several successive carriers is deemed, for the purposes of this Convention, to be one undivided carriage if it has been regarded by the parties as a single operation, whether it had been agreed upon under the form of a single contract or of a series of contracts, and it does not lose its*

international character merely because one contract or a series of contracts is to be performed entirely within the territory of the same State (Art. 1/3).

In practice, it is possible to carry out the carriage service on the basis of the fulfilment of a single contract, as well as to conclude the series of contracts with successive aviation companies to provide the carriage service. This provision of MC stipulates that if an agreement is made between the parties as a single carriage operation, the series of contracts will be accepted as a single contract even if more than one contract of carriage is made with more than one airline company. Therefore, in such cases where more than one contract of carriage is made, the carriage process will not lose its international character even if the carriage is performed entirely within the territory of the same State. It is also worth remembering that this is the case if an agreement on carriage is agreed between the parties as a single carriage operation. In other words, if the passenger has two different tickets that are not even referred to each other from the same aviation company, the passenger's subjective intention to have a single international transport is not taken into account and therefore it is accepted that there are two independent carriage operations between the parties (Golcuklu, 2018).

Finally, it should be stated that, while evaluating whether the carriage is international within the scope of MC, issues such as the nationality of the passenger or the flag state of the aircraft etc. are not important. The important issue in this regard is the elements in the contract concluded between each consumer and the aviation company (Sozer, 1977). Namely, the process of carriage of all passengers on an aircraft may not be subject to the same rules. For example, Ankara-Paris flight with Istanbul connection is not an international route for the passenger landing in Istanbul. Whereas for those traveling to Paris, this carriage is international and MC applies to the disputes arising from the carriage between the parties.

2.4 Reward

Since the notion of "reward" is clearly mentioned in the Art. 1 of MC, there is no doubt that a reward must be agreed between the parties in order for MC to apply to the carriage contracts. Despite the fact that, a rule has been introduced in the continuation of the article that MC applies to the gratuitous carriages, the prerequisite for the implementation of MC is that a reward provision has been agreed in the contract. The payment obligation constitutes the primary liability of the party benefiting from the carriage service.

Although there is a rule that a reward should be decided in the carriage contract, no explanation has been made regarding the legal nature of the reward in MC. As it was mentioned in the introduction section, the legal nature of the reward will be determined by the court solving the dispute by applying *"lex fori"*. For example, in the assumption that the dispute arising from the carriage contract between the person who wants to send a cargo from Istanbul to Berlin and the cargo company comes before the Turkish Courts, the judge initially will decide whether MC applies to the dispute by taking the other elements into consideration. Even if the dispute is subject to MC, the assessment will be made in accordance with Turkish Law in determining the legal nature of the reward agreed in the contract. In this sense, since the notion of reward is examined in a wide scope in Turkish Law, any deed that is valuable in terms of assets can be included in the notion of reward (Golcuklu, 2018). Consequently, any deed valuable is undertaken by the customer within the scope of the liability in the carriage contract, it is accepted that the carriage is performed for a reward according to Turkish Law.

According to the Art. 1.s.2, "*It applies equally to gratuitous carriage by aircraft performed by an air transport undertaking.*" In fact, it is a prerequisite that the carriage will be performed for a reward for the application of MC to the carriage contracts, but an exception has been made that the MC will also apply to gratuitous carriages. In fact, not to determine which free carriages to be covered by the exception is an important deficiency for MC. However, it should be understood from this regulation that the carriages supposed to be for reward but to be performed gratuitous due to a legal reason or a commercial practice will be included in the scope of exemption. For example, the aviation companies do not charge children under a certain age group. The purpose of this regulation in question is to prevent the potential aggrievements that will arise due to not to apply MC because of the gratuitous carriage. The important point here is that the airline company, which is expected to fly for profit, does not charge the consumer due to a justified reason for protecting the consumer. For example, in the case *(Lavergne v. Atis Corp, 767 F. Supp.2d 301)* that the defendant company that was not operating commercially at the time of the accident in which was carrying the friends of the shareholders for free, the judge did not find the defendant company responsible pursuant to MC.

2.5 Aircraft

In Art.1 of MC, it is accepted that MC applies to the carriages performed by "aircraft" however, "aircraft" has not been identified. In this regard, when a dispute comes before the Turkish courts, the judge will decide whether an aircraft exists by applying "lex fori" according to Turkish Law. According to the Art. 3/b of Turkish Civil Aviation Act (TCAA) numbered 2920, dated 1983, the notion of "aircraft" refers to *"all kinds of vehicles that are able to take off and navigate in the air."* Besides that, although TCAA stipulates a dual distinction as state aircraft and civil aircraft, vehicles belonging to both groups will be considered as an aircraft and there will be no difference in the implementation of MC. However, it should be noted that if a state aircraft is involved in a dispute while performing a public service, it may also be subject to a regime separate from the rules applied to the civil aviation industry, from the perspective of administrative law (Erol, 2018).

When a dispute comes before the Turkish Courts, the vehicles that match this definition can be evaluated under MC; another contracting State Court, will use "lex fori" to identify the aircraft in the dispute that comes before it and can decide that the vehicle is not considered to be an aircraft according to its own law and then it can decide that MC is not applicable. For instance, since parachute and telpher do not match the given definition, they are not considered as aircraft, and therefore the Turkish Courts do not apply MC to the disputes arisen from these vehicles (Erdogmus, 2014). It should be stated that, in the event of temporary loss of ability to take off and navigate in the air, the "aircraft" qualification does not terminate, however, the aircrafts, which continuously lose their abilities in question, lose the qualification of being an aircraft (Kaner, 2004).

3 Conclusion

The main purpose played a significant role in signing the Convention for the Unification of Certain Rules for International Carriage, (1999 Montreal Convention) was providing a unification in applying the legal rules on international carriage of person, luggage and cargo. Actually, it is impossible to enact the law regulating each individual issue and make it compulsory for each state. Therefore, the Montreal Convention does not bring a rule for each individual issue, if anything, it sets rules for limited issues. Actually for some issues, MC explicitly states that the authorized State Courts apply their own national laws. Besides that, MC sets some provisions to apply to the carriages. According to the Art.1 which illustrates the prerequisites for application of MC: *"This Convention applies to all international carriage of persons, baggage or cargo performed by aircraft for reward."* In this part of the book, each prerequisite for application of MC is examined. Briefly, to apply MC to a carriage, there should be a contract of carriage regarding persons, luggage or cargo; the carriage should have an international characteristic which is identified by MC; the carriage should be performed for a reward by an aircraft which the legal natures of them are subject to lex fori. To sum up, it can be stated that this part of the book is an interpretation of the Art.1 of the Montreal Convention.

References

Can M., "Türk Hukukunda ve Milletlerarasi Hukukta Deniz Yolu ile Yolcu Tasima Sozlesmesi", Imaj Publication, Ankara, 2011.

Canbolat A.G., "Hava Taşıma Sözleşmesinde Taşıyıcının Sorumluluğu", First Edition, Turhan Publication, Ankara, 2009.

Drion H., "Limitation of Liabilities in International Air Law", Springer-Science+Business Media, B.V., Hague, 1954.

Erdogmus H.F., "Finansal Kiralama Sözlesmesi ve Hava Araci Parcalarinin Finansal Kiralama Yöntemi Ile Temini" PhD Thesis, Istanbul University Social Science Institute, Istanbul, 2014.

Erol Ö.F., "Idarenin Sivil Havacilik Alaninda Hava Tasimaciligina Iliskin Faaliyetleri", First Edition, Oniki Levha Publication, Istanbul, 2018.

Gogen S., Varsova ve Montreal Konvansiyonları Cercevesinde Havayolu Tasiyicilarinin Sinirli Sorumlulugu, Uygulamada Karsilasilan Sorunlar, pp.116–132, Air Carriage Symposium, First Edition, Beta Publication, Istanbul, 2012.

Golcuklu I., "Hava Hukuku" First Edition, Oniki Levha Publication, Istanbul, 2018.

Hobe S./ von Ruckteschell N./Heffernan D. (eds.),: "Cologne Compendium on Air Law", Carl Heymanns Verlag, Cologne, 2013.

Huilbert D. "Limitation of Liabilities in International Air Law", Hague, 1954.

Kaner İ. Hava Hukuku (Hususi Kısım), Second Edition, Filiz Kitabevi, Istanbul, 2004.

Orbay Ortac N. "Havayolu ile Tasinan Yolcularin Olumunden Veya Bedensel Butunlugunun Ihlalinden Dogan Sorumluluk" First Edition, Turhan Kitabevi, Ankara, 2014.

Ozdemir A., "Hava Tasiyicisinin Sorumlulugu: Bagaj ve Yukun Kaybi, Hasari ve Gecikmeden Dogan Zararlar Nedeniyle", Sanem Publication, Ankara, 1992.

Sozer B., Milletlerarası Hava Taşımalarına İlişkin Kurallar ve Uygulanma Şartları, BATIDER, 1977.

Tompkins G. N. Jr. "Liability Rules Applicable to International Air Transportation as Developed by the Courts in the United States: From Warsaw 1929 to Montreal 1999". Wolters Kluwer Law & Business Netherlands, 2010.

Ulgen H., Hava Tasima Sozlesmesi, Banking and Commercial Law Research Institute, Istanbul, 1987.

Uzun T.B., "Uluslararasi Hava Tasimalarinda Tasiyicinin Sorumlulugu" First Edition, Ankara, 2012.

Zeyneloglu A., "Tasima Hukuku", Second Edition, Yetkin Legal Publication, Ankara, 1993.

Niyazi Kurnaz & Ali Kestane

The Effect of Artificial Intelligence on Internal Audit

1 Introduction

The use of information technologies and internet in business activities has created data and information security problems. As a solution tool, information technologies applications have been launched such as cloud software, BigData, ERP and artificial intelligence, acting as a cybernetic system. As a result of the implementation of these applications, the internal audit mechanisms of institutions have also been affected by this phenomenon. This study aimed to determine the effect of artificial intelligence applications on internal audit while making evaluations from a theoretical perspective on the recent technology implementation and the difficulties encountered in practice. The study consists of two main sections. The first part details the conceptual framework of artificial intelligence (AI) technology and the effect of AI technology on internal control is analyzed and evaluated from a theoretical perspective in the second part. The analysis and evaluation results shed light on the future by making suggestions regarding the validity of the internal audit profession and activities in the presence of artificial intelligence in the future and the use of AI technology in internal audit.

2 The Concept of Artificial Intelligence/Conceptual Framework

In recent years, the integration of technological developments into business activities in parallel with computer and internet use has led to the transformation of the human phenomenon, which is at the center of these activities, and the digitization, automation and transformation of a number of business and operations into robotic processes. In this context, the concept of digital business world has emerged. A new era has started in the business world with Industry 4.0, BigData and artificial intelligence applications. This section and following titles include the framework of the concept of artificial intelligence (AI) within the scope of the theme of the study.

2.1 Definition, Purpose and Scope

Different researches on the concept of artificial intelligence are carried out by various researchers. The concept of artificial intelligence, which can be expressed as an effort to develop computer processes based on the human mindset or way of thinking, refers to computers that are configured with elements such as sight, perception, acquisition of information, thinking, and decision-making which are unique to human beings (Serçemeli, 2018: 374). In this context, in case the solution for any problem cannot be determined, people resort to artificial intelligence. It can be explained as the whole of systems that discover or learn by inferring an efficient and correct solution technique (Köroğlu, 2017). Considering the basis of the concept of artificial intelligence, it consists of these four elements: systems that think rationally, systems that think like humans, systems that act rationally, and systems that act like humans (Russel and Norvig, 2010: 1–4).

Systems that think rationally (Laws of Thought): In the 19th century, definitive determinants were studied by the logicians to show the objects in the world and the relations between them. Programs were developed and put into use in the 1960s to solve a problem that could be explained in a logical context. In this regard, thinkers or advocates of logic in artificial intelligence applications predict that smart systems can be implemented through these programs.

Systems that as like humans (Cognitive Modeling Approach): If an absolute theory should be created about the mind, it is possible to transform the relevant theory into a computer program. In this context, the input and output actions of any program can be matched with a human behavior, which can be an evidence for the fact that this program can act like humans.

Systems that act rationally (rational agent approach): The computer programs have a certain function for their purposes, whereas computer agents are a different type of programs that can adapt to changes, act in harmony with the environment, and work autonomously, creating goals and monitoring them. When a rational agent faces any uncertainty, it acts as a tool that works to reach the best result. In the face of other approaches, it is known to be a more advantageous approach in terms of (i) having a more general feature than rational thinking systems, and (ii) clarifying scientific development.

Systems that act like humans (Turing's approach): According to this system or approach, named after its researcher, in the event that it is not possible to distinguish whether the responses to the questions asked by a human are given by a machine or human, the computer passes the test. In this context, a computer can be referred to as intelligent if it has the features of natural language processing, automatic interpretation, information representation and machine learning.

2.2 Artificial Intelligence Infrastructure

Artificial intelligence can be an umbrella term for several different technologies that allow computer systems to perform tasks that normally require human intelligence, such as visual perception, speech recognition, and decision-making. It is possible to list the components in the infrastructure of artificial intelligence as follows (Kennedy and Nesgood, 2020):

- ***Machine Learning (ML):*** It is the use of statistical techniques to enable computers to "learn" with the help of data without being programmed explicitly. Thanks to this learning process, patterns can be identified and previously known rules can be applied to predict the results and provide intuition for abnormalities.
- ***Information Representation (IR):*** This is a subset of ML that tries to model how the connections work in the human brain by applying successive representation layers to teach computers how to learn and make decisions.
- ***Natural Language Processing (NLP):*** This term can be expressed as the use of computational linguistics and artificial intelligence to enable computers to understand and interpret human language, both oral and written.
- ***Visual Perception/Scan:*** These refer to the ability of machines to recognize and extract data/information from images such as pictures and videos. Figure 1 below shows how all of the mentioned subcomponents relate to artificial intelligence, to each other, and to robotic process automation (RPA), a popular technology solution that mimics human actions.

3 The Need for Artificial Intelligence in Internal Audit

Today, the increase in digitalization and automation has paved the way for diversification of information that information users will use for data processing. It has become more difficult to control the large data that is generated with the diversification and intensification of data traffic. In this context, it has become a significant requirement for auditors to store more information on analytical audit procedures than in the past. Due to the integration of the business and the processes of the documents resulting from the transfer of the performed tasks and processes to the digital environment, and the processes being performed over a system, an environment where the auditors can provide higher assurance

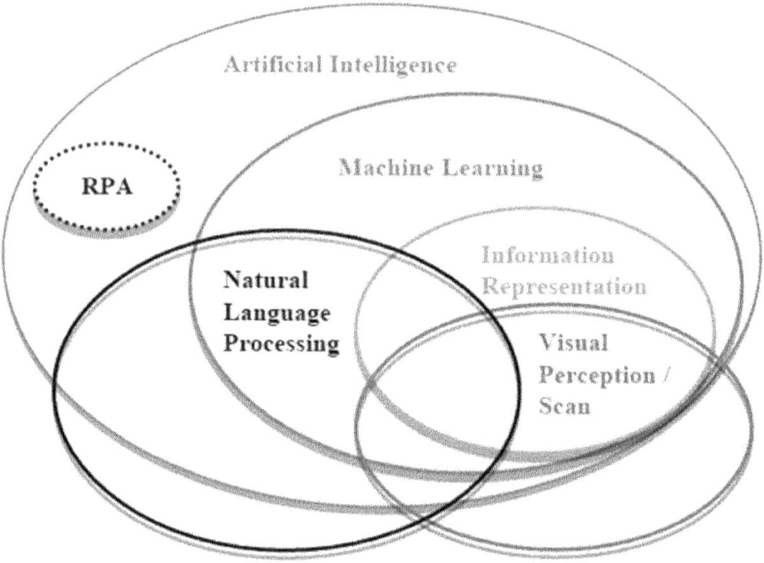

Figure 1: *Subcomponents of Artificial Intelligence.* Source: Kennedy and Nesgood (2020)

in their audit activities has been created with the help of artificial intelligence (Tas and Mert, 2019: 66).

In line with these developments, the use of cognitive technology has started to pose a threat to the professional activities of the auditors who even faced the danger of losing their jobs completely. At this point, it is obvious that the technologies in question have been automating actions such as inventory counting and establishing communication network for many years. However, in order for the auditors to turn this situation into an opportunity, it will be possible to focus on more risky areas during the audit activities. In addition, modeling the intellectual processes for comparing the first results obtained with the use of cognitive technology transforms the daily operations into automation and enables the auditors to improve their professional judgment (Davenport and Raphael, 2017).

Robust data management is the biggest reason or obstacle for many businesses, institutions or organizations against adopting artificial intelligence. In this context, a rapid increase in the collection, processing and storage of new data has revealed the place and importance of ensuring the organization of data in a consistent and proper way, making data accessible, and creating an institutional value while ensuring data integrity in business affairs. At this point, internal audit will be able to address data management, practices and capabilities of the organization on a more solid basis through artificial intelligence (Kennedy and Nesgood, 2020).

4 Difficulties in Application

Artificial intelligence embodies some of the advantages and risks it offers against natural intelligence. Namely, the advantages provided by the system can be listed as the fact that it offers an objective quality rather than acting emotionally, and that all the tasks and operations performed are carried out within a system, which makes it possible to document all the decisions and actions of the system (Dülger, 2018). On the other hand, due to the fact that there is a human supporter and logic errors occur accordingly, artificial intelligence products and services may cause financial damage or reputation loss and ethical problems. Besides, many internal and external stakeholders of an institution cannot adopt artificial intelligence practices. In the absence of an investment in intelligence, artificial intelligence technologies also include many risk factors such as lagging behind competitors (IIA, 2017a).

The data volume and quality generated by enterprises are of great importance in order to carry out audit activities in a successful way. Especially the enterprises that do not have a certain system infrastructure in the generation of such data in accounting systems or those with an unorganized data processing process from past to present will not be able to provide a majority of healthy results with the application of artificial intelligence in enterprises that do not have systematic and integrated systems and lead to greater risks. Therefore, businesses, institutions or organizations that do not have enough data in terms of making a successful modeling may face similar negative consequences and the emergence of great losses may become inevitable (ICAEW, 2017: 9). The institutions that decide to use artificial intelligence technology should provide training to their employees and take serious measures regarding the opportunities and risks of the technology in question, and what should be done to achieve the desired results (IIA, 2017b).

In the process to date, special arrangements regarding artificial intelligence have remained unsatisfactory. Institutions that set global standards and regulatory authorities tend to show an interest in research, discussion documents and advisory guidance services on the related technology. On the other hand, although the work and processes to be carried out will be implemented by artificial intelligence applications, considering the technology in question will be implemented by the human, it is an essential requirement to evaluate the transparency, accountability, and the results from a legal and ethical perspective (IIA, 2017b).

Based on these statements, it is clear that the auditors should increase their awareness of the developing technology and trends and improve themselves in the assurance they can provide regarding the audit activities. Auditors can modernize their profession by learning new technologies such as providing digital services, artificial intelligence and BigData for new industry areas, new production and business models, funding models and new payment systems (ACCA, 2016: 29). In addition, especially the senior management of institutions or organizations in the public or private sector should have a profound information about new technologies. The board of directors must be equipped and conscious in order to fulfill its qualified consultancy and executive duties. Thus, the implementation and adoption of these technology applications will be facilitated. Therefore, it is of great importance to make the corporate governance approach flexible and ready to change.

5 Artificial Intelligence and Audit

In line with the intensive use of computer technology in business operations, the use of artificial intelligence technology is supported to integrate the audit activities of large-scale accounting institutions into automation systems and to create integrated audit activities (Omoteso, 2012: 8490–8491). Artificial intelligence technology institutions and organizations facilitate implementation by automating their technical or administrative business processes and they also tend to increase their use in audit activities.

Today, four major audit firms, namely, Deloitte, EY, PwC and KPMG use artificial intelligence technology to facilitate their audit activities. With the Deloitte "Argus" application, the purchase, sale and credit agreements of the enterprises are scanned and the obtained information is analyzed with key data provided by the auditor into the program (Deloitte, 2018). EY carries out studies on benefiting from drones by using the internet of things and cloud-based information processing in stock counts. As a result of these studies, it will be possible to make an instant inspection of stocks (EY, 2017). With their application called "Clara", KPMG works to make full-time auditing possible. All data that may affect the financial situation of the enterprise to be audited can be examined thanks to this application (KPMG, 2017). On the other hand, PwC uses artificial intelligence technology to enable the instant review of the accounting records with their "GL.ai" application regarding the audit activities, and the results are sent to the audit team (PwC, 2019).

6 The Effect of Artificial Intelligence on Internal Audit

The co-existence of artificial intelligence technology and internal audit profession endangers the future of the profession and creates a concern that this technology can replace internal auditors. Thus, internal audit should provide added value to strategic and operational risks in data analysis, cyber security, policy and procedure formation and talent management in order to adapt to new emerging risks. The risks and opportunities arising from artificial intelligence should be correctly defined in parallel with the change in the role of internal auditors. It is beneficial to remind the risks arising from artificial intelligence, which was also mentioned in the previous sections of the study. These risks are as follows (IIA, 2017a):

- Logic errors occur due to the system being created based on human-based logic,
- Possible financial damage or reputation loss,
- Ethical problems,
- High costs of adopting artificial intelligence applications, and
- Competition risks that arise with artificial intelligence technology that is not adopted.

It is of utmost importance for internal audit activities to identify risks related to artificial intelligence during the determination of targets of institutions or organizations, to include the risk process in question, and to encourage the organization to take risks in the context of artificial intelligence practices. It is also necessary to consider issues such as artificial intelligence (AI) strategy, digital strategy (data and analytics), human factor and talent management (IIA, 2017a).

Artificial intelligence strategy: This explains organizational values by evaluating the management in power and focusing on the implementation of adaptations or restructuring when deemed necessary, and following artificial intelligence practices.

Digital strategy (data and analytics): It contributes to increase the quality and effectiveness of the audit activities by increasing the functionality. In the context of data auditing, assurance should be established regarding the scope and accuracy of internal audit activities.

Human factor: Issues such as ethics, morality and transparency that may exceed expectations in transition to artificial intelligence technology appear as high risk factors. However, it is possible to record all actions in black boxes placed on robots and to report them at any time.

Talent management: It is one of the biggest risks faced by internal audit against artificial intelligence practices. That's because this technology has skills such as the management of machine learning algorithms, the collection, use and modeling of big data while it does not have sufficient skills in risk analysis and management.

Internal audit plays a critical role in ensuring assurance that AI technology is performed correctly and reliably. AI can provide the expected benefit by processing the data in accordance with valid criteria. This situation constitutes one of the main areas of internal audit (IIA, 2017c). Taking these factors into account, auditors should get the answers of the following basic questions during the implementation of AI technology (Kennedy and Nesgood, 2020):

- Do we know where our data is?
- Is the "single version of the truth" known and understood?
- Is the data accessible?
- Is the data reliable (and data integrity guaranteed)?

After receiving answers to these questions, the duties and responsibilities of internal audit against artificial intelligence can be divided into three stages: the establishment phase of AI technology, the operation phase of AI technology and the stage of managing and controlling AI technology (IIA, 2017c).

The establishment phase of AI technology: AI technology can be subjective and unfair because of being a human product. The internal audit needs to contribute to the outputs generated by AI technology, not to produce a biased result, to ensure objectivity, and to reduce the risks of unfair results. In addition, this technology must provide assurance that it is applied in accordance with ethical principles, international regulations and contracts.

Operation phase of AI technology: Performance assessment of businesses, institutions or organizations falls within the scope of internal audit activities. For this reason, the quality of the outputs obtained from AI technology may change depending on the quality of the data processed by the system. It is then possible that errors may occur as a result of the lack of correct communication between the sources for data generation. Therefore, internal auditors are supposed to test the accuracy, reliability, repeatability and completeness of the relevant data. Also, it is necessary to measure success and performance in order to achieve corporate goals on the basis of valid criteria. Regarding the operation of AI technology, identifying and evaluating the significant risks of AI and reporting them to the top management or the board of the organization can be the key role of the internal auditor. That's because at this stage, risks can arise in the form of human-induced logic errors, the internal and external stakeholders of the organization refusing or not adopting AI technology, and the costs of AI technology exceeding the expected benefit.

Managing and controlling AI technology: In order to increase the acceptance level of AI technology in practice, internal audit needs to review levels of accountability and transparency of this technology and improve it with relevant policies and procedures. In this context, the focus of internal audit will be cyber security in terms of information security. That's because, due to the increase in the use of any technology, ill-intentioned people may focus their work in the relevant field. In this regard, a proactive approach to ensuring cyber security of the organization and protecting the rights of third parties is required through internal audit activities. Along with their focus on the risks of AI, internal auditors also need to use AI technology in their activities. By this way, auditors can quickly analyze data, identify data organizations, and discover relationships between data using AI technology.

In addition, auditors should adopt the 4R approach to ensure cyber security and the related institution's cyber resilience should be tested in terms of resisting, reacting, getting rid of cyber attacks and preparing for cyber attacks (IIA, 2017d).

7 Conclusion and Suggestions

Developments in information technologies in recent years have paved the way for the emergence of new applications, and state-of-the-art programs have been created with the integration of enterprises, institutions and organizations. The processes related to business and transactions have increased and diversified and significant problems have emerged in terms of controlling them within the scope of the activities carried out in parallel with the transfer of activities to different geographies around the world. While e-commerce applications emerged in the face of these events, smart systems have been developed and applications such as BigData, Industry 4.0, cloud software, ERP and artificial intelligence have been created and used actively. On the other hand, audit activities have also been affected by the changes and developments. Auditing profession and auditors should definitely gain technological skills accordingly. The interaction of artificial intelligence and audit activities, which is a state-of-the-art application product in global economic circles, aroused global interest and as a result, the position and effects of the use of artificial intelligence against the future of the internal audit and profession came into question. Therefore, this study aimed to determine the effect of artificial intelligence applications on internal audit while making evaluations from a theoretical perspective on the recent technology implementation and the difficulties encountered. As a result of the evaluation, the following key results were reached:

In order to protect the internal audit profession and its activities against artificial intelligence in the future:

- Regulatory and supervisory agencies need to prepare new training techniques and audit programs for the future of the internal audit profession,
- The relevant legal authority should establish the necessary legislation for the use of artificial intelligence technology,
- Audit techniques based on information technologies should be prepared and implemented,
- Professional organizations need to restructure and modernize the training and certification processes regarding the skills of internal auditors,
- Internal auditors should have the ability to use analytical audit procedures in the future,
- Training of internal auditors in information technology auditing is necessary in the context of creativity and innovation skills,
- Institution owners and managers should become aware of the importance given to information technology products and internal audit activities in the face of the digital business world,
- Corporate management approach should be restructured and disciplined by integrating information technology products into business activities,
- The objectivity, transparency and accountability criteria of artificial intelligence applications need to be analyzed in a consistent way,
- Due to the fact that artificial intelligence technology is created based on a logic originating from humans, it is necessary to solve the high cost risks encountered in logic errors, creating financial damage or reputation loss, creating ethical problems and adopting artificial intelligence practices through internal audit activities.

In order to use artificial intelligence technology in audit activities in the future: Auditors should be trained on cyber security activities to ensure information security, The position and role of AI technology in audit activities should be determined, clarifying the strategic plans of the institutions, Audit activities can provide a greater level of assurance with the support of documents produced within algorithms in digital environment, The risk of findings can be reduced to a minimum by directing auditors to higher risk areas, The quality of the assurance provided should be increased with the professional judgment of the auditors, An effective data management can ensure that the assurance and consulting role of internal audit can become the key position of the organization.

Based on the key results mentioned above, future researchers will be able to determine the role of artificial intelligence use in internal audit activities with: Legal and judicial regulations, Corporate management culture, The tendency of emotional intelligence and analytical skills of employees to use artificial intelligence, Evaluation from aspects such as proactive risk management. They will be able to turn the internal auditing profession and its activities into a control center in the enterprises, institutions and organizations, contribute to the protection of its reputation, and increase its validity.

References

ACCA Raporu. (2016). Professional Accountants – the Future: Drivers of Change and Future Skills. https://www.accaglobal.com/content/dam/members-beta/docs/ea-patf-drivers-of-change-and-future-skills.pdf. (14.04.2020).

Davenport, T., & Raphael, J. (2017). 10 Rule; "Creating a Cognitive Audit," http://ww2.cfo.com/auditing/2017/07/creating-cognitiveaudit/ (02.04.2020).

Deloitte. (2018). 16 Artificial Intelligence Projects from Deloitte Practical Cases of Applied AI. https://www2.deloitte.com/content/dam/Deloitte/nl/Documents/innovatie/deloitte-nl-innovatie-artificial-intelligence-16-practical-cases.pdf (15.04.2020).

Dülger, M. V. (2018). Günümüz Yapay Zekâ Teknolojisi ve 'Robot Yargıç/Avukat' Gerçeği. Hukuk ve Daha Fazlası Dergisi. 5, 4–9.

EY. (2017). EY Scaling the Use of Drones in the Audit Process. https://www.ey.com/gl/en/newsroom/news-releases/news-ey-scaling-the-use-of-drones-in-the-audit-process (16.04.2020).

ICAEW. (2017). Artificial Intelligence and the Future of Accountancy. https://www.icaew.com/-/media/corporate/files/technical/information-technology/technology/artificial-intelligence-report.ashx?la=en. (17.04.2020).

IIA. (2017a). Küresel Bakış Açıları ve Anlayışlar: Yapay Zekâ I, https://www.tide.org.tr/file/documents/pdf/GPAI-Artificial-Intelligence-Part-I-Revised.pdf, (18.04.2020).

IIA. (2017b). Küresel Bakış Açıları ve Anlayışlar: Yapay Zekâ II, https://www.tide.org.tr/file /documents/pdf/GPAI-Artificial-Intelligence-Part-II%20Revised.PDF (18.04.2020).

IIA. (2017c). Yapay Zeka: İç Denetimin Geleceği. https://global.theiia.org/translations/ PublicDocuments/TaT-December-2017-Turkish.PDF (23.04.2020).

IIA. (2017d). "Global Perspectives and Insights", The IIA's Artificial Intelligence Auditing Framework, Practical Applications, Part 3.

Kennedy, A. S., & Nesgood, K. (2020). Artificial Intelligence and Internal Audit: A Pragmatic Perspective. https://blog.protiviti.com/2020/01/02/artificial-intelligence-and-internal-audit-a-pragmatic-perspective/ (18.04.2020).

Köroğlu, Y. (2017). Yapay Zekâ'nın Teorik ve Pratik Sınırları. 6. Evrim, Bilim, ve Eğitim Sempozyumu.

KPMG. (2017). KPMG Clara a Smart Audit Platform. https://assets.kpmg/content/dam /kpmg/xx/pdf/2017/05/kpmg-clara-a-smart-audit-platform.pdf (21.04.2020).

Omoteso, K. (2012). The application of artificial intelligence in auditing: Looking back to the future. Expert Systems with Applications, 39(9), 8490–8495.

PWC. (2019). Audit Explorer. https://www.pwc.com/gx/en/audit-services/assets/pdf/audit-explorer-at-a-glance-on-screen.pdf (21.04.2020).

Russell, S. J., & Norvig, P. (2010). Artificial intelligence: A modern approach. Pearson Ed.Ltd.

Serçemeli, M. (2018). Muhasebe ve Denetim Mesleklerinin Dijital Dönüşümünde Yapay Zeka. Turkish Studies, Economics, Finance and Politics, 13(30), 369–386.

Tas, O. ve Mert, H. (2019). Denetimde Yapay Zeka Uygulaması. PressAcademia Procedia, 9, 65–68.

İskender Gümüş

Economic and Social Effects of Minimum Wage Determination: A Critical Evaluation

1 Introduction

The effects of minimum wage in both static and dynamic contexts in the economic literature have been the subject of constant debate. Liberal economists are opposed because the minimum wage impairs employment and production, and they see the minimum wage as a bad social policy implement. On the other hand, minimum wage adherents focus on the target of redistribution that the minimum wage can create. The minimum wage has been used as an important social policy implement, especially during the golden age of the welfare state. Various wage bases are still applied in many developed and developing countries.

In the implementation of the minimum wage, the state may determine a wage base covering the whole country with a law to be enacted, or the state may request that it be determined by labor unions and employers through collective agreements. In addition, the state can also determine the wage base, either nationally or regionally, through minimum wage determination committees. Whichever method is determined, the minimum wage refers to an impact to the labor markets. Low wage payments often occur, which means the exploitation of the worker when determination of wages is released and when no determination occurs. Because in labor markets, the bargaining power of the employee against the employer is weak; therefore state intervention is required. In almost all countries, it is aimed to be guaranteed minimum wages, depending on the economic and financial conditions of that country, that the level of earning employees and their families decent living. Therefore, the necessity of increasing the real income of labor comes in view. Because low wages can be an obstacle to economic development. Considering that a significant part of the society is employed at minimum wage, the economic and social importance of the minimum wage will once again become understandable.

The determination of the minimum wage can produce various economic and social impacts. In this study, the effect of minimum wage on economic development, which is the subject of theoretical and applied research especially in recent years, its effects on employment and unemployment, and its effects on income distribution and poverty will be examined.

2 Minimum Wage in International Standards

In international standards, there is a socio-economic approach in the criteria that will be taken as basis in determining the minimum wage. First of all, the social quality of the minimum wage is prioritized, and the need to consider the needs of the employee and his family is emphasized. It is also an important variable to consider the conditions of the country such as the level of economic development, production and employment. Therefore, it is possible to say that a large amount of criteria is used to decide the minimum wage, depending on the country and period. The reason is that each of these criteria depends on different purposes. The minimum wage in a country can be perceived as a way to ensure a valued standard of living. In this situation, purchasing power will be preferential over other thoughts. On the other hand, the fight against inflation may be a priority in another country or may become a priority in the same country at a later date. Herein, the main factor will be the inflation rate (Eyraud and Saget, 2010: 96).

International Labor Organization (ILO), in its constitution, assuring a wage that would provide sufficient living conditions has been accepted. ILO has also ratified 3 contracts (Contracts No. 26, 99 and 131) and 3 recommendations (Recommendation No. 30, 89 and 135) on minimum wage. On the other part ILO has also worked on minimum wage with international conferences. In the European Social Charter, the right of all employees to fair wages has been guaranteed to ensure an a sufficient level of living for themselves and their families. Fair wages in the European Social Charter, is defined as the wage that will provide a respectable level of life for employees and their families (Korkmaz, 2003; Korkmaz et al., 2013).

3 Economic and Social Effects of the Minimum Wage

The determination of minimum wage is an event that creates some effects on the socio-economic structure of the society. We can group these effects under three titles as its effect on economic development, its effect on employment and its effect on income distribution.

3.1 Effects on Economic Development

The determination of the minimum wage level has important effects on economic development. In times of rapid economic development, wages, meanwhile opportunities to increase the minimum wage, increase. Keeping the minimum wage high can play a prohibitive role, especially in terms of investments, by raising costs in the short and medium range (Gökdere, 1997: 19). Therefore, the effect of minimum wage on economic development should be examined not only in terms of minimum wages, but also with the increase in the levels of all wages. In an economy, the determination of minimum wages and then the rise of all the wages affetcs the costs and prices. However, rising wages and prices are not unlimited. With the perfect competiton conditions, entrepreneurs prefer to make profit and work at least to the point where the capital equals interest. In this case, the opportunities to increase wages are closely related to obtaining minimum profit and the scale of demand. The criteria that determine the level of wages in monopolistic market conditions are the scale of demand and the flexibility of demand that affects it. Producers may not need to increase their production in case of wage increases. Because if the profit falls to a marginal level as a result of wage rise, there is no reason for the producer to increase its production. Thus, when such situations become widespread, economic development pauses or slows down. If it is desired to protect profit margins by transferring such costs to prices, the decrease in demand negatively affects the production volume, and the development of the economy is faced with pause or slowdown. But it is necessary to take a different approach to the issue. In other words, if the increase in wages does not prevent the level of profits from occurring within valid measures, and it means the transfer of workers of a part of the national income, this does not mean a decrease in production. Because, thus, the purchasing power of the masses, namely the workers, increases, which encourages production. However, it is necessary to consider the following situation. The rise in wages does not enforcedly mean that an income is transferred from employers to workers. If the prices increase as much as the wage increases immediately, the worker gains nothing. Profits continue exactly. Workers and low-income consumers again suffer (Talas, 1997: 91–93).

The theory of economics shows that the macroeconomic effect of minimum wage increases on economic development and growth is uncertain. The minimum wage increase can increase labor costs and output prices. It may lead to the profits of companies and a decrease in vocational training and may affect employment negatively. This can also reduce GDP. However, the minimum wage increase enhances the earnings of low-skilled workers who continue their work, and workers who benefit from it have a higher marginal tendency to consume an additional income. Therefore, minimum wage increases can result in higher GDP. On the other hand, if low-skilled workers who lose their jobs receive training to acquire qualifications or increase schooling, if firms start employing higher-skilled workers, economic growth and development can also be mentioned (Sabia, 2015: 2).

Cahuc and Michel (1996) has found that in a model with endegenous growth, minimum wage legislations do not necessarily have negative effects on economic development. These legislations can have positive effects on growth by providing more human capital accumulation. More precisely, the low demand for unskilled labor caused by the minimum wage can create an promotion for workers to raise their human capital. This can increase both a growth-based development in the economy and the level of welfare. Besides, it is possible that a reduction in the minimum wage will reduce the prosperity of each individual in the economy. Accordingly, any reduction in the minimum wage should be accompanied by appropriate education, industrial or employment policies, which could possibly compensate for possible current and future prosperity losses from the lower minimum wage.

Similarly, Sunal and Sezgin Alp (2015) in their work which includes the period covering the years 1987–2012 in Turkey, aims to investigate the causal relationship between the real minimum wages and real GDP growth rate of nominal wages and inflation rates. Accordingly, they have concluded from the increase for the minimum wage that took place between the years 1987–2012 in Turkey, there was no negative effect on economic growth. Consequently, it can be said that the increase in the minimum wage supports economic development.

On the other hand, the minimum wage has a direct effect on the rate of growth with its effect on unemployment. Where the minimum wage increase causes an increase in employment, any increase in productivity will cause an increase in the total demand. The general wage level, which increases with the minimum wage increase, will increase the total demand. This brings along economic development with it (Pürsünlerli, 2003: 32–37).

3.2 Effects on Employment and Unemployment

Another problem arising from the rise of the minimum wage and in paralel with the rise of other wages is about employment. In real life, wages are not determined by market conditions. Governments interfere in the labor market with minimum wage legislation. Because, if the wage is set by market conditions only, some problems may arise. At the beginning of these problems is the tendency of the wages to be drawn down due to the high labor supply and weak bargaining power of the worker.

On the other hand, the interventionist role of the state in the labor markets produce various consequences. Generally, in an economy that is growing and where the workforce is increasing, the level of employment show tendencys to increase year by year. In many developing countries, the marginal productivity of workers living and working outside the traditional part of the country is much higher than that of workers with "zero" or "close to zero" productivity in agricultural or urban areas, such as vending, recycling and similar work. In that case, one of the methods to be used to raise the standard of living of the masses will be to transfer these people who are in the traditional unemployed position to the modern part of the economy as workers. Here, the problem of minimum wages and general wage level occurs. The effect of increasing wages on employment in the long term depends on the result of wage increases at the rate of economic development. However, if the wage, which is the price of labor, rises steadily, even if the economy is developing, employment growth may not be at the same rate as the rate of development due to substituting labor with capital. It is because, through the management is organized by employer in some way and by making a good regulation in the work, it can provide huge savings from the marginalized workers. Otherwise, after a while, the employer may make changes in the working method and equipment in the enterprise and can prefer intensifying capital instead of labor. In turn, if it does not give the desired result for the employer, some enterprises may either restrict their activities or stop them completely. Finally, opening new workplaces may slow down or even stop. Increasing wages, especially minimum wages, brings more or less employment shrinks for some population groups. Especially it may adversely affect the opportunities of unskilled workers, youth, disabled and women to find a job. In this situation, it is imperative that the authorities involved in the determination of national wage policies and, meanwhile minimum wages constantly take into account the effect of wage levels on employment (Talas, 1997).

The increase in the minimum wage increases the wages of relatively unskilled workers and makes the inputs that can replace such workers more attractive. Workers who earn a little more than the minimum wage in the low wage groups usually perform the same tasks as less skilled workers and easily substitute for minimum wage workers (Deere et al., 1995). Therefore, in studies focusing on unskilled labor, a stronger negative impact from minimum wage to employment can be mentioned and findings can be reached that the minimum wage increases unemployment. Supporting this view, Potter (2006), in a study on a sectoral basis for the US economy, draws attention to the negative impact of minimum wage on employment in all sectors, including the construction, retail and health sectors. Neumark and Wascher (1992), on the other hand, has found that the increase in minimum wage had a decreasing effect on youth employment.

Studies that reveal a positive relationship between minimum wage and employment are more common especially in recent years. Katz and Krueger (1992), have investigated the various effects of the minimum wage and have reached the conclusion that employment increased in companies affected by the minimum wage. Card and Krueger's (1994) study reveals that the minimum wage increase does not reduce employment. Addison and Blackburn (1999) also haven't reached the result of a negative employment effect of the minimum wage.

Therefore, although there is a dominant view that the minimum wage and increases in the minimum wage decrease employment and enhance unemployment, there are also studies showing that the minimum wage has a positive effect on employment or no negative impact on employment. Indeed, Türcan-Özşuca (2004), in Turkey sample, the dissolution of the employment and unemployment to retreat wages suggests that it was impossible. Therefore, it is seen as a low probability that the minimum wage level determined significantly below the average wage has a reducing effect on labor demand. Korkmaz and Çoban (2006: 20) also concluded that the increase in the minimum wage has not a negative impact on employment. Furthermore, Akgeyik and Çil-Yavuz (2006) have reached the conclusion that the long-term relationship with a real unemployment rate of the minimum wage and per capita income in Turkey.

3.3 Effects on Income Distribution and Poverty

Minimum wage refers to the minimum level of the wage, which is the interest of labor from production, from production factors. Therefore, the higher the minimum wage, the higher the interest of labor on factor payments from production factors. The minimum wage application has some economic and social effects as it targets the people in the lower income group and has a weak socio-economic characteristics (Dama, 2017). Therefore, the minimum wage must be increased equally to productivity growth and growth rate. Otherwise, there will be a deterioration in income distribution, which increases poverty (Koç and Görücü, 2018: 62).

It is necessary to be careful about the wage policies aimed at ensuring the fair distribution of income through wage increases, and to focus especially on the source of income transfers that are considered to be made. If wage increasing policies increase the wages of one part of the workforce while the other part shrinks their working areas, a situation comes in view such as some wage earners and other wage workers lose their jobs. However, this is not a fair income distribution method. In terms of income distribution justice, it is necessary to consider two different situations. If wage increases are not reflected to consumers due to deficiency or lack of competition, income distribution justice is positively affected. However, if the prices of compulsory consumer goods have increased due to wage increases and thus wage increases are burdened poor, justice can not be achieved in income distribution (Talas, 1997).

It is possible to say that the minimum wage plays a role in reducing the wage inequality between the lowest and the middle part of the income distribution. Because ensuring justice in the income distribution is defended as an aim both in terms of welfare policies and human rights. On the other hand, reducing wage inequality is often confused with preventing relative poverty or, more broadly, income inequality (Gregg, 2000).

On the other hand, the minimum wage is a wage base that will guarantee the minimum livelihood of the worker and his family, as well as a threshold role in the distribution of social benefits to be made in many countries to individuals or households. Along with other income transfers to be made, it affects the social aid policies on the one hand, in order to guarantee the minimum standard of living, and on the other hand it is affected by these policies. Therefore, the minimum wage is used as a social base. For example, in such a system, the pension adjustment with every increase in the minimum wage should maintain the purchasing power of the poor retired. In addition, society as a whole can benefit from the progress made by economic development and growth when minimum wage determination is linked in a similar way (Eyraud and Saget, 2010: 102). Therefore, it should not create a contradiction between the minimum wage level and the system that provides allowances for many poor people to live, whether paid or not (Burkhauser and Finegan, 1993).

When examined, the studies on whether the minimum wage is a successful tool in the fight against poverty and redistribution of income, different results emerge. In their research, Neumark and Wascher (2002) revealed that the minimum wage both saves poor families from poverty and can drag families that have not been poor before. In the study, it is stated that the minimum wage tends to increase the income of the poor families, but there is a transfer which is made from the high-income families to the low-income families through the minimum wage.

In addition, Piketty (2014) emphasizes that investing in vocational education and competence is the best way to increase wages and reduce wage inequalities in the long term. Looking at the minimum wage in a critical perspective, Piketty argues that establishing wage lower limits or wage ranges in the long term will not increase wages five or ten times. According to Piketty (2014), the factors that can provide such an increase are education and technology.

4 Conclusion

Various forms of wage base applications are implemented in most of the developed and developing countries. These practices also frequently cause controversy among the academic community and political decision makers. It is because, the minimum wage affects a large part of the population. The minimum wage increase is a very important macroeconomic indicator that concerns the whole economy as it will also affect the income level, expenditure and savings.

The dominant view on the economic and social effects of the minimum wage; The minimum wage is that it negatively affects economic development, reduces employment and increases unemployment and increases poverty by disrupting income distribution. It is possible to say that the minimum wage increase reveals contrary to the dominant view in recent years, although various empirical studies have supported these dominant views.

It is necessary to open the negative aspects of the minimum wage determination suggested by the dominant view for discussion, which is shaped according to the liberal understanding criticizing the state intervention in wages. Economic growth based on wage rise is always possible. It is because, wage increases revive the economy by increasing the purchasing power. On the other hand, increases in minimum wage can create a new motivation source for working and increase employment. Finally, it can be said that the minimum wage is of vital importance in terms of the distribution of income. The minimum wage level plays an important role especially in increasing the share of low-income groups from national income and decreasing income inequality.

References

Addison, J. T., & Blackburn, M. L. (1999). "Minimum Wages and Poverty". Industrial and Labor Relations Review, 52(3), 393–409.

Akgeyik, T., & Çil-Yavuz, N. (2006). "Türkiye'de Asgari Ücret, Milli Gelir ve İşsizlik İlişkisi (Ekonometrik Bir Analiz)". Maliye Araştırma Merkezi Konferansları, (49) https://dergipark.org.tr/tr/pub/iumamk/issue/749/8069 (12.10.2019).

Burkhauser, R., & Finegan, A. (1993). "The Economics of Minimum Wage Legislation Revisited". Cato Journal, 13(1), 123–9.

Cahuc, P., & Michel, P. (1996). "Minimum Wage Unemployment and Growth". European Economic Review, 40(7), 1463–1482.

Card, D., & Krueger, A. B. (1994). "Minimum Wages and Employment: A Case Study of the Fast Food Industry in New Jersey and Pennsylvania". American Economic Review, 84, 772–793.

Dama, N. (2017). "Sosyal Politika Açısından Asgari Ücret". SETA Perspektif, 161, Ankara.

Deere, D., Murphy, K., & Welch, F. (1995). "Employment and the 1990–1991 Minimum-Wage Hike". The American Economic Review, 85(2), 232–237

Eyraud, F., & Saget, C. (2010). "Asgari Ücret Tespit Düzenlemelerinin Canlanması", Ed. J. Berg & D. Kucera, İşgücü Piyasası Kurallarının Savunusu, Ankara: Efil Yayınevi.

Gökdere, A. (1997). Asgari Ücretin Türk Ekonomisine Etkileri: KOBİ'ler Açısından Yaklaşım, Ankara: TES-AR Yayınları.

Gregg, P. (2000). "The Usage of Wage Floors as Policy Tools". OECD Economic Studies No: 31, 134–146.

Katz, L. F., & Krueger, A. B. (1992). "The Effect of the Minimum Wage on the Fast Food Industry". Industrial and Labor Relations Review, 46, 6–21.

Koç, M., & Görücü, İ. (2018). "Türkiye'de Asgari Ücretin Uygulanması". Social Sciences Studies Journal, 4(13), 58–73.

Korkmaz, A. (2003). Çağdaş Gelişmeler Açısından Asgari Ücret. Ankara: Türk Tarih Kurumu Basımevi.

Korkmaz, A., & Çoban, O. (2006). "Emek Piyasasında Asgari Ücret, İşsizlik ve Enflasyon Arasındaki İlişkilerin Ekonometrik Bir Analizi, Türkiye Örneği, 1969–2006". Maliye Dergisi, 151, 16–22.

Korkmaz, A., Dulupçu, M. A., Gökdere, B., & Songur, H. (2013). Onurlu İnsan Onurlu Yaşam İçin İnsanî Ücret, İstanbul: İGİAD & İLKE Yayınları.

Neumark, D., & Wascher, W. (1992). "Employment Effects of Minimum and Subminimum Wages: Panel Data on State Minimum Wage Laws". Industrial and Labor Relations Review, 46, 55–81.

Neumark, D., & Wascher, W. (2002). "Do Minimum Wages Fight Poverty". Economic Inquiry, 40(3), 315–333.

Piketty, T. (2014). Yirmi Birinci Yüzyılda Kapital, İstanbul: İş Bankası Kültür Yayınları.

Potter, N. (2006). "Measuring the Employment Impacts of the Living Wage Ordnance in Santa Fe, New Mexico." Bureau of Business and Economic Research, University of New Mexico.

Pürsünlerli, E. S. (2003). Asgari Ücretin Vergi Dışı Bırakılması, Ankara: Asil Yayınları.

Sabia, J. J. (2015). Do Minimum Wages Stimulate Productivity and Growth? IZA World of Labor, 221, 1–10.

Sunal, O., & Sezgin Alp, Ö. (2015). "Türkiye'de Reel Asgari Ücretler ve Reel GSYİH Değişmeleri Arasındaki Nedensellik İlişkisi: Enflasyon Oranına Endekslenmiş Bir Nominal Asgari Ücret Politikası". Ankara Üniversitesi SBF Dergisi, 70(1), 111–129.

Talas, C. (1997). Toplumsal Ekonomi. Ankara: İmge Kitabevi.

Türcan-Özşuca, Ş. (2004). "Asgari Ücret İşsizlik ve Yoksulluk". Mesleki Sağlık ve Güvenlik Dergisi, 5(17), 9–13.

www.ingramcontent.com/pod-product-compliance
Ingram Content Group UK Ltd.
Pitfield, Milton Keynes, MK11 3LW, UK
UKHW021240300926
15471UKWH00014B/862